Democracy, Accountability, and Representation

This book examines whether mechanisms of accountability characteristic of democratic systems are sufficient to induce the representatives to act in the best interest of the represented. The first part of the volume focuses on the role of elections, distinguishing different ways in which they may cause representation. The second part is devoted to the role of checks and balances, between the government and the parliament as well as between the government and the bureaucracy. The contributors to this volume, all leading scholars in the fields of American and comparative politics and political theory, address a variety of questions. Do elections induce governments to act in the interest of citizens? Are politicians in democracies accountable to voters in future elections? If so, does accountability induce politicians to represent citizens? Does accountability limit or enhance the scope of action of governments? Are governments that violate campaign mandates representative? Overall, the essays combine theoretical discussions, game-theoretic models, case studies, and statistical analyses, within a shared analytical approach and a standardized terminology. The empirical material is drawn from the well-established democracies as well as from new democracies.

Adam Przeworski is Professor of Politics at New York University and Fellow of the American Academy of Arts and Sciences. He has taught at scholarly institutions in Chile, France, Germany, Poland, Switzerland, and Spain. Professor Przeworski's recent books include *Sustainable Democracy* (coauthor, Cambridge University Press, 1995), *Economic Reforms in New Democracies: A Social-Democratic Approach* (with Luiz Carlos Bresser Pereira and José María Maravall, Cambridge University Press, 1993), and *Democracy and the Market: Political and Economic Reforms in Eastern Europe and Latin America* (Cambridge University Press, 1991).

Susan C. Stokes is Associate Professor of Political Science at the University of Chicago and Executive Director of the Chicago Center on Democracy. Professor Stokes is editor of *Cultures in Conflict: Social Movements and the State in Peru*. She has also been published in numerous journals, such as *Comparative Politics, Comparative Political Studies*, and *Electoral Studies*, and serves as an editorial board member of *Politics and Society*.

Bernard Manin is Professor of Political Science at New York University, Research Director at the Centre National de la Recherche Scientifique, and a member of the CREA (Centre de Recherche en Epistémologie Appliquée), Paris. He is the author of *The Principles of Representative Government* (Cambridge University Press, 1997), and the coauthor of *La social-démocratie ou le compromis* (Presses Universitaires de France, 1979) and *Le régime social-democrate* (Presses Universitaires de France, 1989).

Cambridge Studies in the Theory of Democracy

General Editor
ADAM PRZEWORSKI *New York University*

"It is not current politics but democracy as a form of government that I seek to describe," James Bryce wrote in 1921. The goal of this series is to reinvigorate theoretical reflection about democracy by exposing it to the full range of historical experiences under which democracies have flourished or floundered. Our ambition is to understand what makes democracies work and endure. How do they promote normatively desirable and politically desired objectives, and how do they peacefully handle crises that occur when such objectives are not being fulfilled? We intend to ignore artificial divisions among different approaches, by drawing simultaneously on classical political theory, modern analytical methods, and comparative empirical research. We hope that our conclusions not only will offer some guidance for countries that are still in the process of developing democratic institutions, but also will provide a means of understanding the deficiencies of the well-established democratic systems.

OTHER BOOKS IN THE SERIES
Elster, Jon, ed., *Deliberative Democracy*

Democracy, Accountability, and Representation

Edited by

Adam Przeworski
New York University

Susan C. Stokes
University of Chicago

Bernard Manin
New York University

CAMBRIDGE
UNIVERSITY PRESS

PUBLISHED BY THE PRESS SYNDICATE OF THE UNIVERSITY OF CAMBRIDGE
The Pitt Building, Trumpington Street, Cambridge, United Kingdom

CAMBRIDGE UNIVERSITY PRESS
The Edinburgh Building, Cambridge CB2 2RU, UK   www.cup.cam.ac.uk
40 West 20th Street, New York, NY 10011-4211, USA   www.cup.org
10 Stamford Road, Oakleigh, Melbourne 3166, Australia
Ruiz de Alarcón 13, 28014 Madrid, Spain

© Adam Przeworski   Susan C. Stokes   Bernard Manin   1999

First published 1999

Printed in the United States of America

Typeface Centennial 10/13 pt.   *System* QuarkXPress® [BTS]

*A catalog record for this book is available from
the British Library.*

Library of Congress Cataloging in Publication data

Democracy, accountability, and representation / edited by
Adam Przeworski, Susan C. Stokes, Bernard Manin.
p. cm. – (Cambridge studies in the theory of democracy)
ISBN 0-521-64153-5 (hc.). – ISBN 0-521-64616-2 (pbk.)
1. Democracy. 2. Elections. 3. Representative government and
representation. 4. Responsibility. I. Przeworski, Adam. II. Stokes,
Susan Carol. III. Manin, Bernard. IV. Series.
JC423.D43946 1999
321.8 – dc21   98-50663
                                                     CIP

ISBN 0 521 64153 5   hardback
ISBN 0 521 64616 2   paperback

Contents

Contributors

José Antonio Cheibub, Assistant Professor, Department of Political Science, University of Pennsylvania

Delmer D. Dunn, Professor, Department of Political Science, University of Georgia

John Dunn, Professor of Political Philosophy and Fellow of Kings College, Cambridge University

Jon Elster, Robert K. Merton Professor of Social Science, Department of Political Science, Columbia University

James D. Fearon, Professor, Department of Political Science, Stanford University

John Ferejohn, Carolyn S. G. Munro Professor of Political Science and Senior Fellow of the Hoover Institution, Stanford University

Michael Laver, Professor of Government, Trinity College, Dublin

Bernard Manin, Professor, Department of Politics, New York University, and Directeur des Recherches at the Centre National des Recherches Scientifiques, Paris

José María Maravall, Professor, Universidad Complutense in Madrid, and Director, Instituto Juan March de Investigaciones Sociales

Adam Przeworski, Professor, Department of Politics, New York University

Kenneth A. Shepsle, George Dickson Markham Professor and Chair, Department of Government, Harvard University

James A. Stimson, Professor, Department of Political Science, University of Minnesota

Susan C. Stokes, Associate Professor, Department of Political Science, University of Chicago

Bernard Manin, Adam Przeworski,
and Susan C. Stokes

Introduction

The aim of every political constitution is, or ought
to be, first to obtain for rulers men who possess
most wisdom to discern, and most virtue to pursue,
the common good of the society; and in the next
place, to take the most effectual precautions for
keeping them virtuous whilst they continue to hold
their public trust.

James Madison, *Federalist* no. 57

In framing a government to be administered by men
over men, the great difficulty lies in this: you must
first enable the government to control the governed;
and in the next place oblige it to control itself.

James Madison, *Federalist* no. 51

The Problem of Political Representation

Democracy is a form of rule. Even in direct democracy,
decisions of a majority are binding on everyone, including the
minority that finds them against their opinions or interests. In a
representative democracy – our form of government – these
decisions are made by elected representatives and implemented
by appointed officials to whom the representatives delegate some
of the tasks of governing. The representatives decide what citizens
must and cannot do, and they coerce citizens to comply with
their decisions. They decide how long children must go to school,
how much individuals should pay in taxes, with which countries
men must go to war, what agreements private parties must
adhere to, as well as what citizens can know about the actions of

1

governments. And they enforce such rules, even against the wishes of the individuals concerned. In this sense, they rule.

The question of representation is why would rulers, equipped with such powers, act in the best interests of others, of citizens, or at least some majority thereof. This is what we mean by "representation": acting in the best interest of the public (Pitkin 1967). Such a definition is obviously broad. While the concept of representation has a long history and remains shrouded in ambiguities, we do not focus on its meaning. Our purpose is different. We explore the connection between the institutions that are normally associated with representative democracy and the way in which governments act.

We ask whether these institutions induce governments to act in the best interest of citizens for two reasons. First, there probably is a wide agreement that a government acting in the interests of citizens is a normatively appealing goal. From a normative standpoint, the question is why exactly would the institutions characteristic of representative democracy be conducive to such a goal. Second, defining representation as acting in the interest of the represented provides a minimal core conception, one on which a number of more specific theories converge. It is compatible with a wide variety of views about what representing implies, depending on how the notion of the interests of the represented is interpreted. People holding the view that a government is representative if it acts on the wishes of voters may agree with our minimal definition on the grounds that the interests of the represented can be taken to mean what the represented themselves see as their interests. But the minimal conception stated here is also compatible with the view that a government is representative if it does what according to its own judgment is in the best interest of citizens. Similarly, our definition of representation does not entail a position on whether the representative should do what voters want him to do at the time a policy is adopted or should adopt the policy that voters would approve in retrospect. Such issues have long been in contention among theorists of political representation from Burke (1949 [1774]) to Kelsen (1929). The meaning of representation is notoriously contested. Beyond the notion that representing implies acting in the interest of the represented, there seems to be little else on which theorists agree.

It should be noted, however, that what has been in contention since the establishment of representative government – not to go farther back – concerns primarily the nature of the activity of representing, not the procedures and institutional arrangements that induce political representation. As we have seen, views about what is expected of representatives diverge. But the formal arrangements that initiate, enable, and terminate the activity of representing have been remarkably stable over the last two centuries. Since the establishment of representative institutions, their basic structure has been the same everywhere:

1. Rulers, those who govern, are selected through elections.
2. While citizens are free to discuss, criticize, and demand at all times, they are not able to give legally binding instructions to the government.
3. Rulers are subject to periodic elections.

Except for electoral systems, such formal arrangements have virtually never been questioned since the end of the eighteenth century. It is indeed one of the most striking facts in the history of representation that, while there has been a broad and stable consensus over representative institutions, people have constantly argued over what was supposed to go on during representation.

This discrepancy between agreement over procedure and controversy over substance underscores the uncertainties that have surrounded representative institutions since their establishment. The founders of representative government expected that the formal arrangements they advocated would somehow induce governments to act in the interest of the people, but they did not know precisely why it would be so. Neither do we today, after two hundred years.

There are four generic reasons why governments may represent the interests of the people:

1. Only those persons who are public-spirited offer themselves for public service, and they remain uncorrupted by power while in office.
2. While individuals who offer themselves for public service differ in their interests, motivations, and competence, citizens use their vote effectively to select either those candidates whose interests

are identical to those of the voters[1] or those who are and remain devoted to the public service while holding office.

3. While anyone who holds office may want to pursue some interests or values different from and costly to the people, citizens use their vote effectively to threaten those who would stray from the path of virtue with being thrown out of office.

4. Separate powers of government check and balance each other in such a way that, together, they end up acting in people's best interest.

The first hypothesis should not be dismissed. Many persons who seek public office want to serve the public, and some probably remain dedicated to the public service while in power. If we do not pay much attention to this possibility, it is because this way of securing representation is not distinctive of democracy. Dictators can also be representative: if they know and if they seek to do what people want, nothing prevents them from doing it. The connection between democracy and representation cannot depend on luck: who the dictator happens to be. And, indeed, a central claim of democratic theory is that democracy systematically causes governments to be representative.

This claim is widespread. To take just a few examples, Dahl (1971: 1) asserts that "a key characteristic of a democracy is the continued responsiveness of the government to the preferences of its citizens." Riker (1965: 31) claims that "democracy is a form of government in which the rulers are fully responsible to the ruled." Schmitter and Karl (1991: 76) maintain that "modern political democracy is a system of governance in which rulers are held accountable for their actions in the public realm by citizens." Indeed, our political system was distinguished from all its predecessors as one of "representative government" long before it was identified as a democracy.

Modern democracy is an elitist system or, as Manin (1997) would say, an aristocratic one. By Aristotle's criteria, it is an oligarchy: a rule by the few (Bobbio 1989: 107). Yet it is a competitive oligarchy (Schumpeter 1942; Dahl 1971; Bobbio 1989): we are ruled by others, but we select them and we replace them with

---

[1] Citizens and governments have identical interests if governments want in their self-interest to bring about states of the world that are most desired by citizens.

4

our votes. This is what is distinct about democracies: rulers are selected through elections.

The question, then, is whether the fact that they are elected is sufficient to cause governments to act in a representative manner. The purpose of this volume is to examine whether there are grounds to believe that if elections are contested, if electoral participation is widespread, and if citizens enjoy political liberties, then governments are indeed representative.

As the essays in this volume testify, our questions converge but the answers do not. The volume offers the gamut of facts and opinions: some deeply skeptical, if not outright negative, others unabashedly positive. Given this divergence, one role of the introduction is to analyze why we arrive at different answers. We begin with analytical distinctions, summarize the distinct views, and conclude.

Representation and Its Cognates

Thus far, we have spoken loosely about the best interest of "the people" or "citizens." Yet interests are often in conflict. It is, thus, necessary to ask what interests there are for a government to represent.

1. There are situations in which the same course of action is best for all citizens. Such situations satisfy the conditions of Condorcet's (1986 [1785]) jury theorem: everyone chooses the same course of action in each possible state of the world. Hence, if the state of the world were known, the decision about how to act would be reached by unanimity. But individuals are uncertain which it happens to be. The democratic process is then a search for truth. This can be termed an epistemic conception of democracy (Coleman 1989). If there are disagreements, they are purely cognitive. A government is representative if it acts on the best available knowledge; and if individuals are sufficiently well informed so that each of them or the average one is more likely than not to reach the correct decision, this knowledge is revealed by the verdict of the majority of voters (Grofman, Owen, and Feld 1983). The same is true if the structure of interests is one of pure coordination: individuals do not care whether they drive on the right or the left as long as they drive on the same side. In such situations, the government can represent individual interests, since the common interest is nothing but their sum.

5

2. There are situations in which the structure of interests places individuals in a prisoners' dilemma. If individuals were to make decisions in a decentralized way, each deciding what to do, the collectivity would arrive at a state of the world that would be strictly inferior to a state of the world that could be attained if individuals voted and the decision reached by the vote were coercively enforced. Suppose that each individual decides independently whether to vaccinate himself or herself against a contagious disease, where vaccination has some positive probability of triggering the illness. Each individual would prefer not to vaccinate if all others (or some number of others) did, and the result would be that no one would vaccinate and the disease would be widespread. Yet if individuals vote whether to impose compulsory vaccination, they unanimously decide to do so and, in the centralized equilibrium, few people suffer from the disease.

In such situations, the government cannot represent individual interests, which would be not to vaccinate if others did. Yet the government can represent an interest that is collective in the sense that everyone is better off under the centralized decision than they would have been had they all pursued individual interests. People have to be coerced for their own good; the government is representative in such situations when it pursues the collective interest.

3. In the case of outright conflicts of interests, some people inevitably gain and some lose from any course of action a government chooses. Even under constitutional constraints, majority rule leaves some interests of the electoral minority unprotected. Suppose citizens vote on one issue, linear taxes, and the majority rule equilibrium calls for a major redistribution from the rich to the poor, a redistribution not forbidden by the constitutional guarantees of property. By our definition, the government is representative if it effectuates such a redistribution, that is, if its actions hurt a minority. Note that the epistemic notion, according to which this redistribution would be also in the interest of the minority, makes no sense when interests are in conflict.[2]

Yet governments rarely admit that their actions hurt anyone. President Salvador Allende's declaration that "I am not the president of all the Chileans" was generally recognized as a major blunder and was politically costly. Former British Prime Minister

---

[2] For an attempt to salvage the epistemic notion from Black's (1958) criticism, see Miller (1986).

Edward Heath seems to have been the only politician in recent times who openly declared that he represents class interests, and he was promptly removed from office by his colleagues. There seems to exist a perennial tension between the rationalist origins of democracy and the interest-ridden structure of modern societies.

When the structure of interests is such that any course of action puts individuals in conflict, a government that pursues the best interest of a majority, at a cost to the minority, is representative. This is, after all, what majority rule is about.

Yet since the vote of a majority need not constitute a unique aggregation of individual preferences, there may exist other majorities whose interests the government could pursue. Indeed, it is possible for a government to be elected by one majority and to pursue the interests of another. Since this issue receives little attention in this volume (but see Ferejohn 1986, 1995), let us clarify it at the outset, using an example adapted from Rogowski (1981: 407). Suppose that the electorate has (single-peaked, monotonic) preferences in two (equally weighted) dimensions – social and military expenditures – and the distribution of peak preferences is as follows (0 indicates a preference for the status quo, + for more, – for less):

		Military			
		+	*0*	–	
	+	36	4	12	52
Social	0	15	8	9	32
	–	0	8	8	16
		51	20	29	100

Given this distribution of preferences over {social, military} spending, there are three possible majorities: {0,0}, {0,+}, {+,+}. That is, each of these policy combinations obtains the support of majority when paired against any other policy. Yet no policy outside this set is preferred by a majority to any policy within it.[3] Thus, given majority rule, we can think in two ways: a government

---

[3] To take an example, {+,+} is preferred over {0, 0} by the 36% of voters for whom {+,+} is the ideal point, {0,0} is preferred by the 8% for whom this is the ideal point as well as by the 12 + 9 + 8 + 8 whose ideal points are farther away from {+,+} than from {0, 0}, for the total of 45%, while 15% of voters, with ideal points {0,+} and the 4% with {+,0} are indifferent between {+,+} and {0,0}. Hence, {0,0} defeats {+,+}. Similarly, {+,0} defeats {0,0} and {+,+} defeats {0,+}. Yet, say, {–,–} defeats no alternative in the top cycle.

is representative in the narrow ("mandate") sense if it adopts the policies preferred by the specific majority by which it was elected (say, +,+), or it is representative in a broader ("top cycle") sense as long as it pursues the interests of any majority. In either case, a government is not representative if it pursues a course of action that would be defeated by every majority, that is, as long as it acts in the interest of a minority, including its own.

Note the fluidity of the language just cited: Dahl refers to "responsiveness," Riker to "responsibility," Schmitter and Karl to "accountability," while Pitkin speaks of "representation." To introduce the terminology we agreed to use, let us conjure up an idealized policy process.

This process begins with interests and values by which individuals evaluate different states of the world, outcomes of policies pursued under conditions. When these basic criteria of evaluation are combined with beliefs about the effect of policies on outcomes, they induce preferences over policies. These preferences are signaled to politicians through a variety of mechanisms, such as elections, public opinion polls, or other forms of political expression. "Mandates" are a particular kind of signals that are emitted in elections: they constitute a choice among proposals ("platforms," however vague these may be), offered by competing teams of politicians, by a fixed rule of aggregation, namely one of majority. Once elected, the victorious politicians adopt policies. These policies become transformed into outcomes under the noise of conditions. As the electoral term ends, voters evaluate the outcomes and decide whether or not to retain the incumbent government.

A picture may be of help (Figure I.1). "Representation" is a relation between interests and outcomes. Yet given this idealized picture, we could think of as many as eleven labels that would denote different types of consistency between the different phases of this process. For example, we could say that signals that accurately reflect interests are "rational" or that policies that bring about the intended outcomes are "effective." We will, however, focus only on three of these relations: (1) between signals and policies, which we will call "responsiveness"; (2) between mandates and policies, which Downs (1957) referred to as "reliability," but which, following Stokes (Chapter 3 in this volume), we will call "mandate-responsiveness"; and (3) between outcomes and sanctions, which we will call "accountability."

8

responsiveness (Stimson)

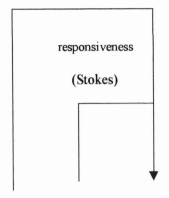

Preferences → Signals → Mandates → Policies → Outcomes

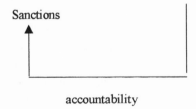

accountability

Figure I.1. Policy process

A government is "responsive" if it adopts policies that are signaled as preferred by citizens. These signals may include public opinion polls; various forms of direct political action, including demonstrations, letter campaigns, and the like; and, during elections, votes for particular platforms. Hence, the concept of responsiveness is predicated on the prior emission of messages by citizens. Stimson (with MacKuen and Erikson 1995[4] and in this volume) examines to what extent the actions of the United States representatives and senators, presidents, and Supreme Court justices follow the unidimensional "mood" of public opinion. Stokes (Chapter 3) does the same with regard to electoral mandates, asking whether governments pursue the policies that

---

[4] Stimson, MacKuen, and Erikson (1995) refer to "dynamic representation," but we argue here that this is not an accurate term.

they advocated in election campaigns. In both cases, the message comes first, and public officials are responsive to the extent to which their actions follow the preferences signaled by citizens, whether via polls or via elections, simply "responsive" in the first case, "mandate-responsive" in the second.

Governments are "accountable" if citizens can discern representative from unrepresentative governments and can sanction them appropriately, retaining in office those incumbents who perform well and ousting from office those who do not. An "accountability mechanism" is thus a map from the outcomes of actions (including messages that explain these actions) of public officials to sanctions by citizens. Elections are a "contingent renewal" accountability mechanism, where the sanctions are to extend or not to extend the government's tenure.

These distinctions highlight the double role of elections in engendering representation, emphasized in this volume by Manin, Przeworski, and Stokes (Chapter 1), as well as by Fearon (Chapter 2). A government may act in a representative fashion because it is responsive or because it is accountable.

If individuals are rational and governments are competent in the sense defined here, and if voters know everything they need to know about the exogenous conditions and about the effect of policies on outcomes, then either a responsive or an accountable government will be representative. People will signal their will in elections, and a responsive government will implement their instructions to generate outcomes that people want. Alternatively, the government will anticipate retrospective judgments of the electorate and, to win reelection, will do the same. Compliance with instructions inherent in the mandate is then equivalent to anticipations of retrospective judgments: they generate the same, first-best actions by the government.

Yet neither a responsive nor an accountable government need be representative. As this is the theme of several chapters, we sketch some of the reasons. We assume first that individuals know what is best for them but are uncertain about some relevant states of the world. We then lift the liberal assumption that individuals are the best judges of their own interests.

With Pitkin, assume first that "normally a man's wishes and what is good for him will coincide" (1967: 156). Individuals know what is best for them. Yet suppose that there is something that people do not know, perhaps because only the government can observe it (e.g., the negotiating posture of foreign governments or international financial institutions) or because the information is costly to obtain (e.g., the level of demand in the major recipients of the country's exports). If people are not certain about exogenous conditions or about the effect of policies on outcomes, then they cannot be sure which policies are in their best interest or how much they can expect from the government.

With such incomplete information, a government may be representative even if it is not responsive to the expressed wishes of the people, and, conversely, it can be unrepresentative even if it follows the signaled preferences.

When people are not certain what is the true state of the world, a betrayal of the mandate no longer implies that the government was unrepresentative. As Stokes (in this volume) emphasizes, if voters' instructions are based on mistaken assumptions, governments may betray them in good faith, which led Pitkin (1967: 163) to maintain that "the represented have no will on most issues, and the duty of the representative is to do what *is* best for them, not what they latently want" (emphasis added).

One way to think about representation under such conditions has been offered by Lord Brougham[5] (cited by Pitkin 1967: 150; emphasis added): "the essence of Representation is that the power of the people should be parted with, and given over, for a limited period, to the deputy chosen by the people, and that he should perform that part in the government which, *but for this transfer*, would have been performed by the people themselves." But this transfer is not innocuous: governments know what citizens do not precisely because they are governments. The counterfactual conjured by the lord and his acolytes is *in modus irrealis*. It calls for imagining what the Peruvian citizens would have done had they known what President Alberto Fujimori of Peru knew when he did in office exactly what he campaigned against in the election. But the citizens of Peru do not know, and neither does anyone else. And if the people do not know what they would have done because the government, by virtue of being the government, knows what people do not, who is to judge its action?

If citizens had really wanted governments to follow their instructions, they could have forced them to do so. As Manin (1997) points out, while this possibility was debated both during

---

[5] And rediscovered independently by Rogowski (1981) and Stokes (1997).

the American and the French constitutional debates, in no existing democracy are representatives compelled to abide by their electoral promises. But even without imperative mandates, voters could at least inform the government what it needs to do in order to be reelected. They could offer the government a contract: if the incumbent delivers what the voter wants, the latter will renew the contract. This is indeed the construction adopted in models of accountability: voters announce to the government that they will vote to reelect it if their income increases by 4%, if streets are safer, if abortion legislation is liberalized, if the country qualifies for the World Cup, and the incumbent decides what to do armed with this knowledge. Yet this construction is obviously artificial: voters make no such announcements. Indeed, democracies have no institutions through which such announcements could be made. We could have them: as voters cast their ballots, they could also include the terms of their personal contracts. But we do not.

Why don't we? The reason may be that we expect governments to do all that is possible under the circumstances to improve our welfare, rather than fulfill contracts. Voters are uncertain about the possibilities. And if governments are not perfect agents, if they want anything different from and costly to citizens, then by revealing what they will be satisfied with, voters allow governments to do less than they could do for them.

Thus, informational asymmetry between governments and citizens can work against the latter. As Cheibub and Przeworski (Chapter 7) argue, when governments know what voters will be satisfied with and voters do not know what governments can do for them, room is opened for moral hazard. Suppose that voters do not announce the terms of the contract to the government but that the incumbent learns, say from public opinion polls, what voters expect. Then the fact that the government adopts policies that follow the trends of public opinion – in other terms, that the government is *responsive* to the public opinion – does not imply that it is *representative*. If voters inform the government that they care most that streets be safe, the government may do nothing about unemployment, even if it could. Contrary to Stimson, MacKuen, and Erikson (1995), responsiveness is not the same as "dynamic representation."

Mandates are not instructions. At best, they signal voters' preferences. Clearly, voters who voted for the victorious party would prefer if the government pursued its announced platform rather than platforms that were defeated. But if voters are rationally ignorant, they must know that they do not know. Hence, while we choose policies that we think represent our best interests or candidates who will represent us as persons, we want governments to be able to govern. And this may mean that they should not be responsive to our expressed wishes.

Indeed, many theorists of democracy argued that governments should not follow the twists and turns of public opinion but should exercise the courage and the authority to do what is best for the society. As Lippman (1956) wrote about citizens, "Their duty is to fill the office and not to direct the office-holder." And Schumpeter (1942) admonished voters that they "must understand that, once they elected an individual, political action is his business not theirs. This means that they must refrain from instructing him what he is do."

Under democracy, people invest governments with the power to rule because they can remove them. If voters do not need to issue any instructions to the incoming government, it is because the incumbents know that voters will have the last say. At the beginning of the term voters need not even have a clear view what to expect or to demand. It is up to the incumbent to guess what voters will reward and what they will punish (Manin 1997). Voters can rely simply on the politicians' desire to be reelected, for, as Hamilton (*Federalist* no. 72) observed, "There are few men who would not feel . . . zeal in the discharge of a duty . . . when they were permitted to entertain a hope of *obtaining by meriting*, a continuance of them."

Yet is this prospect, the prospect of having to render accounts at the time of the next election, sufficient to induce representation? If voters do not observe some conditions that affect the outcomes of government actions, they will sometimes reelect politicians who have not done all they could and will at other times throw out of office governments that did all that was feasible, which led Pitkin (1967: 165) to observe that the incumbent's "reelection is not absolute proof that he is a good representative; it proves at most that voters think so."

Thus, even if individuals know what is best for them, if they are not fully informed about some relevant features of the world, they may not want the government to follow their signals and they may err in their retrospective sanctions. This is why several chapters in this volume explore the relation between elections and representation. What are the conditions, if any, under which using the vote to inform the government about one's preferences induces representation? What are the conditions under which using it to sanction past performance of the government accomplishes this effect? What happens if people use the vote simultaneously for both purposes: to select policies or policy-bearing politicians and to sanction the past performance? We also investigate facts. Do governments follow public opinion (Stimson)? Do they implement mandates (Stokes)? Do they manipulate public opinion (Maravall)? Does their survival in office depend on the outcomes they generate (Cheibub and Przeworski)?

Yet we must also allow the possibility that many people do not know what is best for them. President Chirac of France observed recently that "les politiques courageuses sont rarement populaires," consoling himself with the hope that in the end people will see the light. Why would policies that are in the best interest of citizens not enjoy their support?

People may have inconsistent time preferences. Suppose that the electoral term is divided into two periods: early and late. Suppose that the ex ante preferences of citizens are ($\delta < 1$)

$$UA = U(EARLY) + \delta\, U(LATE),$$

and the ex post preferences are

$$UP = \delta\, U(EARLY) + U(LATE).$$

A responsive government follows policies dictated by UA, and the ex ante signal of voters is "do pleasing things early." But by the end of the term voters will have preferred that the government followed policies implied by UP: "impose hardships early, then please." Hence, Chirac may have been correct that people sometimes object to policies that they find attractive in retrospect.

Inconsistent time preferences are not the same as myopia. Suppose now that there are two periods: the current term and the future beyond it, and that the present value of the future at the beginning of the current terms is

$$W = U(CURRENT) + \delta\, E[U(FUTURE)].$$

Clearly, if they are not myopic, voters should evaluate the performance of the government by looking not just at what will happen or has already happened during the term but also at the legacy the government leaves for the future. If the government produces a bonanza during the current term by cutting all the trees in the country, nonmyopic citizens will think badly of it, even though they lived on champagne during the term. Conversely, if a government embarks on policies that have short-term costs and long-term benefits, nonmyopic citizens will support it.

A government convinced that a long-term future necessitates short-term sacrifices is representative if it does act courageously. But its actions may be unpopular ex ante and disapproved at the end of the term. Effects of policies do not conveniently materialize with the rhythm of the electoral calendar, so the future remains uncertain and people's expectations may be incorrect even if they are not myopic. The present value of the future at the end of the term, the legacy the government leaves, is not something people can easily observe. They must make inferences from what they do see, which is mainly what happened to them or others during the term. But such inferences are not easy and people can reasonably use different rules to make them: "the worse, the worse" but perhaps also "the worse, the better" (Stokes 1996).

If individuals are not the best judges of their own welfare, then who is to judge if a government acts in a representative manner? Pitkin claims that in such situations governments should act on behalf rather than on bequest: on what people "ought to want" rather than what they say they want. But "ought to want" can be taken at least in two ways: (1) "would have preferred the particular outcome with their current preferences, had it already materialized, over what they do want now," or (2) "ought to have different preferences."

The first case is subject to reasoned arguments appealing to people's own hypothetical judgments.[6] The obvious difficulty is that observers may be insufficiently well informed or that they may be interested themselves. Thus, while economists always think that the informed observers are economists (obviously of their particular persuasion), one may reasonably doubt whether their prescriptions are sufficiently well grounded in theory and evidence to warrant overriding people's own judgments. Moreover, even

---

[6] Marxists maintain that an informed, "critical," observer can ascertain what individuals ought to want by looking at their class position. Bartels (1996) suggests that we can tell what people ought to want by looking at what enlightened members of the same groups do want.

when valid, such inferences deteriorate into the second posture if preferences are endogenous. And the second posture is just a way of saying that people's preferences should be disregarded altogether, for reasons base or lofty, as when Henry Kissinger declared that President Salvador Allende of Chile was "elected due to the irresponsibility of the people."

To reject welfarism, one must be willing to accept that individual preferences are not the best standard by which to evaluate collective welfare.[7] For example, observing that "The Arrowian postulates may model the idea of democracy-respecting social choice," Roemer (1996: 37) goes on to ask, "why should distributive justice be determined by a democratic procedure, when citizens vote in a self-interested way?" Governments may pursue ideals and use criteria different from those whom they represent, and they may be "just" or "good" by some normative criteria. But the concept of representation is essentially welfarist. At the limit it can be based on conjectures about what people would have wanted, but it cannot free itself from those whom it represents altogether.

Representation and Elections

The alternative roles of elections in inducing representation are the focus in the first part of the book.

Manin, Przeworski, and Stokes (Chapter 1) distinguish the "mandate" from the "accountability" views of elections: in the first, citizens signal to governments what to do; in the second, they judge whether governments have done what they should have. Having examined the conditions necessary for either mechanism to induce representation, the authors conclude that implementation of electoral promises should be expected whenever what politicians and voters want coincides or whenever reelection-seeking politicians expect voters to stick to their initial preferences. Yet, on the one hand, incumbents may adhere to their promises even if their implementation is not the best for citizens and, on the other hand, they may deviate from the promises in the best interest of the public. Hence, "mandate-representation" – a situation in which mandates are faithfully implemented in the best interest of the electorate – is fragile. In turn, the threat of the electoral sanction

---

[7] On this issue, see the essays in Sen and Williams (1982).

16

is undermined when voters do not observe various things that politicians observe or know. Hence, the fact that governments must render accounts at the polls is insufficient to induce representation. Moreover, when voters use their vote both to choose better governments and to structure incentives for the incumbent, they must sacrifice one goal at the expense of the other.

Fearon (Chapter 2) contests that elections are about taking governments to account. He argues that voters use elections to choose good governments, rather than to sanction the incumbents. Fearon cites several facts that are manifestly inconsistent with the idea that voters think retrospectively. Developing a formal model that includes both a selection of prospective governments and a sanction for the incumbents, he also comes to the conclusion that using the vote for two purposes weakens the power of incentives for the incumbent government.

Stokes (Chapter 3) is particularly concerned with implementation of mandates. She observes that in Latin America's democracies politicians deviate from their mandates with some regularity and shows that they are unresponsive to voters when they switch policies. Pressure from markets, as well as the possibility that voters' preferences may change (or that politicians will somehow escape retrospective sanctions), induces deviations from mandates. Stokes's chapter underscores the complexities of assessing whether a government is representative when it is unresponsive. Does the government think that voters' preferences are ill-informed and that voters will recognize their mistake once the unpopular policies have run their course? Or are unresponsive governments shirking or responding to special interests?

Reflecting on the history of the U.S. Congress, Ferejohn (Chapter 4) poses a puzzle: why would politicians ever voluntarily make their actions more visible to voters? The principal-agent model entailed in the relation of representation is a peculiar one, insofar as it is the agents who decide what principals will know about their actions. Why, then, would politicians, subject to the electoral sanction, make it easier for voters to learn about their conduct? Ferejohn's answer is that under some conditions voters will be disposed to invest politicians with more-extensive powers or resources when citizens are more certain that they will be able to learn what the incumbents did with these powers. In turn, politicians may prefer to have greater resources and be subject to more-extensive scrutiny than have less power.

Reviewing the recent Spanish democratic experience, Maravall (Chapter 5) comes to conclusions opposite to those of Ferejohn. He assumes that since politicians know that they will be judged by voters, they do whatever they can to escape their sanction. Maravall distinguishes mechanisms by which politicians seek to influence public opinion from mechanisms by which they hide their actions from public scrutiny. He is particularly concerned with the role of political parties as a mechanism of accountability.

Finally, the two statistical chapters pose a puzzle. Stimson (Chapter 6) finds that American public officials – legislators, presidents, and even Supreme Court justices – are extremely responsive to public opinion as conveyed by the polls. In turn, analyzing all democracies that existed in the world between 1950 and 1990, Cheibub and Przeworski (Chapter 7) discover that the survival of heads of governments does not depend on economic performance. Both findings run with the grain of the respective bodies of literature (see Cheibub and Przeworski for a summary). Studies of responsiveness typically find a close correspondence between public opinion and policy. Moreover, time-series studies of particular countries, which take as the dependent variable the popularity of the government at the polls or the share of the vote of the incumbent party in elections, also typically find that economic performance plays a role in sanctioning governments. In turn, cross-national studies of the same type, with some exceptions, fail to discover an impact of economic performance on the vote for incumbents. Yet what ultimately matters for accountability is not the popularity or even the share of the vote but survival in office. And while studies of survival of cabinets in parliamentary systems tend to find a clear effect of unemployment, the effect of inflation is problematic. So the findings of Cheibub and Przeworski, who distinguish parliamentary from presidential democracies and discover that economic variables do not matter for the survival in office of the respective heads of governments, are consistent with the tenor of other studies.

If both Stimson's and Cheibub and Przeworski's findings are true, then the puzzle is this: why would politicians choose policies responsive to the public opinion if they do not lose office when they generate bad economic results? One explanation may be that public opinion is not a reliable signal about future retrospective judgments – in particular, that, consistently with Maravall but against Stimson, public opinion is the result, not the cause, of policies. But it may be also true that Fearon is simply correct that voters use elections to choose better governments, rather than to sanction the incumbents.

Representation and the Structure of Government

Although we consider the government as a unitary agent in the first part of the book, in today's democracies power is divided among several agencies or departments, sometimes also between national and local governments. Historically, moreover, a number of key figures in the establishment of representative institutions, such as Locke, Montesquieu, or Madison, to mention just a few, also advocated separating and dividing political power.

Elections are not the only mechanism that may induce governments to act in a representative manner. To use the language of O'Donnell (1991), while elections are a "vertical" mechanism of accountability, democratic institutions are supposed to offer also "horizontal mechanisms": the separate powers of government respond and render accounts not only to citizens but also to one another. Indeed, not all organs of government are elected in democracies: the occupants of legislative and executive powers are elected, directly or indirectly, but judges and bureaucrats almost never are.

The potential importance of separation of powers in generating representation is highlighted by Persson, Roland, and Tabellini (1996), who show that if the separation of powers is organized in a particular way, the government as a whole will be induced to reveal to citizens the true conditions under which it operates and that this information, in turn, will enable citizens to enforce representation through retrospective voting. Although their model ignores the potential role of political parties in promoting collusion, it demonstrates the importance of institutional design. Democracies are not all the same, and the particular features of their institutional system may have profound consequences for the performance of governments.

The second part of the book approaches the government as a composite agent and examines some ways in which its structure affects representation. This part, it will be noted, is less systematic than our analysis of the role of elections. Such a difference is not coincidental. While the arrangements that initiate, enable, and terminate the activity of representatives have been relatively stable and uniform throughout the history of representative democracy, there has been a much wider variance across time and countries in the way governmental power is divided. To be sure, the separation of executive, legislative, and judicial powers can be found in all democracies. The concrete implications of this separation, however, vary widely depending on whether the institutional system is presidential or parliamentary. It seems that the conclusions of Persson, Roland, and Tabellini hold for presidentialism, but not, or much less so, for parliamentarism. Besides, not all countries have a system of checks and balances. Although the principle of the separation of powers and the principle of checks and balances are related, they are not identical. The former requires that the three traditional functions of government be entrusted to distinct organs. The latter prescribes that each branch partially participate in the function primarily exercised by another (e.g., through a presidential veto, judicial review), so that they can hold each other in check (Manin 1994). The consequences of the two systems for representation can hardly be the same. Similarly, the place of the judiciary cannot be the same in the civil-law and common-law traditions. The list of such variations could go on.

Moreover, the concrete functions of governments have enormously changed over time. Yet we continue to conceptualize governmental powers along the lines proposed by Montesquieu 250 years ago. It is at best doubtful that we should still speak of the executive, the legislature, and the judiciary as the three main powers of government. Note, for example, that such a conceptualization makes no room for the bureaucracy. There is also every reason to doubt that we should keep defining the activity of the "executive" branch as carrying out and applying the decisions of the legislature, which was Montesquieu's conception of execution. We are simply lacking a systematic picture of the functions performed by present-day governments.

This volume offers a highly selective view of the consequences of the structure of government for representation, focusing on the bureaucracy and the relations between government and parliament in parliamentary systems.

Citizens' control over the bureaucracy can be only indirect, since democratic institutions contain no mechanisms that would allow citizens to sanction directly the legal actions of bureaucrats. Citizens can at most consider the performance of the bureaucracy when they sanction the behavior of elected politicians. As Dunn and Uhr (1993: 2) suggest, we do not even seem to know how to think about principal-agent relations involved in controlling bureaucrats: "it is by no means clear what place executive officials are meant to play as representatives of the people. Are they agents of the government or of the people? If of the former, are they primarily responsible to the executive which employs them, or the legislature which funds them?" Hence, while the bureaucracy is supposed to serve citizens, it is accountable at most to politicians.

Drawing on the Australian experience from 1983 to 1996, Delmer Dunn (Chapter 10) argues that even such a modest aim is not easy to achieve. When the Labor Party came to power in 1983, the bureaucracy was seen as too independent from ministers and insufficiently responsive. Dunn analyzes the reforms that apparently succeeded in establishing a greater control of ministers over their bureaucracies. He draws broader lessons about the kind of relationship between elected and nonelected officials that best secures responsiveness of the latter to the former.

Laver and Shepsle (Chapter 9) focus on another form of indirect accountability. They argue that in most democracies governments are not accountable to citizens but to the parliament. Thus, political accountability is essentially mediated. Focusing on the motion of no confidence as the privileged mechanism of accountability of the government to the parliament, and using the portfolio approach, they conclude that a government is accountable to its parliamentary principals when it is an equilibrium government. On their view, an agent is accountable to his or her principal when the principal, having the means to do so, has no inclination to replace the agent with a feasible alternative. So if the principal is merely content, though not necessarily happy, with the services of an imperfect agent, that agent may be said to be accountable to the principal.

Elster (Chapter 8) turns to antiquity, more specifically to Athenian democracy, to identify various modalities and mechanisms of accountability. He argues that while all political systems need accountability mechanisms, Athens was special in that individuals could be held accountable for their proposals, not just for their actions. Another striking difference between Athens and modern democracies is that in Athens people could be punished for sheer bad luck: they were held accountable for outcomes, regardless of whether they had been demonstrably incompetent or dishonest.

Conclusion

Finally, John Dunn (Chapter 11) provides a provocative overview of the preceding chapters by situating the issue of accountability in a broader context of democratic theory. He points out that being ruled is an unpleasant necessity. To avoid conflicts, we transpose the "horizontal danger" of killing each other into the "vertical danger" of being coerced by governments. But the necessity does not turn being ruled into a pleasure. Hence, Dunn argues, elections are not about rendering accounts for specific actions: they are an occasion for people to reassert their sovereignty. Elections, in Dunn's view, have two functions under democracy: they offer the losers a chance in the future, and they issue an authorization to rule. Although elections may prevent some abuses, given the intrinsic opacity of the modern-day politics, it is futile to expect that they would serve as an instrument of control over governments.

While Dunn's conclusion reflects the general tenor of other analyses in this volume, it is subject to modalities and degrees. Empirical evidence – accumulated elsewhere as well as offered here – seems to indicate that often what governments do is what people say they want them to do, although it is less clear which comes first. Yet it also appears that while voters sanction incumbent governments for economic performance, this sanction does not extend to the point of throwing out governments that do not perform well. And while the analytical distinction between using the vote to select governments and using it to structure incentives for the incumbents is illuminating, voters probably do some of both: empirical studies of this issue provide highly divergent results. Thus, although we end up with a vague sensation that what governments do has some connection to what citizens want, the modality of this connection remains opaque.

Degrees are even harder to assess. Perfect representation is not a feasible democratic ideal. Even if individuals were best judges of their own interests and even if they could uniquely aggregate their preferences into a collective will, they would not want to bind governments to implement this will. To govern, our rulers must have some latitude and some authority: this much is inescapable. Hence, at times they will do things that surprise us and leave us wondering. But even ex post, when their effects have already materialized, actions of governments are hard to judge. There are so many things we do not know, not even what the government knows. So again, even if citizens could coordinate their ex post evaluations, they have to cast judgments with a fuzzy understanding of the responsibilities. All this means that governments can to some extent escape from public scrutiny and public control. To what extent, we cannot tell: as conceptual discussions of representation indicate, even the yardsticks are difficult to establish, not to speak of their realization.

This is a paltry conclusion. We are not even claiming that, in the standard hand-waving gesture, "further research is necessary." Further research is necessary; while we think that several chapters in this volume have significantly clarified the role of elections in securing representation, our understanding of the effects of the structure of government clearly lags behind. But we should be prepared that results of further research will not remove the basic ambiguities, that answers will depend on assumptions, and divergent assumptions will remain plausible. Does it make sense to think that individual are the best judges of their own interests? Does it make sense to assume that individual preferences are autonomous? Do they neatly order along one dimension? Should we consider a government to be representative when it pursues the interests of a majority different from the one that brought it to office? These are just some examples. The fact is that we can entertain alternative conceptions of representation and that these conceptions will shape the answers.

Yet there are some things we have learned. Perhaps foremost is the importance of information – a theme pervasive in most contributions. The main difficulty both in instructing governments what to do and in judging what they have done is that we, citizens, just do not know enough.

True, we will never know what all governments know, nor would we want to. After all, governing is a part of division of labor, and even if we were to select our rulers at random, not on the basis of the privileged knowledge they already have, they would inevitably acquire what economists term "firm-specific skills." Indeed, we want them to develop such skills. Yet we do not know enough, and the reason is structural, not just volitional. The peculiarity of the principal-agent relation entailed in the relation of political representation is that our agents are our rulers: we designate them as agents so that they would tell us what to do, and we even give them the authority to coerce us to do it. And the rules that our agents impose on us include access to information: to use just one example, the British government barred independent researchers from access to tissues extracted from cows suffering from bovine spongiform encephalopathy ("mad cow" disease).

Yet, to evoke Kant, "All actions affecting the rights of other human beings are wrong if their maxim is not compatible with their being made public." Bobbio (from whom this passage is taken, 1989: 84) comments further that "a precept not susceptible to being publicized can be taken to mean a precept which, if it was ever made known to the public, would arouse such a public reaction that one could not put it into action." We do not want governments to take actions that they would have not taken had we known why they are taking them. But this means that we have to know what the governments are doing and why independently of what they want us to know. Our authorization to rule should not include the authority to hide information from us. To promote representation, democracy requires a "regime of free information" (John Dunn).

Thus, even if elections give governments a broad authorization to rule, this authorization should not extend to informing us. Our information must not depend on what governments want us to know. The institutional implications are obvious: we need independent electoral commissions, independent accounting offices, independent statistical agencies. To coin a term, we need "accountability agencies," independent of other branches of government and subject to direct popular control, perhaps through elections.

These institutional considerations bring us to the second lesson of these analyses: the importance of the institutional structure of government. This is a topic with regard to which we made little headway and where further research is definitely needed. One implication of the ineffectiveness of elections as a mechanism of control over governments is that we may want to be able to control governments independently for their actions in different realms, say, to elect the governors of an independent central bank (Minford 1995). Yet short of multiplying the number of directly elected agencies, the central question is how to design the structure of government in such a way that its various branches would control each other to make the government as a whole act in the best interest of the public.

References

Bartels, Larry. 1996. "Public Opinion and Political Interests." Department of Politics, Princeton University. Unpublished manuscript.

Black, Duncan. 1958. *The Theory of Committees and Elections.* Cambridge: Cambridge University Press.

Bobbio, Norberto. 1989. *Democracy and Dictatorship.* Minneapolis: University of Minnesota Press.

Burke, E. 1949 [1774]. "Speech to the Election of Bristol." In R. J. S. Hoffmann and P. Levack , eds., *Burke's Politics, Selected Writings and Speeches*, 114–17. New York: A. A. Knopf.

Coleman, Jules. 1989. "Rationality and the Justification of Democracy." In Geoffrey Brennan and Loren E. Lomasky, eds., *Politics and Process*, 194–220. Cambridge: Cambridge University Press.

Condorcet. 1986 [1785]. "Essai sur l'application de l'analyse à la probabilité des décisions rendues à la pluralité des voix." In Olivier de Bernon, ed., *Sur les élections et autres textes.* Paris: Fayard.

Dahl, Robert. 1971. *Polyarchy: Participation and Opposition.* New Haven: Yale University Press.

Downs, Anthony. 1957. *An Economic Theory of Democracy.* New York: Harper and Row.

Dunn, Delmer D., and John Uhr. 1993. "Accountability and Responsibility in Modern Democratic Governments." Paper presented at the annual meeting of the American Political Science Association, Washington, D.C., September 2–5.

Ferejohn, John. 1986. "Incumbent Performance and Electoral Control." *Public Choice* 50: 5–25.

1995. "The Spatial Model and Elections." In Bernard Grofman, ed., *Information, Participation, and Choice*, 107–24. Ann Arbor: University of Michigan Press.

Grofman, Bernard, Guillermo Owen, and Scott Feld. 1983. "Thirteen Theorems in Search of the Truth." *Theory and Decision* 15: 261–78.

Kelsen, Hans. 1929. *Vom Wesen und Wert der Demokratie.* Aalen: Scientia Verlag.

Lippman, Walter. 1956. *The Public Philosophy.* New York: Mentor Books.

Manin, Bernard. 1994. "Checks, Balances, and Boundaries: The Separation of Powers in the Constitutional Debate of 1787." In Biancamaria Fontana, ed., *The Invention of the Modern Republic*, 27–62. Cambridge: Cambridge University Press.

1997. *The Principles of Representative Government.* Cambridge: Cambridge University Press.

Miller, Nicolas R. 1986. "Information, Electorates, and Democracy: Some Extensions and Interpretations of the Condorcet Jury Theorem." In Bernard Grofman and Guillermo Owen, eds., *Information Pooling and Group Decision Making,* 173–92. Greenwich, Conn.: JAI Press.

Minford, Patrick. 1995. "Time-Inconsistency, Democracy, and Optimal Contingent Rules." *Oxford Economic Papers* 47: 195–210.

O'Donnell, Guillermo. 1991. "Delegative Democracy?" East-South System Transformations Working Paper No. 21. Chicago: University of Chicago.

Persson, Torsten, Gerard Roland, and Guido Tabellini. 1996. "Separation of Powers and Accountability: Towards a Formal Approach to Comparative Politics." Discussion Paper No. 1475. London: Centre for Economic Policy Research.

Pitkin, Hanna F. 1967. *The Concept of Representation.* Berkeley: University of California Press.

Riker, William. 1965. *Democracy in America.* 2d ed. New York: Macmillan.

Roemer, John E. 1996. *Theories of Distributive Justice.* Cambridge, Mass.: Harvard University Press.

Rogowski, Ronald. 1981. "Representation in Political Theory and in Law." *Ethics* 91: 395–430.

Schmitter, Philippe, and Terry Lynn Karl. 1991. "What Democracy Is . . . and What It Is Not." *Journal of Democracy* 2: 75–88.

Schumpeter, Joseph A. 1942. *Capitalism, Socialism, and Democracy.* New York: Harper & Brothers.

Sen, Amartya, and Bernard Williams, eds. 1982. *Utilitarianism and Beyond.* Cambridge: Cambridge University Press.

Stimson, James A., Michael B. MacKuen, and Robert S. Erikson. 1995. "Dynamic Representation." *American Political Science Review* 89: 543–65.

Stokes, Susan C. 1996. "Public Opinion and Market Reforms: The Limits of Economic Voting." *Comparative Political Studies* 29: 499–519.

1997. "Democratic Accountability and Policy Change: Economic Policy in Fujimori's Peru." *Comparative Politics* 29: 209–26.

Part One

Elections, Accountability, and Representation

Bernard Manin, Adam Przeworski,
and Susan C. Stokes

Chapter One

Elections and Representation

The claim connecting democracy and representation is that under democracy governments are representative because they are elected: if elections are freely contested, if participation is widespread, and if citizens enjoy political liberties, then governments will act in the best interest of the people. In one – the "mandate" – view, elections serve to select good policies or policy-bearing politicians. Parties or candidates make policy proposals during campaigns and explain how these policies would affect citizens' welfare; citizens decide which of these proposals they want implemented and which politicians to charge with their implementation, and governments do implement them. Thus, elections emulate a direct assembly and the winning platform becomes the "mandate" that the government pursues. In a second – "accountability" – view, elections serve to hold governments responsible for the results of their past actions. Because they anticipate the judgment of voters, governments are induced to choose policies that in their judgment will be positively evaluated by citizens at the time of the next election.

Yet both views are problematic. Representation is an issue because politicians have goals, interests, and values of their own, and they know things and undertake actions that citizens cannot observe or can monitor only at a cost. Even if once they are in office politicians may want to do nothing but serve the public, to get elected in the first place they may have to gratify special interests. And once elected, they may want to pursue their private goals or some public objectives that differ from those of citizens. If they have such motivations, they will want to do things other than represent the public. And voters do not know everything they need to know, whether to decide prospectively what politicians should be doing or to judge retrospectively if they did what they should have done. And if voters know that there are some things they do not know, they do not want to bind politicians to implement their wishes. In turn, if citizens do not have sufficient information to evaluate the incumbent governments, the threat of not being reelected is insufficient to induce governments to act in the best interest of the public.

In this chapter we analyze whether voters can enforce representation by using their vote to choose policies and politicians, using it to sanction the incumbent, or using their vote simultaneously in both ways. We then discuss institutional features that may be conducive to inducing representation.

The Mandate Conception of Representation

In electoral campaigns parties propose policies and offer candidates. If voters believe that politicians are not all the same, they may attempt to secure representation by using their vote to choose best policies or policy-bearing politicians. The questions we need to examine are whether (1) electoral campaigns are informative, that is, voters can justifiably expect that parties would do what they proposed, and (2) pursuing the winning platform, the "mandate," is always in the best interest of voters. We will say that "mandate-representation" occurs if the answer to both these questions is positive, that is, parties truthfully inform voters about their intentions and the implementation of these intentions is best for voters under the given circumstances.

The mandate conception of representation is widespread: scholars, journalists, and ordinary citizens rely on it as if it were axiomatic. Keeler (1993), for example, explains the major policy reforms introduced by Reagan, Thatcher, and Mitterand as follows: their respective countries faced economic crises, voters wanted change and expressed this desire at the polls, and the respective governments implemented their mandates. This model seems to account well for policy formation in advanced industrial society (Klingeman, Hofferbert, and Budge 1994). As a French politician put it, "Since the Romans, it is an old law of politics, which we should never lose from our view: governments can last only by the principle by which they were born" (Séguin 1997).

A rudimentary conceptual apparatus may help clarify what is entailed. In elections, parties or candidates present themselves to voters, informing them about their policy intentions.[1] Specifically, they tell voters which policies they intend to pursue, for what purposes, and with which consequences. Once elected, the victorious candidates choose policies, not necessarily the same as announced. Having observed the outcomes of the policies, voters vote again. To introduce an example, suppose that there are two possible platforms: S (for economic "security") and E (for "efficiency") policies.[2] Competing parties or candidates promise to do S or E, and once elected pursue S or E.

Politicians may care both about policies and about being elected and reelected. Politicians have preferences over policies if their reward from holding office or the probability of reelection depends on the policies they adopt. One can think of the reward from holding office in three ways: politicians may have favorite policies and derive utility from implementing them, they may want to advance their private interests, or they may derive satisfaction from the honor attached to office. Politicians have some beliefs about the promises that are more likely to make them win and the policies that voters will in fact appreciate having experienced their results.

Thus, the question about mandate representation is whether (1) the policy of the incumbents will be the same as their electoral platform, and (2) whether pursuing this platform will be best for voters. The conditions under which mandate representation occurs are threefold: when politicians' and voters' interests coincide, when politicians are motivated by the desire to be reelected and they think that voters will reelect them if they pursue policies on which they campaigned, and when politicians are concerned about the credibility of their future promises. We discuss these situations in turn.

1. Interests of politicians coincide with those of voters.[3] Citizens and governments have identical interests if governments want in their self-interest to bring about states of the world that are most desired by citizens. If politicians and voters

---

[1] Candidates also extol their personal virtues, a topic we treat later.

[2] The terminology is Elster's (1994).

[3] Obviously, the question that arises with such formulations is, Which voters? We assume in this chapter that, whatever is the dimensionality of the issue space, a majority rule equilibrium exists and thus there exists a "decisive voter." For complications that arise when this assumption does not hold, see Ferejohn (1986, 1995).

also have the same beliefs about the effects of policies on outcomes ("technical beliefs" in the language of Austen-Smith 1990),[4] then candidates get elected on the platform most preferred by voters and as incumbents they implement this platform in their own interest.

Almost all discussions of representation, beginning with J. S. Mill's *Considerations on Representative Government* (1991 [1861]), assume that electing politicians who somehow mirror or reproduce the composition of the electorate achieves representation. The assembly is representative in this view if it is a miniature of the electorate, a sample of it. The hypothesis underlying this conviction is that if the assembly is descriptively representative, then it will act to represent interests of the represented. As a consequence, discussions of representative institutions focus almost exclusively on electoral systems (for an example, see Rogowski 1981). The pathbreaking, and still unduly ignored, contribution of Pitkin (1967) was to problematize this connection: is it true that proportionality is the best way to secure representation? If each representative puts forth opinions and promotes the interests of his constituency, will the best interest of the collectivity be served?[5] And what if representatives become different from their constituents by the mere fact of being representatives? What if, once elected, they acquire knowledge the constituents do not have and perhaps even interests of their own?

2. Politicians want to be elected and reelected.[6] And they expect that voters will reelect them if they pursue the policies

---

[4] In its pure form, spatial theory of voting is logically incomplete: voters care only about outcomes but they choose on the basis of policies. What is obviously missing are "technical beliefs," as defined earlier. Note that if candidates and voters have identical interests but different technical beliefs, they will have different induced preferences about policies.

[5] One difficulty with this view, manifest in Mill, is that while the assembly may reflect interests proportionately, many decisions entailed in governing do not permit proportional allocations. Indeed, many are dichotomous, and in those the majority prevails while the minority loses. Hence, while proportionality allows all voices to be heard, it does not guarantee that all interests will be proportionately accommodated. Thus, as Pitkin points out, the activity of representing entailed by descriptive representation consists at most of articulating views, not of making decisions.

[6] This is true regardless of whether politicians also have other interests as long as they put a high value on holding office per se.

that they offered in their election campaign. If election-seeking politicians know the preference of the decisive voter, they offer a platform that coincides with this preference. If they expect that voters' preferences will not change or that these preferences will be confirmed by observing the outcomes of implementing the mandate (Harrington 1993a), then the incumbents pursue the announced policy in quest of reelection. And if voters know what is good for them, the outcome is best for voters, so that voters' threat to punish deviations from the mandate is credible.

3. Politicians are concerned that their promises be credible in the future. Even if voters believe that a deviation from the mandate was beneficial for them, they discount future promises of politicians who acquire a reputation of reneging on their campaign promises. Hence, voters may threaten the incumbents to vote against them if they betray their promises, regardless of the outcomes. This threat is implemented by the rival party in Alesina's (1988) model, in which voters are not strategic. In turn, it is implemented by voters in Banks's (1990) model, where, in turn, the credibility of this threat is assumed, rather than derived.[7] Hence, this is at best an incomplete story. We return to it later.

Note that mandate representation is a situation in which policies adopted by incumbents follow their electoral platforms *and* these policies are the best for citizens under the conditions observed by the incumbents. The three possibilities distinguished earlier add up to the conclusion that mandate representation occurs when what politicians and voters want coincides or when politicians care only about winning elections, and to win they must promise and implement policies that are best for the public. But short of this happy coincidence, politicians may have incentives either to deviate from the mandate in the best interest of the public or to stick to it at the cost of the electorate.

---

[7] Banks justifies this assumption referring to the multiperiod model of Austen-Smith and Banks (1989), where the threat of punishing deviations is indeed credible. But in Austen-Smith and Banks, governments never quite fulfill promises: when voters expect little of governments, parties always promise more than they deliver, even though they deliver first best; in turn, when voters expect a lot, platforms and reelection chances are independent of what voters want.

To highlight the weakness of the mandate mechanism, suppose that politicians cannot be reelected even once.[8] Voters know that once elected the incumbent will do whatever he wants. Without the sanction of voting again, voters must guess which of the competing parties or candidates has policy preferences that coincide with theirs and which is impervious to the corrupting sway of office. Yet unless the pool of candidates includes such politicians and unless voters guess correctly who they are, the victorious candidates will not act in the representative manner. If they have policy preferences distinct from those of the decisive voter, they will deviate from the announced policies; if they pursue private benefits, they will extract rents.

Moreover, just to get elected, politicians may have to make promises to special interests. Suppose, in the spirit of the Chicago School of Regulation (Stigler 1975; Peltzman 1976; Becker 1958, 1983), that (1) voters are ignorant, rationally or not, about the impact of policies on their welfare, and (2) to present themselves to voters, politicians need to expend resources, including but not limited to money. Politicians are concerned only with winning elections, but to win they must raise resources. Because voters do not care about policies that have only a small impact on their welfare, politicians can sell to interest groups policies that inflict only a small cost on each individual voter but which concentrate benefits on the particular interest groups and spend on electioneering the resources contributed by interest groups in exchange for these policies. Since policies that raise resources from special interests are costly to voters, politicians choose policies that make them indifferent at the margin between increasing voters' welfare and campaign expenditures, and the welfare of voters is not maximized.

To take an example, suppose that politicians decide whether to

---

[8] In fact, it is enough that the number of elections in which a politician can run is known and finite. Suppose that the politician will not be able to run after the t-th term. Then during the $(t-1)$st election voters will know that in the last term the politician will have no incentives to seek reelection and will vote against him. But if the politician will not be reelected for the t-th term, then he will not have incentives to behave well during the $(t-1)$st term and voters will not elect him. But then the same will be true during the $(t-2)$nd term, . . . , all the way to the first one. Unless politicians care about voters' approval when they leave office for the last time, term limits deprive voters from creating incentives for politicians to represent them.

subsidize the sugar industry. By subsidizing the sugar industry, the government inflicts on each individual an annual cost of $5.75 and benefits the sugar industry to the tune of $1.5 billion. Voters will not want to spend their resources to learn about the sugar policy and its effects: this information costs more than $5.75. Then the government will subsidize, get a campaign contribution from the industry, and maximize its probability of reelection.[9] Indeed, according to the Center for Responsive Policy (*New York Times*, January 24, 1997, p. 3), a sugar price subsidy that adds an extra $50 to a five-pound bag of sugar was supported by sixty-one senators who received on the average $13,473 from the industry political action committee, while it was opposed by thirty-five senators who on the average got $1,461.

The fact is that just to exist and to present themselves to voters, political parties must raise funds. When these funds come from special interests, they are exchanged for favors. Presumably, if Philip Morris Co. Inc. contributed in 1996 over $2.5 million to the Republican National Committee (*New York Times*, January 28, 1997, p. 3), it must have expected at least $2.5 million in favors; otherwise, its management should have been thrown out by stockholders. Exchanges of political contributions for policy favors are distorting through their effects on the allocation of resources. And the social cost of such distortions is likely to be much greater than that of outright theft, which is distorting only through its effect on distorting taxes.

Yet situations in which either politicians deviate from their promises in voters' best interest or stick to them against the interests of a majority are possible even if incumbents face repeated elections and even if electoral campaigns are costless (or publicly funded).

1. Conditions may change in such a way that the implementation of the mandate is no longer best for voters. Suppose

---

[9] This argument is subject to two criticisms. One is that if voters are only rationally ignorant, à la Stigler (1975), governments will be constrained to limit such policies to those that inflict a small cost on voters: hence, the aggregate loss of welfare may not be very large. Clearly what matters is how gullible voters are, and Becker (1983), who drops the assumption that ignorance is only rational, offers not even an intuition about it. Second (see Arnold 1993 and our subsequent discussion), there are several groups and most importantly the partisan opposition that have the interest to diffuse for free information about such policies.

that immediately upon assuming office an incoming government that won the election campaigning for policy S learns something neither it nor the voters knew at the time of the election: the departing government, competing for reelection, hid the sad contents of the treasury, and the electoral victors discover upon assuming office that coffers are empty. Say that S is the better policy when conditions are good, while E is better when they are bad. Then the government faces the choice of deviating from the mandate in the best interest of voters or adhering to it in spite of the changed circumstances. In turn, voters, who would have agreed to changing the policy had they observed what the government observes, must decide whether to believe the government's message, which will appear self-serving, without direct access to this information. And they can err, in either direction. Hence, incumbents will deviate some of the time and voters punish some deviations, good or bad.

Note that even changes of conditions that are endogenous to government policy, but were unforeseen by politicians before they reached office, may be reasons to change course in the interest of citizens' welfare; the 1983 switch of the French Socialist government may be a case in point.

2. To be elected, a candidate must offer the platform preferred by the decisive voter. Suppose a candidate believes that the decisive voter has incorrect beliefs about the effect of policies on outcomes. This candidate then faces a choice of offering a platform that she thinks is better for voters and going down to defeat (perhaps hoping to win the next time around, if the competitor implements less effective policies) or proposing what voters want and having at least a 50–50 chance of winning (if the other competitor offers the same platform). If the incumbent believes that the less popular policy is sufficiently more effective than the one voters prefer, he or she anticipates that, having observed its effects, voters will become persuaded that the correct policy was chosen and will vote to reelect, so that the politician will be able to continue the policy that is in effect better for citizens.

Two situations need to be further distinguished. In one (Harrington 1993a: sec. 4), the two candidates have the same beliefs about the preferences of the decisive voter but different beliefs about the effectiveness of policies, meaning that one of them thinks the decisive voter is wrong. Then they offer the same platform in the electoral campaign but once elected may pursue different policies. If the winner is the candidate who believes that the policy preferred by the decisive voter is significantly inferior to the alternative, the incumbent adopts the policy she prefers, in the belief that voters will be persuaded about its superiority once the outcomes materialize. In such situations, we should observe candidates offering the same platform and then sometimes deviating from the mandate.

In the second situation, the two candidates have the same beliefs about the effectiveness of policies but differ in their beliefs about the preference of the decisive voter. If elected, they pursue the same policy, but to get elected they offer different platforms. If the winner is the candidate who believed that the voters are mistaken, the incumbent switches policies once elected. In such situations, we should observe candidates offering different platforms and then pursuing the same policy regardless of who is elected.

Note that in both of these situations candidates (may) deviate from their platforms once elected, but they deviate believing that they are acting in the best interest of the electorate.

3. Suppose that everything is the same as just described but the incumbent does not believe that voters will be persuaded by the effectiveness of the better policy – either because voters are quite certain which policy is better for them or because the policy choice does not make a great difference. As Harrington (1993a) shows, if voters initially believe that one policy is better than the other, they are harder to convince ex post of the superiority of the alternative.[10] Fearing that if he proposes one platform and pursues another he will not be reelected, the incumbent offers the inferior platform that voters prefer and implements it, against what he believes are citizens' best interests. The mandate will be implemented, but politicians will not act in a representative manner.

To summarize: under some conditions, incumbents may either pursue policies that enhance that welfare of voters by deviating

---

[10] The intuition is the following. Suppose that voters initially believe that policy S is better for them than E by some amount e. If they observe an outcome of implementing E that is better than S by the amount e, their posterior belief will be that E produces outcomes at a level between their initial expectations and their observation, which will still be below S. To be persuaded that E is better than S, the outcome of E would have to be better than the prior on S by more than e.

from the mandate or they may adhere to the mandate even if they think that implementing it is not best for voters. And if implementing the mandate is not the best the government can do, then the threat of punishing incumbents who deviate from it is not credible. Voters may not like governments that betray promises, but they will not punish politicians who made them sufficiently better off by deviating from the mandate.

This impunity is mitigated by reputational considerations (Downs 1957; Ferejohn 1995). Politicians may be concerned about adhering to promises as an investment in credibility. Indeed, the Polish government was said to "be forced to remind itself of the promises of 1993 and to make some concessions to the voters, under the penalty of losing its credibility" (Krauze 1994). If incumbents anticipate that voters will not only look at their past policies but also pay attention to their new promises, that is, if their past performance in office is not fully informative, they must be concerned about being believed, which, in turn, moderates their temptation to deviate from the old promises. A politician who executed a pirouette will have to rely solely on his past performance when seeking reelection, while a politician who stuck to promises will be more likely to be believed next time around. In turn, voters may want to punish politicians who renege on their promises as an investment in information. After all, voters want their choices to have consequences; hence, they want to be able to predict the behavior of politicians from their campaign platforms, rhetoric, or identity. Politicians may claim that unforeseen circumstances are the reason they deviated from their mandates. But they have some explaining to do, which is prima facie evidence that they think they are expected to follow mandates.

While such reputational mechanisms may encourage the incumbents to adhere to electoral promises, a striking feature of democratic institutions, highlighted by Manin (1997), is that politicians are not legally compelled to abide by their platform in any democratic system. In no existing democracy are representatives subject to binding instructions. Citizens' suits against governments that betrayed specific campaign promises have been rejected by courts in several countries, most recently in Poland. No national-level democratic constitution allows for recall, and, except for the U.S. House of Representatives, electoral terms tend to be long – on the average, 3.7 years for legislatures and 3.9 years for presidents (Cheibub and Przeworski, Chapter 7 in this volume). While provisions for impeachment and procedures for withdrawing confidence are common, they are never targeted at the betrayal of promises.[11] Binding national referenda based on citizens' initiative are found only in Switzerland and, in more restrictive forms, in Italy and Argentina. Hence, once citizens elect representatives, they have no institutional devices to force them to adhere to promises. Voters can sanction deviations from mandates only after their effects have been experienced.

Why then are there no institutional mechanisms to force officeholders to be faithful to their platforms? Historically, the main argument was that legislatures should be allowed to deliberate. People want their representatives to learn, one from another. Moreover, when people are uncertain about their judgments, they may want representatives to consult experts.

Another historical argument was that voters may not trust their own judgments. People not only may be afraid of their own passions but, if they are rationally ignorant, they must know that they do not know. Presumably, elections establish the calendar for when the accounts are to be taken. Hence, citizens may want to give the government some latitude to govern and evaluate government's actions at election times. O'Flaherty (1990) argues that this is a reason to elect politicians for fixed terms; in this way citizens can guard themselves against inconsistent time preferences and yet exercise ex post control.

Finally, institutions must allow for changing conditions. No electoral platform can specify ex ante what the government should do in every contingent state of nature; governments must have some flexibility in coping with changing circumstances. If citizens expect that conditions may change and governments are likely to be representative, they will not want to bind governments by their instructions.[12]

Hence, there are good reasons why democratic institutions

---

[11] Occasionally a deviation from mandates provides part of the impetus for impeachment, even though deviation is not the formal justification. Two recent presidents who abandoned their campaign promises, in Venezuela and Ecuador, were impeached, one immediately, with no time allowed for the outcomes to materialize.

[12] Minford (1995: 105) observes in the context of monetary policy that "if voters have little information, they may prefer to let governments have complete discretion, regardless of the lack of credibility, rather than tie their hands."

contain no mechanisms enforcing adherence to mandates. We choose policies that represent our interests or candidates who represent us as persons, but we want governments to be able to govern. As a result, while we would prefer governments to stick to their promises, democracy contains no institutional mechanisms that insure that our choices would be respected.

The Accountability Conception of Representation

Even if citizens are unable to control governments by obliging them to follow mandates, citizens may be able to do so if they can induce the incumbents to anticipate that they will have to render accounts for their past actions. Governments are "accountable" if voters can discern whether governments are acting in their interest and sanction them appropriately, so that those incumbents who act in the best interest of citizens win reelection and those who do not lose them. Accountability representation occurs when (1) voters vote to retain the incumbent only when the incumbent acts in their best interest, and (2) the incumbent chooses policies necessary to get reelected.

To understand why the problem of accountability arises, we must consider again politicians' objectives. Politicians may want to do nothing that well-informed citizens would not have wanted them to do; they may be public-spirited and dedicate themselves fully to furthering the public interest. But they may also want something different from and costly to citizens, whether just some goals that citizens do not share, reelection, or private gains. Politicians may want to pursue their own ideas even if these differ from those of citizens.[13] Some may care most about advancing their careers against fellow politicians, within the government or the same party. Some may seek perks (Niskanen 1971). Some may want to get rich at the expense of citizens, while in office or after leaving it. Some may be most concerned about recognition by foreigners. In all these cases politicians will want something whose pursuit is injurious to citizens. For a lack of a better term and to keep with the standard terminology, we will refer to this something as "rents."

To introduce another term standard in this literature, there are

---

[13] Suppose that in a poor country people want to consume immediately while benevolent politicians want to develop the country by increasing investment.

different ways in which politicians can "shirk," that is, do things that citizens would not want them to do. They shirk if they spend time conspiring against their rivals. They shirk if they act to increase their own wealth. They shirk if they extend clientilistic favors to their families and friends. But the most important way in which they can act against the best interests of their constituents is by choosing policies that advance their own interests or the interests of some special interests to which they are beholden.

The problem facing citizens is then to set up a trade-off for politicians – between extracting rents and losing office or not extracting rents and staying in office – that would induce them to keep rents low, where keeping rents low may mean just doing what voters want. The standard view of how the accountability mechanism operates relies on "retrospective voting." In this view, citizens set some standard of performance to evaluate governments, such as "My income must increase by at least 4 percent during the term," "Streets must be safe," or even "The national team must qualify for the World Cup." They vote against the incumbent unless these criteria are fulfilled. In turn, the government, wanting to be reelected and anticipating the citizens' decision rule, does whatever possible to satisfy these criteria.

Imagine that the conditions under which the government makes decisions can be "good" or "bad." Governments decide whether to implement policy S, which is better for citizens when conditions are good, or policy E, which is better when conditions are bad. Suppose that the rents the incumbents obtain when they do all they can for the public consist just of their salaries and legally authorized perks of office, and suppose that the incumbents value being reelected. To make this analysis less abstract, examine a numerical example in which the legally qualified rents equal $r^* = 1 + e$, where e is some small number, and the value of being reelected is $V = 2$.

Let the structure of payoffs be as follows (the first number in each pair represents government rents, but citizens observe only their welfare, which is the second number):

		Government	
		Implement S	*Implement E*
	"Good"	$1 + e$, 5	3, 3
Conditions			
	"Bad"	3, 1	$1 + e$, 3

41

Suppose now that the electorate knows everything it needs to know. Then, to induce politicians to act as well as they can under the circumstances, voters set their reelection rule as "When conditions are good, vote for the incumbent if the outcome is at least 5. When conditions are bad, vote for the incumbent if the outcome is at least 3; otherwise throw the rascals out." A government facing good conditions knows that by choosing S it will get $r^* = 1 + e$ and it will be certainly reelected, thus obtaining r^* + V > 3, where 3 is the most it can get by choosing E and not being reelected. In turn, a government facing bad conditions knows that by choosing E it will get r^* + V > 3, which is what it would get by adopting S. Hence, the government acts in a representative manner and citizens get the most they can under either conditions. Accountability induces representation (Key 1966). As Fiorina (1981: 11) put it: "Given political actors who fervently desire to retain their positions and who carefully anticipate public reaction to their records as a means to that end, a retrospective voting electorate will enforce electoral accountability, albeit in an ex post, not an ex ante, sense."

Yet suppose that voters do not know what the conditions are. Politicians know these conditions, but voters may be unable to observe them at all or they may be able to monitor them only at a cost. Such conditions may include the negotiating posture of foreign governments or international financial institutions (something citizens cannot observe) or the level of demand in the major recipients of the country's exports (something voters can observe only if they turn into economists). Then voters are in a quandary. If they set the standard the incumbent must meet at 5 and conditions turn out to be bad, the incumbent cannot be reelected whatever he does and he will seek excess rents. In turn, if voters set the standard at 3, the incumbent will be able to extract excess rents when the conditions happen to be good and be reelected by giving voters less than he could have given them. Whatever voters decide to do, politicians will sometimes escape from their control.

One aspect of incomplete information merits particular attention. Note that the voters who animated the previous pages were myopic: they were concerned only with the change of their welfare during the current term. But if voters are fully rational, they should also care at the end of the term about the present value of their future welfare: the legacy the incumbent leaves for the future. If the economy grows because the government cuts all the trees in the country, the voter will live on champagne during the term, but there will be no trees left to cut. In turn, if the economy declined because it underwent structural reforms, voters will have suffered economic deprivation but may have improved their life chances for the future. Yet all that voters observe is the change of welfare during the term, and they have to make inferences about the future on this basis. Say that voters observe that their current welfare declines: should they infer that the government is investing in their future or pursuing some (neoliberal) chimeras of its own or just robbing them blind? Following Stokes (1996a), note that voters can adopt one of three postures:

1. They can extrapolate the present experience into the future. This is the "normal" posture, insofar as this is what models of retrospective voting normally assume.
2. They can assume an "intertemporal" posture (Przeworski 1996), expecting that the worse things have gotten, the better they augur for the future.
3. They can assume an "exonerating" posture, attributing the decline of their welfare to bad conditions, rather than to anything the government did.

It is hard to tell what is rational for people to do under these circumstances. Some empirical work on neoliberal reforms in new democracies (Przeworski 1996; Stokes 1996b) suggests that people are willing to exonerate governments for inflation and to treat increases of wages intertemporally, as forecasting inflation, but that they are risk-averse about unemployment and turn against governments that generate it. Yet other studies come to the conclusion that people are sensitive to inflation and relatively indifferent to unemployment (Rose 1997; Weyland 1996). In any case, there is little on which people can base these judgments.

Accountability models of elections assume typically that while voters do not know something that they need to know to evaluate governments, incumbents do know what they need to do in order to be reelected. The implicit artifice on which these models rely is that voters offer a contract to the government: "if you give us at least this, we will vote for you; otherwise, we will not." Yet voters do not offer such contracts. Note that we could cast not only ballots but also a list of our conditions for reelecting the incumbent. But we do not, and we do not because we want governments to do all they can for us, rather than just fulfill our minimal demands. Indeed, Manin (1997) points out that voters can decide whether to reelect the incumbent on any basis they want, including qualifying for the World Cup, and that they can change their mind between the beginning and the end of a term. At least in this way, voters are sovereign.

Hence, a question arises about how the incumbent will act if information is asymmetric both ways: when voters are not certain about the conditions under which policies are made but incumbents are uncertain what would satisfy voters. It can be shown (Cheibub and Przeworski, Chapter 7 in this volume) that when incumbents very much care about being reelected, they will represent, always pursuing policies appropriate to the conditions they observe, so that voters are better off keeping their expectations secret. When, however, incumbents care less about being reelected and, in turn, voters expect that conditions are likely to be good, voters are better off formulating exacting demands and making them known to politicians. Finally, when incumbents attach less value to being reelected and voters expect conditions to be bad, there is nothing voters can do to prevent incumbents from extracting excess rents when conditions happen to be good. Hence, voters are better off if they can reveal or not reveal their demands strategically. But to do so, they must still know how much the incumbent cares about being reelected and how likely it is that conditions are good.

In sum, accountability is not sufficient to induce representation when voters have incomplete information.

Using the Vote for Two Purposes

In a pure accountability model, voters use the vote only for one purpose, which is to sanction the incumbent, and the entire information available to voters is revealed by the performance of the incumbent. In a pure mandate model, voters compare promises candidates make about the future, and use the vote only to choose the better candidate. In Downs's (1957; also Fiorina 1981) model, voters use the information about the past performance of the incumbent and, if available, of challengers, but this is also a mandate model in the sense that voters use the information about the past only to choose a better government for

44

the future. Indeed, Sniderman, Glaser, and Griffin (1990) claim that purely retrospective voting would be irrational: rational people look forward. Yet this is not right: if voters can credibly employ their vote only to sanction the incumbent, threatening to use it this way is a perfectly rational way of inducing governments to act well in the future.

For all we know, voters do not meditate whether to use the one instrument they have, the vote, to choose a better government or to structure incentives for incumbents. Fearon (Chapter 2 in this volume) offers persuasive stories to the effect that voters want to select good policies and politicians. Yet voting "to keep them honest" seems also ingrained in the repertoire of the democratic culture. The fact remains that voters have only one instrument to reach two goals: to select better policies and politicians, and to induce them to behave well while in office. The question then is what happens when voters try to use the vote for both purposes.

Suppose that, believing that politicians are not all the same, voters are swayed by the prospect of electing better governments. Voters may believe that the challenger is more competent, having a better understanding of the relation between policies and outcomes, or is more honest, being willing to accept lower rents in exchange for holding public office. An election takes place, an incumbent is installed, both the incumbent and the electorate observe the objective conditions, voters set their voting rule, incumbents choose rents, and voters vote again. Having observed what happened during the term, voters vote for a challenger with the probability that the challenger will be better than the incumbent (in the sense that she would have generated higher welfare under the same conditions). Anticipating that voters will vote for the challenger with some positive probability, the incumbent will then require a higher level of rents. Thus the rents that are necessary to induce the incumbent to seek reelection when voters use the vote as a selection device are larger than in the case when voters are only concerned about incentives for the incumbent. Using the vote to choose a better government prospectively is costly to voters in terms of their control over the incumbent (see Fearon, Chapter 2 in this volume).

Note immediately that the following nightmare may arise (Ferejohn 1986; Banks and Sundaram 1993): if voters always think that the challenger is better, then the incumbent can never be reelected, and he will always choose to extract high rents. In turn, if incumbents extract high rents, voters will never vote for them. The incumbent knows that voters will always be swayed by the promises of the challenger and always extract maximal rents, which means that if voters believe that politicians are not all the same, they are certain that the challengers will be better for them. In this situation, voters' control breaks down completely.[14]

Yet, while voters may be gullible, they cannot be that ingenuous. The performance of the incumbent is informative. As Bartels (1988) discovered, in the United States at least, the past performance of a president is a good predictor of his future performance (and not of a challenger's). Thus, voters who use their vote prospectively have good reasons to rely on retrospective information. Harrington (1993b) shows that the more uncertain voters are about the effect of policies on outcomes, the more they should rely on information about past performance. They can observe the past performance of the incumbent and then decide how likely it is that a challenger is better. Nevertheless, as long as voters use their vote to elect a better government, they must lower the power of incentives for the incumbent.

Madison (*Federalist* no. 57) thought that "The aim of every political constitution is, or ought to be, first to obtain for rulers men who possess most wisdom to discern, and most virtue to pursue, the common good of the society; and in the next place, to take the most effectual precautions for keeping them virtuous whilst they continue to hold their public trust." Using the vote for both purposes – to obtain the best rulers and to keep them virtuous – is not irrational: while voters lose some control over the incumbent, in exchange they elect a better government. Yet the system Madison and his colleagues designed makes it possible to strive for one goal only at the expense of the other.

Institutions, Elections, and Representation

Democracies are not all the same, and it is possible that some democratic systems foster representation better than others.

---

[14] This may seem farfetched. But several countries, notably Ecuador and Poland, experienced a series of elections in which the challenger promised to pursue an expansionary policy, was believed by voters, switched upon election to a contractionary one, to be defeated by a challenger promising an expansionary policy, etc.

46

While we have little systematic knowledge about the effects of particular institutional arrangements on voters' control over politicians, some institutional factors merit attention.

1. Voters must be able to assign clearly the responsibility for government performance. Their ability to do so is limited when the government is a coalition. It is also limited when the presidency and the congress are controlled by different parties. It takes an elaborate theory of government to figure out who is responsible for what under such conditions (but see Anderson 1995).

Hamilton argued in *Federalist* no. 70 that accountability is obscured under a plural, that is, cabinet executive: "But one of the weightiest objections to a plurality in the executive . . . is that it tends to conceal faults and destroy responsibility. . . . The circumstances which may have led to any national miscarriage or misfortune are sometimes so complicated that there are a number of actors who have different degrees and kinds of agency, though we may clearly see upon the whole that there has been mismanagement, yet it may be impracticable to pronounce to whose account the evil which may have been incurred is truly chargeable." But a similar ambiguity arises in presidential systems. Bagehot (1992: 67) expressed this view most forcefully: "Two clever men never exactly agree about a budget. . . . They are sure to quarrel, and the result is sure to satisfy neither. And when the taxes do not yield as they were expected to yield, who is responsible? Very likely the secretary of the treasury could not persuade the chairman – very likely the chairman could not persuade his committee – very likely the committee could not persuade the assembly. Whom, then, can you punish – whom can you abolish – when your taxes run short?"

The empirical findings concerning clarity of responsibility, most of them due to Powell and his collaborators, are confusing. Majority-inducing institutions increase the distance between the ideal position of the median voter and of the government (Huber and Powell 1996), but they increase what Powell (1990) measures as the "clarity of responsibility," which, in turn, makes voting for incumbents more sensitive to economic performance (Powell and Whitten 1993). Hence, it seems that majoritarian institutions generate governments that are farther from voters in policy space but more accountable. The relation between citizens' preferences and the actual policies – not studied by Powell – is thus indeterminate.

2. Voters must be able to vote out of office parties responsible for bad performance, and the parties they select must be able to enter government. These may appear to be universal features of democracy, but under some electoral systems they are next to impossible: witness the continued tenure of the Christian Democrats in Italy or of the LDP in Japan, or the weak connection between voting results and electoral outcomes in Bolivia. As Pasquino (1994: 25) put it with regard to Italy, "governing parties seemed to expropriate the voters of the political influence by making and unmaking governments at all levels with very little respect for electoral results."

3. Politicians must have incentives to want to be reelected. This condition becomes problematic when there are limitations on reeligibility, ubiquitous in presidential systems (Cheibub and Przeworski, Chapter 7 in this volume), and when political parties are not continuing bureaucratic organizations that offer their militants career prospects (Zielinski 1997). Paldam (1991) observed that the coefficients of the function relating the probability of reelection to economic outcomes are higher and their estimates are tighter when the party system is stable.

4. The opposition must monitor the performance of the government and inform citizens. Indeed, any reasonable understanding of representation must include the opposition. Citizens have two agents, not just one: the incumbents who govern and the opposition that wants to become the government. The opposition is an agent of citizens because it wants to win office and, in order to win office, it must also anticipate the retrospective judgments that voters will make about the incumbents at election time. Anticipating these judgments, the opposition has incentives to monitor the government and to inform (truthfully or not) voters about the performance of the incumbents.

Yet the existence of an opposition that wants to and can monitor government performance should not be taken for granted. Opposition can collude with the government[15] or it can be so

---

[15] Crain (1977) argued that in a single-member, single-district electoral system incumbents are unlikely to ever run against each other and that they therefore share an interest in raising barriers to entry of challengers from either party. Dasgupta (1993) offered another model of collusion and an argument that we should subsidize new parties.

divided that it spends most efforts on internal fights rather than on the incumbents. The opposition may see no chance of winning and do something else rather than monitor the government (see Pasquino 1994 with regard to the PCI in Italy). And it may or may not have resources to do so; among Powell's (1990) twenty countries, only nine provide resources for the opposition in legislative committees. Yet, conversely, an opposition that always opposes is not any more credible to voters than the government. If every time the government says something, the opposition claims it is false, voters are not any better informed. Thus, the opposition plays a role in informing voters only when it neither always colludes with nor always contradicts the government.

5. The media, the role of which is emphasized by Arnold (1993), thus have a particular role to play. Unless they have clearly partisan interests, they are more credible than either the government or the opposition.

6. Finally, but perhaps most importantly, voters must have some institutional instruments to reward and punish governments for outcomes they generate in different realms. Yet elections are inherently a blunt instrument of control: voters have only one decision to make with regard to the entire package of government policies. Suppose that a government during one term has to make ten decisions, the incumbent makes all decisions against the interest of the majority, and the challenger offers to make one right decision. Then citizens will elect a government that will make nine wrong decisions. Obviously, the question is why would some other challenger not offer to make two right decisions, or three, or four, up to all ten. One answer is the barriers to entry: partisan politics is the most protected industry in the United States. But if there were no barriers to entry, then parties would have an incentive to form, promise to make all ten right decisions, make none right, and get out. If entrance into the electoral system entails fixed costs, competition will be limited; if it is free, then parties do not suffer when they lose. So we get either highly collusive party systems, such as the United States, or completely ephemeral systems, such as in Ecuador, where there is a new party system at each election.[16] In either way, control is limited.

[16] On the importance of electoral systems for the rent extraction by parties, see Meyerson (1993).

Conclusion: Elections as a Mechanism of Representation

Although democracy may not assure representation, it is still plausible that democracy is more conducive to representation than alternative regimes. Yet the conclusion of this analysis must be that citizens' control over politicians is at best highly imperfect in most democracies. Elections are not a sufficient mechanism to insure that governments will do everything they can to maximize citizens' welfare.

This is not an argument against democracy but one for institutional reform and for institutional innovation. We need electoral institutions that enhance clarity of responsibility and make it easy for citizens to reward and punish those responsible. We need moral and economic conditions in which public service would enjoy respect as well as appropriate material rewards. In addition, we need institutions that would provide citizens with independent information about the government: "accountability agencies," in the terms of an Australian Commission on Government Reform (Dunn and Uhr 1993). Such institutions may include (1) an independent board to assure transparency of campaign contributions,[17] with its own investigative powers; (2) an independent auditing branch of the state, an auditor-general (World Bank 1994: 32), in the vein of the Chilean *contraloría*; (3) an independent source of statistical information about the state of the economy; and (4) a privileged place for the opposition in overseeing the publicly owned media.

Yet even if responsibilities are clearly assigned, bad governments can be punished and good ones chosen, voters are well informed about the relations between politicians and special interests, and the rent-seeking behavior of politicians is well scrutinized, elections are just not a sufficient instrument of control over politicians. Governments make thousands of decisions that affect individual welfare; citizens have only one instrument to control these decisions: the vote. One cannot control a thousand targets with one instrument. Thus, for example, separating

---

[17] A question of why private contributions should not be banned altogether naturally appears. Laffont and Tirole (1994) argue that such a ban would be skirted by some politicians. If this is true and if money buys votes, then there would be an adverse selection process in which dishonest politicians would be more likely to be elected.

50

monetary from other political decisions and voting separately, and at staggered intervals, for the directors of the central bank would give voters an additional instrument of control, with results superior both to giving discretion over monetary policy to the government and to delegating these decisions to a central bank independent from voters' control (Minford 1995).

The fact is that during the past two hundred years we have thought little about the institutional design of democracy. Since the great explosion of institutional thinking, when the present democratic institutions were invented – and they were invented – there has been almost no institutional creativity. Except for the never implemented provisions for workers' comanagement in the Weimar Constitution, the discovery of proportional representation in the 1860s was the last major institutional invention. All democracies that have sprung up since the end of the eighteenth century, including the most recent ones, just combine in different ways, often piecemeal, the preexisting institutions. Hence, there is lots of room for institutional creativity.

References

Alesina, Alberto. 1988. "Credibility and Convergence in a Two-Party System with Rational Voters." *American Economic Review* 78: 796–805.

Anderson, Christopher J. 1995. "The Dynamics of Public Support for Coalition Governments." *Comparative Political Studies* 28: 350–83.

Arnold, Douglas. 1993. "Can Inattentive Citizens Control Their Elected Representatives?" In Lawrence C. Dodd and Bruce I. Oppenheimer, eds., *Congress Reconsidered*, 401–16. 5th ed. Washington, D.C.: Congressional Quarterly Press.

Austen-Smith, David. 1990. "Credible Debate Equilibria." *Social Choice and Welfare* 7: 75–93.

Austen-Smith, David, and Jeffrey Banks. 1989. "Electoral Accountability and Incumbency." In Peter C. Ordeshook, ed., *Models of Strategic Choice in Politics*, 121–50. Ann Arbor: University of Michigan Press.

Bagehot, Walter. 1992. "The English Constitution: The Cabinet." In Arend Lijphart, ed., *Parliamentary versus Presidential Government*, 66–71. Oxford: Oxford University Press.

Banks, Jeffrey S. 1990. "A Model of Electoral Competition with Incomplete Information." *Journal of Economic Theory* 50: 309–25.

Banks, Jeffrey S., and Rangarajan K. Sundaram. 1993. "Adverse Selection and Moral Hazard in a Repeated Elections Model." In William A.

Barnett, Melvin J. Hinich, and Norman J. Schofield, eds., *Political Economy: Institutions, Competition, and Representation*, 295–312. Cambridge: Cambridge University Press.

Barro, Robert J. 1973. "The Control of Politicians: An Economic Model." *Public Choice* 14: 19–42.

Bartels, Larry. 1988. "The Economic Consequences of Retrospective Voting." Department of Political Science, University of Rochester. Unpublished manuscript.

Becker, Gary S. 1958. "Competition and Democracy." *Journal of Law and Economics* 1: 105–9.

     1983. "A Theory of Competition among Pressure Groups for Political Influence." *Quarterly Journal of Economics* 98: 371–400.

Crain, Mark W. 1977. "On the Structure and Stability of Political Markets." *Journal of Political Economy* 85: 829–42.

Dasgupta, Partha. 1993. *An Inquiry into Well-Being and Destitution.* Oxford: Clarendon Press.

Downs, Anthony. 1957. *An Economic Theory of Democracy.* New York: Harper and Row.

Dunn, Delmer D., and John Uhr. 1993. "Accountability and Responsibility in Modern Democratic Governments." Paper presented at the annual meeting of the American Political Science Association, Washington, D.C., September 2–5.

Elster, Jon. 1994. "The Impact of Constitutions on Economic Performance." *Proceedings of the World Bank Annual Conference on Development Economics*, 209–26. Washington, D.C.

Ferejohn, John. 1986. "Incumbent Performance and Electoral Control." *Public Choice* 50: 5–25.

     1995. "The Spatial Model and Elections." In Bernard Grofman, ed., *Information, Participation, and Choice*, 107–24. Ann Arbor: University of Michigan Press.

Fiorina, Morris P. 1981. *Retrospective Voting in American National Elections.* New Haven: Yale University Press.

Hamilton, Alexander. 1982 [1788]. *Federalist* 70. In Alexander Hamilton, James Madison, and John Jay. *The Federalist Papers*, edited by Gary Wills. New York: Bantam.

Harrington, Joseph E., Jr. 1993a. "The Impact of Reelection Pressures on the Fulfillment of Campaign Promises." *Games and Economic Behavior* 5: 71–97.

     1993b. "Economic Policy, Economic Performance, and Elections." *American Economic Review* 83: 27–42.

Huber, John D., and G. Bingham Powell, Jr. 1996. "Congruence between Citizens and Policymakers in Two Visions of Liberal Democracy." *World Politics* 49: 291–326.

Keeler, John T. S. 1993. "Opening the Window for Reform: Mandates,

Crises, and Extraordinary Decision-Making." *Comparative Political Studies* 25: 433–86.

Key, V. O., Jr. 1966. *The Responsible Electorate*. New York: Vintage.

Klingeman, Hans-Dieter, Richard I. Hofferbert, and Ian Budge. 1994. *Parties, Policies, and Democracy*. Boulder, Colo.: Westview Press.

Krauze, Jan. 1994. "La Pologne est menacée par l'immobilisme gouvernemental." *Le Monde*, September 19.

Laffont, Jean-Jacques, and Jean Tirole. 1994. *A Theory of Incentives in Procurement and Regulation*. Cambridge, Mass.: MIT Press.

Madison, James. 1982 [1788]. *Federalist* 57. In Alexander Hamilton, James Madison, and John Jay. *The Federalist Papers*, edited by Gary Wills. New York: Bantam.

Manin, Bernard. 1997. *Principles of Representative Government*. Cambridge: Cambridge University Press.

Meyerson, Roger B. 1993. "Effectiveness of Electoral Systems for Reducing Government Corruption." *Games and Economic Behavior* 5: 118–32.

Mill, John Stuart, 1991 [1861]. *Considerations on Representative Government*. Buffalo, N.Y.: Prometheus Press.

Minford, Patrick. 1995. "Time-Inconsistency, Democracy, and Optimal Contingent Rules." *Oxford Economic Papers* 47: 195–210.

Niskanen, William A. 1971. *Bureaucracy and Representative Government*. Chicago: University of Chicago Press.

O'Flaherty, Brendan. 1990. "Why Are There Democracies? A Principal Agent Answer." *Economics and Politics* 2: 133–55.

Paldam, Martin. 1991. "How Robust Is the Vote Function? A Study of Seventeen Nations over Four Decades." In Helmuth Northop, Michael S. Lewis-Beck, and Jean-Dominique Lafay, eds., *Economics and Politics: The Calculus of Support*, 9–31. Ann Arbor: University of Michigan Press.

Pasquino, Gianfranco. 1994. "Shaping a Better Republic? The Italian Case in a Comparative Perspective." Working Paper No. 62. Madrid: Instituto Juan March de Estudios e Investigaciones.

Peltzman, Sam. 1976. "Toward a More General Theory of Regulation." *Journal of Law and Economics* 19: 209–87.

Pitkin, Hanna F. 1967. *The Concept of Representation*. Berkeley: University of California Press.

Powell, G. Bingham, Jr. 1990. "Holding Governments Accountable: How Constitutional Arrangements and Party Systems Affect Clarity of Responsibility for Policy in Contemporary Democracies." Paper presented at the annual meeting of the American Political Science Association, San Francisco.

Powell, G. Bingham, Jr., and Guy Whitten. 1993. "A Cross-National

53

Analysis of Economic Voting: Taking Account of the Political Context."
American Journal of Political Science 37: 391–414.

Przeworski, Adam. 1996. "Public Support for Economic Reforms in
Poland." *Comparative Political Studies* 29: 520–43.

Rogowski, Ronald. 1981. "Representation in Political Theory and in Law."
Ethics 91: 395–430.

Rose, Richard. 1997. "What Is the Demand for Price Stability in Post-
Communist Countries?" University of Strathclyde Studies in Public
Policy No. 282. Glasgow.

Séguin, Philippe. 1997. *Liberation*, May 29.

Sniderman. Paul M., James M. Glaser, and Robert Griffin. 1990.
"Information and Electoral Choice." In John A. Ferejohn and James
H. Kuklinski, eds., *Information and Democratic Processes*, 117–35.
Urbana: University of Illinois Press.

Stigler, George J. 1975. *The Citizen and the State: Essays on Regulation.*
Chicago: University of Chicago Press.

Stokes, Susan C. 1996a. "Public Opinion and Market Reforms: The Limits
of Economic Voting." *Comparative Political Studies* 29: 499–519.

1996b. "Economic Reform and Public Opinion in Peru, 1990–1995."
Comparative Political Studies 29: 544–65.

Weyland, Kurt. 1996. "Risk Taking in Latin American Economic
Restructuring: Lessons from Prospect Theory." *International Studies
Quarterly* 40: 185–208.

World Bank. 1994. *Governance: The World Bank's Experience.*
Washington, D.C.: World Bank.

Zielinski, Jakub. 1997. "Democratic Consolidation: A Role of Political
Parties as Institutions of Accountability." Paper presented at the
annual meeting of the American Political Science Association,
Washington, D.C.

Chapter Two

Electoral Accountability and the Control of Politicians: Selecting Good Types versus Sanctioning Poor Performance

The concept of accountability is not by itself problematic, or at least it should not be. We say that one person, A, is accountable to another, B, if two conditions are met. First, there is an understanding that A is obliged to act in some way on behalf of B. Second, B is empowered by some formal institutional or perhaps informal rules to sanction or reward A for her activities or performance in this capacity. In this sense, employees are accountable to their employers, CEOs to their boards and their boards to stockholders, department chairs to the departments they represent, and elected politicians to their electorates. In the jargon of economic theory, relations involving accountability are *agency relationships* in which one party is understood to be an "agent" who makes some choices on behalf of a "principal" who has powers to sanction or reward the agent.[1]

Most interesting questions about accountability in political and economic contexts concern not its definition but rather the understanding of what activities or performance the agent is

For valuable comments I wish to thank the editors of the volume and John Ferejohn and Jim Snyder.

[1] One might define a weaker notion of "accountability" in which one person is accountable to another if it is understood that the first has a responsibility to act on behalf of the second, independent of whether the second has sanctioning or rewarding instruments. I think this blurs accountability with moral responsibility and does not square with ordinary usage, which typically involves the presumption of monitoring and sanctioning instruments.

accountable for, the nature of the principal's sanctioning or
rewarding instruments, and the problem of to what extent a given
system of incentives will lead the agent to act on behalf of the
principal, that is, to do what the principal would want. In addition,
in the case of *electoral* accountability, additional problems arise
from the presence of multiple principals (voters, but perhaps also
courts and other elected officials in some cases) rather than a
single principal or a collective body that can act as a single
principal. For instance, with multiple principals the question of
saying what the principals would want can be difficult, even theoretically, as Arrow's theorem suggests.

There is an important prior question, however, about whether
elections are best thought of in terms of accountability at all.
Certainly, an important tradition in democratic theory understands elections as mechanisms of political accountability. In this
view, elections are seen as a sanctioning device that induces
elected officials to do what the voters want. The anticipation of not
being reelected in the future leads elected officials not to shirk
their obligations to the voters in the present (Barro 1973; Ferejohn
1986; Fiorina 1981; Key 1966; Manin 1997).

I begin by developing a four-step argument that questions
whether elections are best conceived as mechanisms of
accountability. The four steps may be summarized as follows.
First, voters need not see elections as mechanisms that establish
accountability; instead, they might understand elections as opportunities to choose a "good type" of political leader, one who would
act on their behalf independent of reelection incentives. Second,
if voters can distinguish good types to some degree, then it follows
that electoral accountability is not necessary for elections to
produce public policy that the principals (the voting public) want.
Third, empirical observations about public opinion and elections
in the United States (and probably other democracies) suggest that
in fact voters think about elections more as opportunities to select
good types than as mechanisms establishing accountability and, in
consequence, good behavior by politicians. Fourth, this sort of
understanding is not idiosyncratic or foolish, but may actually
make a good deal of sense if one also believes that repeated
elections *as sanctioning devices* have little ability to induce
politicians to do what the voters would want done.

Even if voters think about elections more in terms of selection than sanctioning, these two understandings are by no means incompatible or mutually exclusive. Indeed, successfully selecting for good types implies sanctioning bad types, which gives bad types an incentive to *appear* as if they were good types. Thus, if the electorate tries to select good types, then bad types may moderate their policy choices in the direction of what the electorate wants, as in the classical theory of electoral accountability. But then, insofar as bad types become harder to distinguish from good types, selection is rendered problematic. This brief argument suggests that selection and sanctioning necessarily interact and that the interaction has a strategic component (at least in the behavior of politicians).

Following the discussion of the four-step argument, I present a simple game model that depicts three views of how elections generate policy outcomes desired by voters: pure sanctioning ("moral hazard," or accountability), pure selection, and a mixed case suggested by the preceding paragraph. Consistent with the fourth point summarized earlier, I show that as the voters' ability to monitor politicians becomes very poor, the mixed case approaches a problem of pure selection, although the voters' ability to sort out good types on the basis of an incumbent's record also diminishes. Analysis of the mixed case also provides insight into the interaction between selection and sanctioning. For example, I show that although the electorate would like to commit to a retrospective voting rule to motivate self-interested politicians optimally, when it comes time to vote it makes sense for the electorate to focus *completely* on the question of type: which candidate is more likely to be principled and share the public's preferences? The simple logic behind this result may help explain the empirical observation that voters tend to think about elections in terms of choosing a good type.

Elections with No Expectation of Accountability

There is no logical reason why elections must be understood as a part of a relationship of accountability or "agency." For example, a group of people might understand elections as a means of selecting or conferring honor on the best or most distinguished person. This sort of understanding can take two forms, one connected with conferring or recognizing honor without any instrumental purpose, and one concerned with selecting the best person with a notion that this person will of her own accord do what is best for the voters.

Thus, in the first case, the voters have no expectation whatsoever that the elected official has a responsibility to act on behalf of the electorate (thus violating the first condition necessary for a relationship to entail accountability). The election might be understood simply as a declaration of who in the group most deserves the honor of political authority. As a logical claim this is simply true. Empirically, Mark Kishlansky's (1986) account of parliamentary elections in early modern England suggests that something like this actually occurred, and Max Weber (1978: 1112–30) had earlier claimed that premodern elections were about the acclamation and recognition of charisma, rather than the selection of a delegate or agent. Echoes of this view can also be found in the "Michigan model" of elections, which sees votes as affirmations of warm feelings for a candidate (Campbell et al. 1960).

In the second case, the voters choose with an eye toward whether the elected official would act on their behalf, but still have *no* expectation that the anticipation of future elections was a device for giving the elected official an incentive to do so (thus violating the second condition). Imagine, for instance, a system in which elected officials can serve only one term in office, so elections cannot serve as a sanctioning device to induce good performance by those elected. But if the voters think they are able to distinguish among types of candidates and that some types are more inclined to act of their own accord in the public interest, then they could still understand the elections as the fundamental mechanism of democratic governance.

Lack of Electoral Accountability Need Not Imply Lack of Responsiveness

This second case suffices to show that lack of electoral accountability need not imply public policy opposed to voter preferences. Imagine again the system in which elected officials can serve only one term in office, and thus are not accountable since they cannot be sanctioned at the polls.[2] Such a system could

---

[2] Of course, they may still be accountable before the law for criminal and civil violations, as is everyone else.

still, in principle, produce public policy in accord with what the voters would want, if the voters are able to distinguish candidates who are simply the *type* who want to do in office what they would want done. Define a good type for a particular voter as a politician who (1) shares the voter's issue preferences, (2) has integrity, in that he or she is hard to bribe or otherwise induce to work against the voter's interests, and (3) is competent or skilled in discerning and implementing optimal policies for the voter. If voters are able to distinguish politicians along these three dimensions, then this lack of accountability need not imply that the public will not get what it wants. The conclusion: *Electoral accountability is not in principle necessary for elections to produce responsive public policy.*[3]

How might voters distinguish between good and bad types? Voters have available a variety of signals and measures, which might be partitioned as follows:

1. General measures of the voter's welfare ("Am I better off than I was four years ago?") or of the health of the economy or society (the "misery index," the crime rate, etc.) that might allow inferences about the types of incumbent politicians.
2. More specific measures of "pork" delivered, policies chosen, or votes cast by incumbent representatives in prior terms in office; party affiliation and location within the party.
3. Information about the personal character of a politician, derivable from all manner of sources, such as life history as reported by the media or the candidate, impressions of how the candidate speaks, body language, sense of humor, involvement in scandals, and group affiliations of the candidate.
4. Policies advocated by the candidate or incumbent in campaign or other political speeches.

Note that this list includes both "prospective" measures such as campaign platforms and "retrospective" measures such as how the economy performed under an incumbent. If people are trying to select good types more than sanctioning to induce good behavior

---

[3] I mean "responsive" either in the weak sense of Stokes (i.e., preferred by some majority) or something stronger (see Stokes, Chapter 3 in this volume). In the public choice literature on what determines how representatives vote on bills in Congress, John Lott (1987) has argued similarly that voters are able to "sort out" officials with similar policy preferences and thus generate outcomes they like.

in the future, then both retrospective and prospective information may be relevant to their decisions, even if it is noisy and often interpreted badly. (By contrast, only retrospective measures are informative in a pure sanctioning view of elections, since promises about future performance are not credible. Voters trying to select good types from campaign speeches face the problem of noisy and misleading signals, but informative signaling is not a priori impossible.)

How Do Voters Think about the Point of Elections?

That voters might understand elections in terms of selection rather than sanctioning is more than an abstract, theoretical point. This conception – elections as a means of selecting the type of leader who will act competently and faithfully in the public interest, independent of reelection incentives – is arguably much closer to the popular understanding in the United States (and probably other democracies as well) than is the understanding that thinks of future elections as a sanctioning device to induce appropriate behavior during an elected official's present term. We can see this by considering how the "elections as selecting a good type" perspective makes sense of a number of striking facts about public opinion and elections in the United States that are perplexing if one adopts an "elections as mechanisms of accountability" view.

Dislike of "Office Seekers"

First, notice that reelection-seeking behavior by politicians is generally regarded with disdain and contempt. People widely and often bitterly deplore the fact that politicians "just want to get reelected!" If one has the view that it is precisely the prospect of reelection that induces politicians to do what voters want, then the trait of cravenly desiring reelection should be highly *valued*, not disdained. We should want to elect those people most desirous of holding office for a long time, because they would be the most inclined to do exactly what we want in order to get reelected and least inclined to risk getting booted by engaging in illicit rent seeking. Note that in Ferejohn's (1986) "moral hazard" model of the electoral control of incumbents, electoral control is easier and more efficient the higher the value of holding office for the incumbent (e.g., how much it pays or how much the person values the status), and the lower the reservation value of the incumbent for not being in office. Among other things, this implies that if we fully believed in the "elections as mechanisms of accountability" model, then we should want to pay politicians very large salaries to reduce their temptation to shirk to a minimum (note that the costs would be spread over an enormous number of taxpayers). But such arguments can hardly be found in the public sphere, possibly in part because paying politicians very large sums would encourage exactly the wrong *types* to run for office – people motivated by financial gain rather than public interest![4]

Term Limits

Second, notice that there is considerable support in the United States for congressional term limits, that the highest office in the United States is subject to a two-term limit, and that a number of Latin American presidents and legislators are allowed to serve for only one term (Carey 1996). These facts would be completely inexplicable if most people subscribed to the "repeated elections as a mechanism of accountability" view. If you believe that the main point of elections is to offer elected officials a future incentive for representative behavior in the present, then how can you possibly support taking away the principal incentive? On the other hand, if most people understand elections as an attempt to choose a good type who will of his or her own accord do what they want, then there need be nothing wrong with term limits. In fact, they could even be a positively good thing, if they would help screen out (through self-selection not to run) craven, opportunistic office seekers, leaving instead candidates more genuinely motivated by

---

[4] Another implication of the pure moral hazard model is that we should want to elect relatively poor people who have a high value for holding onto the office. But in the United States, at least, personal wealth is rarely a political liability, and rich candidates are not discounted on the grounds that they will shirk because they won't care if they lose office. In defense of the moral hazard view, rich politicians might be less likely to shirk to gain monetary rents since their marginal utility for money is likely to be less than their value for office status ("he's so rich he can't be bought").

the desire for public service.[5] Finally, note that the argument *against* term limits that seems to be the most compelling to the U.S. public is definitely not that term limits would make politicians unaccountable, but rather that term limits arbitrarily restrict the free choice of who can be one's representative. They are said to be "undemocratic" for this reason.[6]

The Premium on Principles and Consistency

Third, notice that voters generally put a high value on principledness and consistency in candidates and elected officials, even to the point of being willing of forgive some extremism in policy positions if they believe this can be taken as an indication of these qualities. Thus, many people who would have preferred less conservative policies than Reagan espoused nonetheless appear to have been won over by the sense that he was a man of principle and that they "knew where he stood."[7] Further, notice how politicians can face very significant criticism and loss of support if they change a publicly stated position on a contentious issue. This is true even if

[5] Regarding members of legislatures, there is an argument against term limits on the grounds that if they are too short, the elected officials will not be able to develop the expertise necessary to allow them to hold their own against permanent staff bureaucrats or lobbying interests. But this argues against having short term limits on representatives, rather than for no term limits at all. Regarding presidents in new democracies, there are some other strong arguments in favor of term limits: First, if you can't run for reelection, then you can't use the powers of office to engage in electoral fraud on your own behalf (though you may still be able to commit fraud on behalf of your party). Second, if you know that you will be out of office in (say) six years, then you have to worry more about being prosecuted once out of office for illegal activity you engage in while in office, and the fear of this may then keep you more honest and public-minded while in your one term. Paradoxically, then, term limits for the highest executive office may actually favor democracy, its continuation, and its responsiveness.

[6] There is also the more academic, coordination-problem argument about not wanting to handicap one's own representatives with term limits when other states still do not have them, due to loss of seniority in the legislature (Dick and Lott 1993; McKelvey and Riezman 1992). This has nothing to do with term limits lowering electoral accountability, however.

[7] To some extent, in the 1996 Republican primary campaign Pat Buchanan tried the same tactic pushed farther. He has espoused and stuck to extreme positions in the face of a critical reception and electoral failures, in part because this signals that he is a "man of principle" who really believes that what he is recommending

they change a previously stated position in the direction of what the public seems to want now! "Waffling" is considered a bad thing, even if one waffles toward the median voter.

Again, these facts would make no sense if people thought of elections as mechanisms of accountability. If I think of elections as incentive systems pushing politicians to do what I want, then I should be *happy and approving* when a politician changes position to be more in accord with my views (assuming that I am close to the median, or whatever it is that "the public wants").[8] And if I want elections to induce politicians to do what is in the public interest, I should be upset with candidates and elected officials who espouse or implement policies not thought by a majority to be in the public interest (i.e., extremist policies or policies away from what the median voter wants or thinks best). I should not approve of them for their principled but unpopular stands. By contrast, if I think of elections as a problem of choosing a competent, like-minded type not easily bought by special interests, then it makes perfect sense to be highly concerned with principledness and consistency. Sticking by a position through thick and thin is a *costly signal*, since types who are just office seekers and are easily bought will find consistency and principledness more difficult to manage.

Last-Period Effects

Fourth, if the anticipation of future reelection were the principal factor inducing politicians to vote the way their constituents would want rather than for powerful special interests, we would expect to see systematic changes in representatives' behavior in their last term in office (when they know they will step down due to retirement or a term limit). In other words, we would expect to observe significant *last-period effects*. In addition, if

---

is best for the country. This line of analysis may suggest an explanation for why we tend to see the rise of policy extremists in periods of low trust in government and politicians – in such times, the public's premium on candidates who appear principled and consistent goes up, and this may favor extremists.

[8] The point is not that people never approve of elected officials shifting policy positions in their preferred direction, but that the common reaction of disdain for inconsistency does not make sense from a purely "elections as mechanisms of accountability" point of view.

voters in fact saw the reelection incentive as the principal way that elections encourage public policies they desire, then they would be very reluctant to elect a politician for a term known to be his or her last.[9]

Neither casual empiricism nor more careful empirical studies reveal strong or obvious evidence for these implications. Regarding casual empiricism, I have never heard anyone claim that U.S. presidential shirking on policy or effort goes up markedly in the second term.[10] And voters are clearly willing to reelect presidents for second terms, and sometimes reelect representatives who are thought very likely to be retiring or moving on.[11]

Regarding more-careful empirical studies, there is a large literature on the question of how much U.S. senators and representatives vote against their constituents' preferences, including several studies of voting behavior in the last term (by representatives who do not die in office).[12] With a few exceptions, these

[9] In formal models of elections as a pure moral hazard problem (Barro 1973; Ferejohn 1986), a commonly known last period can cause "unraveling" to occur: anticipating that the incumbent will shirk in her last period, voters would not reelect, but this gives the incumbent an incentive to shirk in the next to last period, which leads voters not to reelect for this period, and so on – the end result being that the politicians are completely unconstrained. Just as in the chain store paradox, this unraveling need not occur if there is lack of common knowledge about which is the representative's last term, even if it is common knowledge that the representative will eventually die or retire. Thus, Bender and Lott's (1996: 82) claim that unraveling is a theoretical implication of politicians' mortality is too strong.

[10] One might argue that for presidents the "judgment of history" is the relevant sanctioning mechanism in the second term, but of course this is quite different from the electoral mechanism. During the 1996 campaign it was sometimes said by liberals that in the second term "we will see the real [more liberal] Clinton" – that is, that he would shirk, ideologically, against the center. This appears to have been wishful thinking.

[11] While one might argue that voters reelect retiring representatives because seniority gives them special powers in Congress, if voters thought reelection incentives were the sole guarantee of good behavior then they would not expect seniority powers to be used on their behalf in a representative's last period.

[12] For a recent review of the literature on "ideological shirking," see Bender and Lott 1996. For studies looking for last-period effects, see Carey 1996; Lott 1987; Lott and Bronars 1993; Kalt and Zupan 1990; Van Beek 1991; Zupan 1990.

studies find no evidence that representatives change their voting behavior systematically in their last term, although they do vote significantly less often (Lott 1987; Lott and Bronars 1993; Van Beek 1991).[13]

This bit of evidence is of a different order from most of the previous examples. The previous examples generally concerned the beliefs and attitudes of the public, which might be justified or not. This fact, if true, could suggest that people actually *are* able to choose "good types" who have similar policy preferences and who are not so easily bought. For this reason it is worth taking a slightly closer look at this literature.

If we assume it is correct, there are three possible explanations for the fact that representatives in their (known) last term do not change their voting behavior as compared with their previous records. First, it could be that the electorate is able to sort out good types with similar issue preferences, as suggested here and by Lott (1987). Second, it could be that representatives are *never* much constrained by the electorate, so that they vote their ideological preferences all the time, last period or not. Third, in principle it might be that representatives will lose some reputational "bond" if they "cheat" in the last period (Barro 1973), such as prospects for higher office, party-guaranteed pensions, or political career prospects for their children.

The evidence from the literature on congressional voting seems to favor the first explanation, although more could be done to rule out the second. For the third, there are simply not enough plausible "bonds" available to explain the result for retiring congressmen, and those present for some politicians (children's career prospects in politics, aspirations to higher office) seem to have little effect anyway.[14] Regarding the second possible explanation, there seems to be no doubt that, when voting, representatives put some weight on constituent interests as opposed to personal, party leadership, or special interest preferences. The

---

[13] The major exception is Zupan 1990, which is credibly criticized by Lott and Bronars 1993.

[14] Lott 1990; Van Beek 1991. See Carey 1996 for a careful analysis that finds that aspirants to statewide office systematically alter their last period congressional voting in the direction of the state party delegation, which controls nominations. As Carey notes, however, too few congressmen run for higher office for this to explain the general result concerning the absence of a last-period effect.

amount of the weight is hard to estimate.[15] In an innovative essay, Levitt (1996) uses the voting records of a state's House delegation to estimate constituent interests for senators from that state and finds that senators put three to six times less weight on constituent preferences in voting than they do on "personal ideology" (where this should be understood as personal and probably interest-group preferences). The variation – from three to six times less weight – depends on whether one considers only the influence of the state's median voter, or also those voters in the senator's "support constituency," which essentially means voters of the same party. While Levitt's technique seems a big improvement on earlier methods (Kalt and Zupan 1994), the nagging suspicion remains that constituent interests are not adequately estimated, so that the senator-specific effects may contain unmeasured constituent interests. For one thing, in Levitt as in most other studies, the votes used to measure a senator's position are the same for all senators, so that no account is taken of the fact that politicians almost surely put more weight on constituent interests on issues that their constituents care a lot about. Brady and Schwartz's (1995) study of the effect of positions on abortion on election prospects and voting in the Senate tends to support this view.[16]

Levitt's and other evidence in this literature would seem to suggest the following points relevant to this chapter. First, there is no doubt that U.S. congressmen "shirk" to some degree in their voting on bills, in the sense that they do not mirror the ideological preferences of their geographical constituencies (whom they are normatively bound to represent).[17] Nor, it seems, do they perfectly

---

[15] See Kalt and Zupan 1994 and the several critiques of their methodology in *Public Choice* 76 (June 1993). As Bender and Lott (1996: 78) observe, the hypothesis that politicians shirk completely in every period is inconsistent with the finding that in their last term they vote significantly less often (Lott 1987).

[16] Another problem with Levitt's and Kalt and Zupan's approaches is that, in both, average ideological shirking across senators is effectively constrained to be zero, so that systematic bias introduced by, say, the greater power of business lobbies, cannot be estimated. See Bender and Lott 1996 for this point with respect to the Kalt and Zupan methodology. In Levitt, the problem arises from the assumption that the average ideological position of a state's House delegation is an unbiased estimate of voter ideological preferences in the state.

[17] Authors in this literature often bemoan the following problem. What counts as "shirking" depends on which constituency (geographic, electoral, interest group?) representatives are representing, and theory does not tell us which is

mirror the ideological preferences of their "electoral support" constituencies, although the extent of the average deviation is unclear. Second, diverse evidence suggests that the threat of electoral sanctioning does matter. For example, Levitt (1996: 436–38) finds that senators give twice as much weight to (median) constituent preferences in the year before elections as compared to four years or more before elections. He also finds that senators in marginal seats put considerably more weight on constituent preferences than do senators in safe seats.[18]

Third, it nonetheless appears that voters are to some extent able to use elections to select politicians who have roughly similar issue preferences. Otherwise, it is hard to explain the absence of strong last-period effects coupled with the fact that representatives' voting does reflect constituent preferences to a nonnegligible degree. In addition, some studies provide more-direct empirical evidence of electoral sorting – politicians who deviate more from their constituents' preferences are more likely to lose reelection bids (Lott and Davis 1992; Lott and Bronars 1993; Wright 1993; Brady and Schwartz 1995; Levitt 1996: 437n23). It appears, then, that both mechanisms of electoral control – selection and sanctioning – operate to some degree, although if Levitt (1996) is correct, there remains considerable "slack" in the electoral agency relationship.

How Should Elections Be Understood?

Are people wrong to think about elections primarily in terms of choosing a good type rather than as mechanisms of accountability? Are they mistaken to disdain reelection-seeking politicians, to support term limits, and to put so much emphasis

the right one (e.g., Bender and Lott 1996; Poole and Romer 1993). From a normative perspective, however, it seems to me that the issue is clear. Representatives are normatively bound to represent their *geographic* constituencies, and not just the people who voted for them. Thus a representative who votes in accord with the median of her supporters rather than the median of the district is shirking or the median voter in the district has mistaken what is really in his own interests.

[18] There is abundant evidence that U.S. representatives are powerfully motivated by the desire for reelection, and that in consequence they pursue at least some activities that their constituents desire (e.g., Mayhew 1974; Cain, Ferejohn, and Fiorina 1987).

on principledness, consistency, and the character of candidates and elected officials?

These attitudes and beliefs make perfect sense if people also believe that (1) repeated elections do not work well as a mechanism of accountability, because they believe that their ability to observe what politicians do and to interpret whether it is in the public interest is so negligible; and (2) there actually is relevant variation in types of candidates for political office, and these can be distinguished to some extent, either by campaigns or observed performance in office. This is not to say people would be *justified* in having these beliefs – that requires saying whether the beliefs are correct. But neither belief is crazy on the face of it.

Consider the second belief – that a range of types exists and can be distinguished to some extent. A "good type" for a given voter means a candidate with similar policy preferences, who is relatively honest and principled (hard to buy off), and who is skilled. Certainly candidates vary in their policy preferences and general competence, and almost surely they vary in principledness and integrity. *Any* variation in types in this sense, and *any* ability to distinguish them through campaigns or performance in office, would make it reasonable for voters to think about elections at least in part as exercises in sorting among types, independent of a relationship of accountability. The more difficult it is to distinguish types, the more fallible the sorting process – and everyone believes it is highly fallible, since everyone believes there are many corrupt and incompetent politicians. But this need not make it any less rational to try to sort on quality in these dimensions, especially if it is true that elections are not very good as mechanisms of accountability.

So now consider the first belief – that repeated elections do not work well as mechanisms of accountability. There can be no doubt that formidable problems are involved in monitoring and evaluating incumbent behavior to make informed judgments about whether to reelect. Voters face a severe agency problem, because their information about politicians' behavior is inevitably poor and because their sanctioning instrument (reelect/don't reelect) is so crude. Voters have neither the time to follow policy debates in Washington nor the training and skill to evaluate conflicting "expert" arguments about what is best. In any event, elected officials can do an enormous amount of business entirely out of public view. Further, when policy is produced by a legislature, it is difficult to see how one can hold individual members responsible for it unless one has a detailed empirical and theoretical understanding of legislative procedure and politics (which even full-time students of Congress do not agree on).

Finally, even if the public *could* better observe and interpret what elected officials do, it is not clear that the electoral sanction is a subtle enough instrument to induce politicians to do what the public wants.[19] For example, because policy is typically multidimensional, elected officials may be able to play one coalition against another in electoral politics, staying in office while pursuing policies that no majority prefers to available alternatives (Dewatripont and Roland 1992; Ferejohn 1986).

Given the difficulty of the agency problem voters face, then, it might be entirely reasonable to imagine that the best available solution is to try to elect good types of candidates, and to view repeated elections as repeated opportunities to *sort among types* rather than as mechanisms for controlling problems of moral hazard for elected officials. In this view, one votes against an incumbent if economic or other circumstances are bad not in order to give the new officeholder an incentive to work harder or more responsibly, but rather just to try a new random "draw" from the pool of types. In economic jargon, elections may be more about an adverse selection problem – sorting good from bad types that want to mimic them – than about controlling moral hazard.

This perspective has been given a formal statement by Banks and Sundaram (1990), who analyze repeated elections as a species of "bandit problem" from statistics.[20] A voter chooses each period between an incumbent and a challenger, where all candidates are

---

[19] Maravall (Chapter 5 in this volume) provides some dramatic examples of how politicians can exploit the crudeness of the sanctioning mechanism. Why, then, do we use this simplistic incentive scheme for political offices? Why not tie presidential pay to GNP growth (or some weighted average of measures of welfare), as a *Saturday Night Live* skit had Ross Perot suggesting during the 1992 race? This sounds ridiculous, but it is interesting to try to spell out exactly why. Holmstrom and Milgrom (1991) point out that if a job involves many tasks that vary in how easily they can be monitored and evaluated for performance, then making compensation contingent on performance for the most monitorable tasks will suboptimally direct activity away from the less monitorable tasks. Since politicians' jobs involve many tasks and responsibilities that vary in their ease of monitoring, this argument would seem quite relevant.

[20] See also Rogoff and Sibert 1988; Rogoff 1990. For informal discussions, see Lott 1987; Ferejohn 1993.

characterized by an unobserved "competence level." The voter observes her welfare each period, which is the incumbent's competence level plus a stochastic error term. The question is when to dump the present incumbent for a return to the pool of challengers. With two candidates, optimal behavior involves a myopic decision rule where the voter dumps the incumbent if performance falls below a certain level. This is retrospective voting, but it is aimed solely at finding a good type rather than at giving politicians incentives not to shirk in office.

Note that under this conception of elections as pure selection problem, the voter may well want to be able to reelect the same person over and over (i.e., not to have term limits), but the reason has nothing to do with electoral accountability. Rather, voters simply want the option of "keeping good ones." This fits nicely with what seems to be the most popularly convincing argument against term limits, which sees them as restricting democratic choice – "if you have a good representative, why force him or her out?"

The Interaction of Selection and Sanctioning

In the preceding section, I suggested that if voters' ability to monitor politicians' behavior in office is very poor, they might reasonably focus on trying to select good types, even if politicians vary little in desired qualities. This is a claim about what would constitute rational behavior in a particular situation, and it could be wrong or in need of major qualification. For example, it could be that the inability to monitor politicians also effectively undermines the ability to sort among types. Or it could be that a small amount of variation in politicians' types would rationally have only a very small effect on voter behavior.

One way to investigate and assess claims about what would constitute rational behavior is to consider a simple game-theoretic model of the situation, which I develop next. While neither the model nor its results should be taken too literally, it proves useful for a further purpose as well.

Thus far, I have described two ways that elections might bring about a correspondence between public policy and what the public desires. Elections might work either as a sanctioning device that induces politicians to choose in the public interest so they can retain their jobs, or as a selection device that allows the public to choose leaders who will, of their own accord, do what the public wants.[21] Of course, as the empirical literature cited earlier suggests, there is no reason to think that only one of these mechanisms operates. Even if people tend to think about elections as selection devices, *selection can imply sanctioning and vice versa*. If people try to select good types at the polls, then this can imply that bad behavior is electorally sanctioned and thus that bad types have an incentive to mimic the behavior of good types. But this mimicry might in turn reduce the ability to select.

Clearly, then, selection and sanctioning interact. A simple game-theoretic model is also valuable for analyzing the nature of this interaction. I next consider three variants of a model in which an incumbent politician chooses a policy, and then the electorate, uninformed about the policy but informed about its overall welfare, chooses whether to retain the incumbent. The first two variants depict in stark terms the cases of elections as a pure selection device and elections as a pure sanctioning mechanism. The third variant combines selection and sanctioning. Technical details are confined to an appendix.

I will consider three variants of a simple two-period game between two players, the electorate (or median voter), E, and an incumbent politician, I. For all three variants, the sequence of events is the same.[22]

1. The incumbent chooses a policy, represented as a real number x. (In the pure selection case, the incumbent simply implements a given policy rather than making a strategic choice.)
2. The electorate does not observe the policy chosen, but does observe a measure of its welfare that depends partly on the policy x and partly on random factors. The observed measure of welfare is $z = -x^2 + \varepsilon$, where $-x^2$ is the electorate's utility for the policy x and ε is a random variable drawn from a symmetric, strictly unimodal probability density function f with mean zero. Thus, the

[21] This distinction is implicit in the small formal literature on electoral control under the heading of moral hazard versus adverse selection (see Banks and Sundaram 1993, 1996; Ferejohn 1993). In the public choice literature on "ideological shirking" (e.g., Kalt and Zupan 1984), Bender and Lott (1996: 75) label the selection view the "ideology-ensuring-performance hypothesis."
[22] The model both draws on and tries to extend the small formal literature on the electoral control of politicians. See in particular Austen-Smith and Banks 1989; Banks and Sundaram 1990, 1993, 1996; Ferejohn 1986; Harrington 1993a, 1993b; Larocca 1997; Reed 1994; and Zielinski 1997.

electorate's ideal policy choice is $x = 0$, but the electorate cannot tell exactly what the government did because x is not directly observed and the electorate's welfare level z is a noisy measure of x.[23]

3. After observing its welfare level z in the first period, the electorate chooses whether to reelect the incumbent or to draw a new officeholder from a "pool" of aspiring politicians.

4. The second period begins, with the new or old incumbent choosing a policy y, and the electorate receiving utility $-y^2 + \varepsilon'$, where ε' is another draw from the density f. The game then ends. (From the viewpoint of the first period, all second-period payoffs are discounted by a common factor $\delta \in (0, 1)$.)

A strategy for the electorate will be a rule saying whether to reelect the incumbent as a function of its observed first-period welfare, z. Intuition suggests that a sensible rule for the electorate would take the form of a *performance criterion* of "cut rule." For example, "reelect if welfare is at least as great as the level k, and elect a new incumbent otherwise." In fact, for each of the three variants of the model, the optimal rule for the electorate takes this form, which looks like "retrospective voting" in the sense that Fiorina (1981) and others have argued is typical of how voters decide in practice.[24] Of course, if voters are rationally seeking to influence their future welfare with their votes, then their retrospective judgment has a prospective purpose. The question then arises of how to choose the performance criterion k to best motivate or select politicians in the future. I proceed to consider this problem for the three variants in turn.

Pure Selection

In the case of elections as a pure selection problem, candidates vary in their level of competence or skill at producing outcomes the electorate likes.[25] For simplicity, suppose there are two types – good ones, who are both able and willing to implement the

---

[23] The case where the electorate observes a noisy measure of the policy chosen ($z = x + \varepsilon$) yields qualitatively similar results.

[24] I do not demonstrate this here. See Banks and Sundaram 1996 for a proof of the optimality of a simple cut rule in a similar model.

[25] As in Rogoff 1990; Banks and Sundaram 1990.

electorate's optimal policy $x = 0$, and bad ones, who can at best implement a suboptimal policy $\hat{x} > 0$. Thus, good types are expected to produce a welfare level of zero on average, while bad types produce $-\hat{x}^2$ on average. Assume further that in the "pool" of aspiring politicians, a fraction $\alpha \in (0, 1)$ are good types and $1 - \alpha$ are bad types, and that the first-period incumbent was initially drawn from this pool (e.g., in an open-seat race).

So in this case of pure selection, the electorate faces the decision-theoretic problem of drawing an inference about the incumbent's competence from its observed welfare level z, and then reelecting if the updated belief that the incumbent is good is higher than α, the probability that a new incumbent would be a good type. This is a simple matter of applying Bayes's rule. In the appendix, I show that when the distribution of "noise" f is symmetric and unimodal, the electorate increases its estimate that the incumbent is competent if it observes welfare z greater than $k = -\hat{x}^2/2$, which is the outcome halfway between the expected performance of competent and incompetent types. Thus, $k = -\hat{x}^2/2$ is the retrospective performance criterion in this case. If not attained, the incumbent is dumped.

Two interesting comparative statics results follow. First, the better the expected performance of the less competent type (the smaller $\hat{x}$), the *more demanding* is the optimal performance criterion (k rises as $\hat{x}$ falls). For example, suppose that competent types are expected to produce noninflationary growth of (on average) 2%, while incompetent types are expected to produce 0%. Then a rational electorate infers the incumbent is more likely to be a competent type than a new draw would be if it observes growth of at least 1%. However, if an incompetent type is expected to produce growth of 1% on average, then the electorate's performance criterion rises to 1.5%. Intuitively, the more the bad type's expected performance resembles the good type's, the higher the performance needed to increase the electorate's estimate of competence. This observation will prove important later, in the analysis of the mixed case.

Second, making it harder for the electorate to monitor the incumbent's behavior (i.e., increasing the variance of the noise ε) has no effect on the optimal-performance criterion (k is independent of the density function f). However, worse monitoring does make it harder for the electorate to select good types. The probability that a good type is reelected is the probability that

73

$z > k$, or $1 - F(k)$; the likelihood that a bad type is reelected is the probability that $z = -\hat{x}^2 + \varepsilon > k$, or $1 - F(\hat{x}^2 + k)$. As the variance of the noise term ε increases, both these terms approach 1/2, so that good and bad types are almost equally likely to be reelected. As monitoring improves, by contrast, the probability that a good type is reelected eventually approaches 1 and the probability that a bad type is reelected approaches 0.[26]

Pure Sanctioning (Moral Hazard)

In the case of elections understood purely as mechanisms of accountability, all politicians are the same type. They are all venal, or have policy preferences distinct from the electorate's. Assume, for example, that the incumbent and all aspiring politicians in the model maximize their own utility in a given term in office by choosing $x = 1$. This might arise either because the politicians are systematically more ideologically extreme than the median voter, or because wealthy special interests offer venal politicians various benefits for choosing policies the median voter dislikes.

In particular, for the model, assume that an incumbent's utility is given by $W - (1 - x)^2$ in the first period and $W - (1 - y)^2$ in the second. $W > 0$ is a politician's value for office independent of policies chosen, which presumably includes pay and perquisites but, for national office, is probably mainly a status value – "ego rents," as Rogoff and Sibert (1988) put it.[27] Because the second period is the last, politicians maximize utility in the second period by setting $y = 1$, which yields them W. For the first term in office, however, an incumbent has to consider the effect of the policy choice on the probability of being reelected, which depends in turn on the performance criterion set by the electorate.

---

[26] Here and elsewhere, when I equate the quality of monitoring with the variance of ε, I mean variance parameterized as in the case of standard bell-shaped curves like the normal and logistic distributions. There are in principle an infinite number of ways to increase the variance of a distribution, and for some peculiar ways (e.g., readjusting probability weight only in the tails), some of the claims given in the text would be weakened.

[27] As is typical in this literature, I will assume W to be exogenous, even though W can presumably be manipulated through salary choice by the principal. For a variety of reasons (some of them worth exploring), representatives' pay is not much used for incentive purposes.

In this case of pure sanctioning, it is important to see that *any performance criterion set by the electorate is credible*, in the sense that the electorate is willing to reelect or not according to any criterion. Because in this case all politicians are alike (somewhat bad), the electorate is always indifferent between keeping and dumping the incumbent, since it gets the same second-period outcome ($y = 1$) either way.[28] And because the electorate is always indifferent between candidates, the electorate can choose the performance criterion to motivate the incumbent optimally and have it be credible that this criterion will in fact be employed. As I show later for the mixed case, introducing even a tiny possibility of variation in politicians' types radically changes this – if politicians vary in policy preferences, even a little, then voters are no longer generically indifferent between the incumbent and possible replacements.

What, then, is the performance criterion that will motivate the incumbent to choose a policy as close as possible to the electorate's ideal of $x = 0$? At first glance, one might think that the higher the electorate sets the standard, the greater the incentive for the incumbent to choose a policy in the public's interest. This is mistaken, however. If the electorate holds incumbents to too high a standard for reelection, then, since reelection is relatively unlikely anyway, politicians have an incentive to shirk a lot – the marginal impact of shirking on the (low) probability of reelection is small. Similarly, if the electorate sets a low threshold for reelection that is easily obtained, then incumbents have an incentive to shirk substantially. As shown in the appendix, the optimal cut rule k^* is chosen to maximize the sensitivity of the likelihood of reelection to shirking by the incumbent.

This basic moral hazard model produces a natural comparative statics result concerning the public's ability to monitor: the worse the electorate's ability to monitor (the greater the variance of ε), the worse the electorate does in terms of policy (the incumbent chooses an x closer to 1). Worse monitoring implies that a given

[28] This point is also stressed by Austen-Smith and Banks 1989, who consider a similar two-period model with moral hazard. It does not seem to be entirely an artifact of having only two periods, however. Voter indifference between candidates obtains as well in the infinitely repeated case of this model with no term limits, which I have examined, and in the case presented by Ferejohn (1986), who considers an infinite horizon model where incumbents observe their randomly fluctuating marginal cost before they choose "effort" each period.

amount of shirking has a smaller effect on the incumbent's probability of reelection, which reduces the force of the electoral sanction. Conversely, as monitoring approaches perfection (the variance of ε shrinks towards 0), the incumbent's policy choice approaches the voter's ideal point, $x = 0$.[29]

The Mixed Case: Selection and Sanctioning

As I argued earlier, a number of empirical observations suggest that voters think about elections more in terms of selection than as sanctioning mechanisms to influence future incumbents. The pure moral hazard model just presented (and likewise, that of Ferejohn 1986) allows no place for variation in politicians' motivations and dispositions, and so cannot capture this dimension of democratic governance that seems to loom large in the minds of voters. While perhaps better, the pure selection model is also crucially deficient. Surely voters do think that some politicians are intrinsically more capable or competent at producing good outcomes than others, and voters are interested in sorting out the relatively competent ones. But everyone recognizes that politicians make important policy *choices* while in office that are not well monitored by the electorate. Thus Ferejohn and others are absolutely right to say that the voter-politician relationship involves moral hazard in a central way. A theoretical model that captures the voter's decision problem simply but usefully must combine the elements of adverse selection and moral hazard.

There are numerous ways that selection and sanctioning might be combined in a game model,[30] in part because there are at least

---

[29] Interestingly, as monitoring worsens, the electorate's optimal-performance criterion becomes *less* demanding. I have analyzed the infinite horizon version of the pure sanctioning model, and the result appears to obtain there as well, at least for normally distributed noise. While in the two-period case the probability of reelection is always 1/2, in the infinite horizon case it can either increase or decrease as monitoring worsens (and it is typically well above 1/2).

[30] Banks and Sundaram 1993, 1996 are the only fully game-theoretic election models I know of that incorporate both elements; see the appendix for a discussion of relevant differences. Reed (1994) claims to consider moral hazard and adverse selection, but in his model the voters observe the policies implemented perfectly, so there is no moral hazard in the usual sense of "hidden actions." Reed's analysis is also incomplete or incorrect, as discussed in the appendix.

three dimensions along which good and bad types can differ: policy preferences, integrity, and intrinsic ability or competence. I will consider a simple formulation that builds on the games just considered, and in which good and bad politicians differ with respect to policy preferences.[31]

Suppose that everything is the same as in the pure sanctioning case described earlier, except that now all politicians initially have an $\alpha \in (0, 1)$ chance of being a "good type," which will mean a politician with the same policy preferences as the electorate (i.e., quadratic with the ideal point at $x = 0$, so that a good type's one-period utility function in office is $W - x^2$). The electorate now might have an incentive to try to sort out good types rather than just optimally motivate bad types. In fact, as argued informally here and formally in the appendix, even if there is only a *tiny* chance of finding a good type (α close to zero), it makes sense for the electorate to focus *completely* on the problem of selection when casting its vote! And, ironically, this is true even though the rationality of trying to select on type at the polls can undermine the efficacy of elections as mechanisms of accountability.

That it makes sense for the electorate to focus entirely on the problem of selection at election time is easy to see. Since the second-period behavior of all bad types will be the same (they all choose $y = 1$), at the polls the electorate maximizes its utility by choosing the candidate most likely to be a good type (who would choose $y = 0$). This holds even if the probability of drawing a good type from the pool of aspiring politicians, α, is negligible.

There is an important substantive point here that is probably more general than this simple model. If politicians do not vary in type, as presumed by the pure sanctioning view of elections, then voters are completely indifferent between candidates – all politicians will respond the same way to any given set of electoral incentives. But this indifference is fragile. Introduce *any* variation in politicians' attributes or propensities relevant to their per-formance in office, and it makes sense for the electorate to focus *completely* on choosing the best type when it comes time to vote. This result supports and even strengthens the claim made in the previous section, that it would be rational for voters to try to sort

---

[31] Depending on how we interpret what gives rise to the politicians' preferences, types in the model may also be seen as differing in integrity.

good from bad types of politicians even if there is in fact little variation or it is difficult to discern.[32]

In the model, the fact that the electorate rationally focuses on type at election time has an additional consequence of interest. Namely, the performance criterion that would be optimal ex ante for motivating bad types of politician is generally not optimal (and thus not credible) ex post, for the purpose of selecting good types. The electorate could minimize shirking by bad types by committing in advance to use the cut rule k that maximizes the marginal impact of shirking on the bad type's probability of reelection, as in the pure sanctioning case analyzed earlier. But here's the rub: the more effective this performance rule is in motivating a bad type of incumbent to choose a policy close to $x = 0$, the smaller the practical difference between good and bad types, which makes selection harder. As shown for the pure selection case, the more that bad types choose public-spirited policies, the *better* the performance the electorate will need to see to conclude that the incumbent is likely enough to be a good type to be worth reelecting.

Thus, the more bad types are expected to try to appear good (i.e., the less they shirk the public interest), *the higher the performance standard they will be held to after the fact.* And choosing policies more in line with what the public desires will not necessarily increase one's odds of reelection if the public responds by demanding a better performance in order to reelect.

This result suggests, then, a possible problem with elections as a mechanism of accountability. The problem is that the electorate cannot commit to keep its standards for reelection constant. If there is variation in politicians' policy preferences, then the more incumbents serve public rather than special interests, the higher the performance level the electorate will demand for reelection,

---

[32] It is hypothetically possible that in a model with more than two periods, there might be equilibria in which the electorate can commit to keep incumbents thought less good than a new draw would be because failure to do so would lead to "punishment" by future incumbents. This seems intuitively farfetched, in part because such a scheme would probably not be renegotiation-proof – if later incumbents were made worse off by punishing the electorate, they would have an incentive to renegotiate to the original terms. Banks and Sundaram's (1993) model uses a trigger-strategy punishment by the politicians, but to encourage the electorate to drop incumbents if "rewards" fall below a certain level rather than to keep them.

which may undermine politicians' incentives not to shirk in the first place. The result can be a sort of "trap" that makes both sides worse off. I show in the appendix that if the proportion of good politicians is not too large (typically, no more than about 1/2), then voters would be strictly better off if they could commit in advance to use the performance criterion that optimally motivates bad types.[33]

It can also be shown that because of this commitment problem for the electorate, bad incumbents shirk strictly more in the equilibrium of the mixed case than in the case of pure moral hazard, with the amount of the difference being independent of α, the fraction of good types.[34] Ironically, then, introducing a small chance that some politicians are public-spirited can make the public worse off relative to the pure sanctioning case, by undermining the ability to electorally control bad types. (Of course, as the fraction of good types grows, eventually the public is made better off by their presence, despite the increased shirking by bad types.)

I also show in the appendix that, in accord with earlier arguments, as the electorate's ability to monitor becomes very poor, bad incumbents choose their preferred policy (almost) and the electorate's problem approaches pure selection. At the same time, however, worse monitoring lowers the electorate's ability to distinguish good types based on performance, so that the efficacy of selection falls as well.[35] This is not a coincidence – bad types are willing to choose very different policies from good types only if the electorate has a hard time telling the difference between them (i.e., if selection based on performance is not very effective).

There are thus two senses in which it can be reasonable for voters to focus on the problem of selecting good types. First, since bad types are all the same regarding how they will perform for any given set of electoral incentives, the only basis for preferring

---

[33] The latter rule is not, however, ex ante optimal for the electorate, because in addition to the sanctioning effect that motivates bad types there is a "selection effect" – the better the performance of bad types in the first period, the harder it is to sort good from bad for the second period.

[34] See the appendix. A perfect Bayesian equilibrium obtains in the model when the incumbent has correct expectations about the performance criterion the electorate will employ, and chooses a policy with this expectation.

[35] In the limit, as the variance of ε grows very large, good types' probability of reelection approaches 1/2 from above and bad types' from below.

one candidate to another at election time is some variation in type (policy preferences, personal rectitude, competence, etc.). Second, if voters have a difficult time monitoring whether incumbents chose policies in their interests, then the electoral sanction will not deter shirking by bad types, leaving electorates the option of sorting them out by performance and other measures, albeit poorly.

Two other results deserve mention. First, how does the efficacy of electoral selection vary with the voters' ability to assess whether politicians are choosing good policies? There are two opposing effects. On the one hand, worse monitoring increases the amount of shirking by bad incumbents, which means that the expected performance of good and bad types diverges. This effect increases the voters' ability to sort good from bad. On the other hand, as monitoring worsens, the probability that a bad type will satisfy the performance criterion (for any given amount of shirking) goes up, which tends to make selection less effective. In numerical analyses of the case of normally distributed noise, I have found that the relationship between monitoring and the efficacy of selection takes the form of an inverted "U." When monitoring is very good, selection is ineffective (although unimportant) because bad types closely mimic good types. When monitoring is very poor, selection is ineffective because bad types frequently meet the performance standard despite their shirking. In between, when voters are moderately able to assess politicians' choices, the difference between good and bad types' odds of reelection is greatest.

The second result, consistent with those of Banks and Sundaram (1996) and Lott and Reed (1989), concerns a cross-section-versus-time-series effect. In equilibrium, all politicians shirk at least as much or more in their second term, due to the last-period effect for bad types. But at the same time, second-term politicians *as a group* may shirk less on average than first-termers, because selection implies that more good types hold office in the second term than the first.[36] Thus time series studies of particular representatives would be expected to find increased "ideological shirking" with greater tenure, while cross-sectional comparisons should find less shirking by longer-serving representatives. The empirical evidence is largely consistent with this prediction,

---

[36] The formal condition for the expected second-period policy to be better for the electorate than the expected first-period policy is $F(-k^*) - F(k^*) > (1 - \sqrt{-2k^*})/\alpha$.

although the evidence for increased shirking with greater tenure is slight (for examples, see Kalt and Zupan 1990; Zupan 1990; Levitt 1996).

To summarize, this section has posed two "ideal typical" views of how the electoral control of politicians might work, arguing that a good theory needs to incorporate both and also to consider that the two mechanisms interact. Even if voters focus their attention on the problem of selection – and, as suggested by the model, they can have good reasons for doing so even when selection is difficult – this implies that to some degree elections will act as sanctions establishing an accountability relationship.

Analysis of the model also produced the unexpected finding that the problem of adverse selection in elections can, in principle, worsen the problem of moral hazard. If politicians vary in their policy preferences and integrity, which they surely do, then (rational) voters will be drawn to choose at election time on the basis of beliefs about type, and ironically this imperative may reduce the flexibility of elections as mechanisms of accountability. In essence, the performance criterion that would minimize politicians' incentive to shirk is not credible because at the polls voters would want to apply a higher standard in order to sort good types from bad optimally.

Though of theoretical interest, I suspect that the practical and empirical relevance of this commitment pathology is small, in part due to concern that the model is unusually spare. Moreover, even in the model as it stands, in numerical analyses I have found it almost impossible to generate large welfare losses for the electorate due to the commitment problem.[37] Even though shirking by bad types increases when a chance of good types is introduced, the increase is typically quite small, especially when monitoring is poor but even when monitoring is relatively effective. For example, almost regardless of monitoring ability, the electorate does better in the mixed model than in the pure sanctioning case if at least one in five hundred political aspirants is a good type.[38]

---

[37] In these analyses I used a normal distribution for ε; almost surely the claim holds for any bell-shaped distribution.

[38] Some might say that one in five hundred is too optimistic. Also, the simulation results described all assume that politicians' value for office W is at least as great as their value for maximum shirking in a period – that is, $W > 1$. If $\delta W < 1$, then the commitment problem can cause nontrivial welfare losses.

Conclusion

The main justification for freely contested and regular elections is that these are supposed to bring about democracy, or rule according to the will of people. As the editors note in the volume's introduction, the tradition of democratic theory contains surprisingly little on exactly how elections are supposed to produce this result, or on how well they might be expected to. How, if at all, do elections bring about a correspondence between public policy and what the electorate desires? And under what conditions is the correspondence strong or weak?

The main points of this chapter may be summarized as follows. First, following the small formal literature on electoral control, I have argued that there are *two* principal mechanisms by which elections might bring about public policy that voters desire – sanctioning and selection. Elected officials might be motivated to choose policies the public desires either because this will help get them reelected (sanctioning), or because the electorate is able to select "good types" who are principled, competent, and share the electorate's ends, independent of reelection incentives. This simple point is missed if the voter-politician relationship is understood purely as a relationship of accountability based on the electoral sanction.

Second, I suggested that in fact voters think about elections much more as opportunities to try to select good types than as sanctions to deter shirking by future incumbents. A number of empirical observations support this claim. The popular dislike of office seeking, support for term limits, the premium put on politicians being principled and consistent, and the absence of concern about "last-period effects" all suggest that voters think about elections primarily in terms of selection.

Third, analysis of a simple model of electoral control in which voters face both adverse selection (the problem of distinguishing good from bad) and moral hazard (imperfect monitoring of agents who might shirk) suggested two reasons why it may be reasonable for voters to focus on selecting good types. Once at the polls, the electorate can't commit to ignore type in favor of implementing an ex ante optimal sanctioning scheme – variation in type is what is relevant to voter payoffs at the moment of choice. Also, if the electorate's ability to monitor what politicians do is poor, then the force of the electoral sanction is weak and voters are left with selection as a (noisy) means of getting the public policies they desire.

Finally, the mechanisms of selection and sanctioning inevitably interact, with consequences for the efficacy of democratic rule. Even if voters focus on selecting good types, this implies accountability, since bad performance in office will be sanctioned when it suggests the incumbent is a bad type. In the model examined here, where voters could only distinguish types of politicians by observing their performance in office, the electorate's ability to monitor determines the interaction between selection and sanctioning. Good monitoring induces bad types to act like good ones, so selection becomes difficult but also less important. Bad monitoring leads bad types to shirk more, which makes selection possible, but also makes it a noisy and fallible enterprise for the voters.[39]

The importance of monitoring for making elections somewhat effective instruments of popular rule in the model accords with common sense (though I hope the strategic logic described provides stronger and more developed foundations for the common sense). Almost surely, politicians are most inclined to choose policies and other actions that the public desires when the probability of exposure for failure to do so is highest. The standard liberal observations about the importance of effective media and an informed, interested public follow immediately.

As Downs (1957) stressed, however, voter's incentives to be interested and well informed about politics are far from strong, a point amply confirmed by empirical studies of what most voters know about politics. The preceding arguments about monitoring, selection, and sanctioning are all based on a model in which people assess politicians' types by looking at noisy measures of their performance in office. As noted earlier, there are other, less attention-intensive ways of trying to assess types. For example,

---

[39] As throughout, "monitoring" refers here to the electorate's ability to assess whether politicians are choosing policies in the public interest. I have not distinguished among the several reasons why voters may have trouble making this assessment – stochastic relationships between policies chosen and outcomes observed (what is modeled here), lack of knowledge about what policy is in one's own best interest (Harrington 1993a), asymmetries of information between politicians and voters concerning policy (Larocca 1997), and so on. Differences among these may have significant consequences for accountability and responsiveness.

how does the politician look and sound when giving a speech? What sort of person does he or she seem like? It is an interesting and open question as to how well voters can select "good types" based on this sort of information, and quite relevant to the question of how well elections serve democracy.

Appendix

Pure Selection

Derivation of the electorate's decision rule proceeds as follows. Let $\alpha'(z)$ represent the electorate's updated belief that the incumbent is a good type, conditional on observing welfare level z. Bayes's rule states (in odds-ratio form) that the posterior odds that I is a good type, $\alpha'(z)/(1 - \alpha'(z))$, equals the prior odds, $\alpha/(1 - \alpha)$, times the likelihood ratio, $f(z)/f(\hat{x}^2 + z)$. (The likelihood ratio derives here from $Pr\,(z \approx 0 + \varepsilon)/Pr(z \approx -\hat{x}^2 + \varepsilon)$. Thus, $\alpha'(z) > \alpha$ if and only if $f(z) > f(\hat{x}^2 + z)$. Intuitively, the posterior belief that the incumbent is a good type increases if it is more likely that the electorate would observe z if the incumbent were good than bad. The optimal performance criterion is then defined by the welfare level k that satisfies $f(k) = f(\hat{x}^2 + k)$.

As indicated by Figure 2.1, for f such that $f'(z) = 0$ only at $z = 0$, there is a unique cut rule k that satisfies this equality. Further, when f is symmetric as well, we can specify the performance criterion exactly. It must be $k = -\hat{x}^2/2$, since $f(k) = f(-k) = f(\hat{x}^2 + k)$.

To see the claim in the text about monitoring, consider a logistic distribution $F(z) = e^{z/a}/(1 + e^{z/a})$, where $a > 0$ parameterizes variance (greater a implies higher variance). Observe that since the optimal cut rule $k < 0$, $\lim_{a \to \infty} 1 - F(k) = \lim_{a \to \infty} 1 - F(-k) = 1/2$, $\lim_{a \to 0} 1 - F(k) = 1$, and $\lim_{a \to 0} 1 - F(-k) = 0$, as claimed. The same holds for a normal distribution.

Pure Sanctioning

The electorate's optimal cut rule k^* is found by considering how the incumbent would choose given any particular rule k, and then choosing k so as to induce the smallest choice of x possible. As argued in the text, because the electorate is indifferent between all candidates in the second period, it is optimal for it to implement any cut rule.

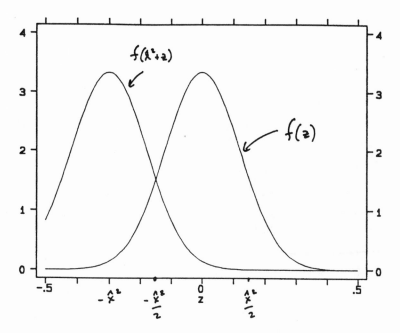

Figure 2.1. Pure selection

Given a k, the incumbent chooses x to maximize

$$u(x) = W - (1-x)^2 + \delta(1 - F(x^2 + k))W, \tag{1}$$

where $1 - F(x^2 + k) = 1 - Pr(-x^2 + \varepsilon < k) = 1 - Pr(z < k)$ is the probability that the incumbent will be reelected given x and k. Notice that the right-hand side of (1) implicitly incorporates the fact that the incumbent will choose $y = 0$ in the second period, by subgame perfection.

The first-order condition is $u'(x) = 2(1 - x) - \delta W f(x^2 + k)2x = 0$, which yields

$$f(x^2 + k) = \frac{1-x}{x}\frac{1}{\delta W}. \tag{2}$$

Provisionally assuming that the second-order condition is also satisfied, equation (2) implicitly defines the incumbent's best response x as a function of k; call it $x(k)$. The right-hand side of (2) is decreasing in x, so that E gets the smallest x possible by choosing k so as to maximize the left-hand side, given $x(k)$. The assumption that $f(\cdot)$ is strictly unimodal and has mean zero implies that $f(\cdot)$ reaches its maximum value at $f(0)$. Thus, to induce the

85

minimum possible value of x, E chooses k^* such that $x(k^*)^2 + k^* = 0$.

Letting $x^* = x(k^*)$, we can solve directly for x^* from

$$f(0) = \frac{1-x^*}{x^*} \frac{1}{\delta W}. \tag{3}$$

Thus, $x^* = 1/(1 + \delta W f(0))$ and $k^* = -x^{*2}$.

As the variance of a normal or logistic $f(\cdot)$ increases, $f(0)$ falls, increasing the equilibrium amount of shirking (x^* increases), and making the performance criterion less strict (k^* falls). (It is worth pointing out that the solutions for x^* and k^* hold for *any* strictly unimodal distribution for ε.)

It remains to check that the second-order condition is satisfied at x^* and k^*. This condition requires that

$$u''(x) = -2 - 2\delta W[f(x^2 + k) + 2x^2 f'(x^2 + k)] < 0 \tag{4}$$

at x^* and k^*, which is true since $x(k^*)^2 + k^* = 0$, $f(0) > 0$, and $f'(0) = 0$.

The Mixed Case: Selection and Sanctioning

The game is solved for pure-strategy perfect Bayesian equilibria (PBE) in which the electorate uses a cut rule in deciding whether to reelect the incumbent. Specifying strategies is simplified if we immediately apply subgame perfection to the new or old incumbent's choice of a policy y in the second period of the game: For all prior histories of play, good types maximize their utility by setting $y = 0$, and bad types by choosing $y = 1$. With this understood, a pure strategy for the incumbent in the first period amounts to a choice of $x \in \mathbb{R}$ for each type. A pure strategy for the electorate is a function $s_E(z) \in \{0, 1\}$, which gives the electorate's decision to keep (1) or drop (0) the incumbent for each possible observation $z \in \mathbb{R}$. Attention is restricted to functions of the form $s_E(z) = 1$ if and only if $z \geq k$.[40] Let $s = (x_g, x_b, k)$ represent a strategy triple where the first two elements are the good and bad type's first-period policy choices and the third is the electorate's cut rule. A system of beliefs for the electorate is a

---

[40] See Banks and Sundaram 1996 for a proof of the optimality of such cut rules in a similar model.

function $\alpha'(z) \in [0, 1]$, which gives the electorate's posterior belief that the incumbent is a good type after having observed welfare level z.

A pure-strategy PBE is then defined as an s and a system of beliefs $\alpha'(z)$ such that each player's strategy is optimal given beliefs at every one of the player's information sets, and the electorate's beliefs are formed using Bayes's rule whenever possible.

Working backward by considering the electorate's choice of whether to keep or drop the incumbent, observe that E's expected utility for reelecting the incumbent is $\alpha'(z)0 + (1 - \alpha'(z))(-1) = -(1 - \alpha'(z))$, while the expected utility of drawing a new incumbent from the pool is just $-(1 - \alpha)$. Thus optimal choice for the electorate entails keeping the incumbent if $\alpha'(z) \geq \alpha$. In odds ratio form, Bayes's rule says that

$$\frac{\alpha'(z)}{1-\alpha'(z)} = \frac{f(x_g^2+z)}{f(x_b^2+z)} \frac{\alpha}{1-\alpha},$$

so that E keeps the incumbent if $f(x_g^2 + z) \geq f(x_b^2 + z)$ and not otherwise. Further, E is indifferent when it observes $z = k$, implying that in equilibrium k satisfies

$$f(x_g^2 + k) = f(x_b^2 + k). \tag{5}$$

Next, consider what choices of x_g and x_b would be optimal for the incumbent in the first period, given the expectation that the electorate is using the cut rule k. The bad type's maximization problem is exactly the same as in the pure sanctioning case considered earlier, so condition (2) again implicitly defines a bad type's best response $x(k)$. Good types choose x to maximize $W - x^2 + \delta(1 - F(x^2 + k))W$, which has its first-order condition $-2x - \delta f(x^2 + k)W2x = 0$ satisfied uniquely by $x = 0$. (That this is a maximum is apparent from inspection of the objective function.) So good types have a dominant strategy of choosing their ideal point $x = 0$, regardless of δ, W, and k.

Thus, condition (5) reduces to $f(k) = f(x_b^2 + k)$, which implies, since $f(\cdot)$ is symmetric and quasi-concave, that in any equilibrium $k \leq 0$ and

$$k = -x_b^2/2. \tag{6}$$

This last equality says how the electorate's performance criterion k responds given the policy choice expected from bad

87

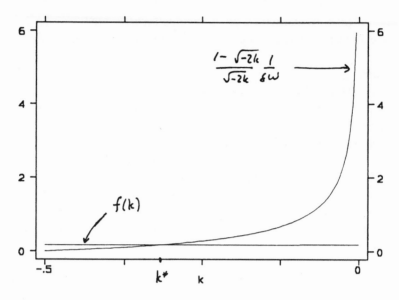

Figure 2.2a. Poor monitoring (high-variance noise)

incumbents.[41] As in the pure selection model, the better the bad types' expected performance (smaller x_b), the higher the level of welfare E needs to observe to conclude that the incumbent is more likely a good type than a new draw would be.

But of course the cut rule k also determines which x_b is optimal for the incumbent through condition (2). A PBE requires that the bad type's choice of x_b imply a cut rule k (through condition (6)) that in turn induces bad types to want to choose x_b (through condition (2)). Formally, $x_b = \sqrt{-2k}$ from (6), and substituting for x in (2) yields the condition that implicitly defines "interior" candidates for equilibrium k^*'s:

$$f(k) = \frac{1 - \sqrt{-2k}}{\sqrt{-2k}} \frac{1}{\delta W}. \tag{7}$$

Figures 2.2a–c graphically depict the determination of such k^*'s in three cases. The following claims are apparent from inspection of the figures: (a) There exists either one or three interior solutions to (7) (omitting nongeneric cases involving a tangency). (b) If $f(\cdot)$

---

[41] Note also that $k \leq 0$ and $x_b^2 + k \geq 0$ imply that in any equilibrium good types will be reelected with a probability of at least 1/2, while bad types are reelected with probability at most 1/2.

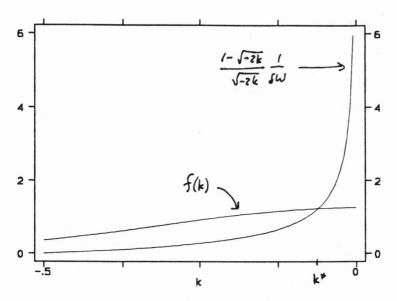

Figure 2.2b. Moderate monitoring (moderate-variance noise)

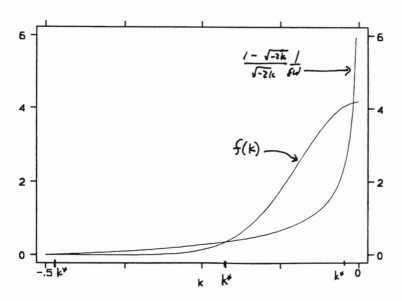

Figure 2.2c. Good monitoring (low-variance noise)

is normal or logistic, then for large enough variance there is a unique interior solution that approaches $k = -1/2$ (thus, $x_b = 1$) as variance increases. If the interior solution is indeed a maximum, then this implies that as monitoring worsens, bad types' choice of policy ultimately approaches $x_b = 1$, or total shirking. (c) For interior solutions, shirking need not decrease monotonically as monitoring improves (i.e., variance of f decreases), although for small enough variance there will exist an interior solution that involves almost no shirking (Figure 2.2c).

I next show that neither $x_b = 0$ nor $x_b = 1$ can be part of a PBE, so that if a PBE exists it involves at least one of the interior solutions to (7). At $x_b = 0$, $u'(0) = 2 - 2\delta W f(k)(0) > 0$ for all $k \in [-\infty, \infty]$, so bad incumbents always have an incentive to shirk at least a little. For $x_b = 1$, observe that $u'(1) = -2\delta W f(1 + k) < 0$ for all finite k, which means that the incumbent wants to choose $x_b < 1$ for any finite cut rule. And since neither $k = -\infty$ (sure reelection) nor $k = \infty$ (certain replacement) can support an equilibrium – in both cases E would optimally deviate to $k = -1/2$, ex post, since $x_b = 1$ would be expected – any pure-strategy PBE must involve an interior solution to the bad type's first-order condition given earlier.

For cases like Figure 2.2a, where there is only one interior solution, this must be a maximum since $u'(0) > 0$ and $u'(1) < 0$ for all finite k. For cases with three interior solutions to the first-order condition, I next show that the "middle" solution corresponds to a minimum, and thus is not a candidate.

Using the facts that at a solution to (7), $x^2 + k = -k$, $f(k) = f(-k) = (1 - \sqrt{-2k})/(\sqrt{-2k}\ \delta W)$, and $f'(-k) = -f'(k)$, algebra applied to the second-order condition (4) can be shown to imply that $u''(k) < 0$ if and only if

$$f'(k) < \frac{1}{2}\frac{1}{(-2k)^{3/2}\delta W}.$$ (8)

Differentiating the right-hand side of (7) with respect to k gives $1/((-2k)^{3/2}\delta W)$ as the slope of this function. Since at a "middle" interior solution to (7), $f'(k) > 1/((-2k)^{3/2}\delta W)$, it follows that the second-order condition (4) cannot be satisfied. So we can say that the "middle" interior solution to (7) cannot support a PBE, and that at least one of the other two solutions (in this case) must support a PBE. Without specifying functional forms, we cannot say which one or both supports an equilibrium.[42]

---

[42] In simulations using a normal distribution for ε, I have not found a single case in which multiple equilibrium obtain. I have been unable to show that this is necessarily the case.

This completes the derivation of equilibrium in the mixed case. I conclude with a comparison of the mixed and pure moral hazard models that demonstrates and elaborates several of the claims about the models made in the text.

Comparison of Mixed and Pure Moral Hazard Models

In the pure moral hazard case, the best the electorate can do is to induce politicians to choose the policy x_{mh} that satisfies conditions (3). This policy is defined implicitly by

$$f(0) = \frac{1 - x_{mh}}{x_{mh}} \frac{1}{\delta W}.$$

Suppose now that we introduce into the pool of candidates a very small fraction (α close to zero) of good types of politician who have policy preferences similar to the electorate or who are uncorruptible by interest group bribery, as in the mixed case. Writing (7) in terms of $x_b = \sqrt{-2k}$, where x_b is the equilibrium choice of bad types in the mixed case, we have

$$f(0) = \frac{1 - x_{mh}}{x_{mh}} \frac{1}{\delta W} > f\left(\frac{x_b^2}{2}\right) = \frac{1 - x_b}{x_b} \frac{1}{\delta W},$$

since $f(z)$ is maximized at $f(0)$ and $x_b > 0$. It follows immediately that regardless of how small α is, *bad types of politicians shirk more when there are some good types than when they are all the same* $(x_b > x_{mh})$.[43] This is a "pathological" result – introducing a sufficiently small chance that there are public-spirited politicians who will actually *lower* the public's utility, essentially by making the public unable to commit not to select on type at the polls. The imperative of selection then reduces the flexibility of the elections as a sanctioning instrument and leads to suboptimal motivating of bad types of politicians.

In more technical terms, lower hemicontinuity of the equilibrium correspondence fails at $\alpha = 0$; there exist equilibria in the $\alpha = 0$ case that are not the limit of any sequence of equilibria as α approaches zero. This result is in marked contrast to Banks

---

[43] Note, in fact, that $\alpha \in (0, 1)$ plays *no* role in determining equilibrium strategies in the mixed case.

and Sundaram (1996), who consider a closely related model of elections that combines moral hazard and adverse selection. They find that the equilibria of their game with a small amount of type heterogeneity (adverse selection) "converge to equilibria of the 'pure moral hazard' case," so that "adding a 'little bit' of uncertainty about agent types will only move the agents a little bit away from their myopic actions" (1966: 25). A related implication is that the electorate "can . . . never lose from the introduction of 'better' types of agents" (1966: 5). Neither result holds in the model considered here, and it is natural to wonder why.

The crucial difference appears to be that my model ends in two periods, whereas Banks and Sundaram (1996) consider the case of an electorate with an infinite horizon and politicians who are constrained to serve at most two terms.[44] In pure moral hazard models with an infinite horizon and any commonly known, finite term limit, the electorate cannot commit to condition reelection on performance, and, in consequence, incumbents are completely uncontrolled in any subgame perfect equilibrium ("unraveling" occurs). By contrast, in a two-period, pure moral hazard model, voters can credibly promise to reelect incumbents who perform well. This allows equilibria in which politicians do not shirk completely in the first period, as shown here and by Austen-Smith and Banks 1989. I have considered the infinite-horizon, two-period term-limit case of the mixed model analyzed earlier, and find that Banks and Sundaram's (1996) result is reproduced there – introducing a small chance of a good type leads to a small improvement over the total shirking equilibrium of the pure moral hazard case.

The interesting question is whether the commitment problem discovered here would appear in an infinite horizon model with no term limits and both adverse selection and moral hazard. Banks and Sundaram 1993 satisfies these conditions, but there the politicians' choice variable is not policy but effort (as in Ferejohn 1986), and adverse selection is introduced by varying politicians' marginal costs for effort. It is easy to see that even in the two-period model considered here, if politicians vary only in their

---

[44] Another difference that may be significant is that ideal-point preferences are not covered in the large class considered by Banks and Sundaram, which is formulated more with "effort" in mind rather than policy choices. Ideal-point preferences fail Banks and Sundaram's Assumption 6.

marginal costs for moving policy toward the median voter, then the electorate will be indifferent among all types in the second period and thus optimal sanctioning will be ex post credible. I suspect this is why no commitment problem appears in Banks and Sundaram 1993. (If correct, this would also indicate that the choice of "effort" or policy as the politician's choice variable is nontrivial.)

Thus far, I have been unable to analyze the infinite-horizon, no-term-limit case of the model with politicians who vary in policy preferences. For the reasons given in footnotes 29 and 32, I would conjecture that the commitment problem will appear here as well as in the two-period case.

A final significant point about the mixed model is that moral hazard is not necessary to generate the commitment problem pathology discussed earlier. Consider the same model but with perfect monitoring – assume the electorate observes the policy choice x directly, and so can condition the incumbent's reelection on it. Consider a rule for the electorate that says, "we will reelect if you choose our optimal policy, $x = 0$." A bad type of incumbent will want to mimic a good type and choose $x = 0$ provided that $W - 1 + \delta W \geq W + 0$, or $\delta W > 1$. And in this event, the electorate is willing to reelect if it sees $x = 0$, since its posterior that the incumbent is good is then $\alpha'(x = 0) = \alpha$, implying indifference. So in this case adding a small chance of good type has no effect – the electorate gets an expected payoff of approximately $0 + \delta(-1)$ whether $\alpha = 0$ or is very close to 0.

Suppose, however, that $\delta W < 1$. In this case the best the electorate can do when all politicians are bad types ($\alpha = 0$) is to employ the rule "we will reelect if you choose a policy $x \leq \hat{x}$," where $\hat{x}$ is defined by $W - (1 - \hat{x})^2 + \delta W = W$, or $\hat{x} = 1 - \sqrt{\delta W}$. $\hat{x}$ is the policy choice that leaves a bad type indifferent between choosing $\hat{x}$ to get reelected and shirking completely and not getting reelected.

But if some politicians are good types ($\alpha > 0$), the electorate will infer that the incumbent is a bad type if it sees $\hat{x} > 0$, which implies that it should dump the incumbent in favor of a new draw who has some chance of being a good type in the second period. Thus what was an equilibrium when $\alpha = 0$ collapses, leaving a radically different and unique PBE in which bad types shirk completely, choosing $x = 1$ and being tossed out of office for sure. In this case, then, introducing a tiny chance of public-spirited politicians completely undermines elections as a mechanism of accountability.

James D. Fearon

(It is not difficult to show what these arguments go through if we consider an infinite horizon model with no term limits and no moral hazard.)

This last example also suffices to show that Reed's (1994) analysis is either mistaken or incomplete. Reed's model is essentially identical to that just analyzed, except that he considers a case where incumbent's ideal points are uniformly distributed. Reed solves for the $\hat{x}$ that is optimal for the electorate ex ante, but never asks if ex post it would be rational for the electorate to implement this rule in all states of the world. The example just given suggests that it almost surely is not, and that if it is under a uniform distribution, this would be an exceptional case.

One claim from the text remains to be demonstrated: that for small enough α, the electorate would be better off if it could commit in advance to use the performance criterion k^* that optimally motivates bad types (defined following equation (3)). To see this, we write the ex ante expected payoff for the electorate in the mixed case as follows:

$$u_E^{mix} = \alpha(0 + \delta[F(k)(-(1-\alpha))]) + \\ (1-\alpha)(-x_b^2 + \delta[F(x_b^2 + k)(\alpha - 1) + (1 - F(x_b^2 + k))(-1)]),$$

where the k and x_b are equilibrium values in the mixed case. Algebra simplifies this to

$$u_E^{mix} = -(1-\alpha)(x_b^2 + \delta[1 - \alpha(F(-k) - F(k))]).$$

Note that the term in brackets captures the payoff improvement due to the possibility of selecting a good type for the second period. In a similar fashion, the electorate's ex ante expected utility for commiting to the rule k^* defined for the pure moral hazard case is found to be

$$u_E^{mh} = -(1-\alpha)\left(x_{mh}^2 + \delta\left[1 - \alpha\left(.5 - F(k^*)\right)\right]\right),$$

where $x_{mh} < x_b$ is the bad type's policy given k^*. From algebra, it follows that $u_E^{mh} > u_E^{mix}$ when

$$x_b^2 - x_{mh}^2 > \delta\left[\alpha\left(F(-k) - F(k) - \left(.5 - F(k^*)\right)\right)\right].$$

For α close enough to 0, this necessarily holds, since $x_b^2 - x_{mh}^2 > 0$ and k and k^* are bounded between 0 and $-1/2$. In simulations with a normal distribution and $\delta W = 2$, the statement typically holds for all α less than about 1/2. For $\alpha > 1/2$, the utility loss from

94

suboptimal selection in the second period is greater than the gain from better motivation of bad types in the first period.

References

Austen-Smith, David, and Jeffrey Banks. 1989. "Electoral Accountability and Incumbency." In Peter Ordeshook, ed., *Models of Strategic Choice in Politics*, 121–50. Ann Arbor: University of Michigan Press.

Banks, Jeffrey, and Rangarajan Sundaram. 1990. "Incumbents, Challengers, and Bandits: Bayesian Learning in a Dynamic Choice Model." University of Rochester. Mimeographed.

1993. "Adverse Selection and Moral Hazard in a Repeated Elections Model." In William A. Barnett, Melvin J. Hinich, and Norman J. Schofield, eds., *Political Economy: Institutions, Competition, and Representation*, 295–313. Cambridge: Cambridge University Press.

1996. "Electoral Accountability and Selection Effects." University of Rochester. Mimeographed.

Barro, Robert. 1973. "The Control of Politicians: An Economic Model." *Public Choice* 14: 19–42.

Bender, Bruce, and John Lott. 1996. "Legislator Voting and Shirking: A Critical Review of the Literature." *Public Choice* 87 (1): 67–100.

Brady, David, and Edward Schwartz. 1995. "Ideology and Interests in Congressional Voting: The Politics of Abortion in the U.S. Senate." *Public Choice* 84: 25–48.

Cain, Bruce, John Ferejohn, and Morris Fiorina. 1987. *The Personal Vote.* Cambridge, Mass.: Harvard University Press.

Campbell, Angus, P. Converse, W. Miller, and D. Stokes. 1960. *The American Voter.* New York: John Wiley and Sons.

Carey, John. 1996. *Term Limits and Legislative Representation.* Cambridge: Cambridge University Press.

Dewatripont, M., and G. Roland. 1992. "Economic Reform and Dynamic Political Constraints." *Review of Economic Studies* 59: 703–30.

Dick, Andrew R., and John R. Lott. 1993. "Reconciling Voters' Behavior with Legislative Term Limits." *Journal of Public Economics* 50: 1–14.

Downs, Anthony. 1957. *An Economic Theory of Democracy.* New York: Harper and Row.

Ferejohn, John. 1986. "Incumbent Performance and Electoral Control." *Public Choice* 50: 5–25.

1993. "The Spatial Model of Elections." In Bernard Grofman, ed., *Information, Participation, and Choice*, 107–24. Ann Arbor: University of Michigan Press.

Fiorina, Morris P. 1981. *Retrospective Voting in American National Elections.* New Haven: Yale University Press.

Frank, Robert. 1988. *Passions within Reason: The Strategic Role of the Emotions.* New York: Norton.

Harrington, Joseph. 1993a. "The Impact of Reelection Pressures on the Fulfillment of Campaign Promises." *Games and Economic Behavior* 5: 71–97.

———. 1993b. "Economic Policy, Economic Performance, and Elections." *American Economic Review* 83 (1): 27–42.

Holmstrom, Bengt, and Paul Milgrom. 1991. "Multi-Task Principal-Agent Analyses." *Journal of Law, Economics, and Organization* 7 (1): 24–52.

Kalt, Joseph, and Mark Zupan. 1994. "Capture and Ideology in the Economic Theory of Politics." *American Economic Review* 74 (June): 279–300.

———. 1990. "The Apparent Ideological Behavior of Legislators: Testing for Principal-Agent Slack in Political Institutions." *Journal of Law, Economics, and Organization* 33 (April): 103–31.

Key, V. O. 1966. *The Responsible Electorate.* New York: Vintage Books.

Kishlansky, Mark. 1986. *Parliamentary Selection: Social and Political Choice in Early Modern England.* Cambridge: Cambridge University Press.

Larocca, Roger. 1997. "Informative Representation." University of Chicago. Mimeographed.

Levitt, Steven D. 1996. "How Do Senators Vote? Disentangling the Role of Voter Preferences, Party Affiliation, and Senator Ideology." *American Economic Review* 86 (June): 425–41.

Lott, John. 1987. "Political Cheating." *Public Choice* 52 (March): 231–46.

———. 1990. "Attendance Rates, Political Shirking, and the Effect of Post-Elective Office Employment." *Economic Inquiry* 28 (1): 133–50.

Lott, John, and Stephen Bronars. 1993. "A Critical Review and an Extension of the Political Shirking Literature." *Public Choice* 74 (December): 461–84.

Lott, John, and Michael Davis. 1992. "A Critical Review and an Extension of the Political Shirking Literature." *Public Choice* 76 (May): 125–49.

Lott, John, and W. Robert Reed. 1989. "Shirking and Sorting in a Model of Finite-Lived Politicians." *Public Choice* 61 (1): 75–96.

Manin, Bernard. 1997. *Principles of Representative Government.* Cambridge: Cambridge University Press.

Mayhew, David. 1974. *The Electoral Connection.* New Haven: Yale University Press.

McKelvey, Richard, and Raymond Riezman. 1992. "Seniority in Legislatures." *American Political Science Review* 83: 1181–1206.

Poole, Keith, and Thomas Romer. 1993. "Ideology, 'Shirking,' and Representation." *Public Choice* 77 (2): 185–96.

Reed, W. Robert. 1994. "A Retrospective Voting Model with Heterogeneous Politicians." *Economics and Politics* 6 (March): 39–58.

Rogoff, Kenneth. 1990. "Equilibrium Political Budget Cycles." *American Economic Review* 80: 21–37.

Rogoff, Kenneth, and Anne Sibert. 1988. "Elections and Macroeconomic Policy Cycles." *Review of Economic Studies* 55: 1–16.

Van Beek, James. 1991. *Public Finance Quarterly* 19 (4): 444–56.

Weber, Max. 1978. *Economy and Society.* Vol. 2. Berkeley: University of California Press.

Wright, M. B. 1993. "Shirking, Political Support, and Agency Costs in Political Markets." *Public Choice* 76 (June): 103–24.

Zielinski, Jakub. 1997. "Parties and Elections in Emerging Democracies." Paper presented at the 93rd annual meeting of the American Political Science Association.

Zupan, Mark. 1990. "The Last Period Problem in Politics: Do Congressional Representatives Not Subject to a Reelection Constraint Alter Their Voting Behavior?" *Public Choice* 65 (May): 167–80.

Chapter Three

What Do Policy Switches Tell Us about Democracy?

Carlos Menem was the presidential candidate of the Peronist party in Argentina in 1989. The economic context was bad: inflation was high (although hyperinflation would not break out until after the election), and the government's hard currency holdings were perilously low. The incumbent government of Raúl Alfonsín, of the Radical Party, attempted numerous emergency plans to stabilize prices and reduce the government's current account deficit.

Menem's campaign called for stabilizing the economy without imposing hardships on workers or the middle class. A book he and his running mate coauthored during the campaign called for a *revolución productiva*, or productive revolution (Menem and Duhalde 1989). With mildly expansionary policies to exploit unused industrial capacity, Argentina would overcome depressed real wages, high unemployment, and price instability. At the very moment when the incumbent Alfonsín government was imposing austerity measures and currency devaluations – called *paquetazos* – Menem on the campaign trail invented the term *salariazo*, a big upward shock to wages. Consistent with the Peronist tradition, Menem championed a development model that included state ownership of heavy industry, utilities, and oil. Also consistent with the Peronist tradition, he expressed distrust of Argentina's export bourgeoisie, epitomized by the conglomerate Bunge y Born. Early in the campaign Menem called for a moratorium on payments of Argentina's foreign debt, although he later moderated that position

Research was supported by a SSRC-MacArthur Foundation Fellowship in International Peace and Security. John Baughman, David Laitin, Steve Pincus, Adam Przeworski, and Pieter van Houton provided useful comments.

with a call for a five-year cessation of repayment and renegotiation on terms favorable to Argentina. Finally, he warned Britain that blood might again flow in the Malvinas, or Falkland Islands.

Menem won the election in May. Once in office, he named Miguel Roig, a former vice-president of Bunge y Born, as his economics minister. When Roig died of a heart attack eleven days after taking office, Menem turned the selection of a replacement over to Bunge y Born's president, who chose Nestor Rapanelli, another vice-president of the firm. Other early actions by Menem also contradicted his campaign pronouncements or Peronist tradition. Having called for a moratorium and then five-year cessation of payments on the foreign debt, Menem named the presidential candidate from the right-wing Unión del Centro Democrático as his chief debt negotiator in Washington. To put it in the U.S. context, imagine that Ronald Reagan ran for reelection in 1984 and after winning named Walter Mondale as director of the Office of Management and Budget.

Menem also sold off all state firms for which buyers could be found, even at bargain-basement prices, eliminated subsidies, laid off workers from government ministries, liberalized trade, and eliminated job security laws – much to the dismay of the Peronist unions, a major portion of which would soon break with the Peronist party. By August 1989, only three months after the election, the language of *salariazo* was long forgotten. Menem introduced his austerity program exhorting Argentineans to accept "a tough, costly, and severe adjustment" requiring "major surgery, no anesthesia" (cited in Smith 1991: 53).

A similar story can be told about Alberto Fujimori in Peru, who ran against the conservative Mario Vargas Llosa in 1990. Fujimori campaigned against an International Monetary Fund (IMF)-style austerity program and in favor of continued state intervention in the economy. Again and again on the campaign trail Fujimori repeated the promise that "my government will not engage in a policy of *paquetazos*" (Universidad del Pacífico 1990: 31). The "antishock" (*el anti-shock*) became the mantra of his campaign. On August 8, less than two weeks after his inauguration, Fujimori imposed one of the largest packages of price adjustments in Latin American history, followed by the full menu of neoliberal reforms.

In twelve of the forty-four presidential election campaigns that took place in Latin America between 1982 and 1995, the winning

99

candidate pronounced himself[1] in favor of some combination of job creation, growth, higher real wages, industrial policy, a gradualist approach to inflation stabilization, and limited repayment of the foreign debt, only to impose austerity and a withdrawal of the state from the economy immediately upon coming to office (see Table 3.1). All of these immediate, drastic policy switches were in the same direction: from "welfare-oriented" campaigns to "efficiency-oriented" policies (the latter term is borrowed from Elster 1994)

Obviously, mandate representation is fragile in Latin American presidential politics. Voters cannot "justifiably expect that parties would do what they proposed" in campaigns (see Manin, Przeworski, and Stokes, Chapter 1 in this volume). Yet the critical question is, Does this fragility signal a broader breakdown in representation?

The answer, according to some, is yes. Observing Menem's and Fujimori's spectacular changes of course, Guillermo O'Donnell concluded that representation was not a feature of Latin American democracies. These were not representative but "delegative democracies," a distinct subtype and one inferior in normative terms (O'Donnell 1994).

The answer to the question I offer here is that representation of a more retrospective sort, involving ex post accountability rather than ex ante mandates, had been a feature of Latin American politics. This is the good news. The bad news is that the breakdown of mandate-representation, even though compensated by representation-as-accountability, implies citizens who are badly informed about the choices they face. And citizens who are ill-informed by the political culture and rhetoric of politicians will have difficulty discerning instances when politicians do unpopular things for good reasons from instances when they do unpopular things for bad reasons.

In what follows I offer an explanation of policy switches. It builds on field research in Peru, Argentina, Bolivia, and Ecuador and a cross-national statistical database I have constructed allows me to explore further this and alternative explanations. The database includes observations for all competitive presidential

[1] Only one woman ran for president, Violeta Chamorro of Nicaragua in 1990. Chamorro, who won and served as president from 1990 to 1995, ran on and implemented what I am calling an efficiency-oriented program.

Table 3.1. Presidential Elections and Policy Switches in Latin America's Democracies, 1982–95

Country	Year	Country	Year
Argentina	1983	Ecuador	1984
	1989[a]		1988[a]
	1995		1992[a]
Bolivia	1985	El Salvador	1984
	1989[a]		1989
	1993		1994
Brazil	1989	Guatemala	1985[b]
	1994		1990[b]
Chile	1989		1995
	1993	Honduras	1985
Colombia	1982[a]		1989
	1986		1993
	1990	Nicaragua	1984
	1994		1990
Costa Rica	1982[b]	Peru	1985
	1986		1990[a]
	1990[a]		1995
	1994[a]	Uruguay	1984
Dominican Republic	1982[a]		1989
	1986		1994
	1990[a]	Venezuela	1983
	1994[b]		1988[a]
			1993[a]

[a] Denotes an election followed by a policy switch.
[b] Denotes an election after a vague campaign, one in which candidates make no policy proposals.

elections in Latin America between 1982 and 1995, as well as economic data for the same period and countries.

Explaining Policy Switches

Consider a two-period world in which politicians run for office once and then run for reelection at the end of the

101

term.[2] They have beliefs about which policy is best for voters, and they must decide whether to reveal or conceal these beliefs in the campaign before the first election. Unlike the beliefs of voters, politicians' beliefs about the relative effectiveness of policies are fixed and unchanging. Once elected, they must decide which policy to implement. Politicians care about maximizing voters' utility income and about holding office. Formally, the utility they derive from a term in office can be expressed as

$$u(k,y) = k + \theta(y),$$

where k is the value of holding office and y is per capita income.

Voters also have beliefs about which policy is best, beliefs not known to politicians. In contrast to the politicians, voters' beliefs are not fixed but may change once policies are implemented and their results observed. Voters ex ante beliefs about how their utility income will be affected by alternative policies can be conceived as a Bayesian prior; once outcomes in the first term are observed, the voter will develop new beliefs, which will tend to be a weighted average of their old, "prior" beliefs and the outcomes they observed. Voters don't know politicians' beliefs before the first election, whether a given politician is of the type who believes that policy a is more effective than b, or the reverse. But they know that if the incumbent enacted policy a in his first term, a is more likely to continue if the incumbent is reelected than if he is defeated by a challenger. Voters must make two choices: whom to vote for in the first election and then whether to support the incumbent or the challenger in the second election.

To get a sense of how voters' beliefs may change, consider the voter who initially believes that her utility income will grow more under welfare than under efficiency policies. In the first election she votes for the politician who promises welfare policies. If a majority of voters (or the median voter) shares her beliefs, the politician sending the welfare message in the campaign wins the election. Suppose then the politician switches to efficiency policies. If by the end of the term the utility income of voters, who initially preferred welfare policies, grew more than expected but not much more, they may still believe that welfare policies are more effective and support the challenger. If their utility income grew by much

---

[2] The discussion in this section draws heavily on the work of Harrington (1993a, 1993b).

more than they had expected, they may infer that the prior beliefs on which their prowelfare preferences rested were incorrect, and that efficiency policies were in fact better. In this case they will support the incumbent for reelection.

Voters' uncertainty and the consequent endogeneity of their preferences in turn influence the electoral strategies of politicians. Consider a candidate who believes that voters far underestimate the relative effectiveness of efficiency over welfare policies. If voters' beliefs were certain and fixed, the candidate would face three choices. Either he could campaign on an efficiency program and lose; he could campaign on a prowelfare program, implement efficiency policies (which, he believes, will maximize income), and fail to be reelected; or he could campaign in favor of welfare policies, implement them, and improve his chances of winning reelection but at the cost of pursuing what he believes to be inferior policies. But if voters' beliefs are endogenous, this trade-off is softened. The politician may campaign in favor of welfare, switch to efficiency, and – if incomes rise enough – still be reelected at the end of his term. Yet note that because voters consider both their prior beliefs and the results they observe in formulating their preferences after the first term, all things equal the standard to which a politician will be held if he switches policies will be higher than if he enacted the policies that he campaigned on. At a given level of realized income, the popularity of a policy switcher will be dragged down by voters' prior beliefs. Politicians who anticipate this higher standard will therefore only switch if they believe their preferred policies to be far superior to those initially favored by voters.

This model is of interest because it offers a reasonable account of politicians' strategy in switching policies and – like our Latin American examples – switching right away, and not only after conditions have changed. It is also of interest for normative reasons. Politicians who switch are representative; within the bounds of what they know and believe, they are attempting to serve the interests of citizens as best they can. Because they anticipate that voters' beliefs are inaccurate, and hence that their (induced) preferences over policies will change, politicians violate mandate responsiveness *in order to act* as good representatives.

Another condition will induce representative politicians to switch. This is when they find themselves sharing power with other parties in postelection coalitions or facing an opposition majority in the legislature. In either case, competing parties may insist on deviations from the leading party's campaign platform.

The foregoing discussion suggests several empirical tests that will help us decide whether politicians who switched policies early in their term were attempting to represent constituents' interests. If welfare-to-efficiency policy switches are carried off by representative politicians, we expect:

- Politicians who switch believe that voters far underestimate the relative effectiveness of efficiency over welfare policies. They believe that they must dissimulate to win the first election but that switching to efficiency policies once in office is both good for voters and improves their or their party's prospects of prevailing at the next election.
- Policy reversals are associated with situations of voter uncertainty about the impact of policies on outcomes.
- All else equal, the economy improves more under switches than under consistent policies.
- Policy switches are associated with shared rule, that is, minority and postelection coalition governments.

In the next section I test the hypothesis that Latin American policy switches were for the most part carried out by politicians who were attempting to represent. I do so by testing the accuracy of each of these propositions in the Latin American setting.

Beliefs and Switches

Some politicians who switched from welfare-oriented campaigns to efficiency policies believed that if they pursued welfare policies they ran the risk of creating economic havoc. They believed that a majority of voters nonetheless preferred welfare policies and, hence, that to advocate efficiency policies in campaigns would be tantamount to accepting defeat. Yet they anticipated that voters would come to support them or their parties in subsequent elections, despite their switches to policies that voters feared.

Some politicians who reversed campaign pronouncements in favor of expansionist policies believed that if they fulfilled the

104

policy expectations created in their campaigns they risked precipitating an economic collapse. These were the fears of Carlos Andres Pérez in Venezuela. His predecessor, Jaime Lusinchi (1983–88) presided over an expanding economy, with GDP growth averaging over 5% in the last two years of Lusinchi's term. Yet Pérez observed disquieting signs in the economy and was exposed to economists who foretold a dark future should the new government not adopt a course of austerity and liberalization. His fears were reinforced by observations of the presidential term of Alan García in Peru (1985–90; Naim 1993). García, a friend and colleague in the Second Socialist International, implemented a heterodox stabilization program; his term ended in recession and hyperinflation. Economists whom Pérez attempted to recruit to his cabinet reinforced the message that avoidance of austerity and liberalization would bring chaos. Moisés Naim, a young economist who would serve as Pérez's first minister of development, was cautious when the president-elect approached him, and he expressed unwillingness to serve unless the new government adopted radical reforms. "I told him, 'Venezuela is about to experience the worst bout of inflation in its history'" (interview, January 1993).

The fear that departure from orthodoxy might produce economic chaos was reinforced by messages that politicians received from markets. Here I use the term "market" in a broad sense, to refer to investors, currency speculators, and others whose uncoordinated actions, in aggregate, could produce inflation, devaluations, and capital flight; and to officials in international financial institutions, private creditor banks, and foreign governments, whose actions were coordinated and intended to keep Latin American governments on an orthodox policy path. Against the backdrop of a region in crisis, these market actors helped shape the belief that welfare-oriented policies constituted a risky path.

Consider the forces at work on Alberto Fujimori of Peru. At the outset of his campaign, only months before the election, Fujimori had been a blank slate on which his neo-Keynesian advisors inscribed their theories. Although the advisors found this mathematician a quick study, they were later to understand that he saw their models more as electoral tools than as a blueprint for policy. As president-elect, Fujimori came under intense pressure from international financial institutions and governments in the United States and Japan to change his policy orientation. Pressure was exerted during an international tour, with stops in Miami, New York, and Tokyo, where political leaders and officials from international financial institutions admonished Fujimori to turn to an orthodox economic path (see Stokes 1996 for more details). When Fujimori returned to Peru at the end of the tour, domestic forces redoubled the pressure. A former advisor reported to me the following illustrative anecdote. One evening shortly after their return, he found Fujimori watching two television political talk shows simultaneously. On both, conservative economists were offering their views on how the incoming government should handle macroeconomic policy, and both were advocating tight fiscal controls. Fujimori turned to the advisor and said, "You see, *everyone* wants a shock." The view of Fujimori's early advisors was that this pressure, combined with that applied by international financial institutions (IFIs) and governments on his international tour, persuaded him to change course. Whatever the theoretical merit of his campaign economic promises, such as *el anti-shock*, and whatever their mass appeal, no good could come of a policy course that had so many powerful opponents.

If politicians like Pérez and Fujimori thought departure from orthodoxy would produce bad economic results, why did they not simply campaign in favor of efficiency-oriented reforms? The answer is simple: they feared they might lose. Hence, some policy switchers displayed just the belief structure that the model discussed earlier predicts will induce a policy switch: they believed that the policies preferred by a majority of voters would in fact induce bad results but thought they couldn't win if they revealed their true intentions.

How did presidential candidates in Latin America make inferences about voters' preferences? In part from public opinion polls. Major candidates in most countries in the region ran their own surveys and focus groups. Those who couldn't afford to had access to surveys that were available to the public. Candidates also drew on their knowledge of the preferences of major voting blocks. In Argentina, Carlos Menem's strategists believed important voting blocks were vigorously opposed to the liberalization that the Menem team was planning; they dissembled in order not to lose the support of these constituents. The best source is Menem himself, who in a 1993 magazine interview explained why the decision to pursue austerity and large-scale privatizations, taken well before the election, was not revealed to the public until later: "The three golden rules of behavior are to be perfectly informed, keep that information secret and act with surprise. That's what I did all my life. If in the election campaign I tell the people 'we are going to renew relations with England,' I lose 20% of the vote. If I tell the people 'I'm going to privatize telephones, railroads, and Aerolíneas [the national airline],' I have against me the whole labor movement" (cited in Nunn 1994). This reasoning was repeated by Roberto Dromi, a Menem insider and early cabinet member, whom I interviewed in 1994.

> **Stokes**: If Menem knew in the campaign that he would pursue austerity and liberal reforms once in power, why did he not say so in the 1989 campaign?
> **Dromi**: In this country, ten percent of the labor force were government employees. We knew that if we talked of privatizing Aereolíneas Argentinas, we would have the airline workers on our backs; if we talked of privatization, we would have those workers on our backs. We thought we might lose the support of Left Peronists, the unions, protected industries, and public employees. And we were not confident of winning. At first we thought Cafiero would win the primaries; then we thought Angeloz would win the election.[3]

Alberto Fujimori also thought that in order to win he had to persist in campaign messages emphasizing economic security, despite an intuition that these messages might not predict the eventual course of his policies. An anecdote, reported to me by Fernando Villarán, a campaign advisor, reveals Fujimori's thinking at the time. Villarán was suspicious of candidate Fujimori's dogged insistence on *el anti-shock*. Some adjustment is coming, Villarán told Fujimori, so you shouldn't place so much weight on the antishock. He admonished Fujimori, "try to think more like a statesman, not like a politician." Fujimori replied, "If I don't think like a politician now, I'll never get to be a statesman." The difference between Menem and Fujimori was between clear policy intentions that remained hidden and vague intuitions that

---

[3] Antonio Cafiero was Menem's rival to become the Peronist candidate for president. Ricardo Angeloz was the candidate of the incumbent UCR party.

campaign pronouncements might not be carried out. Yet in both cases, the perception that voters would reject the candidate if he announced other-than-welfare policies induced one to mask his intentions, the other his intuitions.

In contrast, when candidates favoring promarket policies believed they could advocate them openly without risk of losing, they did so. They may not have feared losing because they believed voters shared their beliefs, but it seems to have been more common in Latin America that politicians expressed neoliberal policy intentions when no credible opponent could pronounce welfare beliefs and hence threaten their election. This was the case of the Chilean Convergencia Democratica, a coalition of Christian Democrats and Socialists, in 1989. Patricio Aylwin was the Convergencia's presidential candidate. He and his strategists believed there was little to fear in electoral terms by advocating a continuation of the Pinochet regime's neoliberal model because their opponents on the right could not credibly shift to a welfare position (see Arriagada and Graham 1994; Angell and Pollack 1990). Despite virtually ignoring the social concerns that, as polls showed, most voters shared, Aylwin went on to defeat the right by a margin of 28.5 percent.

If politicians who intended to pursue neoliberal reforms hid these intentions because they feared losing elections, we would expect to see an association between close races and the election of politicians making welfare-oriented pronouncements. Consider an election in which two candidates compete, one who believes that efficiency policies will be better for voters than welfare ($y \mid E > y \mid W$), and one with the opposite beliefs ($y \mid W > y \mid E$). If he believes voters prefer $W > E$, in a tight race the candidate with beliefs $E > W$ will hide these intentions and advocate W. An extreme example is the Ecuadorean presidential runoff of 1992. Here both candidates, Jaime Nebot and Sixto Durán-Ballen, had neoliberal intentions. But in the close race, with the perception that voters feared such reforms, both hid their intentions and declared that they would forgo austerity measures and increase social spending. Under these circumstances voters have no choice but to elect a politician pronouncing W, who may or may not believe what he is saying. But once in office, some of the politicians who masked their true beliefs will switch policies. In contrast, in lopsided races the front-runner will not need to mask his true intentions, which in some cases will be E and in others W; hence the probability of victory of a candidate campaigning on E is higher.[4]

The dynamics of several campaigns illustrate these effects. In Peru in 1990 Mario Vargas Llosa was a distant front-runner for a full year, during which he expounded a radical version of neoliberalism. On the insistence of strategists who wanted to send a clear signal that radical measures would be taken to liberalize the economy, Vargas Llosa's television ads ended with the message, "it will cost us, but together we will make the Great Change." Despite conflicts within the campaign over this strategy, and despite some polling and focus group data showing soft support among poor people, the campaign persisted with a message of imminent austerity until after the general election (see Vargas Llosa 1993; Salmon 1993; Daeschner 1993). Fighting for survival against Fujimori in the runoff, Vargas Llosa turned control over to a faction that had pushed all along for a less strident message. Yet Vargas Llosa is an ideologue and he had difficulty evincing a softer image. Postelection polls indicate that people were not persuaded by his partial shift away from neoliberalism. For example, when asked by pollsters, Why did you not vote for Vargas Llosa?, 46% answered because he "represented the interests of the rich," and another 17%, "because of his right-wing ideas"; these were the two most common answers (Apoyo, May 1990).

In Venezuela in 1988, Carlos Andrés Pérez pulled ahead of his opponent in public opinion polls in October, for reasons that seemed to have to do more with the COPEI candidate's personality than with policy. Pérez then began to hint at exchange rate liberalization, one element of what eventually would be the *Gran Virage*, or the "Great Turnaround."

The expectation of an association between close races and the victory of welfare candidates finds confirmation in the probit model in Table 3.2. The dependent variable in the first model is a dummy variable for the election of politicians who in their

---

[4] If voters' choices were entirely governed by economic policy position, adopting a less popular position would simply drive down the leading candidate's popularity, and the dynamic described here would not occur. Then we would expect all candidates to converge on the preferred position of the median voter. Yet in most campaigns they did not converge, either because of credibility problems (e.g., candidates with a rightist history could not persuade voters that they would pursue welfare policies) or because voters weighed some other policy dimension or criterion (e.g., identity or competence).

Table 3.2. Probit Model, Dependent Variable ELECTION OF WELFARE-ORIENTED CANDIDATE, 38 Observations

Variable	Coefficient	Standard Error	t-ratio	Prob |t| ≥ x	Mean
Constant	0.80	0.63	1.28	0.20	
GDP[a]	−0.21	0.09	−2.27	0.02	1.88
INFL[b]	−0.02	0.01	−1.90	0.06	23.79
TRANS[c]	0.07	0.03	2.33	0.02	14.79
MARGIN[d]	−0.07	0.03	−2.06	0.04	11.72

Maximum Likelihood Estimates
Log-Likelihood   −14.86
Restricted (slopes = 0) Log-L   −25.86
Chi-Squared (4)   22.00
Significance Level   0.000

Frequencies of Actual and Predicted Outcomes[e]

		Predicted 0	Predicted 1	
Actual	0	12	4	16
	1	2	20	22
		14	24	38

[a] Average change in GDP during two years leading up to the election. *Source*: *International Financial Statistics*, IMF.
[b] Average inflation rate in the two quarters before the quarter of election. *Source*: *International Financial Statistics*, IMF.
[c] Number of years since transition to democracy.
[d] Difference in rote shave between winning candidate and closest competitor.
[e] Predicted outcome has maximum probability.

campaign advocated welfare policies. The model includes the independent variable MARGIN, which is the difference in vote share between the first- and second-place candidates, which I use as a proxy for the perceived closeness of the race throughout. The sign on the coefficient relating MARGIN to victory of a welfare candidate is negative and significant at the 96% level. (The model as a whole predicts thirty-two of thirty-eight of the outcomes

110

correctly (84%) at the Pr = .5 level, and has a chi-square of 22, which is significant at the probability level p = 100.)

In sum, both qualitative evidence from campaigns and statistical analysis of cross-national data offer evidence that fear of losing elections induced politicians to hide their policy intentions.

Yet the critical question is whether politicians dissimulated and switched because they thought efficiency policies were in the best interest of voters, or because they found efficiency policies advantageous for themselves whether or not they would be good for voters.

Argentina in 1989 offers strong evidence that policy switchers were sometimes motivated by the belief that the economy would perform unexpectedly well under neoliberal programs, and hence that voters, who opposed these policies ex ante, would favor them ex post. This view, repeated to me by several Menem strategists, was most fully elaborated by Roberto Dromi. The interview partially quoted earlier continued as follows:

> **Dromi**: In this country, ten percent of the labor force were government employees. We knew that if we talked of privatizing Aereolíneas Argentinas, we would have the airline workers on our backs; if we talked of privatization, we would have those workers on our backs . . . .
>
> **Stokes**: But you believed these measures [privatization, fiscal adjustment] were necessary to lower inflation. If you stated your intentions, you might have won the support of the ninety percent of Argentine workers who didn't work for the government and who suffered from inflation.

At this point in the interview, which took place in Dromi's law office, he pulled from the shelf *Nuevo Estado, Nuevo Derecho* (Dromi 1994), a book he had authored, and opened to the epigraph, a quotation from Machiavelli's *The Prince*, which he then read aloud:

> [T]here is nothing more difficult to try, nor more doubtful of success, nor more dangerous to deal with, than to take it upon oneself to introduce new institutions, because the introducer makes enemies out of all those who benefit from the old institutions and is feebly defended by all those who might benefit from the new ones. This feebleness arises, in part from the fear of the opposition, who have the laws on their side, in part from the skepticism of

111

men, who do not truly believe in novelties until they see them arising out of firm experience.[5]

Dromi then continued:

> **Dromi**: We knew that Argentines would disapprove of the reforms we planned, but would come to see that they were good. And we also wanted to send a message.
> **Stokes**. A message to whom?
> **Dromi**. To God and the devil, to Morgan Guaranty, the U.S. government, the World Bank.

Dromi aptly captures two pieces of our story. First, whatever the "spontaneous" preferences of these Peronists, they perceived themselves to be constrained by markets. The best policy, given market constraints, was neoliberalism. Second, he anticipates a shift in the beliefs of voters regarding policy. Ex ante, before the "firm experience" of promarket reforms, their posture is one of skepticism. Ex post, when they have been instructed by experience and can observe tangible results, Menem and his strategists believed, voters would come to support neoliberal reforms and the government that had put them in place.

Evidence from other countries is less clear. In Peru, Fujimori's strategic choices appear to have been conditioned by extremely short-term considerations. With no real party and a highly tactical orientation, the candidate's guiding principle was to win the election and worry later about how to govern. This was the sense of his comment to Villarán quoted earlier, that he had to win the election before he could concern himself with statesmanship. In part this posture reflected Fujimori's personality traits of pragmatism and tactical acumen. The setting, combining economic crisis with a serious security threat from Shining Path guerrillas, also discouraged taking the long view. It is unlikely that Fujimori in mid-1990 was looking forward as far as 1995, when a successor could run for reelection, much less to 2000, when he would first be eligible to run for reelection under the term limits then in force. In switching to efficiency reforms, Fujimori seems

---

[5] The translation of Machiavelli (1996) is Paul Sonnino's. The excerpts are from chapters 26 and 6. Dromi's rendering in Spanish differs in some details from Sonnino's.

to have been trying not to maximize his own future electoral prospects, but to avoid the risks he began to see as associated with policies unpopular with markets, and thus try to put himself in the best possible political position vis-à-vis both markets and public.

If Fujimori's time horizon was shorter than a presidential term, Carlos Andrés Pérez's was longer. Pérez was sixty-seven years old in 1988; given Venezuela's six-year presidential terms and stringent term limits, he could not have been focused on personal reelection. More likely his focus was on finishing out a long and successful political career. Success meant ruling over an expanding economy and hence creating the conditions for party reelection in 1994, as well as going down in history books as a wise and courageous leader. Pérez would have been willing to wait through some hard times in order later to be acknowledged as having been correct in subjecting Venezuela to a "Great Turnaround." What he certainly did not anticipate was what in fact happened: riots in response to price adjustments, challenges from the military, and impeachment, which kept him from even serving out his full term. Hence Pérez departs from the representation model: reelection pressures were not foremost among his concerns. Instead, what he cared about was maximizing voters' welfare and hence his own prestige over a longer period. But Pérez is consistent with the model in that the politician who changed course anticipated that the shift would later be regarded as having been good for Venezuela.

To summarize, we have seen that in some settings politicians were motivated to dissimulate and switch because they anticipated that voters, informed by experience of the effects of efficiency policies, later would be induced to change their preferences.

Voter Uncertainty

Having established a convergence between the representation model and the underlying beliefs of Latin American policy switchers, I now turn to test a number of the model's predictions. First, the representation model links policy switches with voter uncertainty. Recall that if voters are uncertain about the relative effectiveness of policies, sufficiently good performance of a policy previously considered inferior may cause people to change their beliefs. The more uncertain voters are regarding policies, the more their ex post assessments will be driven by performance rather than policy; and the greater voter uncertainty, the more likely politicians will be to switch when they think voters underestimate the advantages of efficiency policies. This likelihood increases because very uncertain voters will pay more attention to outcomes (which politicians anticipate will be good) rather than policies.

There are good reasons to expect that economic policy anywhere will be associated with greater uncertainty than other sorts of policies, and that uncertainty in the historical setting of post-debt-crisis Latin America would run especially high. Economies are complex systems, "delicate watches" (Hirschman 1977); any intervention is likely to have unpredicted secondary effects, and predictions even by experts may be far off. And even greater uncertainty than usual was attached to Latin American economic policy at the historical juncture of the post-debt-crisis years. The economies were subject to huge external shocks, beginning with the exhaustion after August 1982 of new international loans. At the same time, the air was full of debates about the need for a drastic shift in the economic "model." Little wonder that common citizens might have trouble distinguishing the effects of external conditions from those of domestic policy, or sorting through the claims and counterclaims about the benefits of alternative policy approaches.

If policy switches are linked to voter uncertainty, we should expect ex post judgments of governments that switched to be more sensitive to outcomes than when governments were consistent. Using the LACAP database,[6] I studied the impact of economic

---

[6] The data are from the Latin American Campaign and Policy (LACAP) database, a cross-national statistical database I have constructed. The LACAP database includes observations for all competitive presidential elections in Latin America between 1982 and 1995. I culled information from published sources (newspapers, transcripts of campaign speeches, and party manifestos) concerning the economic policy positions of the major presidential candidates. This information permitted a coding of the winning candidates' campaigns, according to the expectations of future policy that it would have created among attentive voters. All campaigns were coded as either efficiency-oriented, welfare-oriented, or too vague to create any expectations as to the direction of future policy. Published information, the secondary literature, and, in some countries, interviews with government officials allowed me to code each government as pursuing an initial set of economic policies that were welfare or efficiency oriented. The combination of the two codings, of campaigns and then of early

Table 3.3. OLS Regression, Dependent Variable INCUMBENT PARTY VOTESHARE, 23 Observations

Variable	Coefficient	Standard Error	t-ratio	Prob $|t| \geq x$	Mean	Standard
Constant	−12.69	2.43	−5.23	0.000		
SWITCH[a]	−8.58	3.73	−2.30	0.033	0.39	0.49
DIFGDP[b]	1.04	0.54	1.94	0.068	3.27	4.37
GDP*						
SWITCH	2.49	0.69	3.590	0.002	1.49	3.88
R-squared	0.786					
Adjusted R-squared	0.752					
F[3,19]	23.26					
Prob Value	0.000					

[a] Dummy variable for politicians who switched. *Source*: LACAP.

[b] Difference between the average GDP growth rate in the two years leading up to term and average growth rate during the last two years of the term. *Source*: *International Financial Statistics*, IMF, table 3.

outcomes on the change in the incumbent party's vote share before the first election (the one bringing it to power) and the second. Economic outcomes were measured as the difference between average GDP growth rates in the last two years before the first election and the last two years before the second. The model estimated in Table 3.3 regresses economic outcomes (DIFGDP), a dummy for policy switches (SWITCH), and an interaction term (GDP*SWITCH) on end-of-term vote share.

We are interested here in contrasting the impact of changes in GDP growth rates on vote share between switchers and non-switchers. Statistically, this entails comparing the coefficient on GDP among these two subsamples. Following Gujarati (1995:

policy, allowed me to code each government as acting consistently with its campaign or as switching policies once in power (vague campaigners were treated separately). The LACAP database also incorporated information about economic conditions, political institutions, majority status of governments, and other variables.

512ff.), the effect of GDP change in the base category, non-switchers, is given by the coefficient on DIFGDP. We see that the coefficient is positive and significant at the 93% level. The effect of GDP change among switchers is given by the sum of the coefficient on DIFGDP and the interaction term: 1.04 + 2.49 = 3.53. Hence, whereas a 1% percent increase in GDP over the course of the term among nonswitchers was associated with about a 1% increase in vote share, among switchers the same change in GDP was associated with a 3.5% increase in vote share.[7] The impact of economic contraction was similarly magnified among politicians who switched policies early in the term. Ex post assessments by voters of mandate-unresponsive governments were more than three times more sensitive to economic outcomes than of mandate-responsive governments.

The interpretation is that politicians were prone to engage in bait-and-switch tactics as a function of voter uncertainty, uncertainty that politicians were able to sense. It is also likely, however, that policy switches themselves created additional uncertainty. Consider the voter who places her faith in a politician who in the campaign opposes a fiscal shock on the grounds that it will exacerbate inflation. Imagine her confusion when that same politician within weeks of taking office announces a fiscal shock – claiming that it is needed to control inflation. Whether uncertainty was more cause of effect or switches, it is fair to infer that voters were uncertain about the impact of policy. Without this uncertainty politicians, who wanted to be reelected later, would have been hesitant to impose policies that they knew to be unpopular.

The model in Table 3.3 lends support to an additional feature of the representation model. Recall that voters are conceived as weighing both their prior beliefs and their observations of the

---

[7] The significance of the difference between the two coefficients is tested by the t-statistic associated with the coefficient on the interaction term, which is significant at the 99% level. The analysis performed here compared policy switchers and nonswitchers, the latter including both those who consistently pursued efficiency reforms and those who consistently pursued welfare. When the sample is restricted to those who ran for office on "welfare" messages, and the comparison is of consistent welfare governments and those that switched to efficiency, the results are the same – that is, switchers are held to a higher standard (lower intercept) and their end-of-term vote share is more sensitive to outcomes (larger coefficient on DIFGDP).

outcomes of policy in formulating ex post beliefs about the relative effectiveness of policies. When their prior belief is that welfare reforms will produce better outcomes than efficiency, the same level of performance will generate less ex post support for governments implementing efficiency than welfare policies. When voters' prior beliefs favor welfare, they will elect a candidate giving a "welfare" message; hence politicians who switch (to efficiency) will be held to a higher standard than those who are consistent.

Our expectation is that, holding economic outcomes equal, end-of-term vote shares will be lower for policy switchers than for nonswitchers. The constant, –12.7 in the model in Table 3.2, is the y-intercept for nonswitchers. It indicates that under the condition of no change in GDP, the vote share of consistent politicians at the end of their term will be 12.7 points lower than their share in the election that brought them to office.[8] The constant for the subsample of switchers is the sum of the constant and the coefficient on the SWITCH dummy: $(-12.7) + (-8.6) = -21.3$. Hence, when the difference between beginning and end-of-term growth rates is 0, incumbents who switched policies lose almost twice as many votes as nonswitchers. The penalty for incumbency is high; for switching it is much higher, sufficient to keep politicians to their mandates unless they believe that voters far underestimate the effectiveness of efficiency policies.

Economic Conditions

If the representation model of policy switches is correct, some politicians carrying out welfare policies believe efficiency policies would be more effective, but not enough to overcome voters' prior skepticism. In contrast, politicians who switch anticipate much better performance of efficiency than welfare policies. If politicians' beliefs have any bearing on reality, "good" – representative – switches should be associated with better economic performance than consistent welfare policies.

As a first step toward measuring the impact of switches on performance, we must explore whether there were differences in

---

[8] This heavy burden of incumbency is consistent with the findings of Remmer 1991.

Table 3.4. Probit Model, Dependent Variable SWITCH, 22 Observations

Variable	Coefficient	Standard Error	t-ratio	Prob |t| ≥ x	Mean of X
Constant	2.44	2.05	1.20	0.23	
GDP[a]	0.33	0.20	1.68	0.09	1.15
INFL[b]	0.07	0.05	1.44	0.15	16.54
STATUS[c]	−0.08	0.04	−1.9	0.06	48.05

Maximum Likelihood Estimates

Log-Likelihood	−8.70
Restricted (Slopes = 0) Log-L	−15.16
Chi-Squared (3)	12.92
Significance Level	0.005

Frequencies of Actual and Predicted Outcomes[d]

		Predicted		
		0	1	
Actual	0	6	4	10
	1	1	11	12
		7	15	22

[a] Average change in GDP during two years leading up to the election. *Source*: *International Financial Statistics*, IMF.
[b] Average inflation rate in the two quarters before the quarter of election. *Source*: *International Financial Statistics*, IMF.
[c] Proportion of parliamentary seats controlled by president's party.
[d] Predicted outcome has maximum probability.

initial economic conditions faced by consistent welfare politicians and by policy switchers. Table 3.4 reports a probit model of policy switches and includes two measures of initial economic conditions: average annual change in GDP during the two years leading up to the election, and the inflation rate in the two quarters leading up to the election. GDP growth is associated with a heightened probability of a switch (significant at the 96% level); higher inflation shows some signs of predicting a switch, although the significance of the coefficient is less (83%).

Recall the model of the election of welfare-oriented politicians

Table 3.5. OLS Regression Model, Dependent Variable CHANGE IN GDP GROWTH RATE End of Presidential Term versus Beginning of Term, 18 Observations

Variable	Coefficient	Standard Error	t-ratio	Prob $|t| \geq x$	Mean
Constant	1.20	1.27	0.95	0.36	
SWITCH	3.90	1.86	2.09	0.05	0.50
GDP	−0.86	0.23	−3.68	0.00	−0.04

R-squared	0.48
Adjusted R-squared	0.42
F[2,15]	7.04
Prob Value	0.007

in Table 3.2. It showed that the opposite economic conditions – slow growth and low inflation – favored the election of welfare-oriented candidates. Hence, when growth and inflation are low, voters prefer governments that will emphasize growth; when they are high, they prefer governments that will control inflation. But welfare-oriented politicians who are elected under conditions of *relatively* high growth and inflation are more likely to switch to efficiency once in office. It appears that politicians were somewhat attentive to voters' preferences even when they defied their mandates, an attentiveness that we would expect less in rent-seeking politicians.

Taking into account these differences in initial conditions, what effect did switching policies have on economic outcomes? Using OLS, I regressed the difference between the two-year average growth rate before the first and second elections on a dummy for SWITCH and on the GDP growth rate at the beginning of the term, included as a control for initial economic conditions (see Table 3.5; the sample is restricted to elections won by welfare-oriented candidates). When GDP change at the beginning of the term was 0, a switch produced a 3.9% increase in the GDP growth rate at the end of the term; without a switch, the change in growth rate was 1.2% (significance level of the difference between the

119

two y-intercepts = 95%). Note the negative association between GDP growth rate at the beginning of the term and change in the growth rate at the end (the correlation coefficient between the two measures is –.57). The lower the initial GDP, the more room for improvement. Yet this improvement is improved on, as it were, by the switch to efficiency policies. The interpretation, consistent with the representation model, is that politicians switched from welfare campaigns to efficiency policies when they thought doing so would produce very good results, and they did.

Argentina and Peru provide two examples of these economic outcomes. When Menem came to power, the economy had contracted on average 0.6% in the preceding two years. The average growth rate in the two years leading up to Menem's reelection in 1995 was 5.5%, so that the difference between the two growth rates was 6.1%. Given the model in Table 3.5, the expected value of the difference in GDP growth rates under a switch to efficiency policies was 3.4%; had he not switched, the expected value would have been 0.7%. Whether or not Fujimori was deeply persuaded that he was doing the right thing for voters when he switched to efficiency, the results, at least in terms of overall growth, were spectacular. Inheriting an economy that had contracted under García on average nearly 7% for two years, Fujimori produced average growth rates of 9.5% in the two years leading up to his reelection; without a switch the expected difference in growth rates would have been 7.2%. The contrasting case is Carlos Andrés Pérez, who came to power in a growing economy and produced growth rates of –2.5% on average in his last years. These results go some way toward explaining reelection of the first two politicians despite their enactment of initially unpopular policies, and the inexorable slide of Pérez into unpopularity, impeachment, and his party's loss of the presidency in the election following his ouster.

To summarize, at least some Latin American politicians violated mandate representation because they thought voters' beliefs were wrong and that it was in voters' best interests to pursue policies that were ex ante unpopular. To put it negatively, these politicians thought that if they did what they had promised in the campaign all hell would break loose in the economy, saw all hell beginning to break loose as speculators bet against the currency and international actors threatened financial isolation, and believed there was a good chance their political careers would end after this term – perhaps even sooner – if they did not act to reassure markets. They sensed that voters were skeptical of austerity and neoliberal reforms but were also uncertain about the effects of any policy. Given this uncertainty, they believed voters might become persuaded, in light of outcomes, that efficiency had been the right course after all.

Majority Status

Recall the objective function of our "representative" politicians: they value holding office as well as per capita income. In certain institutional and electoral settings, they may face a trade-off between these two objectives. If they enter office as coalition partners, or as a minority government, they may be forced to deviate from their campaign platforms. The Comparative Manifestos Project found most deviations from party manifestos in Belgium and the Netherlands, countries where electoral rules and party systems encourage coalition governments (see Klingemann, Hofferbert, and Budge 1994: chaps. 12, 13). Huber and Powell (1996) contend that proportionality systems, with their higher incidence of shared executive power, do not so much undermine representation as foster a different conception of it, the "proportionate influence vision." "Proportionate influence" maximizes the representation in government of the full range of constituencies, whereas "majority control" systems maximize the representation of the majority.

Coalition and minority governments were a cause of policy switches in Latin America. Politicians who ran on welfare programs were more likely to win by smaller margins (see Table 3.2), which in turn increased the probability that they would have to share power or face an opposition majority in the legislature. Probit models show that postelection coalition and minority status was associated with an enhanced probability of a change of policy. The independent variable STATUS measures the proportion of parliamentary seats controlled by the president's party. The coefficient relating STATUS to probability of a switch is positive and significant, and remains so in specifications that include the MARGIN of victory in the election. A collapsed version of STATUS, a dummy variable for nonmajority governments, has the same effect: postelection coalition and minority governments are nearly twice as likely as majority governments to change policies.[9]

Because Latin American legislatures tend to be constitutionally weak and de facto even weaker, the statistical result may over-estimate the effect of majority status on the probability of switches. Presidents in many Latin American countries have wide-ranging executive decree powers and use these powers even more extensively than constitutions allow. Party indiscipline further weakens legislatures (but see Shugart and Carey 1992). Further-more, in some instances the anticipation of positive results from efficiency policies prevailed over concerns about dealing with the opposition or coalition partners. The Menem government is a case in point. Legislative elections for one-half of the congress are held every two years in Argentina, one concurrent with presidential elections, the second two years and the third four years into the presidential term[10] At the time of Menem's victory the Peronists won sixty-six seats; they were the largest party but did not control an absolute majority of the lower house. Yet my interviews and secondary accounts (e.g., Palermo and Novoa 1996) suggest that not the political opposition but markets, as well as future electoral strategies, shaped Menem's strategems.

Minority status played a larger role in inducing the policy reversal of Jaime Paz Zamora of Bolivia (1989–93). Paz Zamora was a leader of the Movement of the Revolutionary Left (MIR), a Marxist party. Paz Zamora found himself in the presidency after running third in the presidential race. Constitutional rules at the time turned the selection of the president over to the Congress if no candidate won an absolute majority of the vote. Although some campaign statements were ambiguous, we have little reason to believe that Paz Zamora was a convert to neoliberalism, or that he necessarily believed that a continuation of his predecessor's

[9] I follow Powell 1990 in merging preelection coalitions with majority gov-ernments, and in treating postelection coalitions as intermediate between majority and minority governments. His concern is discernibility: will voters be able to distinguish which party is responsible for policy and hold it accountable at the end of term? Mine is with the ability of nonwinning parties to induce pro-grammatic changes, either on minority governments or on coalition partners. I reason that leading parties are relatively more beholden to opposition majorities than to coalition partners.
[10] Presidential terms were six years long from 1983 until 1995, when they were shortened to four years.

"New Economic Program" of market liberalization was best for his constituents. Paz Zamora became president thanks to a post-electoral coalition between the MIR and the rightist Democratic National Action (ADN), led by former dictator General Banzer. Hence Paz Zamora would have had great difficulty enacting a program that diverged much from the one supported by the right. The continuation of neoliberalism in Bolivia was carried out by a cabinet staffed largely by members of Banzer's ADN, who occupied ten of eighteen positions. These included the posts of finance and planning, as well as defense and foreign affairs. Bolivia thus illustrates a policy reversal carried out by a postelection coalition government, one in which policy bore the imprint of a range of parties, and not just the one of the president.

Alternative Hypotheses

New Information

It is worth contrasting the representation explanation of switches with the one frequently offered by new governments after they deviated from their mandates. They claimed that upon coming to office they learned that the fiscal deficit was larger than their predecessors had acknowledged. Incumbents hid the larger-than-acknowledged deficit during the campaign because it reflected not just incompetence but corruption. The switch to unpopular policies was the fault of a profligate and perhaps venal prior government.

On the face of it, this official scenario for a policy shift is not unreasonable. But if we dig deeper, we can see that it does not hold up.

In a subset of cases (Peru under Alberto Fujimori, Argentina under Carlos Menem, Venezuela under Carlos Andrés Pérez), the new government reversed itself not only by imposing a surprise one-time fiscal adjustment, but by pursuing a whole menu of policies at odds with the specific pronouncements and general tenor of the campaign. The unforeseen need for austerity would not have forced, say, a Menem to liberalize trade or a Fujimori to eliminate job security regulations for private industry. In these cases, at least, new information about fiscal conditions could at most contribute to the change of course but could not be the whole explanation. What's more, in Argentina and Peru politicians knew that they would change course, or intuited that they might, well before they came to office and could have gained private information about the deficit. The deficit story is more excuse than explanation; this comes through most clearly in Ecuador in 1992, where the new government of Sixto Durán made claims about the size of the deficit that it inherited from its predecessors, claims that were later shown to be exaggerated (see Stokes 1995).

If not in Argentina, Peru, or Ecuador, were larger-than-expected deficits the explanation elsewhere? If this were true, we might expect some association between the size of the deficit and the probability of switches. But no such association appears. In probit models, the government deficit as a proportion of spending had no impact on the probability of a switch (not shown). These models tell us little about the difference between the size of the deficit anticipated by the new government in comparison with the deficit it actually found. Still, the irrelevance of deficits to our story is revealing.

If the surprise deficit justification were true, we would also expect switches to be more common when the new government was in opposition before the election. Incumbents, the story goes, hide the size of the deficit from the public during the campaign; if the incumbent party wins the election, then the new government ought not be surprised by the size of the deficit, which cannot therefore constitute new information motivating a change of course. Incumbent parties were reelected to the presidency thirteen times in Latin America between 1982 and 1995, whereas challengers defeated incumbents twenty-five times. Were the challengers more likely than incumbents to switch?[11]

The answer, again, is no. Challengers were not more likely to change policies than were incumbents. The sign on the coefficients in various models for a dummy variable for incumbent governments – that is, ones whose predecessor was from the same party – was negative, as expected, but it was far from significant (not shown). The surprise deficit explanation is further undermined.

In sum, if the surprise deficit explanation of policy switches were true, we would expect switches to be restricted to fiscal

[11] Presidential term limits might be expected to encourage short time horizons and policy switches. Analysis of the cross-national dataset reveals no significant impact of term limits on the probability of a switch. See Carey 1996.

adjustments, which they were not; we would not expect that new governments planned to change course before they came to office, which they sometimes did; we might expect that bad fiscal conditions would increase the probability of a switch, which they did not; and we would expect reelected incumbent governments to be less likely to switch than ones made up of the erstwhile opposition, which they were not. For all of these reasons we should reject this, the most common official explanation for the change of course.

Weak Political Parties

Political parties in Latin America are weak. Compared with parties in other regions, they have difficulty imposing internal discipline in legislatures, form and fall apart frequently, and suffer sharp oscillations in voter support from election to election (Mainwaring and Scully 1996; Coppedge n.d.). We know parties are weak and party systems volatile; what we don't know is whether the ones with weaker parties are also the ones in which campaigns predict policy least well.

I generated scores on an index of party system volatility.[12] As Coppedge found for a somewhat different time period, volatility in Ecuador, Brazil, and Peru was very high compared to typical scores for advanced industrial countries. Other countries not studied by Coppedge, such as Guatemala, had volatility indices off the scale in comparison with Europe and the United States. Party system volatility had no discernible impact, however, on the likelihood of a switch; indeed, in some models (not shown) the sign on the coefficient was negative. The result suggests that if sharp elite-popular polarization, market pressures for costly signals, and close races induced a logic of inconsistency, strong political parties were insufficient to impose mandate responsiveness.

---

[12] The formula for volatility I used was

$$V = \frac{1}{2}\sum_{i=1}^{p}|Pi,t - Pi,t - 1|$$

where Pi,t is the percentage of the vote won by party i in the election at time t. This is the formula Coppedge uses in his study of party system volatility in Latin America, following Bartolini and Mair 1990.

125

Conclusion

What do policy switches tell us about democracy? The first lesson is that, in democracies, mandates may be widely and severely violated. The Latin American countries under discussion were all democracies by most reasonable criteria: they upheld institutional guarantees of freedom of association and expression, nearly universal adult suffrage, and free, fair, and competitive elections on a regular schedule (Dahl 1971). Political power, furthermore, was held by the elected political leadership (Schmitter and Karl 1991). Such conditions, however, were not sufficient to bind governments to their mandates. When politicians were under pressure from actors with preferences contrary to voters', and when politicians viewed voters' preferences as erroneous and unstable, mandates were bad predictors of policy.

The finding is contrary to previous studies (Klingemann et al. 1994; Budge, Robertson, and Hearl 1987; Krukones 1984; Fishel 1985). In the settings of these earlier studies, the conditions I have specified for mandate deviations did not hold. And my study contradicts earlier work, in particular of Klingemann and associates, which attributes whatever mandate inconsistency did appear with weak political parties and coalition governments.

The second lesson relates to the link between mandates and representation. We have seen that sticking to mandates is not the only way politicians can represent citizens' interests, and that governments may have to violate mandates in order to represent. They violated mandates in particular because they anticipated being held accountable at the end of the term. Hence, in these settings governments had to choose between mandates and accountability, and by choosing accountability they were choosing to represent. Remaining faithful to campaign promises, at least for some Latin American policy switchers, would have meant governing in a way they considered bad for citizens; it would have meant failing to represent.

O'Donnell, then, would seem to be wrong when he infers from mandate violations in some Latin American countries the absence of representation. And yet one is hesitant to dismiss his instinct that something is amiss in these democracies. If the analysis of the previous pages is correct, then citizens were seriously ill-informed about the choices they faced and about the likely consequences of these choices. In general we would consider a democracy in which

126

citizens' beliefs are correct to be superior to one in which citizens' beliefs are incorrect. Why, we must ask, did citizens hold erroneous technical beliefs in the first place? Their beliefs were erroneous in part because politicians chose not to persuade them, but instead, in the heat of campaigns, told them what they wanted to hear. A scenario more in line with our sense of how democracy ought to work would be one in which politicians informed the people about the real choices they faced, and hence campaigns served as a meaningful moment of public discussion.

A defender of these democracies might point out that it matters little that citizens hold erroneous ex ante beliefs if they at least are capable of making good ex post judgments of incumbent governments by the end of the term. Given that our beliefs will from time to time be incorrect, retrospective accountability is a second chance to judge policies, a safety mechanism allowing us to reward politicians who knew better than we what consequences would follow from policies. Of course, we would hope that such safety mechanisms would not be a habitual necessity, and that citizens in general would be well informed about the choices before them.

Yet the defense is not fully persuasive. And one is not entirely comforted by the prospect of politicians saying one thing, doing another, and then being judged retrospectively. Even if campaigns were not used to inform citizens, we would hope that the experience of being won over to unpopular policies might enrich the political culture and make citizens better prospective decision makers in the next election. But this brings us to perhaps the most disturbing part of the Latin American story: not that politicians dissimulated *before* elections but that they dissimulated *after*. Even when they were secure in office, many policy switchers did not attempt to persuade people that the policies they had voted against would in the end prove superior. Instead, new presidents offered a false justification: that matters were not as they had thought (e.g., budget deficits were bigger) and they were constrained to take the unpopular course. Governments chose false justification over persuasion undoubtedly because people would resent learning that they had been actively misled in campaigns, and because the false justification lay the blame on the new government's political opponents.

The cost to citizens of this continuing dissimulation was potentially high. If they didn't know the real reasons why the government was changing course, they might also be misled when the government did unpopular things not for good reasons but for bad. Consider an example. A new government justifies a shift toward privatization with the argument that the unanticipatedly high fiscal deficit requires that it rid itself of inefficient state-owned enterprises. To make its case, it exaggerates the size of the deficit and the degree to which state-owned enterprises represent a drain on the treasury. As the program proceeds, enterprises begin to be sold off at below their market value to investors who reward cabinet members with kickbacks. The public, ill-informed about key facts, will be less capable of discerning painful but necessary measures from rent seeking.

Hence the basic lesson of recent Latin American policy switches. Violations of mandate are not inconsistent with representation narrowly construed. But they should still raise alarms about the quality of democracies in which they are endemic.

References

Angell, Allen, and Benny Pollack. 1990. "The Chilean Elections of 1989." *Bulletin of Latin American Research* 9 (1): 1–24.

Apoyo, S. A. Various dates. "Informe de opinion." Lima: Apoyo, S.A.

Arriagada Herrera, Genaro, and Carol Graham. 1994. "Chile: Sustaining Adjustment during Democratic Transition." In Stephan Haggard and Steven B. Webb, eds., *Voting for Reform: Democracy, Political Liberalization, and Economic Adjustment*. Washington D.C.: World Bank and Oxford University Press.

Bartolini, Stefano, and Peter Mair. 1990. *Identity, Competition, and Electoral Availability: The Stabilization of European Electorates, 1885–1985*. Cambridge: Cambridge University Press.

Budge, Ian, David Robertson, and Derek Hearl, eds. 1987. *Ideology, Strategy, and Party Change: Spatial Analysis of Post-War Programs in Nineteen Democracies*. Cambridge: Cambridge University Press.

Carey, John M. 1996. *Term Limits and Legislative Representation*. Cambridge: Cambridge University Press.

Coppedge, Michael. N.d. "Democratic Consolidation and Party-System Volatility in Latin America." Johns Hopkins University. Unpublished manuscript.

Daeschner, Jeff. 1993. *La guerra del fin de la democracia: Mario Vargas Llosa versus Alberto Fujimori*. Lima: Peru Reporting.

Dahl, Robert. 1971. *Polyarchy: Participation and Opposition*. New Haven: Yale University Press.

Dromi, Roberto. 1994. *Nuevo estado, nuevo derecho*. Buenos Aires: Ciudad Argentina.

Elster, Jon. 1994. "The Impact of Constitutions on Economic Performance." Paper prepared for the World Bank annual conference on Development Economics, Washington, D.C., April 28–29.

Fishel, Jeff. 1985. *Platforms and Promises*. Washington, D.C.: Congressional Quarterly Press.

Gujarati, Damodar N. 1995. *Basic Econometrics*. 3d ed. New York: McGraw-Hill.

Harrington, Joseph E., Jr. 1993a. "The Impact of Reelection Pressures on the Fulfillment of Campaign Promises." *Games and Economic Behavior* 5: 71–97.

1993b. "Economic Policy, Economic Performance, and Elections." *American Economic Review* 83: 27–42.

Hirschman, Alberto O. 1977. *The Passions and the Interests: Arguments for Capitalism before Its Triumph*. Princeton: Princeton University Press.

Huber, John D., and G. Bingham Powell Jr. 1996. "Congruence between Citizens and Policymakers in Two Visions of Liberal Democracy." *World Politics* 49: 291–326.

Klingemann, Hans-Dieter, Richard I. Hofferbert, and Ian Budge. 1994. *Parties, Policies, and Democracy*. Boulder, Colo.: Westview Press.

Krukones, Michael G. 1984. *Promises and Performance: Presidential Campaigns as Policy Predictors*. Lanham, Md.: University Press of America.

Machiavelli, Niccolò. 1996. *The Prince*. Paul Sonnino, trans. Atlantic Highlands, N.J.: Humanities Press.

Mainwaring, Scott, and Timothy R. Scully, eds. 1996. *Building Democratic Institutions: Party Systems in Latin America*. Stanford, Calif.: Stanford University Press.

Menem, Carlos, and Eduardo Duhalde. 1989. *La revolución productiva*. Buenos Aires: Pena Lillo.

Naim, Moisés. 1993. *Paper Tigers and Minotaurs: The Politics of Venezuela's Economic Reforms*. Washington, D.C.: Carnegie.

Nunn, José. 1994. "Post-Modern Politics? The Paradoxes of Peronism." Buenos Aires. Unpublished manuscript.

O'Donnell, Guillermo. 1994. "Delegative Democracy?" *Journal of Democracy* 5 (1): 55–69.

Palermo, Vincente, and Marcos Novoa. 1996. *Política y poder en el gobierno de Menem*. Buenos Aires: Grupo Editorial Norma.

Powell, G. Bingham, Jr. 1990. "Holding Governments Accountable: How Constitutional Arrangements and Party Systems Affect Clarity of

Responsibility for Policy in Contemporary Democracies." Paper presented at the annual meeting of the American Political Science Association, San Francisco.

Remmer, Karen L. 1991. "The Political Impact of the Economic Crisis in Latin America in the 1980s." *American Political Science Review* 85 (3): 777–800.

Salmon Jordan, Jorge. 1993. *Entre la vanidad y el poder: Memoria y testimonio.* Lima: Editorial Apoyo.

Schmitter, Phillipe C., and Terry Lynn Karl. 1991. "What Democracy Is . . . And What It Is Not." *Journal of Democracy* 2: 75–88.

Shugart, Matthew Soberg, and John M. Carey. 1992. *Presidents and Assemblies: Constitutional Design and Electoral Dynamics.* Cambridge: Cambridge University Press.

Smith, William C. 1991. "State, Market and Neoliberalism in Post-Transition Argentina." *Journal of Interamerican Studies and World Affairs* 33 (4): 45–82.

Stokes, Susan C. 1995. "Democracy and the Limits of Popular Sovereignty in South America." In Joseph Tulchin and Bernice Romero, eds., *Essays on the Consolidation of Democracy in Latin America*, 59–81. Boulder, Colo.: Lynne Rienner.

1996. "Democratic Accountability and Policy Change: Economic Policy in Fujimori's Peru." *Comparative Politics* 29 (2): 209–25 [January 1997].

Universidad del Pacífico. 1990. *El debate.* Lima.

Vargas Llosa, Mario. 1993. *El pez en el agua: Memorias.* Barcelona: Seix Barral.

Chapter Four

Accountability and Authority: Toward a Theory of Political Accountability

We take it for granted that modern government must be democratic in the sense of deriving its authority directly or indirectly from the people. But democratic governments differ greatly in producing policies that are responsive to the popular will. In part, this variation may be traced to the diverse representational structures of various democratic governments. Electoral institutions are employed not only to choose good public officials, but as mechanisms to hold incumbents accountable to the public, and, in these ways, they may make policies more or less responsive to public wishes.[1] Accountability is, on this view, a property of institutional structures, whereas responsiveness is a consequence of interaction within such structures. Put another way, responsiveness is a measure of how much accountability an institutional structure permits.

Of course, responsiveness is not an unmitigated virtue. Most of us want government to be responsive when it comes to matters like building roads and universities, establishing a system of

Special thanks are due to Lewis Kornhauser, Bernard Manin, Paquale Pasquino, Adam Przeworski, Susan Stokes, and members of the Colloquium on Law, Economics and Politics, New York University School of Law, for useful comments on an earlier draft of this paper.

[1] Whether or not popular responsiveness is a value is a deeper issue of democratic theory. Many writers would regard responsiveness as a populist virtue that is either normatively unattractive or incoherent as a criterion for evaluating democratic institutions. For example, see Riker 1982.

131

welfare and social security, and deciding how protective we will be of natural resources. What government should do in these cases is not a matter of justice or morality but depends on what cooperative projects citizens wish to undertake. But in the administration of programs in which the dispensing of justice is concerned, and perhaps in the case of managing monetary policy, popular responsiveness is not so attractive. We may want our judges to be accountable to someone in order to ensure that they are not venal or partisan but not because we wish their decisions to respond to popular preferences. Thus, how much and what kind of accountability there should be is a delicate matter to be decided in view of how much popular responsiveness is desired.

There are at least three serious limits to accountability within democratic institutions. First and most obvious is the structure of the voting rule itself. Officials in majoritarian institutions might not be accountable to minorities – at least not to insulated and underprivileged ones – but more consensual voting rules are not accountable to majorities. More generally, electoral heterogeneity makes it possible for officials to play off some voters against others to undermine their accountability to anyone. This is, it seems to me, a consequence of a government being democratic. Second, institutions of accountability operate in real time – either sporadically or periodically – and this provides officials with opportunities to avoid electoral responsibility for particular actions by grouping unpopular with popular actions. This is a practical problem of agency relations in any government. Third, and the main focus of this chapter, elected officials typically enjoy an immense informational advantage over the voters that limits how accountable such principals will be to the voter desires. This is a consequence of the complexity of modern government. These three impediments – each quite imposing – operate together to limit optimism as to the possibility of fully accountable democratic rule.

The only hope, short of finding virtuous politicians (or politicians whose interests are identical to their electors) is that institutions may be designed, or may evolve endogenously, in such a manner as to encourage accountability. Mechanisms that recommend themselves take advantage of competition in one of two ways. One possibility is to put agents into conflict with one another so that their competitive interaction produces policies that take account of popular preferences. I have argued elsewhere

(Ferejohn 1986), however, that there are rather severe limits on the desirable effects of explicit competition among ambitious officials. Alternatively, as I explore here, principals may have "outside" opportunities to pursue their own well-being that are competitive with their governmental options. Agents are therefore forced, implicitly, to compete with other options available to the principal in order to attract her support, and this circumstance may induce more-accountable agency. The wish to attract the support of principals can, as is shown here, induce officials to behave much more responsively than they would were such support not an issue. In particular, agents faced with this competitive circumstance would willingly offer principals tools to control and monitor officials. There are, of course, limits in just how accountable agents subjected to this form of competition will be, as we shall see, but these limits are relatively favorable to the principals.

The point of this chapter is, therefore, twofold: first, to sketch an endogenous conception of accountability in which public officials are induced to make their actions relatively controllable by their principals, in order to attract resources and support; and, second, to employ the comparative statics of this theory to develop hypotheses, some of which might be testable, as to the conditions under which political agents will make themselves more or less accountable to the public. The theory outlined here is only suggestive, since it rests on some arbitrary choices of preferences and beliefs. Moreover, the present analysis lacks genuine "dynamical" implications. The degree of accountability is endogenous in that it depends on choices made within the model, but political accountability does not "evolve" in any interesting sense. A richer model would be needed for such implications to emerge. The theory is intended, in that sense, to point the way toward a fuller theory of endogenous accountability but not to provide a completed one here.

The Agency Model in Politics

Recent thinking about democratic accountability has been dominated by the agency model. There are at least two applications of this model found in the literature. Public officials are in an agency relationship with their electors, and the electorate is limited, for one reason or another, in its capacity to figure out what their agent is doing and why he or she is doing it. Moreover, even if the public could observe the actions of its agents, voters do not agree on what they wish their agents to do. And, worse yet, the set of tools that voters have for rewarding and punishing the agents' behavior in office is very limited. Thus, even if voters could coordinate on their best feasible strategies, their agents would nevertheless be able to secure economic rents from the relationship.

Analogously, executive agencies are in an agency relation with the legislature, which, again, is at an informational disadvantage in observing either agency actions or characteristics. This relationship has similar issues of informational disadvantage and disagreement among principals. In this setting, however, the principal has more leverage over the agent for two reasons. First, Congress organizes itself along party lines and, insofar as the majority party can remain cohesive, it may be able to act as a unified principal with respect to executive agencies. Second, the range of rewards and punishments available to Congress is relatively large compared with those available to ordinary voters. Third, Congress is not as informationally disadvantaged as is the electorate with respect to governmental institutions. Thus, one would expect that Congress would be relatively more successful in controlling agencies than voters are in controlling electoral officials.

While the language used here is of recent vintage, the use of the agency model to understand political institutions and relationships is not at all new. Indeed, two robust theories of constitutional interpretation propounded by scholars and judges over the past couple of centuries seem to have taken an agency perspective. On the first account – the compact theory, which is traceable to Madison and Jefferson in the Virginia and Kentucky Resolutions of 1798 and subsequently to John Calhoun in various of his writings – the U.S. Constitution was an agreement among the states, as sovereign entities, to create a new federal entity with limited and specified powers. The relation of the federal government to the states, therefore, was one of agency in that federal officials were given authority to employ their delegated powers subject to supervision by the states. In recognition of the newly created agency relation, the states were careful to place themselves, or their representatives, in supervisorial positions. They retained the power to conduct federal elections; participated in the election of the president and the conduct of foreign and high policy; and reserved a role for themselves in punishing (impeaching) errant federal officials. This theory seems to explain the structure and position of the Senate in the legislative process, the fact that its members were to be selected by state legislatures, and its special role in checking executive powers (in treaties, appointments, and impeachment proceedings), the structure of the electoral college and the use of unit-rule voting in the House when selecting a president, as well as the role of the states in constitutional decision making. Each of these features has the purpose and, to some (no doubt, much lesser) extent, the effect of protecting state interests (this is a way to interpret Wechsler's [1961] classic exposition of federalism).

The alternative theory is currently more popular in the legal academy, if not among the current justices of the Supreme Court. On this account, the Constitution was created by the People (the fashion among partisans of this view is to capitalize this term) acting in its sovereign capacity, which entailed making decisions in separate state conventions. The People constituted a national government and directly delegated some of its powers to it, but subjected the exercise of governmental powers to continuing direct and indirect supervision. The same people, assembled in the states (again in conventions), created the state governments (which had, with the theoretically embarrassing exception of Texas, never actually been sovereign) and in each state delegated certain powers to those governments as well. This theory distinguishes sharply between state governments – as agents of the People – and the People assembled in the states.

This theory – popular sovereignty theory – explains the special powers of the House of Representatives with respect to taxation, the preponderance of the popular representation in selecting the president both in the electoral college and in the House itself, and the special place allotted to the People (perhaps assembled in conventions in both Articles V and VII) in adopting or changing the Constitution. It also explains state representation in the Senate, the Senate's sharing of executive powers of appointment and treaty making, and the use of the unit rule in the electoral college, as indirect rather than direct means of supervising the fundamental agency relation between the People and the national government.

Indeed, the pattern of parallel agency relations may best be interpreted as an instance of the People placing its agents in a competitive relationship in order to limit the degree of opportunism that either state or federal officials can exhibit. I read Madison's arguments in *Federalist* (Rossiter 1961) nos. 45–46 and Hamilton's argument in *Federalist* nos. 26–28 in this way. In those essays Publius considers what would happen in the event of usurpation by either the national or state government and argues, in effect, that structure of the federal relationship would provide the means and the motive for a checking response. Madison argued that just as the national government would check potentially tyrannical state governments, the states would serve as counterbalances to congressional usurpations and prevent the national government from overawing the people, partly by the fact of holding the preponderance of military power in the militias but, even more importantly, by serving as a focal point of political resistance to the concentration of power. The federal system, on this account, is a collection of parallel and competitive agency relationships within which officials at all governmental units are more accountable to the people than they would be in alternative, unitary arrangements.

Political Agency

Modern agency theory, then, is attractive as a mode of understanding fundamental political relationships both because it seems to pick out important phenomena and because it resonates deeply with robust and long-lived perspectives in constitutional thought. There is a problem, however, with the application of agency theory to public organizations. In economic applications, it is natural to think of the principal as designing or choosing a contract to structure its relationships with its agent. The firm, from this perspective, either designs an incentive system for its laborers or it chooses to employ a standard-form wage contract. Of course, this is just a harmless story. With sufficient competition among potential agents, it makes no difference if the agent is the one who designs the contract. Competition among potential agents will induce each of them to offer contracts that are optimal from the principal's viewpoint. In this respect, competition among agents serves to limit the capacity of agents to earn monopoly rents from their agency.

But electoral competition is generally not sufficient to eliminate the monopolistic opportunities available to officials, however temporarily they may enjoy them. Consider a model in which an elected official receives a lump-sum payment upon being elected and then must decide either to do what her constituents want and get reelected, or to do what she wants instead, forgoing the chance of reelection. Suppose further that constituent utility depends jointly on the state of the world (which the incumbent gets to observe privately) and on the incumbent's action (which is known only to the incumbent). In this case, the constituents can do no better than establish a threshold utility level and reelect the incumbent only if that level is attained. Obviously, the incumbent will follow her constituents' wishes only if the cost of doing so is less than the (discounted) value of reelection, which depends both on the level of the utility threshold and the value of office. This means that voters cannot rationally set such a high threshold that incumbents will choose not to be reelected and that they must reward incumbents with a relatively substantial payment upon reelection. Moreover, as I have argued previously (Ferejohn 1986), potential officials – challengers for office – cannot generally make credible promises to voters that they would behave differently when in office. This is because potential agents are motivationally identical to the incumbent and any such pledge would be discounted by rational voters.[2]

Electoral punishment in this kind of a model is a fairly blunt instrument, and incumbent officials will be, at best, only moderately responsive to public wishes.[3] It is also clear that there will be a difference between the agency contract that voters would choose and that which would be offered by an incumbent official. Officeholders would prefer to offer a contract that limits the ability of the voter to observe official actions, which has infrequent elections, and substantial postelection payments. Voters would prefer contracts that have easily monitored agents and frequent

---

[2] It is, of course, possible that potential officials are not all the same and that voters, knowing this, attempt to distinguish good from bad types. This structure would mitigate but not eliminate the problem studied in this chapter. For an analysis of a such a model, see Jim Fearon's contribution to this volume (Chapter 2).

[3] If votes are the principal tool available to ordinary citizens, the analysis here suggests that officials have an interest in keeping that tool blunt. The institution of the Australian ballot, for example, by making vote selling difficult, may be understood as a severe limitation on the capacity of principals to control agents.

elections. But they also concur with officials in wanting high post-election rewards – these are necessary for any electoral control to occur. Because voters and incumbents have conflicting tastes among contracts, we need to worry about the way in which political agency relations develop.

In a sense, we can understand the choice of contract as an asymmetric or one-sided bargaining game that precedes the agency interaction. Someone, either the agent or the principal, makes an offer that can be accepted or rejected by the other before the agency relationship actually begins. The asymmetry of the bargaining arises from one of two possible assumptions. We might assume that voters employ constitutional means to fix agency relations with officials. The officials then indicate their acceptance of these terms by choosing to run for office. Or, more realistically, we could assume that incumbents are in a position to make initial offers in virtue of their position as incumbents. Voters might either accept or reject this initial offer, but, given their incapacity to deal with other potential officials, their capacity to reduce the opportunistic incentives of incumbents is quite limited. If we think, as I do, that explicit constitutional means to control agents are fairly weak – there are simply too many ways that professional political officials can shield their actions from outside observation – the combination of agency costs with bargaining circumstances that are disadvantageous to voters suggests that political officials will be relatively unaccountable to their constituents.

There are empirical reasons to doubt, however, that the fact of agent design actually leads to badly suboptimal outcomes for political principals. In fact, it seems that political agents have, over the course of American history, frequently made their actions more observable by their constituents, and therefore permitted them increasingly to attach specific rewards and punishments to more-observable outcomes. For example, the first congresses were, as a matter of conscious design, usually quite difficult for outsiders to follow. While the Constitution specified that "each house shall keep a journal of its proceedings, and from time to time, publish the same, excepting such parts as may in their judgment require secrecy" (Article I, section 5), the publication of proceedings of the early congresses was sporadic and casual. The Senate, perhaps conceiving of itself as an advisory council as much as a branch of the legislature, generally met in closed sessions attended by executive branch officials. However, each of these practices was superseded relatively rapidly in the early years of the Republic and replaced by the practices and expectations of open meetings, with visitors and press present, and regular publication of the proceedings of each chamber. Indeed, within a very few years, the Senate itself was transformed from a closed council to a highly public showplace of the rhetorical talents of the leading orators of the day.

More recently, congressionalists can point, with some perplexity perhaps, to the institution of the recorded teller vote, the opening up of committee markup sessions, recording within-committee roll call votes, the enactment of various forms of campaign finance reform, and the introduction of cameras into congressional proceedings. Each of these reforms was adopted in the early 1970s, ostensibly with the purpose of "opening up" the political process to the public. More recently, the Republican 104th Congress pried the window open a bit more widely by publishing committee roll call votes, making it more difficult to conduct closed committee meetings, and prohibiting proxy voting in committees. Whether these reforms all had the effects their proponents intended,[4] certain empirical consequences followed. For example, following the institution recorded teller voting, attendance at roll calls roughly doubled. Similarly, when roll call votes began to be recorded in committees, participation on roll calls increased from around 40% to over 90% (Hall and McKissick 1997). Other recent institutional changes arguably fit the same pattern: in 1974, House Democrats decided to permit secret ballots on individual committee chairs, rather than voting in public on the whole slate of seniority-designated chairs, and, after a few committee chairs were deposed, this measurably increased the responsiveness of Democratic chairs to their party caucus.[5]

A similar tendency toward openness was exhibited within the federal bureaucracy, but here perhaps it was Congress, acting as a principal, taking the lead in increasing the level of scrutiny of

[4] One effect of forcing open committee meetings and recording internal votes probably was to shift decisions to other, less formal settings, such as party task forces.

[5] It seems possible that the opening of congressional processes to public view lies behind the relentless decline in public approval of congressional performance over roughly the same period. It is true the decline in approval is not confined to Congress, but then the increasing public access to previously closed processes is not confined to Congress either.

139

agency activity. The most famous example is the 1967 Freedom of Information Act, which opens most federal agencies to popular and press scrutiny. More recent are federal requirements that policy-making meetings that involve nonfederal employees must be open to the public. Numerous other requirements are embedded in various congressional acts governing administrative procedures, which demand that agencies develop a record of proceedings that can be examined by outsiders, and that this record bear some systematic relationship to subsequent decisions. Congress also often requires that agency decisions be subjected to judicial oversight. The result is, arguably, one in which federal agencies are required to be accountable and, presumably, responsive to public expectations and sentiments.

The puzzle, of course, is why agents would ever redesign contracts in this way. Why would they make their actions more easily monitored when, by all accounts, the result is to induce them to take actions (e.g., showing up for roll call votes) that they would refrain from otherwise? Surely such contracts make agents worse off, by reducing their opportunities to act on their own preferences, out of the public glare.[6] It seems at least a little surprising from the agency theory perspective that the political process has increasingly been "opened up" to external view and the politicians have made themselves more and more vulnerable to criminal punishment (among other forms) over time. Why would agents behave this way? Why wouldn't they work to perpetuate a situation in which they have great opportunities to take advantage of their official positions, without fear of competitors or retaliation?

Agent-Designed Contracts

I think there are several possible answers to these questions, but I want to focus on one that grows out of the agency relation itself. I want to argue that increasing the degree of accountability

---

[6] One might think that by making it easier for the public to monitor goings-on in committee, it became possible for interest groups to focus on these situations too, and condition their payments to members on their observed behavior. In effect, by opening committee proceedings, and making members' actions verifiable, the conditions for a viable market for votes are created. But the benefits to members to extract rents from interest groups will be dissippated in competition for office in such a way that agents are left no better off with reforms than without them.

in an agency contract can increase the power of the agent, all things considered, and therefore that agents have an incentive to make themselves accountable. This argument focuses on the willingness of the principal to enter into or invest in the agency relationship in the first place. Here the idea is as follows. It is straightforward to establish in a standard agency model with moral hazard that the principal would like to get some direct measure of the agent's effort, in addition to the observation of output. Depending on the specific information structure, she would be willing to pay something for the possibility of such an observation (or audit).[7] This implies that there are agency relations that a principal would enter into if he could obtain an audit that she would not find worthwhile without an audit. Thus, one way that agents might compete for the business of a principal is to commit to such an audit as part of the contractual arrangement. A simple example is if, knowing very little about how your car works, you face a choice of which of two automobile repair shops to take your car to. If one of the shops is, for example, part of a national chain that reviews and evaluates the work of its mechanics (and had a reputation to maintain in this regard), you might be willing to pay more to take your car there rather than to a small, unaffiliated repairman.

Consider a single principal who can divide her current income between two activities: a private one exhibiting decreasing returns, and an activity involving the employment of an agent whose behavior can only be imperfectly observed. Now assume that the agent first designs the information structure of the contract – by permitting the principal to observe an ex post signal of the agent's action – and the principal subsequently decides how much to invest in the agency relationship (thereby establishing the consequences of firing the agent, conditional on available information). Following this investment by the principal, the agent privately observes the state of the world and chooses an act conditional on that observation. The principal subsequently observes the outcome (which is a function of the agent's action and the privately observed state of the world) and the value of the signal of the agent's action, and then decides whether or not to fire the agent.

Thus, the sequence of actions is as follows: the agent chooses

---

[7] This issue is explored in Rajan and Sarath 1995 and in Gjesdal 1982.

an information structure (σ), which is modeled by permitting the principal to observe, ex post, a signal of his action $s = a + \theta$, where θ has the distribution function $G^\sigma(\theta)$ with (differentiable) density function $g^\sigma(\theta)$. In view of σ, principal chooses how much (x) to invest in the relationship, investing her remaining income (I – x) in a private production process, H(.). The agent then privately observes the state of the world, a random variable (ε) that is distributed on [0,1], according to F(ε), and selects an action, (a(ε)). The one-period reward to the principal of investing x in the agent is simply O = xa(ε)ε, while the agent earns Wx – a(ε). The principal then observes the outcome and the signal (s = a(ε) + θ) and reelects the agent if and only if the agent's performance is "satisfactory" (which means that the value of output and the signal fall in an acceptable region), and then the next period begins.[8] If the agent is fired, he is replaced by an identical agent from an inexhaustible supply. We assume that both the principal and the agents employ the same discount rate, δ, and that the relationship between them continues indefinitely. Thus, principal's expected utility can be written as follows:

$$EU^P = \int_0^1 xa(\varepsilon)\varepsilon dF(\varepsilon) + H(I - x) + \delta V^P, \tag{1}$$

where $V^P = EU^P$ is the "continuation" value the principal expects to receive from future play and x $\leq$ I. The agent's expected utility can be written similarly: $EU^A = Wx - a(\varepsilon) + p(a)\delta V^A$, where p(a) is the probability of reelection given that the agent did action a and $V^A = EU^A$ is the agent's continuation value. As is standard in agency models, the principal wishes to maximize her discounted expected utility subject to the constraints that the agent will subsequently choose optimal actions, and that the agent prefers to participate in the relationship. Less standard is the fact that the principal is restricted to using a "firing rule" and cannot condition ex post payments on observed outcomes in any more refined fashion. Thus, the principal picks her optimal firing rule subject to the restrictions that the agent maximizes $Wx - a(\in) + p(a)\delta V^A$, for each ε and that for each ε, $Wx - a(\varepsilon) + p(a)\delta V^A \geq Wx + p(0)\delta V^A$.

While the agency relationship is fairly standard, the main

[8] Rajan and Sarath (1995) show that the principal would generally prefer that (be willing to pay more for) θ and ε be negatively correlated, but we omit such considerations here.

departure of this chapter is to model "contract design" explicitly. Here the principal and agent jointly design the contract in an asymmetric bargaining game: the agent first proposes an information structure, σ, which indicates how observable his actions will be ex post, and the principal then chooses x, the amount she wishes to invest with the agent. Refusal of the agent's offer of information structure, σ, would amount to choosing x = 0. To keep matters simple, the design stage occurs before any informational asymmetry arises, so that neither the principal nor the agent has any private information to divulge.

We seek to characterize stationary Bayes perfect equilibria in this game. Stationarity, while restrictive, is natural in this setting since the decision problem itself is stationary – preferences and opportunities of all players are time independent – and, because agents are replaced in equilibrium, the implementation of history-dependent strategies would seem especially difficult.

The agent has two moves in each stage game. First, he picks an information structure σ, and following the principal's choice of an investment level, he picks an action, a, that depends on all prior moves in the game. The principal, after observing the information structure, chooses how much to invest with the agent, $x: \Sigma \to \mathbb{R}^+$, and after the outcome and signal are observed, she decides whether or not to retain the agent. Thus, the agent's stage game strategies are pairs, $t^A = \langle \sigma, a \rangle$, where $\sigma \in \Sigma$ and $a \in A$ such that $a: E \times \Sigma \times X \to [0,\infty]$. The principal's stage game strategies are pairs, $t^P = \langle x, r \rangle$ where $x(\sigma)$ is the principal's investment choice and r is reelection decision rule, where $r: A \times S \times \Sigma \times X \to \{0,1\}$.

A stationary Bayes perfect equilibrium of this game can be written as follows:

$$< \sigma^*, x^*(\sigma^*), a^*(\varepsilon, \sigma^*, x^*), r^*(a^*, s(a^*, \theta), \sigma^*, x^*) > 0,$$

where $s(a^*, \theta)$ is the realized value of the action signal, σ^* is a best response for the agent, given optimal play by all actors in the remainder of the game, x^* is a best response to σ^*, given subsequent optimal play, $a^*(\varepsilon, \sigma^*, x^*)$ is optimal for the agent given σ^*, x^* following the observation of ε, assuming the principal is playing her optimal reelection rule, r^*, and r^* is a best response to all previous actions, given the value of the signal, s.

The principal may employ one of two methods of controlling the agent: either she could reelect the agent if output is greater than some threshold (we may call this "output monitoring"); or she could reelect the agent only if the agent appears to take a sufficiently good action (s is greater than some threshold level, which we can call "action monitoring"). Suppose, for the moment, that σ and x are fixed and that the principal can observe a signal of action, s, which is distributed according to G^σ with a mean of a and standard deviation of σ, and that she engages in action monitoring. Therefore, the agent will be reelected only if $s = a + \theta \geq s^*$. Thus, in a stationary equilibrium, once the principal picks s*, the agent will rationally choose an a that satisfies

$$g^\sigma\left(s^* - a\right) = \frac{1}{\delta V^A},$$ (2)

if any exists, or else will pick a = 0. The second-order condition ensures that for a satisfying (2), $\frac{dg^\sigma}{ds} > 0$ so that, if g^σ is unimodal and a is positive, a(s*) > s*. Taking account of this relationship, the principal will then choose s* so that the agent's participation constraint is satisfied with equality. This entails that the following relationship hold:

$$a\left(s^*\right) = \left[G^\sigma\left(s^*\right) - G^\sigma\left(s^* - a\left(s^*\right)\right)\right]\delta V^A = \left[p(\phi) - \sigma - p\left(\alpha^*\right)\right]\delta V^A$$ (3)

where $p(a) = 1 - G^\sigma(s^* - a)$. We may also use these equations to find the relationship between the continuation values and the basic parameters:

$$V^A = Wx - a\left(s^*\right) + p\left(a\left(s^*\right)\right)\delta V^A = Wx + p(0)\delta V^A,$$ (4)

or,

$$V^A = \frac{Wx}{1 - \delta p(0)} = \frac{Wx - a\left(s^*\right)}{1 - \delta p\left(a\left(s^*\right)\right)},$$ (5)

which implies that V^A does not depend on s* and, therefore, not on a either. In this formulation the agent's actions do not depend on any information advantage, since under action monitoring he has none. The principal chooses s* so that the agent is indifferent between choosing a = a(s*) and a = 0. By inspection of equations (4) and (5), a(s*) depends on the parameters δ, W, and x and increases as any of these numbers increase. Moreover, from equation (3), as the signal becomes more informative (σ goes to 0 or, equivalently, as the right hand side of (3) gets large), a(s*) must increase as well. If the signal of the agent's action is sufficiently informative, the principal can induce her official to act as a nearly perfect agent.

Using equation (1) and the stationarity assumption, we may write the principal's utility as

$$EU^P = \frac{1}{1-\delta}\left[\bar{\varepsilon}a(s^*)x + H(I-x)\right],$$ (6)

from which, after substituting for a(s*) from equations (3) and (5), we obtain:

$$EU^P = \frac{1}{1-\delta}\left[\bar{\varepsilon}(p(a)-p(0))\frac{\delta W x^2}{1-\delta p(0)} + H(I-x)\right].$$ (7)

Plainly, with action monitoring, the agency relationship is very valuable to the principal and so she will invest heavily in it if W and δ are large, and σ is small; thus x depends positively on W, δ, and $1/\sigma$. Moreover, because of the convexity of the first term inside brackets in (7), $x = I$ for sufficiently large values of $[p(a) - p(0)]\delta W I^2$.

Now suppose that the principal ignores the action signal and engages instead in output monitoring. In this case the agent is reelected only if output exceeds some threshold value, K. In this case it is clear that the agent's best action is $a = K/\varepsilon$ if $Wx - K/\varepsilon + \delta V^A \geq Wx$, and $a = 0$ otherwise. Note that under output monitoring, the agent is reelected with probability one if and only if he chooses $a \geq K/\varepsilon$, so that the probability terms can be ignored. Substituting into (1), we can write principal's expected utility from investing in the agent as

$$\frac{1}{1-\delta}K\Pr\left(\varepsilon \geq \frac{K}{\delta V^A}\right) = \frac{1}{1-\delta}K\left(1 - F\left(\frac{K}{\delta V^A}\right)\right),$$

which is maximized at K* satisfying,

$$\frac{1 - F\left(\dfrac{K^*}{\delta V^A}\right)}{f\left(\dfrac{K^*}{\delta V^A}\right)} = \frac{K^*}{\delta V^A},$$ (8)

which has a unique solution if F satisfies the monotone likelihood property defined earlier. The relationship of V^A

145

and W is more complicated in this case because the participation constraint is binding only for $\varepsilon = \dfrac{K^*}{\delta V^A}$, so that the agent's expected utility is

$$V^A = \int_0^{\frac{K^*}{\delta V^A}} Wx \, dF(\varepsilon) + \int_{\frac{K^*}{\delta V^A}}^1 Wx - \frac{K^*}{\in} + \delta V^A dF(\varepsilon) \qquad (9)$$

$$= Wx + \delta V^A \left[1 - F\left(\frac{K^*}{\delta V^A} \right) \right] - \int_{\frac{K^*}{\delta V^A}}^1 \frac{K^*}{\in} dF(\varepsilon). \qquad (10)$$

This expression becomes much simpler to work with if we assume that F is uniformly distributed, which we will for the remainder of this chapter. Then (8) reduces to $K^* = \dfrac{\delta V^A}{2}$ and $EU^P = \dfrac{1}{1-\delta} \left[\dfrac{\delta V^A}{4} + H(I-x) \right]$. The expected utility of the agent, from (10), is then written

$$V^A = Wx + \frac{\delta V^A}{2} + \frac{\delta V^A}{2} \left(\log\left(\frac{1}{2} \right) \right) = Wx + \frac{\delta V^A}{2} (1 - \log(2)), \qquad (11)$$

which implies that

$$EU^P = \frac{1}{1-\delta} \left[\frac{\delta}{4} EU^A + H(I-x) \right] = $$
$$\frac{1}{1-\delta} \left[\delta \frac{Wx}{4 - 2\delta(1 - \log(2))} + H(I-x) \right]. \qquad (12)$$

As in the case of action monitoring, the principal's choice of x depends positively on W and δ and converges to I as these values increase. An important thing to note is that, in the case of output monitoring, the returns to the principal of investing in the agency relationship is linear in x, whereas the return to investment is quadratic in the case of action monitoring. Thus, if the principal has a sufficiently large income that could be invested with the agent, she will invest more with the agent under action monitoring than she would under output monitoring. This is because the principal's optimal choice of x under output monitoring depends only on W, δ, and I, while under action monitoring, x is increasing in $1/\sigma$ as well, eventually exceeding the principal's investing under output monitoring. Moreover, it is evident that, under either form of monitoring, the agent is made better off by increases in x. Indeed, fixing the values of the other parameters, the agent generally has an incentive to pick σ small enough to induce the principal to choose a large value of x and engage in action monitoring.

The consequences of this setup can be made clear in a simple example. Suppose that only two information structures may be proposed by the agent: either he makes his action completely observable ex post, or he keeps that information private. Assume further that the distribution of ε is uniform on [0,1]. Then, the principal decides on how much of the income ($x \le I$) she receives (exogenously) to invest in the agent. She keeps the remainder for immediate consumption (no savings are permitted across periods). This determines the one period reward functions, $U^p = xa(\varepsilon)\varepsilon + I - x$, and $U^A = Wx - a(\varepsilon)$.

Suppose first that the agent chooses to make his actions ex post observable, and the principal's best response is to invest x^a in the agent. In this case the principal can require that the agent pick $a = \delta V^A$ as a condition for reelection and the agent will always comply. Clearly, if I is sufficiently large, the principal will choose to invest all of her current income in the agent. Thus, the agent's expected utility is simply $Wx^a = WI$ and that of the principal is $\delta W \dfrac{(I)^2}{2}$.

If, however, agent actions are not observable ex post, the principal will adopt a reelection rule based only on the value of output. The agent will be reelected if and only if $xa(\varepsilon)\varepsilon$ exceeds some cutoff value (K). The previous analysis shows that the principal's optimal choice of K is $K^{**} = \delta V/2$ and that the agent will choose $a^{**} = K^{**}/\varepsilon$ if and only if ε exceeds 1/2, and will choose $a^{**} = 0$ otherwise. Then, the principal invests all her income with the agent only if $\delta WI \ge 4\left[1 - \dfrac{\delta}{2}(1 - \log(2))\right]$, which holds for large values of W, I, and δ. But it is also clear that there are values of I, W, and δ such that the principal will invest in the agent with action monitoring but not with output monitoring. Thus, whether the agent chooses to make information on his actions available to the principal depends on a comparison of the agent's expected utility under action or outcome monitoring, taking account of the principal's best responses.

This example shows that by decreasing σ (in this case, choosing $\sigma = 0$ rather than infinity) the agent can induce the principal to contribute more to the agency relationship and thereby earn more rents himself.[9] This occurs because the agent will work harder if x is increased, but not so much harder that his expected utility is reduced. The same story is demonstrable in the more general setting set out earlier. Here the agent will choose σ at the outset to maximize expected utility, taking account of subsequent reactions by the principal and himself. Because of the distributional assumptions, the agent's choice boils down to a decision to be in one of two monitoring regimes: either pick σ small enough that the principal monitors the signal, or large enough that the principal monitors output. Thus, the choice in the more general setting turns out to be essentially the same as in the simpler example: choose whether to reveal your action ex post. This simplicity would, of course, be lost in a more complicated model, but the logic would likely be preserved.

This story has a number of implications that will be discussed shortly. For now, I shall point out only some of the most obvious ones. To the extent that the actions of elected officials can be monitored, citizens will be willing to invest more in government. Thus, if there are exogenous forces leading to an "opening up" of governmental processes, this will permit the reformed political process to extract more wealth from society. It is of course true, in the crudest sense, that governmental growth and openness have proceeded in parallel, though much finer-grained empirical observation would be needed to see how firm that descriptive generalization really is. There is, based on the argument given here, some reason to think that these phenomena are causally linked: that the increase in governmental authority has been brought about by the provision for increased agent observability. Perhaps an even stronger hypothesis might be ventured: that the authority of government has expanded in exactly those areas that observability has increased. Of course, this is not an explanation of governmental growth because the model is too simple to exhibit

[9] The reason for the qualifier is that without further restrictions there may be corner solutions.

endogenous dynamics. But it does point to a possible consequence of transparent governmental processes.

Perhaps more provocative is the hypothesis that those parties or factions that are interested in pursuing governmental solutions to social problems should also be in favor of more open or "democratic" processes. In this sense, we should expect liberal or left parties to be more interested in opening up the process, not out of a principled commitment to visibility, but out of a determination to make a large government politically possible. Openness or reform, on this account, might be part of a strategy that would make a larger public sector politically feasible.

We could put the matter less manipulatively as follows. Suppose that, for some exogenous reason (e.g., a scandal), governmental processes have suddenly become more open. Then, on this analysis, we should expect that large governmental programs would become relatively more attractive to the electorate. Indeed, one way to understand the growth of government in the early post-Watergate era, a period that was not economically propitious for government growth, is as a manifestation of this phenomenon. Conversely, the renewed popular concern over campaign finance, and increasing popular concern about the capture of government by special interests, should be expected to make large governmental programs politically vulnerable.

Heterogeneous Principals

While the previous section of this chapter concerned how open or observable (endogenously designed) governmental processes would be, it should be clear that the informational issue is a special case of the more general issue of controllability. Informational asymmetries are only one reason that a principal is hard to control, and I have shown that the agent has an interest in offsetting the effects of some of those asymmetries. But, on the same logic, the agent has a more general interest in facilitating some degree of control over his actions by the principal, whatever the source of uncontrollability may be.

I argued previously (Ferejohn 1986) that in typical institutional settings heterogeneous principals will often be unable to control agent opportunism, and suggested that such principals will either find ways to mitigate the effects of heterogeneity or will forgo the advantages of entering an agency relationship. The source of the controllability issue in that essay was located in the incapacity of heterogeneous principals to commit to a coordination scheme that would limit the agent's opportunities to exploit the heterogeneous interests of his supervisor. I suggested in that setting that the principals had a shared interest in limiting the space within which the agent could choose actions to a single dimension, if they could credibly do so. Alternatively, while the agent may take actions in a high-dimensional space, the principals have an interest in evaluating agent actions according to a one-dimensional statistic on these actions. I conjectured in that article that the apparently quite general tendency of political life to be organized along left-right terms might be explained in this way. Obviously, this story, as it was sketched out, was seriously incomplete.

Even though principals may share an interest in placing limits on the space of agent evaluations, they have conflicting interests over exactly which statistic on output should be employed to evaluate agent performance. Control of officials is, in this sense, plagued by a coordination problem, and it is difficult to see how that problem might be solved. If we think of political principals as voters, with only sporadic involvement in the political process, it is difficult to be sanguine about the chances that public officials will be much restrained in their agency. My speculations in that essay had, as a result, a kind of magical or functionalist quality that some of our brethren find troubling. Fortunately, from the present viewpoint, I was silent as to whether the principals themselves would design the solution. If it was them, the fact that they have diverse interests would seem to lead to a potentially intractable collective action problem. Perhaps, this problem could be avoided either by letting solutions evolve (still magical) or, as suggested shortly, by positing that the agents construct their own evaluation space.

In the previous section I argued, within a standard political agency model, that agents have an interest in making themselves accountable in order to get the principal to trust them with more resources. Extending that insight to the present case, we can see that the agent has an interest of the same kind in mitigating the effects of principal heterogeneity. The reason is straightforward. Heterogeneous principals cannot control agent opportunism and will therefore not invest in the agency relationship. If the agent can construct a contractual arrangement that prevents playing one principal off against the others, accountability will be enhanced and the principals will be more willing to invest in the relationship.

According to the model in my earlier article, agents seeking to enhance their powers have an interest in making their actions auditable in a single dimension. This might be done by providing statistics on agent actions that are confined to a single dimension. Within a pure moral hazard model, the agent is indifferent as to which dimension is picked out by providing an audit statistic, just so long as they coordinate on a single dimension. Thus, agent design converts the problem to one of pure coordination rather than a bargaining game. Admittedly, hands will need to be waived to provide an ex ante account of the political life of a particular republic, but, I think, there is less pressure to move toward magical accounts in pure coordination problems.

Thus, the conjecture is that the agents themselves have an interest in limiting competition to a single (perhaps left-right) continuum; and where they succeed in doing this, the principals will be willing to invest more in the relationship – government will be larger. It seems true, for example, that simplified left-right politics is more characteristic of northern European countries than of southern ones (where particularistic issues more often dominate), and one might argue that this is what makes northern European states more inclined to support larger governments. Moreover, within the American polity, periods in which the left-right structure is dominant – the New Deal period in American history is probably the best example – are relatively propitious for governmental growth. Perhaps, one might argue for the same explanation in postwar Great Britain.

Parties and Candidates

The previous discussion focused on a principal selecting a single agent, but in actual settings we sometimes observe the principal selecting parties or selecting among candidates who are organized into parties. From the present perspective the parties, as collectivities, would have systematically different interests with respect to agency contracts than individual candidates. Specifically, parties might collectively prefer to make official action relatively observable in order to attract popular support to all candidates of the party, whereas individual officeholders might prefer to have more opportunities to avoid monitoring. Thus, where there are multiple agents in the parties, there may be a collective action problem among them that is similar to that among heterogeneous principals. Insofar as parties are able to restrain their individual candidates from avoiding audits, they should be more successful in attracting electoral support.

Additionally, insofar as parties differ in support for governmental activity in general, we might expect the party most favorable to large government to prefer to implement contracts that provide for more observability. Left parties ought, on this account, to be relatively favorable to reform policies, but they should be especially supportive of intraparty reforms. For example, Democrats might generally prefer to reform congressional practices by changing party rules rather than rules of the chambers, whereas Republicans would be expected to have the opposite preference.

Similarly, while parties might have a collective incentive to limit the dimensionality of competition in order to provide assurance to voters that they can expect to exert some control over officials, individual candidates would have an incentive to differentiate themselves from their copartisans, by offering specific services to their constituents, in order to attract additional support. Insofar as individual candidates succeed in offering distinctive promises, the party itself might be expected to suffer at the polls.

Moving inside the polity, numerous congressional observers have noted the willingness of relatively homogeneous parties to yield authority to their leadership (Aldrich 1995; Rohde 1991). The apparently sharp consolidation of decision making in Newt Gingrich's inner club is a recent manifestation of this phenomenon, but the evolution of congressional leadership structures can be explained in similar terms (see the essays in Dodd and Oppenheimer 1997). Less often remarked on is the possibility that persistent House-Senate differences may be illuminated by attention to principal heterogeneity. That House districts are relatively small and that incumbents have an interest in making them safe might lead one to believe that House parties will typically be more homogeneous than Senate parties and, for that reason, more willing than Senate parties to delegate authority to leadership structures. The highly individualist and chronically gridlocked Senate, exhibiting perhaps the most striking feature of modern congressional politics, may be traceable to the relative

intractability of the collective action problem facing the members
of that chamber.

References

Aldrich, John. 1995. *Why Parties: The Origins and Transformation of Parties in America*. Chicago: University of Chicago Press.

Dodd, Lawrence, and Bruce Oppenheimer, eds. 1997. *Congress Reconsidered*. Washington, D.C.: Congressional Quarterly Press.

Ferejohn, John. 1986. "Incumbent Performance and Electoral Control." *Public Choice* 30 (Fall): 5–25.

Gjesdal, F. 1982. "Information and Incentive." *Review of Economic Studies* 49: 373–90.

Hall, Richard, and Gary McKissick. 1997. "Institutional Change and Behavioral Choice in House Committees." In Lawrence Dodd and Bruce Oppenheimer, eds., *Congress Reconsidered*, 212–28. 6th ed. Washington, D.C.: Congressional Quarterly Press.

Rajan, Madhav, and Bharat Sarath. 1995. "Correlation of Signals and Value in Agencies." Unpublished manuscript, September.

Riker, William. 1982. *Liberalism versus Populism*. San Francisco: Freeman.

Rohde, David. 1991. *Parties and Leaders in the Postreform House*. Chicago: University of Chicago Press.

Rossiter, Clinton. 1961. *The Federalist Papers*. New York: Mentor.

Wechsler, Herbert. 1961. "The Political Safeguards of Federalism." In *Principles, Politics and Fundamental Laws: Selected Essays*, 184. Cambridge, Mass.: Harvard University Press.

Chapter Five

Accountability and Manipulation

The main point of this chapter is to discuss some of the ways politicians try to survive in office and to increase their margin of maneuverability to design and implement policies. I assume that, in addition to policy preferences, politicians want to win elections, stay in power, and maximize their autonomy in case their policies diverge from voters' preferences. I also assume that manipulative strategies consist of attempts by politicians to avoid the cost of such divergence.[1] My discussion attempts to link agency theory and Machiavellian politics in order to interpret some aspects of the control of politicians by citizens in a democracy. To provide illustrations of typical political strategies and their consequences, I also draw from evidence pertaining to recent Spanish politics, examining some conjunctures of the Socialist government from 1982 to 1996. This long period in office, most of it with an absolute Socialist majority in Parliament, was marked by four consecutive electoral victories as well as by the troubled waters of unpopular economic policies, high unemployment, a dramatic reversal of position over NATO, and a long string of financial scandals.

Democratic theory has traditionally considered that, although the interests of citizens and politicians may diverge, elections are the instrument whereby citizens can ensure that politicians will act on their behalf and carry out their policy preferences. As a

I wish to thank, in addition to the three editors, Peter Lange, Ignacio Sánchez-Cuenca, Ana Rico, Alberto Penadés, Andrew Richards, and Gösta Esping-Andersen for their comments on an early draft of this chapter.
[1] The concept of manipulation that I use in the discussion differs from that of Riker in that voters' preferences are not considered as given, strategies largely deal with information, and the main political initiatives do not correspond to the former losers but to incumbents (Riker 1982, 1986).

154

consequence, as Dahl (1970: 1) put it, "a key characteristic of a democracy is the continuing responsiveness of the government to the preferences of its citizens." At election time, voters will listen to promises from competing politicians, look for clues about their trustworthiness, compare, and choose accordingly. The choice would be both meaningful and consequential. Elections would thus act as a prospective mechanism for the responsiveness of politicians – under perfect information, *rebus sic stantibus*, politicians will adhere to the mandate. But elections would also protect citizens' interests as a retrospective mechanism: voters will examine past performance and, as a result, reward or punish politicians. In Key's (1966: 76–77) words, "The only really effective weapon of popular control in a democratic regime is the capacity of the electorate to throw a party from power. . . . Governments must worry, not about the meaning of past elections, but about their fate at future elections." Thus, because in democracies politicians suffer the consequences of their policies and unpopular policies make them lose elections, governments will respond in anticipation to the interests and preferences of citizens.[2]

We can examine this relationship between politicians and citizens within the framework of agency theory. An agency relationship arises in those situations in which one actor, the agent, acts on behalf of another, the principal, and is supposed to implement the preferences and interests of the latter. The voters, as principal, will select an agent out of several competitors in an election, invest him with power, and expect him to respond to their policy preferences: that is, to adhere to electoral programs and political promises on whose grounds the selection of the agent was made. The agent will be politically accountable when the principal can hold him responsible for past performance and, therefore, reward him with reelection or punish him with defeat. A perfect agency relationship would reflect a view of political representation according to which "the rulers should be identified with the people; their interest and will should be the interest and will of the nation . . . let the rulers be effectively responsible to it,

---

[2] This argument plays an important part in Sartori's (1987: 155–56) theory of democratic representation: "If it is true – and it is most of the time – that the leader subject to periodical electoral removability is concerned with how the voters will react to his actions, it follows that he will be monitored (at least, when sensitive issues come up) by the anticipation of what that reaction, whether positive or negative, might be."

promptly removed by it, and it could afford to trust them with power of which it could itself dictate the use to be made" (Mill 1991: 24).

But are politicians controlled by citizens through elections as traditional democratic theory and perfect agency assume? There is substantial comparative empirical evidence that elections do indeed influence policy prospectively, and that policies can be predicted out of the "issue agendas" that emerge from interparty competition (Klingemann, Hofferbert, and Budge 1994). Politicians concerned about reelection listen to public opinion when they take policy initiatives. As Stimson, MacKuen, and Erikson (1995: 559) vividly put it, "politicians are keen to pick up the faintest signals in their political environment. Like antelope in an open field, they cock their ears and focus their full attention on the slightest sign of danger." The evidence has shown that public opinion drives policy; that, either through electoral replacement of the incumbents or rational anticipation of the latter to policy moods of the citizens that might change over time, governments reflect in their policy initiatives the preferences of voters; that party election programs make it possible to predict the course of action of the winners; and that subsequent policies are congruent with thematic electoral promises.

So democratic governments appear to be responsive, the cause being elections and the anticipation of elections. Yet this view of democratic responsiveness faces several problems. First, it takes voters' policy preferences as exogenous. Second, although considerable empirical evidence shows that prospective evaluations influence the vote (Lewis-Beck 1988), no institutions other than elections exist to force incumbents to implement subsequently their original promises.[3] Third, citizens may be myopic in their preferences: should responsive incumbents care about such policy preferences or about their consequences? Politicians might think that if their policies adhere to the ex ante configuration of preferences that are temporally inconsistent, they may pay the costs later on, when the long-term negative consequences emerge. Thus, politicians will want to influence public opinion, not just respond to it. Can they do so? Considerable evidence exists on the

[3] Manin (1995: 209–14) has examined how two crucial mechanisms of control, imperative mandates and revocable representations, disappeared in the institutional configuration of democracy at the end of the eighteenth century.

relative malleability of such opinion (Page and Shapiro 1983, 1992; R. Shapiro and Jacobs 1989): politicians can manipulate citizens' preferences and obtain a margin of autonomy for their policies. Jacobs and Shapiro (1994: 9–16) have termed this influence, rather benevolently, as "the leadership effect." Manipulation of public opinion is usually intended to have effects on retrospective accountability at election time; sometimes, however, politicians try to influence opinion prospectively, so that they obtain from citizens a mandate to do what the politicians want. The latter may be attempted through referenda; although their results are usually not imperative, they may provide useful backing for politicians who have to take difficult decisions – and they might also occasionally provide them with serious frights (as in the cases of the Spanish referendum on NATO in 1986, or the French and Danish referenda on Maastricht in 1992 and 1993).

Democratic governments are accountable when citizens can judge their record retrospectively at election time, and punish or reward them accordingly. Politicians anticipate such judgment when they undertake policy initiatives and pay attention to the interests of the voters. So, rather than look at promises, citizens assess past performance. As Fiorina (1981: 6) put it, "Elections do not signal the direction in which society should move so much as they convey an evaluation of where society has been." On the basis of such evaluation, in Key's (1964: 544) succinct dictum, "the vocabulary of the voice of the people consists mainly of the words 'yes' and 'no.'" That is, governments survive or are thrown out of office. A vast evidence indicates, for example, that the performance of the economy has a great influence on the support for incumbents at election time: when economic conditions are bad, citizens vote against the ruling party (Fiorina 1981; Lewis-Beck 1988; Norpoth, Lewis-Beck, and Lafay 1991). Yet Cheibub and Przeworski (1996) also provide exhaustive empirical findings, covering the period from 1950 to 1990 for 99 democracies and 123 dictatorships, that show that the survival of heads of democratic governments is not sensitive to this performance. Elections appear to be mechanisms that displace rulers in ways that are random with regard to economic performance. If it is the case that the life and death of governments are independent from the evolution of the economies, then the mechanisms of democratic accountability must be critically examined. And we all know that politicians often opt for unpopular policies, that these can be ineffective, that political promises can be broken.[4] That is, policies frequently appear to be unresponsive to the preferences and the interests of citizens, and they are also poorly evaluated retrospectively. Yet it is not exceptional that politicians manage to survive. How do the mechanisms of accountability operate? When governments lose, is it because their policies are unpopular? And, on the contrary, when they survive, is it because their policies are popular? What is it that they do to remain in power? How do they try to manipulate accountability?

Machiavellian politics assumed that strategies could determine the survival of politicians, accommodating the governed to unpopular initiatives or to breaches of promises: "A prudent Prince neither can nor ought to keep his word when to keep it is hurtful to him and the causes which led him to pledge it are removed. . . . No Prince was ever at a loss for plausible reasons to cloak a breach of faith. . . . It is necessary, indeed, to put a good colour on this matter, and to be skilful in simulating and dissembling. But men are so simple, and governed so absolutely by their present needs, that he who wishes to deceive will never fail in finding willing dupes. . . . He must therefore keep his mind ready to shift as the winds and tides of Fortune turn" (Machiavelli 1992: 46). How can this be done under the conditions of modern democracy, where modern princes are in a less favorable position than in early sixteenth-century Florence?

To examine the context of such strategies, agency theory provides useful clues. An agency relationship will face problems of accountability when the interests of principal and agent do not coincide, the former can not easily determine whether it is in his interest that the policies of the latter are being taken, and his capacity to reward good agents and sanction opportunistic and self-interested ones is limited. Thus democratic accountability entails prospectively an "adverse selection" problem for the principal: how to avoid choosing a bad agent; retrospectively, it turns into a "moral hazard" problem: whenever the principal's (i.e., the citizens') information is unverifiable, there will arise the possibility

---

[4] Promises may be different in their nature and strength, and this will influence the possibility of assessing their implementation. Promises may refer to policy proposals, but also to general goals and values, or to procedures of decision making. And candidates may give them high salience in their programs or, on the contrary, state them in conditional terms as "potential" pledges (Schedler n.d.).

of politicians who, once elected, will not advance the preferences and interests of citizens, and whose survival is unrelated to their performance. The principal may commit retrospectively two errors: to reward an agent who has shirked or to punish an agent who has worked in the principal's interest. Indeed, the control of agent by principal depends on three requirements: that the actions of the agent and the conditions under which it operates can be publicly known; that both parties are symmetrically able to anticipate fully all possible contingencies that might arise during their relationship; and that the agent can be bound costlessly by the principal to carry out the preferences and interests of the latter (Sappington 1991). Therefore, the control of politicians by voters faces problems of information, monitoring, and enforcement.

Problems of monitoring arise when citizens have information that is either incomplete or asymmetrical. In the first case, they will find difficulties in establishing whether a causal connection exists between the actions of politicians and performance, either because of technical reasons or because the costs involved in finding out are greater than the potential benefits. But the activity of opposition parties, social movements, and civic associations can lower such costs: political mobilization and intensities of interests can thus facilitate democratic accountability as informational instruments. When, on the other hand, information is asymmetrical, politicians will be able to manipulate to their advantage information to which they have privileged access, while vast areas of politics remain opaque to voters. These might have difficulty in assessing whether good or bad outcomes are due to governmental policies or to "objective conditions" whose responsibility cannot be attributed to the government.

Also, new contingencies, which can never be fully anticipated, will arise once the elected politician is in office. These may make citizens uncertain about whether their initial preferences respond now to their real or long-term interests. Such new contingencies partly explain why democratic mandates are never imperative, and why they resemble "relational contracts" – that is, agreements that frame the agency relationship when complete and enforceable contracts that specify the behavior to be adopted are impossible. In such contracts, "the parties do not agree on detailed plans of action but on goals and objectives, on general provisions that are broadly applicable, on the criteria to be used in deciding what to do when unforeseen contingencies arise, on who has what power to act and the bounds limiting the range of actions that can be taken" (Milgrom and Roberts 1992: 131). So, the mechanisms of democratic accountability largely operate on implicit procedural contracts rather than on substantive issues. Rewards depend essentially on whether rules have been followed: for instance, on whether the behavior of politicians was honest, the truth was said, information was displayed when needed, the parties acted in good faith. This respect of rules and procedures by politicians is generally valued by citizens: for example, according to a recent Spanish survey,[5] when asked about the main qualities to be demanded from a politician, 56% of people chose "to be honest" as the first one, 12% selected "to keep promises," while only 5% opted for "to be able to take decisions, even if unpopular." However, under such lax controls, voters may find it hard to discern whether the "objective conditions" are indeed different from those anticipated before the politician came to office, whether they are really beyond the control of the agent, and whether they are being manipulated.

Citizens will have limited information on their interests and on whether they are being taken care of by a perfect agent. Did politicians deviate from promises out of concern for the welfare of citizens – "the general interest"? Did they campaign, on the contrary, on popular policies that they knew were ineffective, only to renege once in office in order to adopt effective ones? Is it in the interest of citizens to punish such politicians, voting them out of office in order to enforce the predictability of policies out of future campaign promises? Or should they reward them with reelection because they cared about the "objective interests" of citizens more than about their ex ante preferences?

The enforcement problem has to do with the capacity of voters to sanction or reward politicians effectively. If they are to bear the full impact of their actions, politicians must, first of all, have incentives in their reelection. A basic condition for "no cheating" to be an equilibrium is that the present value of the future gains from not cheating outweighs the temptation to cheat.[6]

---

[5] Survey of the Centro de Investigaciones Sociológicas, April 1995.

[6] This requires several conditions, which include the present reputation of the agent (its political capital value), the value it attaches to holding office in the future (the premium earned for what it supplies), and a discount rate low enough so that future gains are greater than the temptation to cheat. See the discussion of such conditions in firms in Shapiro 1983.

Enforcement then depends on whether the principal, or citizens, can prevent or ensure such "future gains." Punishing incumbents for bad performance must in addition not entail excessive costs to citizens. But in democratic politics, elections are about policy package deals and relative choices. And the vote is a particularly crude sanctioning instrument: in the words of O'Flaherty (1990: 134), "politics can be nothing more than meting out rewards and punishments, and doing so in a ham-fisted manner." For one, governmental action is multidimensional, and voters may want to reject some policies but retain others that they value. Incumbents will fully play a balancing game, making popular and unpopular policies interdependent. Also, citizens may dislike the opposition even more intensely. As Jensen and Meckling (1976) put it, in examining agency relationships in firms, "the size of the divergence (the agency costs) will be directly related to the cost of replacing the manager." Elections are not just about sanctioning an agent who has performed poorly, but about whether to appoint an alternative one. Thus governments will play a comparative game: the discrediting of the opposition is probably a more usual electoral resource than explanations of past actions or promises about the future. So, although in Ferejohn's (1986) model the importance of challengers lies entirely on their availability and it is the existence of willing alternative office seekers that gives the voter whatever leverage he has on the incumbent, it is also the case that the latter may use to his advantage citizens' mistrust toward the opposition. His room for maneuver is a function of both his reputation as agent and the reputational characteristics of the opponent.

If democratic accountability depends on whether voters have information to assess performance, responsibility can be assigned, and incumbents can be punished or rewarded, then the strategies of politicians who want to remain in office and benefit from a wide margin of maneuver will be manipulative regarding one or more of these requisites. But they will have to do so in a restrictive scenario. Obviously the incumbents will face the strategies of the opposition politicians, who want to replace them and who will manipulate the information in the opposite direction: they will, for example, attribute the responsibility for good news to exogenous factors and for bad news to the government. And more generally, incumbents will deploy their strategies in a scenario occupied by a plethora of actors with crisscrossing interests that will be providing citizens with very heterogeneous information relevant for the accountability of the government. This information will be related to policies or policy outcomes; but it may also deal with the activities of politicians previous to holding office, their private lives, and different strategies of discredit. Critical information of this kind may both paralyze the agendas of the incumbents and raise new dimensions of political liability. True or false, it clearly has a major impact among citizens: it may indeed be the case that politicians lose office more easily due to private scandals than to failed policies. So, the flow of information on the performance of the agent and the instruments for monitoring him have a particular complexity in politics.

This political scenario in which the mechanisms of accountability operate has changed very much in recent times. The media often take up the role of the opposition in Parliament: that is, the opposition follows, rather than leads, the media. The parliamentary political agenda is generally set by the information flow of newspapers and radio and television programs. In fact, parliamentary debates have a comparatively limited impact, except on rare occasions. Thus, a motion of no confidence may be presented not just when it might be viable in parliamentary terms, but also when the challenger who is likely to lose hopes nevertheless to raise his political stature through the media. And politicians cultivate the media more than Parliament in the explanation and defense of their policies. Bruno Kreisky, the Austrian chancellor, estimated that 80% of his schedule was dedicated to relations with the media.[7] The judiciary has also acquired a major role in the mechanisms of political accountability and in the definition of the political agenda. That is, politics has become more judicialized and justice more politicized. Politicians often react to this political influence of media and judiciary, contrasting their own democratic support to the nonelected nature of these powerful actors. They would like them to reflect the political majority of the day – for instance, attributing to Parliament the nominations to the judiciary, or introducing participatory democracy within the media (as Andreas Papandreou, the Greek prime minister, attempted to do through legislation). Such reactions are implicitly or explicitly supported by an argument that opposes democracy to pluralism. Of course, the argument

---

[7] Personal interview of the author with Kreisky, June 18, 1982.

would be more credible if the institutions of democracy performed satisfactorily as instruments of accountability, providing information on incumbents and facilitating their monitoring; on the contrary, it would appear to be cynical if democratic accountability were to be critically dependent on the institutions of pluralism.

Yet the control over politicians can hardly be ensured by pluralist institutions when democratic institutions (such as Parliament or parties) are impotent instruments of accountability. Such control requires independent media, real pluralism of information, and fairness of coverage. And centers of vast economic and informational resources have interests of their own, which do not overlap with those of citizens, that guide their strategies toward the government of the day. They may use pressure, threats, blackmail, or sheer destabilization: to paraphrase Harry Truman, they can raise the heat considerably inside the kitchen. Such strategies will manipulate citizens; the latter will use information that will facilitate their monitoring of incumbents, but they will also be misled with disinformation.[8] And, although citizens will suspect or be aware of the latter, they will also grant credit to the former, for shedding light over issues that democratic institutions had not revealed. So, when politicians complain of the treatment they get from the pluralist institutions, their best strategy is to facilitate monitoring through Parliament and parties.

In this complex scenario of political accountability, incumbents will be backed by their own party, often held together by powerful instruments of discipline. They will face an opposition in Parliament supposed to play a crucial role in providing information on incumbents and monitoring them. Media and judiciary will be influencing the definition of agendas and shedding light (or

---

[8] When citizens suffer informative manipulation from multiple sources, a limited interest in politics on their part may paradoxically facilitate the control over politicians. As Ferejohn (1990: 11–12) puts it, "because citizens care so little about politics, political evaluations and attachments are relatively stable and slow to shift. Thus, competitors for office are induced to regard them as external "facts" about their environment and not really subject to intentional manipulation. In a sense, citizens are able to act "as if " they have precommitted to a reward scheme. Thus, the fact that citizens do not pay much attention to new information and that politicians know this implies that politicians are limited in their ability to take advantage of the heterogeneity of their constituency to build new coalitions."

shadows) on politicians. And centers of economic and informational power will pursue their own interests, developing strategies that will both help and distort the monitoring of incumbents. In this scenario, facing demands for political responsiveness and anticipating accountability, what will modern princes do? Remember that we assume that they are interested in their own political survival, independently from the median voter's position. That is, they want to remain in power and to maximize their margin of maneuver for unpopular policies or breaches of promises. To achieve these goals, politicians will develop strategies directed toward their own party and toward public opinion – or citizens. And they will try to rally them against the opposition, the hostile press, the conspiring centers of power, and the inquisitive judges, whose credibility they will try to undermine.

The role of parties in the mechanisms of political accountability has not been sufficiently studied. Politicians have often been treated in two contradictory ways: either as simple reflections of parties considered as unitary actors (mostly when examining western European politics), or as autonomous from parties viewed as irrelevant (generally when analyzing Latin and North American politics). Many effects of different party systems remain unclear. Take, for instance, the rather trivial argument that in systems of proportional representation, with multiple and centralized parties, governments are closer to the median voter and more representative of the issue preferences of the electorate (Huber and Powell 1994; Dalton 1988); this says little about their accountability or electoral vulnerability. Think of the Italian case, where the median voter was fed up with the unaccountable median politician. Also, while coalition governments are generally considered to be less accountable due to difficulties in the attribution of responsibility, the internal symmetrical information shared by the different partners of such governments, who will compete against each other in future elections, may help monitoring by citizens. It has also been pointed out that political competition reduced to two parties decreases the level of control over officeholders (Ferejohn 1986); that decentralized parties and single-member constituencies hamper the attribution of political responsibilities and hence accountability; that in multiparty systems "voice" has little room as a mechanism of internal democratic control and "exit" is the only alternative for dissidence (Hirschman 1970; Fiorina 1981). As what regards the internal

164

affairs of parties, they have been generally considered as irrelevant for democracy. To quote Dahl (1970: 5), "if political parties are highly *competitive*, it may not matter a great deal if they are not internally democratic or even if they are internally rather oligarchical. . . . If the main reason we need political parties at all is in order for them to facilitate democracy in the *government of the country*, then might not parties that are internally oligarchic serve that purpose just as well as, or maybe even better than, parties that are internally more or less democratic?"

Oligarchical parties may indeed be more competitive, and party discipline may be necessary for electoral victories and stable governments. But party members are not just organizational soldiers: they join the party for reasons other than the particular interests of their leaders. Parties, as organizations, embody an agency relationship between members and leaders, and this relationship is relevant to citizens in general. In such a relationship, the interests of activists as principal and those of leaders as agent may not coincide. We may assume that the activists have policy preferences and want power in order to implement them, but, as their preferences may be distant to those of the median voter, they will be willing to make concessions. There is a limit to such concessions, though: activists are not recruited among centrist voters. People join parties due to ideological motivations; if they want their party to be in power, it is in order to implement policies they believe in, not merely for the spoils of office. As for the leaders, besides policy preferences, they want power both within and without the party, and to maximize their autonomy in case their political initiatives do not coincide with those of activists (either because they want to attract votes or because their policies, once in office, are not popular among activists). So "the mark of a successful political party is that it can move to the center and appeal to voters while simultaneously retaining the loyalty and effort of its activists" (Wintrobe 1993: 254). Politicians, as agents, will have to develop strategies toward two principals, leading them to believe that their interests (which only partly overlap) are being taken care of in the best possible way. Party democracy will depend on whether activists have information on leaders' strategies and policies, can monitor their performance, and can reelect or dismiss them accordingly.

But parties are also intermediaries between leaders and citizens. Oligarchical parties may hamper democracy if they are

165

an obstacle to political accountability, if their leaders use them in order to manipulate information and prevent monitoring. Democratic political parties may, on the contrary, be important instruments of accountability. If citizens vote a party platform, they will expect that the party will control its leaders regarding promises on policies. If, according to widespread democratic theses, parties are to operate as a crucial connection between citizens and the governmental process, they must follow voters' preferences and control the government, both if they are in power or in opposition. Parties provide citizens with informational shortcuts based on historical images, all the more relevant when other information is limited or missing (Popkin 1993); such shortcuts may or may not be misleading about governmental performance. Leaders may try to protect themselves behind such historical party images, the resilient partisan identity of voters, or the internal solidarity of party members ("partisan patriotism"). But parties have interests that do not necessarily overlap with those of their leaders. They have a longer-term horizon, an "intertemporal brand-name," and, as Moe (1990: 241 n. 22) puts it, they "expect to play the political game again and again, into the distant future." So, in difficult times, parties may opt for a "scapegoat strategy": that is, to change a leader who has become a liability, even if the responsibility for unpopular policies is more collective. Thus, the relationship between parties and leaders is relevant for democratic accountability, and, in principle, both should not be seen as mirror images of each other. Parties are not monolithical actors but arenas of political struggle. It is the combination of such internal struggles and external competition that shapes their organizational structures, the way decisions are made, the mechanisms of control over the politicians that the parties endorse.

When party members, as principal, cannot monitor the activities of their leaders and the party itself becomes an instrument for the manipulation of information, the capacity of citizens to control politicians will suffer. Yet born as vehicles for popular participation, defined as such by many constitutions, parties have become machineries dominated by oligarchies with their own goals. That is, they have increasingly turned into organizational weapons – instruments for competition and power – rather than part of the mechanisms for the democratic accountability of politicians. To use Michels's (1962: 79) words, "in a party . . . democracy is not for home consumption, but is rather an article made for export." Most of western Europe, where parties have a long tradition and dominate politics, shows a combination of what Manin (1995) has called *la démocratie du public* and *la démocratie de partis*: that is, parties compete at election time with images, symbols, and personalities, rather than specific policy positions, while in their internal life the power of oligarchies is overwhelming. This bureaucracy is reinforced when a system of public financing of parties diminishes the incentives to expand the number of militants and promote their rights (Pradera 1995). Members of such parties usually have in fact more rights as citizens than as activists; and, lacking channels for "voice," they can only opt for "exit" or for silent "loyalty" (Hirschman 1970). Sometimes, in joint-stock companies shareholders have more rights and administrators more responsibilities. If internal democracy is limited, electoral systems of proportional representation with closed and blocked lists of candidates will transfer decisions from the citizens to the party bureaucrats: citizens will vote for a party, activists will have little say on candidates, and bureaucrats will choose the future members of Parliament. Thus, parliamentary representatives will lose their freedom: they will no longer be accountable to their constituencies but to the party oligarchy.

But I do not intend to discuss in this chapter the impact that different formulas of party organization have on the democratic accountability of politicians. Internal polycentrism or factionalism may not lead to greater accountability than a centralized leadership, as the examples of the French PS and the Italian PSI show. Collusion between plural oligarchies is possible in such organizations. Also, while undisciplined and divided parties make the control of politicians difficult, if only because they blur the attribution of political responsibilities, and are usually punished by voters, parties that are not regarded as internally democratic can be electorally successful, as the case of the British Conservative Party has shown over a long period of time. This complex relationship between party organization, democratic accountability, and electoral performance needs much more careful analysis. What I intend to show here are the strategies followed by politicians and the role that the party has played as intermediary between politicians and citizens in one particular setting: that of a party with an absolute majority in Parliament and a highly centralized leadership. Such conditions are supposed to facilitate the attribution of responsibility and hence accountability. This was the Spanish experience for more than a decade.

Let us start with the strategies directed by politicians toward their own party. To keep control of the party in difficult circumstances is crucial for them: incumbents will try to get protection for their unpopular policies or breaches of promises under the party's mantle, that is, quelling internal opposition and manipulating party loyalties rooted in past political experiences. If they are successful, their credibility vis-à-vis citizens will increase: with limited information, a sympathetic voter will think that if the party backs the politician it will be due to good reasons. And if things turn out badly externally, the politicians who control their party will at least be able to survive internally and have a chance in the future to stand again for office. If they fail to control it, they will face political death.

If we turn to examine the Spanish example, for the politicians who had taken hold of the leadership of the PSOE beginning in 1974, party unity and discipline were the central organizational concerns. This was due to several reasons: memories of past fratricidal struggles, the attribution of the defeats in the 1977 and 1979 elections to factional disputes, and the breakdown of the UCD government and party due to internecine confrontations. They believed, therefore, that electoral success and governmental stability required strict party discipline. As a result, from the end of the 1970s onward the Socialist Party was a small but tightly knit organization. Its membership, which had stood at 101,000 in 1979, amounted only to 112,000 in 1982, when it won the general elections for the first time.[9] The ratio between members and voters was one of the lowest of all western European socialist parties, close only to the French PS: it was 1 : 54 in 1979, 1 : 90 in 1982. The leaders' control over the party was achieved through three main instruments: the very large powers of the Federal Executive Committee, the system of majoritarian representation in internal party elections, and the Spanish electoral system of proportional representation with closed and blocked lists of candidates.

The Federal Executive Committee decided on global party

---

[9] Figures from the Secretary of Organization, Federal Executive Committee, PSOE, Madrid.

strategy and had a decisive influence on the final say over lists of candidates to the Spanish Parliament, to regional assemblies, and to local councils in large towns. While Felipe González provided the ideas and strategy, the deputy leader, Alfonso Guerra, controlled the organization: they had both accumulated vast personal loyalties ever since the party was reconstructed in the final years of Franco's dictatorship, but the leadership also had powerful instruments for the control of the organization. Thus, internal party elections were regulated by a majoritarian principle: delegates to congresses were elected in accordance with the rule that "winner takes all." And bloc voting procedures were established so that large territorial delegations would have a unitary vote attributed to the head of the delegation. Although there were some exceptions to these rules,[10] the oligarchical trends were very strong and the possibility of protest votes very limited. The percentage of congress delegates who held public office either by election or by appointment went up in the 1980s: it represented 57% in 1981, 61% in 1984, 67% in 1990. And the leadership became more and more rigid: while in the 1979 congress, only 42% of the Executive Committee was reelected, the proportion went up to 76% in 1981 and 1984, to 81% in 1988, and in 1990 only one member who did not want to stand again was replaced.[11] Ever since 1979, the congresses of the PSOE produced majorities of over 80% of votes on policies. The PR system with closed and blocked lists for Parliament also attributed large powers to the party oligarchy; deputies knew that their survival as future candidates depended on the sympathies that they could muster within it, to the cost of their representative function and of the mediatory role between citizens and the governmental process that parties are supposed to fulfill.

Such mechanisms of power probably contributed to the strong competitiveness of the party during the 1980s. But within the party, they led to an uncritical delegation of decisions to the leadership, the languishing of internal debates, the inhibition of information. This could be useful in the short-term (i.e.,

---

[10] Such exceptions were that political resolutions were voted by individual delegates, that a minority surpassing a threshold of 20% of the vote could have 25% of the delegates, and that "currents of opinion" (but not "organized tendencies") were accepted from 1983 onward.

[11] Figures from Craig n.d.

correspond to the interest of the present leaders) but costly in the long-term horizon. The connections with society, the capacity to provide warning lights, and the anticipation of demands of accountability for broken pledges all suffered. Concern over these costs was expressed in an internal document written to González:

> The party has been changing very much. The density of the power relations cannot be compared to that existing at any other time. Endogamy, clientelism, "praetorian guards" have been reinforced. The ideological and political poverty is today very great. People think that, as deputies, all kinds of precautions are necessary in order not to be a victim of sectarianism. If this were true, if one should be more concerned with the apparatus than with voters, then the consequences of the internal politics of the party would be of a very serious nature indeed. The party needs reflection: serious, wide, and audacious. Not because this will shed light miraculously on anything, but because it will allow us to foresee problems, to act and to react. . . . The question is that many sectors of the party can be described as follows: too many mafias, too little principles.[12]

Such an organizational weapon was very successfully used by the government in difficult situations. The connection between party and public opinion was well perceived by the leaders: while Guerra used to say that "when we convince the party, then we shall be able to convince society" (on the issue of NATO), González argued that "society will help us to convince the party" (on the moderation of socioeconomic policies). To ensure the support of the organization, leaders appealed to "partisan patriotism," used past symbols and memories, and when internal criticism was voiced they argued that "the dirty linen should not be washed in public," that once an issue had been debated and decided upon activists should obey it, that party membership was voluntary (and, thus, that "loyalty" and "exit" were the only options). In October 1986, González himself warned against "serious indications of oligarchization and intolerance within the PSOE," and in February

---

[12] Document written by the author to Felipe González, July 8, 1987. This document and those mentioned in notes 18, 24, and 31 were part of a series written between December 1979 and September 1990, as a member of the Federal Executive Committee (1979–84 and 1988–94) and of the cabinet (1982–88).

1990 he declared that "there is fear within the party."[13] Yet the party remained mostly an instrument for power. On some delicate policies (such as the reversal over NATO or economic policies) and over a prolonged period of time, this instrumental and disciplined party provided crucial help for the government in rallying acceptance from citizens. But its growing internal rigidity, its incapacity for circulating information and monitoring its leaders, its lack of internal criticism, and the opacity of its internal politics became eventually very damaging, both for the government and for the long-term interests of the party. Thus it played an impotent role in the string of scandals that emerged in the 1990s.

The internal evolution of parties became a growing public concern during the 1990s, while their discredit in public opinion rose. Partisan disaffection became an important issue in western European politics during the decade, although this disaffection was often unrelated to the internal democracy of the organizations. As a result, different formulas with which to change their internal life and increase their attraction were discussed – none highly imaginative or successful. In Spain, the constitution of 1978 declared parties to be "a fundamental instrument for political participation" and required that "their internal structure and operation must be democratic" (Article 6). Thus, when the PSOE promised a "new democratic impulse" in the elections of 1993, this included a law promoting such internal democracy within parties, protecting the rights of activists, and reforming party finances and electoral lists. Some of the party leaders had come to accept that internal party politics could hamper not the information of citizens on politicians but the information of politicians on citizens and on themselves – that is, their rational anticipation of accountability. Following these elections, the PSOE formed a minority government with the support of the Catalan nationalists; the law was drafted but it was never passed, either because of incapacity or unwillingness. It is indeed difficult to imagine why politicians would want to transform parties from instruments of power into potential arenas for democratic accountability.

Let us now examine more closely politicians' strategies in critical conjunctures. These strategies will be addressed to the two

---

[13] Speech by Felipe González to the "Autumn School" of the PSOE, Madrid, October 1986, and statement of González in a meeting of the Federal Executive Committee held on March 20, 1990.

principals, the party activists and the voters, and will try to manipulate information and monitoring, both internally in the organization and externally among citizens. Rather than allowing bottom-to-top internal monitoring within the party, which would be facilitated by competition for the leadership, incumbents will try to transform the party into an instrument for the external manipulation of citizens. They will also use political explanations strategically in order to structure public opinion and shore up political support for the politicians who provide the account and for the unpopular policies.[14]

1. A first strategy consists of concealing policies – that is, preventing a critical dimension of politics from emerging in the public realm. The strategies will try to extend total opacity over such policies, which might have to do with actions or nonactions. Nonactions by governments refer to the exclusion of potential issues from the political agenda, knowing that public opinion would force them to take unwanted decisions. Pollution or poverty are well-known examples of issues that were in the limbo of politics over a long time (Bachrach and Baratz 1970; Crenson 1971; Lukes 1974; Gaventa 1980). When a latent issue enters the public domain, it is normally as the result of political struggles in which segments of the population, extramural actors, and different agencies of political pluralism confront governments. These confrontations illuminate previously unknown facts, extend information, augment public sensitivity over the issue, and eventually help voters in assessing the performance of governments. Actions, on the contrary, refer to underground initiatives and hidden faces of power, public knowledge of which governments will try to avoid. Examples are numerous: they often refer to affairs of security and defense, usually protected under the label of "reasons of state." But they extend to many other issues: three recent examples are bovine spongiform encephalopathy in Great Britain, the public provision of AIDS-contaminated blood supplies in France and Japan, and the Iran-Contra affair in the United States.[15]

[14] The impact of such explanations will, of course, depend on the verisimilitude of the accounts, the politicians who provide them, and the different predispositions of voters. See Stone 1989; Kuklinski and Hurley 1996; McGraw and Hubbard 1996.

[15] Wintrobe defines as a typical "Iran-Contra" strategy one in which politicians first break the law, then lie to the public, and finally, if discovered, blame the whole affair on the unauthorized actions of subordinates (Wintrobe 1993).

The illegal financing of parties (and the associated political corruption) may be considered as another illustration of underground political activity. Hidden over a long time, the use of under-the-counter commissions, false receipts, and a wide panoply of predatory instruments related to executive power as a method of financing the parties (and as a source of personal enrichment) has turned into a major issue in many democracies. Its political impact has recently been dramatic in Japan, South Korea, and southern Europe. In Italy, over several decades party bureaucracies were transformed into Asiatic satrapies, into *nomenklaturas* that used every public resource as private property (Flores D'Arcais 1990). In France, Greece, and Spain, the presence of the Socialist parties in government after a long exclusion from power, presenting themselves as holders of moral banners, made revelations about their involvement in illegal finances particularly scandalous.

Let us look a bit more closely at the Spanish case as an example that has many similarities with other experiences. The illegal financing of parties emerged publicly as an issue in January 1990, with a scandal over the enrichment of the brother of the vice-president of the government, Alfonso Guerra, which gradually revealed a complex network for the illegal financing of the Socialist Party and was followed by a string of successive scandals over the following five years.[16] From the initial scandal onward, the issue was brought into the open by the press and then by the judiciary.[17] The opposition only followed when the issue was already on the agenda, and it stayed silent about its similar underground economic activities.[18] Parliament only debated, more or less heatedly, what was already being discussed outside it. This

---

[16] These scandals involved the underground activities of Juan Guerra, brother of the deputy leader of the party and vice-president of the government; Filesa, a company set up by several members of the party close to the secretary of administration; Luis Roldán, director general of the Civil Guard; Gabriel Urralburu, president of the regional government of Navarra and secretary general of the party in the region.

[17] There is a good study that compares the evolutions of the Juan Guerra affair and other scandals under different regimes and shows the very different role played by the press: see Jiménez 1995.

[18] These activities were revealed in three affairs of illegal finances: they involved the mayor of Burgos; Rosendo Naseiro, the national treasurer of the Popular Party; Gabriel Cañellas, president of the regional government of Baleares.

limited role of the opposition and Parliament was due, on the one hand, to the existence of a monolithic party with a parliamentary majority that blocked any investigation; on the other, to inter-partisan complicity. As the leading political analyst of *El País* wrote, "denunciations for illegal financing affect the great majority of political parties. . . . The normal operation of representative institutions is paralyzed or obstructed when all (or nearly all) parties collude in a strategy of concealment or silence" (Pradera 1993). The result was that the provision of information for political accountability was mostly due to the press and the judges.

What did the accused politicians do? Their strategies were directed toward the party and toward public opinion. And the first reaction was the use of "denials" (McGraw, Best, and Timpone 1995): that is, the denial that any offense had been committed. In other words, the agent first reacted by denying to the suspicious principal that he had been involved in illegal activities for his own profit using agency privileges. Defensive strategies directed toward the party tried to quell internal protest and suppress demands for internal accountability stemming from potential competitors for organizational power. In fact, the underground economy of the party had been a secret affair, used to finance not just elections but control over the organization. It was based on the opacity of internal party politics, sectarianism, and informal nuclei of power. As none of the elected bodies knew about such economic activities, denials were first addressed to them, then to the party as a whole, and finally to Socialist voters.

Evidence was declared to be false, and the sources of information were discredited. The fact that many media had been involved in virulent antisocialist campaigns helped this strategy for some time. Conspiracies, which did in fact exist,[19] and external enemies were denounced; a rhetoric of "them against us" was systematically used to rally support. "Us" involved stressing identity, a history of past struggles, loyalty, and "partisan patriotism." "Them" comprised a threatening and dark coalition of adversaries:

---

[19] The conspiracies were organized with great skill and vast resources. They were mostly financed by a banker, Mario Conde, imprisoned after the Bank of Spain discovered a major fraud, and spearheaded by a newspaper, *El Mundo*, and its editor, Pedro J. Ramírez. Such conspiracies tried to force the government to drop charges against Conde. They found the cooperation of some strongly antisocialist magistrates and public prosecutors. The goal, eventually, was to bring down the government. See Ekaizer 1996.

powerful sectors of the press, the judiciary, big business, banks. The politicians involved exhibited, to use Michels's (1962: 218) words, "a notable fondness for arguments drawn from the military sphere. They demand, for instance, that, if only for tactical reasons, and in order to maintain a necessary cohesion in face of the enemy, the members of the party must never refuse to repose perfect confidence in the leaders they have freely chosen for themselves."

The party, which had been unable to exert monitoring (i.e., to detect what was going on), was now unable to play any role as mediator between citizens and politics. It was, most of the time, an internally manipulated instrument that served to manipulate citizens – that is, an obstacle to democratic accountability. Only gradually, as the scandal continued, did internal tensions increase. But dissident voices were accused of complicity with the enemy, of being "victims of the Stockholm syndrome."[20] That is, the reaction tried to prevent "voice" and restrict internal options to "exit" or "loyalty." After a bitter discussion in the Federal Executive Committee, in which once again informers were discredited and information on the scandal denied, a report written to González denounced "the sectarian tendencies and paranoid outbursts referring to alleged internal enemies. . . . They see enemies everywhere, generate vague and infamous suspicions on supposed accomplices."[21] The internecine struggle went on for four years; the result was that, although Guerra and his followers were able to win the 1990 congress of the party, their power slowly declined. Thus, Guerra was sacked as vice-president in March 1991, and, although he survived as deputy leader in the 1994 congress, his position became minoritarian. This internal change in the party was mostly due to the divergent views of González and Guerra about the model of the party and the strategies of accountability, to the growing evidence about what had been going on, to the succession of additional scandals, and to the increasing disaffection of public opinion.

Whenever hidden policies emerge in the open as scandals, politics becomes a battle for public opinion (Lang and Lang 1983). In this Spanish example, the initial strategy of politicians toward citizens consisted also of the denial of information and the dis-

---

[20] These were accusations formulated by Alfonso Guerra in a meeting of the Federal Executive Committee held on September 12, 1990.

[21] Document written by the author to Felipe González, September 15, 1990.

175

crediting of informants. An argument that was repeatedly used in the battle for public opinion was that no political responsibilities could be accepted until penal responsibilities had been established. Only then could the principal expect the agent to resign or dismiss him on fair grounds. The contrary would make politicians very vulnerable to defamation, accusations without proof, and public trials without guarantees. It would thus be easy for powerful extraparliamentary actors to throw from office politicians backed by the popular vote. This is an argument that may end up, as I argued earlier on, opposing democracy to pluralism. The consequence is also an extraordinary politicization of justice and a judicialization of politics.

Over time, however, as the accumulation of evidence became overwhelming and additional scandals erupted, the strategy gradually shifted to "excuses" (McGraw, Best, and Timpone 1995): that is, to the rejection of full or partial responsibility. The problem was presented as one of isolated individual corruption, rather than of illegal partisan activities: a "scapegoat strategy." Although the number of "scapegoats" actually became quite large, the leadership never accepted any institutional wrongdoing, although it was also unable to tell a convincing story of what had actually happened. Finally, the strategy tried to minimize electoral punishment by emphasizing the resulting costs to the voters themselves. The opposition, as the alternative agent, was accused of being involved in similar practices. If the choice on this matter was between Scylla and Charybdis, then the principal ought to look at other dimensions of politics, such as leadership, policies, and traditional partisan identities.

The electoral defeats of incumbents in Greece in 1989 and France in 1993 were largely the product of popular rejection of similar scandals. In Spain, however, the government was able to survive a general election in 1993, largely due to the remaining popularity of González, his promise to "regenerate" the party and politics, sympathy with some governmental policies, and mistrust toward the opposition. But the impact of the economic scandals was important: at the time of elections, 89% of the people thought that very much or considerable corruption existed in Spanish politics; 56% believed that it was present in every party, while 34% thought that its incidence was greater in some of them. Of the latter, 71% considered that it was particularly concentrated in the Socialist Party. Another survey also carried out in 1993 revealed, however, that 64% viewed the opposition in bad terms. But the string of scandals continued. In 1995, corruption was the main political concern for 36% of Spaniards, preceded only by unemployment and terrorism.[22] The consequence was that the government could not survive the following election, held in 1996. But, as had been the case in Greece, the defeat was limited: the Socialists managed to maintain 37.5% of the vote, against 38.8% won by the Popular Party.

2. Let us now turn to what politicians do when they try to transform unpopular policies into palatable ones, thus avoiding sanctions from citizens. I will assume that governments have mandates that are not controversial: that is, that they are not tied by a narrow electoral victory, that they dispose of sufficient executive and legislation power. As agents, politicians will try to have unpopular policies that do not correspond to electoral undertakings assessed according to "rules of exception" rather than to "rules of transgression" (Schedler n.d.). That is, they will argue that the former are due to unforeseen conditions that justify the violation of promises, and will deny that they fooled voters ex ante with inconsistent, unrealistic, or deceptive pledges.[23] The new position may also be presented as a display of "statesmanship." As Salmon (1993: 31) has noted, "the hallmark of statesmanship often consists in a leader bypassing his or her party . . . supporting or implementing policies that are disliked both by it and by public opinion." And the strategies deployed to persuade the principal, citizens, will be either prospective or retrospective. In the first case, the incumbent will wish to obtain the support of the principal before embarking on a policy course so far unpopular. That is, it will try to influence public opinion in order to appear as responsive when undertaking initiatives that carry political risks. In the second case, the incumbent will not try to influence the policy preferences of citizens, but to survive the costs of unpopular policies at election time through justifications and compensations. The policy initiatives will not depend on the support that these find

---

[22] The figures are from surveys of DATA, S.A., in May–June 1993 (for the Spanish team of the Comparative National Election Project, led by José Ramón Montero and Richard Gunther), and the Centro de Investigaciones Sociológicas, December 1993 and April 1995.

[23] "Rules of exception" refer to changed circumstances, new information, modification in voters' preferences, or popular opposition to specific parts of the program. See Schedler n.d.

among citizens, but the government will try to minimize electoral costs.

In both the prospective and the retrospective cases, the bluntness of the electoral choice can be used strategically by the government; this is so when the issue space is multidimensional and/or when the opposition is not trusted. Although situations are analytically different, they may have similar substantive implications for how agents can behave. I argue that, in the Spanish case, because a majority of voters favored positions of the PSOE in different dimensions of policy and because, even if they disagreed with the party's position on a critical issue, they trusted the government more than the right, they eventually had little choice when votes had to be cast. I focus here on the strategies of political survival of the government, hardly on why it would decide to follow an unpopular policy. It could well be argued that the government chose an intertemporal trade-off (costs today vs. benefits tomorrow) and that, even if unresponsive, it was representative: that is, if voters had been an assembly of self-governing citizens with the same information as the government, they would have made a similar choice. I am only concerned here with the strategical management of policy choices that are politically risky – with the strategies of survival deployed by an agent that tries to persuade the principal ex ante or ex post to accept such policy choice.

There is substantial empirical evidence on governments' capacity to mold public opinion, in spite of political competitors and media interested in the contrary and capable of providing alternative information to citizens. Page and Shapiro (1983, 1992), for instance, have shown that 25% of 357 significant changes in policy preferences in the United States between 1935 and 1979 were due to such influence of the government; they have also examined more closely the official rhetoric, and the use of lies and deception in several cases having mostly to do with foreign policy. In fact, this area of policy seems to provide a large number of cases of prospective manipulation. And referenda are a typical instrument used by governments to obtain public backing before undertaking either a risky initiative or a reversal in promised policy courses. European integration provides examples, such as those of Great Britain in 1974, Denmark and France in 1992 and 1993. I will examine here the Spanish referendum over NATO membership, held in 1986, as an illustration of the agent's capacity to influence the principal's view of what the latter's best interests are.

Spain had joined NATO in May 1982, a decision taken by a conservative government widely expected to be routed in elections due only a few months later. The decision was backed by Parliament, with the opposition of the Socialist and Communist parties. This opposition reflected a wide hostility toward NATO in Spanish society, largely due to a long history of international isolation, a military agreement between the U.S. and Spanish governments under Francoism, and an unsuccessful negotiation with the European Community since the return to democracy. Thus, in October 1981, when Parliament debated the decision of the government, only 18% of citizens supported it, while 52% rejected NATO membership.[24] The Socialist Party argued that the admission of Spain would increase international tensions, carry costs without benefits for the country as it would not provide protection against its main security risks nor contribute to membership in the European Community, and was of sufficient importance to call a referendum on it. In the parliamentary debate González committed himself to call a referendum on NATO if the Socialists were to win the next elections. Such positions were confirmed by the congress of the PSOE held in November 1981. But membership had been completed at the time of the elections, in October 1982. In the electoral manifesto, the PSOE maintained the commitment of the referendum and promised to freeze entry into the integrated military command of NATO until citizens had decided on the issue of membership.

When the Socialists won the elections the question no longer was whether to enter into NATO but whether to leave it. The dilemma was substantially different: as González put it, "not getting married is less traumatic than getting divorced." The traumas of divorce referred to its effects on membership in the European Community and on international tensions over the deployment of Pershing II and Cruise missiles. Foreign leverage (particularly exercized by Helmut Kohl) used these arguments quite forcefully, in order to both maintain Spain in NATO and replace the referendum by a general election. But González also used uncertainty with skill: while he expressed solidarity with western European governments that were facing domestic problems over the deployment of the "euromissiles," he exerted

---

[24] Survey of *El País*, October 1981. There is an interesting book on Spanish politics and NATO: see Val 1996.

strong pressure on these governments to accelerate the admission of Spain as a member of the European Community. As a result, the European summits of Stuttgart and Fontainebleu, held in June of 1983 and 1984, opened the doors to membership.

So the government faced two dilemmas: whether to remain in NATO or to leave the Alliance, and whether to call a referendum or to replace it with a general election. And it had to respond to the party and to the electorate. The order of decisions of the government was as follows: the party had to be convinced first, then the electorate; the policy position had to be made clear first, then the decision on the referendum would be taken examining the reaction of public opinion. Of course, the problem of the government was that, in opposition, it had made strong promises, that the context had now changed, and that it perceived the situation differently. If it were to take Spain out of NATO, the external costs would be serious; if it were to break its pledges, its electoral support and the party's cohesion would be damaged. But it had two cards to play: the first was the progress on admission to the European Community; the second, that the conservative opposition wanted to keep the country in NATO.

In the fall of 1984, negotiations over European Community membership were at an advanced stage. Although France had raised most of the difficulties ever since Spain requested admission in 1977, Mitterrand now declared that Spain would be a member of the community as of January 1, 1986. In a parliamentary debate on the State of the Nation at the end of October 1984, González unveiled the position of the government, which defended the permanence of Spain in NATO. The change of course was defended with three main arguments: first, the situation itself had changed, and the consequences of exit were very different from those of not entering; second, external constraints were powerful, as European security arrangements had to be stable and a country that wanted to be part of western European institutions had to share defense policies as well; third, the position of the government entailed compensations that made the policy package acceptable. These compensations included a withdrawal of U.S. troops from the military bases that had been established in Spain since 1953, under Franco; independence from the integrated military command of NATO; and a pledge that no nuclear weapons would be stored in Spanish territory. That is, the package emphasized the inevitability of the decision, the remaining autonomy on defense, the minimization of costs, and the benefits of "Europeanization." Eventually, the position of the government was presented in terms of the general, nonpartisan interest (the slogan was *En interés de España*). The conservative opposition, however, rejected joining the government on this platform: it opposed the restrictions to full membership in NATO and the possibility of calling a referendum, and, hoping to put the government in a tight spot, declared that it would campaign for abstention.

So the government could not play the second card, and the Socialists were on their own. Convincing the party was not very difficult: González had vast and solid loyalties, and the control of the leadership was very strong. A congress held in December 1984 backed the government: while most members (76%) of the former Federal Executive Committee were reelected, González won 71% of the votes for his new policy on NATO and over 80% for every other issue discussed. Thus the organizational weapon was ready to be used to rally voters. They, however, were less easy to convince. After the policy reversal of the PSOE, in October 1984, the distribution of views on NATO among citizens did not vary, with 52% against membership and only 19% in favor of remaining in the alliance.[25]

The consequence was that the second dilemma of whether to call the referendum or replace it by a general election became dramatic. After the change in the policy position, influential actors strongly defended abandoning the pledge to take it to the popular vote: foreign prime ministers, domestic bankers, businessmen, newspaper editors, and politicians argued that simply to call a referendum on such an issue would be an irresponsibility and that a defeat that appeared as likely would be a catastrophe. The decision on the referendum was then postponed for some time. But shortly after Spain joined the European Community in June 1985, the government started the last year of its mandate. Polls taken in October and November 1985 indicated that two-thirds of citizens demanded to vote in a referendum on NATO, that 46% of them opposed membership in the alliance, and that the proportion of supporters remained at 19%.[26] It was clear that the referendum could be lost. But popular exigencies for the government to call it

[25] Survey of *El País*, October 1984.

[26] The figures are from polls of Sofemasa and the Centro de Investigaciones Sociológicas carried out in October and November 1985.

increased, rather than diminished, and the government did not know the electoral costs and the general political discredit that dropping the pledge on the referendum would entail. Additional considerations were also expressed in an internal document written to González:

> The credibility of democracy is at stake. It is not only a problem of personal credibility: it affects the whole political system. About 70% of citizens demand to be consulted through a referendum. It is true that the results are uncertain, and this uncertainty will remain until the very end. But most important is that citizens are ready to listen to reasons, and we must provide them. Our society today is particularly sensitive to Europe: it understands that membership entails costs, but is ready to accept them. People demand information and leadership. And while they may have confidence in you, they demand to be consulted. On this issue, a gap between what Parliament might decide and the preferences of society would be very damaging for Spanish politics as a whole.[27]

Eventually the government decided to be responsive prospectively, rather than accountable retrospectively – that is, to call a referendum in March 1986, rather than include the issue among the many others on which it would be held accountable at the time of the next election, due a few months later. The result of the referendum was not binding, but the government assured citizens that it would comply with it. It tried to obtain a mandate for a change of policy course that was very unpopular. The logic it used was "you will see in the future that what we want to do is best for you, but we need your acquiescence first." Probably such initiative can only be undertaken by governments and prime ministers still largely untainted from the tenure of office, confident that they can mobilize voters into supporting something different from their initial preferences.

Such mobilization was not easy. In the last month, support for NATO increased only from 21% to 26%, and opposition declined only from 39% to 36%.[28] The visible mobilization corresponded overwhelmingly to the anti-NATO coalition, while the conservatives were using the occasion to discredit the government. And while the pro-Socialist press was torn by its traditional pacifist

[27] Document written by the author to Felipe González, November 22, 1985.
[28] Surveys of Instituto Alef on February 2–4 and February 28 to March 1–3, 1986.

stance and the dramatic situation of the government, the right-wing press was much more active in attacking the PSOE and González than in defending NATO membership. Facing a very likely defeat, the Socialists intensified their campaign over the last two weeks. They insisted very much on all the previous arguments: that, due to the changed circumstances, the external constraints, and the compensations, the position of the government was the best possible option, that the others entailed serious costs, and that "Europeanization" was at stake. But they increased the drama with two additional resources: the resignation of González as prime minister in case of defeat, and the risk of an unpopular opposition throwing the government out. The campaign thus became plebiscitarian, facilitated by the conservatives' strategy. The confusion of citizens, as a principal being required by its agent to change its policy preference, was considerable: they were uncertain about the true nature of the external constraints, the costs of sticking to the initial preference, the altruism or opportunism of the opposition. And although the *horror vacui* in case of the government being defeated was very extensive, the uncertainty lasted until the very last moment: the final published survey before voting day predicted that the government would get only between 40% and 46% of the votes, while the "no" vote would reach between 52% and 56%.[29]

The vote eventually backed the government: 53% supported its position, and 40% rejected it. A postreferendum survey revealed how close it had nevertheless been:[30] 27% of the voters had made up their decision in the last three days, and an additional 21% in the last two to three weeks. The percentages were similar for the electorate as a whole and for voters of the PSOE in the earlier general election of 1982. Only 12% of the voters declared that they had voted yes because they had always believed that Spain should join NATO. The reasons of the government had a clear influence on voters: 44% had been convinced that its position best represented the general interest (against 30% who had not); more particularly, 27% of those who voted yes argued that they had done so because Spain had to share the responsibility of European defense, and 17% because of the restrictive conditions on NATO

---

[29] Reported by *El País*, March 6, 1986. Similar results were predicted by surveys of Emopública, Sigma Dos, Aresco, Técnicas de Comunicación.

[30] Survey of the Centro de Investigaciones Sociológicas, March 1986.

membership that the government had established. Former PSOE voters more frequently provided reasons of loyalty: in 41% of the cases they had voted yes because that meant supporting their party or the government. Their support was crucial for the final result: they provided 67% of the yes vote; in contrast, former voters of the Popular Party, the centrists, and the Communist Party represented only 7%, 5%, and 1% respectively. The government had won by mobilizing its previous electorate.

A few months later, in June 1986, the PSOE again won the general elections, with 44% of the vote and an absolute majority of the seats. This percentage was four points below its 1982 result. According to a postelection survey,[31] of those previous Socialist supporters who switched their vote to another party or to abstention, only 28% had voted yes in the NATO referendum; the rest had mostly voted no (47%), abstained, or provided a blank vote (16%). So the policy change had a cost for the government, albeit limited. And honoring the pledge to call a referendum had carried serious risks indeed. The government was able to survive them with a strategy that emphasized changes in circumstances, external constraints, compensations, and the costs that punishing the incumbents would carry for the voters. So the agent adapted the principal to the former's policy preference and could claim to be prospectively responsive.

3. The strategies of a government as agent vis-à-vis its citizens as principal are much more often addressed to the latter's retro-spective evaluation at election time than to its prospective support for embarking on a risky policy course. Referenda are exceptional initiatives; strategies for surviving unpopular policies, betrayed promises, and political reversals at election time are, on the contrary, part of what politics is normally about. I will not discuss why politicians follow such paths: they may have made opportunist electoral promises that they never intended to fulfill; they may have had access to new information; the "objective conditions" may have unexpectedly changed; the constraints may be over-whelming. Governments, for whatever reason, might think that popular but inefficient policies will eventually generate more political costs than unpopular but efficient ones. Eventually, citizens' preferences will be temporally inconsistent; if the government is responsive, its electoral support will suffer when

[31] Survey of the Centro de Investigaciones Sociológicas, July 1986.

184

the time of being held accountable comes. Over the past fifteen years many governments have undertaken economic policies that combined in different ways the betrayal of electoral promises, unpopularity, and also poor performance. Yet their political consequences have not been inevitably disastrous. The principal appears to have considered that performance was not attributable to the agent, that the latter was doing as best he could, that alternative courses of action or another agent would lead to worse material outcomes. How can the agent influence such benevolent considerations?

I shall examine, by way of illustration, the Spanish experience of economic policies between 1982 and 1996. The Socialist government had not made promises comparable with those of the PS in France or the PASOK in Greece before their electoral victories of 1981. It did not commit itself to vast nationalizations, state- and demand-led growth, or irreversible steps toward socialism or *changer la vie*. But it promised growth and the creation of 800,000 jobs over four years. Its record on economic growth was rather satisfactory: over that period, the average annual rate was 2.4%, an improvement over the rate of 0.6% in the previous four years, and equivalent to that of the European Community as a whole. In contrast, its performance over jobs was dramatic: the unemployment rate went up 3.7 percentage points, reaching 21.2% of the active population.[32] Cheibub and Przeworski (1996) have shown that unemployment is the only outcome that appears to affect the political survival of heads of government in parliamentary democracies. Yet after his initial electoral victory of 1982, González was able to win three consecutive elections – in 1986, 1989, and 1993.

The paradox not only lies in the "objective condition" of high unemployment but in the "subjective condition" of a deep unpopularity of the government's economic policies. We may divide the Spanish experience into four main phases: first, harsh economic adjustment and tough economic conditions (1982–85); second, rapid growth and intense job creation (1986–91); third, sharp economic deterioration and growing unemployment (1992–94); and, fourth, renewed economic growth and lower unemployment (1995 and 1996). No clear connection existed between such

---

[32] The figures on economic performance over time are from *Economie Européenne* (1995: tables 3 and 10, pp. 102 and 116).

"objective conditions," "subjective conditions" (i.e., popular evaluation of the economic situation and of economic policies), and
political support for the government. Pessimism over the economy
and hostility toward economic policies were always considerable,
but much less so in the first period of hardship, when voters
were clearly prospective and their views on the economy were
influenced by their hopes in the new government. At the end of this
first period, in June 1986, the PSOE won its second election, with
21.2% of the active population unemployed. In the following phase
of prosperity, economic policies became much more unpopular.
When new elections were called in October 1989, the annual rate
of growth had stood on average at 5.2%, while unemployment had
fallen by 4 percentage points. Support for the government fell by 5
percentage points of the overall vote, although it managed to win
for the third time. In the following phase of economic crisis, growth
fell to 1.4% on annual average and unemployment went up again
to 22.8% of the active population. This time such deterioration was
reflected in a massive pessimism about economic conditions and
an intense hostility toward economic policies. Yet the government
managed to win again for a fourth time, in June 1993. Then, after
two years of strong economic recovery, the PSOE was thrown out
of power in March 1996.

Economic policies were disliked both by the party and the
electorate, and performance had no clear influence on their views.
On the contrary, social policies were always more popular and
their support, rather than weaken, increased over time. Let us
consider, for example, popular assessments of the evolution of
education, health care, and the economy at four points in time. In
1986, after a long crisis and when an economic recovery was
starting, only 20% of citizens believed that the economy had
improved over the past years, while the percentages for education
and health care were 52% and 46% respectively. In 1988, in the
middle of a phase of strong growth and job creation, positive
assessments of the economy went up to 31% (still below negative
ones, which amounted to 35%), but represented only 13% for
employment policies (negative ones reached 46%). The views on
education and health care hardly varied: the percentages of
positive assessments were 52% and 41%. In 1993, in the middle
of a new recession, only 29% of citizens considered economic
policy as "good," while the percentage for education policy was
61%. Finally, in 1995, when economic growth had picked up again,

only 20% of people thought that the economy had improved, but the corresponding percentages for education and health care were 68% and 65%.[33]

Voters tended to support the government if they approved of social policies, even if they disliked economic policies, and this was quite independent from the economic cycle. The same happened within the party, where the ministers of the economy were always unpopular. Their power was only a delegation of González, who used to recall the advice of Olof Palme that the prime minister ought to back the minister of the economy in 98% of the occasions [sic]. González also used social policies to defend his economic policy both within the party and toward public opinion. His arguments were that there was little margin for options in macro-economic management; that, although economic efficiency was a means for social policies, it was also their necessary requisite; and that the political identity of the government depended not on a distinct macroeconomic program but rather on choices over social policies. That the combination between social and economic policies was not an easy one is reflected in the following report written to González:

> In a first moment, a governmental discourse based on technical rationality dazed our supporters. To listen to members of a socialist government speaking of liquid assets or the stational evolution of M-3 produced astonishment. The government not only connected with demands for social reform, but it also seemed to master cryptical knowledge. This impact has now vanished. Unemployment, conflict over industrial reconversion, failed concertation with unions, strikes, insecurity: all this has eroded the faith in our quasi-thaumaturgical virtues. On the contrary, we now have an image of "job destroyers." True, in the name of a future recovery, but we do not explain well why we should have hope in the future. Our policies appear considerably distant and indifferent regarding the anguish of so many of our citizens; we are far from expressing sufficient concern over their conditions. The government seems to consider itself the only economically rational agent. To declare that there is no alternative macroeconomic policy is a terrible expression of pragmatism. If this is so, then we have to establish the differences in a lot of other policies. These differences are so far not sufficient enough. We must reinforce our fairer and more

---

[33] Surveys of Centro de Investigaciones Sociológicas, May 1986, February 1988, April 1995, and of DATA, S.A., May–June 1993.

humane policies: this is what was expected from us, and this is what is still expected.[34]

Anticipating elections, governments look at opinion polls and organize their strategies accordingly. In the Spanish case, the government knew that when citizens considered its record in office, they sympathized more with social policies. The campaigns thus gave more prominence to this dimension of accountability. The strategy thus resembled what Nagel (1993) has called "reinforcing the winning dimension" – a heresthetical device used by incumbents in order to maintain a winning majority. The result was that, when asked in postelection surveys about their main reason for supporting the Socialists, a large proportion of voters answered its overall policy record: the percentages were 29% in 1986, 37% in 1989, 23% in 1993, when popular social policies could successfully compensate for the more unpopular aspects of such a record.

The government also knew that, in a *démocratie du public*, the attraction of the leader is important: thus, González was a major factor in the campaigns. The percentages of Socialist voters who declared that González had been their main reason for supporting the government were 22% in 1986, 14% in 1989, 23% in 1993.[35] But perhaps the most crucial influence of leadership was on the undecided voters. This was clearly revealed in a panel study of the 1993 general election: surveys had indicated since January 1992, with few exceptions, that the PSOE was behind the conservative Popular Party in electoral support, and the prediction that the government would be defeated lasted until the very last day. Eventually the PSOE won by a difference of 4 percentage points. Its victory was due to a last-minute decision of a substantial proportion of the electorate; as Barreiro and Sánchez-Cuenca have shown, these voters were situated on the left, most of them being former supporters of the party unhappy with the policy record of the government, and they eventually rallied round González, stimulated by a campaign centered on him (Barreiro and Sánchez-Cuenca 1996). Thus, when election time comes and citizens, as principal, have to evaluate the performance of the agent under conditions of imperfect information, they look for clues. A "good

---

[34] Document written by the author to Felipe González, March 22, 1984.

[35] Postelection surveys of the Centro de Investigaciones Sociológicas, July 1986, November 1989, June 1993.

guy" might lead them to assume that he did his best under conditions that were not totally under his control, and that he pursued the principal's interest as best he could. This consideration might be reinforced by distrust toward the alternative agent. This additional strategy of highlighting the costs for the principal of sanctioning the agent was systematically pursued by the Socialists.

Finally, loyalty to the party and the historical image of the PSOE were important reasons given by Socialist voters to explain their continuing support. If we look at the three elections of 1986, 1989, and 1993, partisan loyalty was what moved 14%, 15%, and 14% of the Socialist electorate to vote for the PSOE; in addition, 20%, 22%, and 24% indicated that the main reason for their vote had to do with the traditional identity of the party (in terms of democracy or the left). As Popkin (1993: 23) argues, "party loyalties are not easily changed. They reflect past political battles that have shaped the ways in which voters thought about politics and government." Thus, the influence of such informational shortcuts rooted in historical images, together with the overall policy record of the government and the personal attraction of the party leader, helps to explain the capacity of the Socialists to survive in office.

To sum up, the Spanish government framed its economic performance with a strategy that used a panoply of different arguments vis-à-vis the party and the electorate to avoid punishment for policies that these two principals thought were not in their best interest:

The Inevitability of Such Policies. This was due to the inheritance of previous governments (*la herencia recibida*): the government presented its tough economic policies as an antidote to previous mismanagement. If they were harsh, that was due to others' mistakes. They were also determined by exogenous constraints. When the government announced its program of economic adjustment, González argued that the government would do by itself what the International Monetary Fund would force it to do otherwise. Later on, the European Community was often used by the government as a justification: that is, as a source of overwhelming economic exigencies referring to antiinflationary policies, fiscal discipline, and industrial reconversion. González was himself more careful in this respect, in order to avoid an anti-European backlash; economic globalization took the place of the

189

European Community, his argument being that even without the Maastricht requirements economic competitiveness would require similar measures. The alternative would be worse: isolation, protectionism, sanctions from the European Community or from the international economic community. The consequence might be called the TINA ("there is no alternative") syndrome: economic conditions would be worse if other policies were implemented. This strategy thus leads to what César Luis Menotti, the Argentinean soccer trainer, called "the shrinking of spaces" (*el achique de espacios*): a reduction of the space for policy options.

The Promise of Light at the End of the Tunnel. That is, things will improve, but only after crossing a "valley of tears." This argument is intertemporal; the trade-off is the opposite to a popular Spanish saying: rather than "bread today, hunger tomorrow" (*pan para hoy, y hambre para mañana*), the promise consists of "hunger today, bread tomorrow." The government made systematic use of such an intertemporal discourse: it used different metaphors, such as "entering the European first division" or "not missing the train of modernity," in order to make it worthwhile crossing the tunnel. Other policies were presented as a risk, as a delay of the end of the problem, as involving worse intertemporal trade-offs because they would lead to a bleaker future.

The Offer of Present Compensations. These consisted of social policies but also of popular political initiatives that no alternative government would allegedly provide (a reform of abortion is an example). As I have argued, the government inserted unpopular policies in more-attractive "policy packages." Social policies tried to reduce hardship, avoid distributional opposition, and build support constituencies. Social and political compensations tried to provide clues about the political identity of the government to disoriented voters, activate associations with historical party images, and attract complicity and understanding among supporters. Sometimes, parliamentary or extraparliamentary confrontations with ideological antagonists over popular policies (such as reforms of education or abortion) served to provide additional clues and gather support from citizens unhappy about other initiatives of the agent.

The Popular Leadership in Contrast to the Mistrusted Opposition. The alternative agent was used over a very long time as a disincentive for the principal to punish the incumbent. When the credit of the opposition is low, either because of its past policy record or poor leadership, the autonomy of governments increases – that is, its accountability diminishes because of the enforcement problem that the principal faces. The historical image of the party, associated with its democratic and leftist past, was used as a powerful symbolic instrument to mobilize voters suspicious of the true identity and intentions of the opposition.

The success of such arguments in defending unpopular economic policies, which is part of the manipulation of accountability, varies according to the situation in which the government finds itself. A new government that undertakes unpopular policies will use more successfully the first two arguments. In such case, the strategy will try to influence a pattern of prospective voting. Voters will attribute hardship to the past, be pessimistic in retrospect, support a government that has taken over after a discredited predecessor even though things are bad, and be optimistic prospectively. But the past is rapidly forgotten, honeymoons do not last long, and voters have a limited memory of past performance. And when a government that has aged launches unpopular policies, it will have to rely more on the last two arguments, which will be handled conservatively: that is, emphasizing the risks of losing progress made over the past years, of missing opportunities, of changing an experienced agent. This strategy will try to induce retrospective voting: it will claim credit for achievements of the past. Voters will be pessimistic, and their support for the government depends a lot on resignation and on whether they see the opposition as worse.

The passing of time did matter for the strategies of the Spanish government. After winning in unexpected fashion in 1993, it followed the same strategy in 1996. The economy was in fact performing much better. But other issues and time had made the government more vulnerable, past achievements less effective, and González less credible. Among such issues, the emergence of the scandals that I discussed earlier had a decisive influence. And yet, insisting on social policies and the leadership of González, the Socialists managed to reduce an initial disadvantage close to 10 percentage points in opinion polls to 1.3 at election time. As agents, incumbent politicians can skillfully manage a repertoire of strategies for manipulating accountability and do well. And if the principal eventually decides to replace them, they will stand by, waiting for the next election, the rapid erosion of memory of the principal, and unhappiness of the latter regarding its choice of a new agent.

Thus, politicians do not face in passivity the uncertain verdict of citizens. They develop typical strategies of survival that are not irrelevant for democratic accountability. Rather than look at principals (i.e., citizens), I have focused on what it is that agents (i.e., incumbent politicians) do, if they are interested in staying in power and maximizing their political autonomy, when their policies are unpopular. What they do is manipulate to their advantage the problems of information, monitoring, and commitment of citizens when assessing whether the incumbent is pursuing their interest, and whether he should be rewarded in elections.

Agents operate in complex scenarios, with multiple interests involved in political struggles and competing to persuade citizens. While this variety of sources of information increases the monitoring capacity of citizens, contradictory information that generates mistrust regarding their reliability may be used by incumbents to their advantage with strategies of discredit. And while the incumbent party is an important aspect of democratic accountability as far as it involves agency relationships between voters and party, activists and leaders, its predominant role in contemporary democracies as an instrument for power (winning elections and protecting the government) serves politicians to manipulate accountability. A party that is both unitary and transparent, democratic and disciplined, is a rare political animal. Most of the time, democratic accountability and political success, both in elections and in office, are not easily compatible. So, difficult choices have to be made.

Unpopular policies may be kept out of the political domain or be publicly known. When a formerly secret policy emerges publicly, incumbents will use strategies of concealment of political responsibility and will mobilize "partisan patriotism" and discipline to get protection under the party's mantle. I have used the example of illegal party finances to illustrate the margin of maneuver of politicians for disorienting citizens and avoiding punishment. In such cases, politicians' collusion may paralyze democratic institutions as mechanisms of accountability. When this happens, as it often does, politicians will surrender their own control to other institutions (the press, the judiciary), and democratic accountability will be distorted.

When governments publicly embark, for whatever reasons, on unpopular policy courses, they have two options. One is to get the ex ante acceptance of citizens, so that, after changing their initial policy preferences, governments may appear as responsive. Referenda are a typical example, and I have examined the strategies of the Spanish government to get an unpopular position over NATO backed by citizens. The other option is to win the ex post approval of citizens at election time, with retrospective strategies. I have discussed, as illustrations, the strategies of the Spanish government for surviving its unpopular economic policies and large unemployment. Both options require that the agent persuades the principal that the policy course is not due to the former's responsibility, but to the inheritance of past administrations, to unexpected changes in "objective conditions," or to overwhelming and unanticipated external constraints. The principal's approval also depends on the discrediting of alternative options, an acceptable intertemporal trade-off, and additional policy initiatives that will make the "package" more palatable. In some circumstances (for instance, a recently elected government), mistrust toward the alternative agent, the historical image of the party, and personal qualities of the incumbent ("leadership," "good guy" image) will be part of the manipulative strategy.

This is not a study of the probabilities of survival that are associated with such strategies. But the illustrations from recent Spanish politics show that this repertoire of strategical resources can be skillfully used. This may help us to understand why incumbents often manage to survive negative "objective conditions," political reversals, and unpopularity. Machiavellian *virtú* is part of the explanation: the fate of politicians is not inexorably tied to their performance, and to some extent they can manipulate accountability. As a result, governments may dispose of "relative autonomy" vis-à-vis citizens. What this means is that, on the one hand, short-term political opportunism is not a necessary condition for survival, and that an agent may work in the long-term interest of the principal; but also, on the other hand, that an agent who has shirked, that is, been a "bad government," may also be rewarded if he is a "good politician."

References

Bachrach, Peter, and Morton S. Baratz. 1970. *Power and Poverty*. Oxford: Oxford University Press.

Barreiro, Belén, and Ignacio Sánchez-Cuenca. 1996. "Análisis del cambio de voto hacia el PSOE en las elecciones de 1993." Instituto Juan March, Madrid. Unpublished manuscript.

Cheibub, José Antonio, and Adam Przeworski. 1996. "Democracy, Elections, and Accountability for Economic Outcomes." Unpublished manuscript.

Commission Européenne. 1995. *Economie européenne*. No. 60. Brussels.

Craig, Patricia. N.d. "The PSOE in Parliament." Instituto Juan March, Madrid. Unpublished manuscript.

Crenson, Matthew A. 1971. *The Un-Politics of Air Pollution*. Baltimore: Johns Hopkins University Press.

Dahl, Robert A. 1970. *After the Revolution? Authority in a Good Society*. New Haven: Yale University Press.

Dalton, Russell. 1988. *Citizen Politics in Western Democracies: Public Opinion and Political Parties in the United States, Great Britain, West Germany and France*. Chatham, N.J.: Chatham House.

Ekaizer, Ernesto. 1996. *Vendetta*. Barcelona: Plaza & Janés.

Ferejohn, John A. 1986. "Incumbent Performance and Electoral Control." *Public Choice* 50: 5–25.

1990. "Information and the Electoral Process." In John A. Ferejohn and James H. Kuklinski, eds., *Information and Democratic Processes*, 3–19. Urbana: University of Illinois Press.

Fiorina, Morris. 1981. *Retrospective Voting in American National Elections*. New Haven: Yale University Press.

Flores D'Arcais, Paolo. 1990. "La democracia tomada en serio." *Claves* 2: 2–14.

Gaventa, John. 1980. *Power and Powerlessness*. Urbana: University of Illinois Press.

Hirschman, Albert O. 1970. *Exit, Voice, and Loyalty*. Cambridge, Mass.: Harvard University Press.

Huber, John D., and G. Bingham Powell Jr. 1994. "Congruence between Citizens and Policymakers in Two Visions of Liberal Democracy." *World Politics* 46: 291–326.

Jacobs, Lawrence R., and Robert Y. Shapiro. 1994. "Studying Substantive Democracy." *PS: Political Science and Politics* 27: 9–16.

Jensen, Michael, and William Meckling. 1976. "Theory of the Firm: Managerial Behavior, Agency Costs, and Ownership Structure." *Journal of Financial Economics* 3: 305–60.

Jiménez, Fernando. 1995. *Detrás del escándalo político*. Barcelona: Tusquets.

Key, Vernon O. 1964. *Politics, Parties, and Pressure Groups*. New York: Crowell.

1966. *The Responsible Electorate*. New York: Vintage Books.

Klingemann, Hans-Dieter, Richard I. Hofferbert, and Ian Budge.

1994. *Parties, Policies, and Democracy*. Boulder, Colo.: Westview Press.

Kuklinski, James H., and Norman L. Hurley. 1996. "It's a Matter of Interpretation." In Diana C. Mutz, Paul M. Snyderman, and Richard A. Brody, eds., *Political Persuasion and Attitude Change*, 125–44. Ann Arbor: University of Michigan Press.

Lang, Gladys E., and Kurt Lang. 1983. *The Battle for Public Opinion: The President, the Press, and the Polls during Watergate*. New York: Columbia University Press.

Lewis-Beck, Michael S. 1988. *Economics and Elections: The Major Western Democracies*. Ann Arbor: University of Michigan Press.

Lukes, Steven. 1974. *Power: A Radical View*. London: Macmillan.

Machiavelli, Niccolò. 1992. *The Prince*. New York: Dover Publications.

Manin, Bernard. 1995. *Principes du gouvernement représentatif*. Paris: Calmann-Lévy.

McGraw, Kathleen M., Samuel Best, and Richard Timpone. 1995. " 'What They Say or What They Do?' The Impact of Elite Explanation and Policy Outcomes on Public Opinion." *American Journal of Political Science* 39: 53–74.

McGraw, Kathleen M., and Clark Hubbard. 1996. "Some of the People, Some of the Time: Individual Differences in Acceptance of Political Accounts." In Diana C. Mutz, Paul M. Snyderman, and Richard A. Brody, eds., *Political Persuasion and Attitude Change*, 145–70. Ann Arbor: University of Michigan Press.

Michels, Robert. 1962. *Political Parties*. New York: Free Press.

Milgrom, Paul, and John Roberts. 1992. *Economics, Organization, and Management*. Englewood Cliffs, N.J.: Prentice-Hall.

Mill, John Stuart. 1991. *On Liberty*. London: Routledge.

Moe, Terry M. 1990. "Political Institutions: The Neglected Side of the Story." *Journal of Law, Economics, and Organization* 6: 213–53.

Nagel, Jack H. 1993. "Populism, Heresthetics, and Political Stability: Richard Seddon and the Art of Majority Rule." *British Journal of Political Science* 23: 139–74.

Norpoth, Helmut, Michael Lewis-Beck, and Jean Dominique Lafay, eds. 1991. *Economics and Politics: The Calculus of Support*. Ann Arbor: University of Michigan Press.

O'Flaherty, Brendan. 1990. "Why Are There Democracies? A Principal Agent Answer." *Economics and Politics* 2: 133–55.

Page, Benjamin I., and Robert Y. Shapiro. 1983. "Effects of Public Opinion on Policy." *American Political Science Review* 77: 175–90.

1992. *The Rational Public: Fifty Years of Trends in Americans' Policy Preferences*. Chicago: University of Chicago Press.

Popkin, Samuel L. 1993. "Information Shortcuts and the Reasoning Voter."

In Bernard Grofman, ed., *Information, Participation, and Choice,* 17–35. Ann Arbor: University of Michigan Press.

Pradera, Javier. 1993. "Jeringas, agendas y silencios. El poder de los medios de comunicación." *Claves* 32: 48–55.

———. 1995. "La maquinaria de la democracia. Los partidos en el sistema político español." *Claves* 58: 16–27.

Riker, William H. 1982. *Liberalism against Populism.* San Francisco: W. H. Freeman.

———. 1986. *The Art of Political Manipulation.* New Haven: Yale University Press.

Salmon, Pierre. 1993. "Unpopular Policies and the Theory of Representative Democracy." In Albert Breton, Gianluigi Galeotti, Pierre Salmon, and Ronald Wintrobe, eds., *Preferences and Democracy,* 13–39. International Studies in Economics and Econometrics, vol. 28. Dordrecht: Kluwer Academic Publishers.

Sappington, David E. M. 1991. "Incentives in Principal-Agent Relationships." *Journal of Economic Perspectives* 5: 45–66.

Sartori, Giovanni. 1987. *The Theory of Democracy Revisited. Part One: The Contemporary Debate.* Chatham, N.J.: Chatham House Publishers.

Schedler, Andreas. N.d. "The Binding Force of Electoral Promises." Unpublished manuscript.

Shapiro, Carl. 1983. "Premiums for High Quality Products as Rewards for Reputations." *Quarterly Journal of Economics* 98: 659–79.

Shapiro, Robert Y., and Lawrence R. Jacobs. 1989. "The Relationship between Public Opinion and Public Policy: A Review." In Samuel Long, ed., *Political Behavior Annual,* 2: 149–79. Boulder, Colo.: Westview Press.

Stimson, James A., Michael B. MacKuen, and Robert S. Erikson. 1995. "Dynamic Representation." *American Political Science Review* 89: 543–65.

Stone, Deborah. 1989. "Causal Stories and the Formation of Policy Agendas." *Political Science Quarterly* 104: 23–35.

Val, Consuelo del. 1996. *Opinión pública y opinión publicada. Los Españoles y el referendum de la OTAN.* Madrid: Centro de Investigaciones Sociológicas.

Wintrobe, Ronald. 1993. "Fourteen Ways to Credibly Escape a Credible Commitment (and Still Be Re-Elected)." In Albert Breton, Gianluigi Galeotti, Pierre Salmon, and Ronald Wintrobe, *Preferences and Democracy,* 247–64. International Studies in Economics and Econometrics, vol. 28. Dordrecht: Kluwer Academic Publishers.

Chapter Six

Party Government and Responsiveness

Political scientists have long written about the prospects of party government – democratic governance wherein citizens choose between programmatic parties to achieve the public policy they desire. They have written, in the main, in a context of concern whether *anything* might mediate citizen preferences into policy, often with the view that parties represented the best hope in a not very promising scenario. This work has a tone that is both wistful and gloomy: wistful because programmatic parties, if only they could spring to life, offer a neat package by which policy responsiveness might be facilitated,[1] gloomy because the prospect for programmatic parties runs afoul of American politics and culture, a dream of the ideal polity only to be realized elsewhere.

In this chapter I revisit this familiar theme, asking whether programmatic political parties can be the mechanism by which citizen preferences become translated into public policy. The topic is worth another visit because (1) the programmatic parties we have prescribed for fifty years seem at last to be an emerging reality of American politics, and (2) we have evidence in hand that responsiveness of a longitudinal sort seems to work, and work pretty impressively. The present context, neither wistful nor gloomy, turns the question on its head. Given the existence of programmatic parties, and given the fact of dynamic responsiveness

---

[1] A note on usage: earlier work and an earlier version of this chapter used the term "representation," where here I employ "responsiveness." While one could drive a conceptual wedge between the two, I treat them as interchangeable. The change to "responsiveness" here is for consistency with other chapters of this volume. That will create some inconsistency here when I refer to the original work by its proper title.

of public policy to citizen preferences, we can ask the more normal scientific question, Are parties the mechanism by which the translation occurs?

This question has some limited answers in the empirical findings of "Dynamic Representation" (Stimson, MacKuen, and Erikson 1995). There the process is captured in a single coefficient in a multivariate model, which suggests that the electoral connection, traditionally conceived, *does* account for some portion of successful policy responsiveness.

We may conceive the relationship in principal-agent terms. The principal, the electorate, wishes policy responsiveness from its agent, the elected policy maker. The agent is motivated to shirk by such things as ideology and commitment to the collective goals of a political party or faction. The principal can sanction shirking behavior through the mechanism of elections. Two models of agent accountability are "adverse selection," whereby agents who have strayed too far are eliminated in the election period following their actions; and "moral hazard," in which the agents themselves enforce the principal-agent relationships by molding their behavior to anticipated preferences of the principal in order to sustain the flow of benefits from the relationship. In adverse selection the sanctioning is effected by principals. In moral hazard it is the behavior of agents that restrains shirking.

Citizen preferences in this model are exogenous relative to current policy activity. But they are allowed to respond to policy at previous occasions. That response is expected to have a negative feedback character, as in the thermostatic conceptions of Durr (1993) and Wlezien (1995). Liberal policy activity at $t - 1$, for example, produces a (weakly) more conservative public at t. This is the expected response of a moderate public to a two-party system in which the two parties do not fully converge – the result of the Downs model in which there is strong elasticity in the ideological tails.[2] With D and R platforms that are "too left" and "too

---

[2] Elasticity at the tails would be expected if those at the extremes are more attuned to ideological distance, for example, because they care more about ideology, or if they are more important to electoral victory than their mere numbers. Both of these conditions are true of American politics. Understanding of and attention to ideology decline as one approaches the middle of the spectrum, and the relative extremes are disproportionately likely to number among the cadre of party workers and to be regular campaign contributors – they are considerably more important than their numbers.

right," the center of public opinion is always moving contrary to the position of the party in power.[3]

The questions for this principal-agency conception become, (1) How well does the agency relationship work, to what degree does the behavior of agents match the preferences of principals? and (2) What mix of adverse selection and moral hazard accomplishes the result? The answers, from the "Dynamic Representation" analysis are (1) that the principal-agent match is exceptionally tight, and (2) albeit with interesting variation between institutions, the moral hazard conception is dominant; agents are much more adept at anticipating the preferences of principals than are principals in sanctioning agent behavior after the fact.

All this is based on analysis of fully aggregated national public opinion and fully aggregated national policy making. Here I step back from that analysis and look more carefully at *political parties* as mediators of electoral signals. I disaggregate the macropolicy indicators to the political parties and ask whether the parties in Congress (also) faithfully represent changes in public opinion. I explore alternative modes of responsiveness in which, on the one hand, the electorate uses the mix of parties to effect its policy preferences (adverse selection) or, on the other, voters act as a deterrent, motivating aspiring politicians to produce responsiveness without (actual) electoral sanctions (moral hazard).

I begin with a summary statement of Dynamic Representation theory and findings.

The Dynamic Representation Setup

Dynamic Representation models the microbehavior of voters and of elected politicians, derives macroproperties of both and a model connecting them, and estimates the model. That is a lot of steps, hard to summarize briefly.

Voters and Electorate

Voters in this conception structure most of their attitudes toward issues of public policy around general orientations toward

[3] In empirical estimations to come, this exogeneity of preferences is enforced by associating current policy activity with lagged public preferences. This crude expedient rules out elite leadership explanations of concurrence between mass and elite; this year's debate may not move last year's preferences.

"government." Whether the issue is control of handguns, regulation of environmental quality, spending to improve public education, or dozens of other policy debates, citizens who like or trust government want more, those who dislike and distrust want less. This is operationalized in the macroconcept, public policy mood, a time series summarizing preferences aggregated over voters and over issues (excepting a few that don't belong). With a mathematics analogous to principal components, the latent mood concept is estimated from data series of all domestic public policy survey questions asked in identical format over time by all survey organizations. This concept and measure stand in for "preferences" in the analysis to come.

Politicians

Elected politicians in this setup care about public policy and about reelection. Typically more extreme in their personal views than those they represent, they face an ubiquitous choice between personal ideal points and most expedient positions on each occasion of policy choice. The distribution of member ideal points is a product of elections, thus ultimately under the control of the electorate. Member calculation of the most expedient position we presume to take account of both static knowledge of constituent preferences and of dynamic information that points to likely changes of relevance to future election prospects. Postulating that politicians act rationally, that they are well informed about global movements in public sentiment, and that consensus exists about those global movements, we predict that strategic politicians will adjust expediency calculations to changing information about preferences and change their behaviors at the margin to adapt. In this "rational anticipation" theory, individual (and, because of consensus, macro-) decision making will track global changes in preference. The result is a dynamic responsiveness of voter preferences independent of election-induced changes.

This is a moral hazard conception. The action in it arises from agents – that is, politicians, who do the anticipating and the adapting. All it requires of the principal, the electorate, is that it threaten sanctions for shirking and *perhaps* every now and then carry out the threat.

Macrospecification

Public policy-making activity is modeled as a function then of public opinion, of current government composition, and of exogenous influences on policy (of which the only candidate is the Vietnam War, which produced more-conservative policy behavior, independent both of opinion and of government composition). Since government composition is endogenous with respect to public opinion, reduced form models are estimated (without composition) alongside full specifications to deal with the separate questions, Does public opinion influence policy making? and By what mechanism?

Measurement of policy making is attacked by way of derived multiple measures of activity that capture diverse meanings and differing threats to validity. The concept then becomes a latent variable in a simultaneous, full-information estimation of structural and measurement models. The estimation technology is the Kalman filter DYMIMIC specification of Engle and Watson (1981) and Watson and Engle (1983), described in detail by Kellstedt, McAvoy, and Stimson (1996).

Summary of Macrofindings

The Dynamic Representation setup is estimated for House and Senate (to be further pursued in this chapter) and also for the presidency and the Supreme Court. The general finding across all is that they *do* respond to changing public preferences as predicted. The mechanism of response varies pretty much as the Founders intended, with (1) the House immensely sensitive to changing currents of public preference, reacting immediately and decisively to every change, (2) the Senate behaving more in line with the electoral connection, not anticipating the public very well, but promptly correcting its position as a result of elections, (3) the presidency both anticipating and following elections, and (4) the Supreme Court responding to global opinion change, but too weakly for any mechanism to receive strong support.

With the benefit of new data in hand and to illustrate this structural estimation, which is a building block of later analyses, I replicate the responsiveness estimations for House and Senate. These are reduced form estimations in order to leave out the effects of party composition so that they can later be empirically determined. For each chamber a model is estimated in which policy making is a function of exogenous variables and simultaneously of measurement models that map the latent concept to four endogenous indicators: (1) median percent of all roll call votes cast for the liberal side of ideologically polarized votes, (2) percent of all votes in which the liberal side wins, (3) a combined measure of ADA and ACA/ACU ratings, and (4) a "key vote" measure that averages median coalition size and "Who wins?" criteria. The metric of the latent dependent variable is unidentified with unrestricted measurement models. Thus it is set to the scale of the median coalition size variable (by fixing the measurement parameters for that indicator), the desired variable for later analyses.[4]

Table 6.1 shows these reduced form estimates for the two chambers. Given measurement scales all in the same percentage metric and quite similar variances, the coefficients are easily interpreted. The opinion coefficient of central interest for responsiveness shows roughly comparable effects across chambers, each unmistakably moved by the influence of changing global preferences. Although the two would show quite different mechanisms at work in full models (i.e., with party composition included), in both cases a little over a third of the variation in policy making is directly attributable to public opinion in these simple models. Latent variable estimates (products of both left- and right-hand-side variables) along with the policy mood variable appear in a summary Figure 6.1. Each of the three will reappear in later analyses.

Old work summarized and updated, I am ready now to proceed with reconceptualizing the setup for a novel focus on parties.

A Model of Party Government

The textbook portrait of American political parties is one of mixed collections of actors who agree at election times to use a

[4] The resulting latent variable estimate, called a state variable, will have the mean and variance of the median coalition indicator but is a function (weighted by empirical communality estimates) of all of the indicators and of the exogenous variables. The results of Table 6.1 will not be directly comparable to those reported in Dynamic Representation because a different indicator (for comparability in analyses to come) is chosen for metric setting.

**Table 6.1. Public Opinion and Public Policy: Kalman Filter Reduced
Form Estimates: Coefficients and Standard Errors (in Parentheses)**

Variables	House of Representatives	Senate
Dynamics (Y_{t-1})	0.247	0.466
	(0.096)	(0.095)
Public Opinion$_{t-1}$	0.375	0.345
	(0.056)	(0.113)
Cumulative Vietnam Deaths	−0.189	
	(0.023)	
Intercept	22.259	9.232
	(4.273)	(8.125)
Number of Cases	39	39
Measurement Model (Communalities)		
Median Liberal Coalition Size	.917	.915
Percent Liberal Wins	.907	.995
Net Group Ratings[a]	.816	.670
Key Vote Average[b]	.554	.449

[a] Scored as average of ADA and ACA/ACU rating reflected in the liberal
direction.
[b] Average of Percent Key Vote Liberal Wins and Key Vote Median Liberal
Coalition size.

common label, but then quickly revert to a diversity of views that
makes contests over public policy direction almost as large within
party groupings as between them. A bit of a caricature by scholars
whose preference for the neatness of European parliamentary
democracy was always apparent, this textbook view exaggerated
intraparty differences relative to interparty ones. The parties have
always had some programmatic character; observers were simply
more impressed with the variety that could be assembled under
one tent than with the fact that the two tents were different. But
things have changed, and what was once merely an exaggeration
is now a simple falsehood.

American political parties are no longer such diverse collections as they once were. Except by the strange comparative

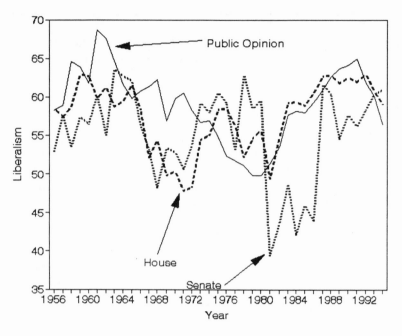

Figure 6.1. Public opinion and estimated latent policy variables for House and Senate: 1956–94

standards that emerge in intraparty contests, most Democrats are liberals, most Republicans conservative. As the differences within parties shrink, the difference between them grows. These are far from novel observations, but we have not fundamentally revised the notion that the American party system is nonprogrammatic.

The evidence is telling. Figures 6.2 (House of Representatives) and 6.3 (Senate) display averages of party aggregate ADA ratings and ACA/ACU ratings (reflected to measure liberalism). These are combined to get beyond the idiosyncrasies of a single rating organization (although it truly doesn't matter) and for a little smoothing to let the over-time pattern emerge more clearly.[5] What we see in both (but more clearly in the Senate) is growing differences between the parties over time as the Republicans become homogeneously conservative, the Democrats homogeneously liberal.

Table 6.2 summarizes the party differences by decade. The largely parallel movements in the two chambers produce party

[5] ACA ratings are unavailable for a few early years where the scale becomes simply the ADA rating.

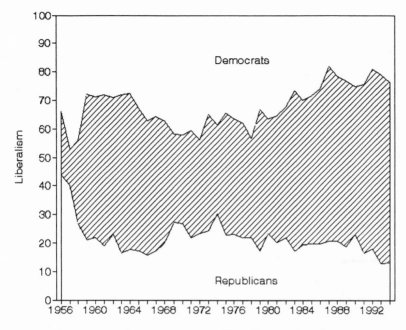

Figure 6.2. House of Representatives liberalism ratings by party

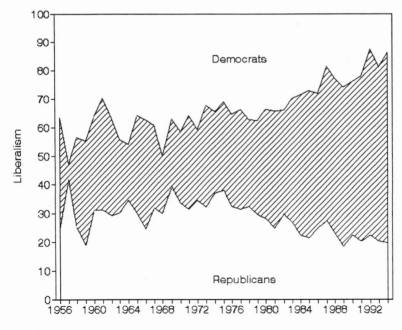

Figure 6.3. Senate liberalism ratings by party

205

Table 6.2. Polarization of Party
Behaviors over Five Decades: Ideological Differences in Party Stance
by Chamber

Decade	House	Senate
1956–59	28.9	28.0
1960–69	47.9	29.5
1970–79	38.1	30.7
1980–89	52.1	47.1
1990–94	60.7	60.9

Note: Cell entries are average between
party differences on scales that are the
average of ADA and reflected ACA/ACU
ratings.

differences that are on average about twice as large in the 1990s
as in earlier periods. The differences now are so large as to near
an upper limit where it is no longer possible to distinguish between
party and ideology in the votes. Although it is swimming against
the tide to assert that American political parties have a programmatic character, it is clearly not swimming against the
evidence. But it is obviously also contrary to that evidence to assert
that the programmatic behavior is timeless.

But all these data are highly aggregated, so a more tangible
illustration may be useful. If a voter looked to the U.S. Senate in
the first year of our analysis and asked, "Are the parties different
or similar?" he or she would have seen mixed evidence. On the
one hand, the distributions of our measure of ideology had
remarkably different central tendencies, Republicans conservative
and Democrats liberal. But on the other hand, it was also the case
that the distributions overlapped one another almost completely.
The most liberal Republican (ADA = 90) was more liberal than all
but fourteen of the forty-seven Democrats. And the most conservative Democrat (ADA = 0) was more conservative than all but
three of the forty-seven Republicans of 1956. One could be
impressed *either* by difference or by similarity. By 1996, in

contrast, the central tendencies were much more dissimilar than in the earlier year. But, more noticeably, the overlap in the range of positions had all but disappeared. The most liberal Republican of that year (ADA = 55) was more liberal than exactly two Democrats (ADA = 40). *And neither the lone liberal Republican nor the two conservative Democrats returned for the 105th Congress.* For the first time we may now say, in the U.S. Senate all Democrats are liberals, all Republicans are conservatives, period. The story of nonprogrammatic parties is now utterly at odds with the data.

A Role for Voters: Do Voters Mix Parties to Achieve Ideal Points?

Begin with the unrealistic assumption that the national electorate is a unitary actor. "It" has policy preferences that are necessarily moderate and, in particular, median. This moderate electorate faces a choice between parties D and R, which are always more extreme than the electorate. If the electorate wishes to see its preferences enacted, its decision rule is obvious. Not having a moderate party to choose, it may only signal its preferences for moderate policies by mixing the too liberal policy program of D with the too conservative program of R.[6] The electorate may approximate its ideal point, E, by choosing the proper mixture of D and R, in this conception, setting the level of α in (1).

$$E = \alpha D + (1 - \alpha)R. \tag{1}$$

Now, the electorate's preferences will change over time, and so we add the minor complication of subscripting E and α:

$$E_t = \alpha_t D + (1 - \alpha_t)R, \tag{2}$$

where E_t is now our concept public policy mood, the ideal point of a unitary electorate. Equation (2) is an ideal type in which the electorate's ideal point E_t is perfectly represented with public policy by programmatic parties that maintain constant programs over time. This is a simple metering problem; the electorate can

---

[6] This idea of moderate electorate balancing ideological parties is developed in the political economy context by Alesina and Rosenthal (1995).

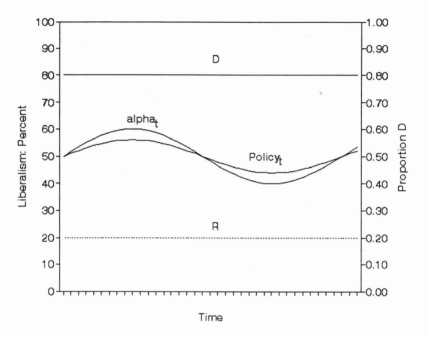

Figure 6.4. Responsiveness by electoral connection: An ideal type where party positions are fixed, but party mix varies

finely adjust to hotter (D: more government) or colder (R: less) to get just the blend it prefers. Figure 6.4 shows this ideal type with hypothetical values. There, constant party positions (D, R) with variable blending (α_t) produces variable policy outcomes.

We can generalize (2) by time subscripting D and R to represent party programs that change over time, which is a party-centered variation of the full "Dynamic Representation" model, an electorate with changing preferences chooses between changing party programs (at the level of individual candidates) to get the policies it prefers. It might succeed either because it chooses the correct mix (α) of D_t and R_t *or* because the parties anticipate E_t and change to produce a representative policy outcome *even with a constant mix*. This is our second ideal type, "rational anticipation," where a constant α and variable party programs produce the representative result, as in (3):

$$E_t = \alpha D_t + (1 - \alpha)R_t \tag{3}$$

and graphed with hypothetical values in Figure 6.5.

208

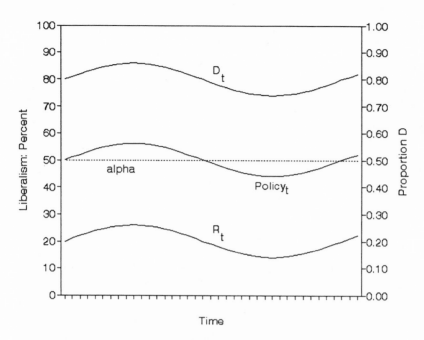

Figure 6.5. Responsiveness by rational anticipation: An ideal type in which party positions vary, but party mix is constant

The major empirical task of this chapter will be an evaluation of equation (2), changing mixtures of constant parties, against equation (3), fixed mixtures of changing parties, as alternative explanations for observed opinion and policy changes.

We do not, of course, have a unitary electorate. At the level of the individual voter facing a single electoral contest, the decision problem is complicated. It isn't particularly problematic that individuals may appear anywhere in the distribution of possible preferences. Movement of the central tendency of the distribution over time will have the "unitary" effect postulated. But it is problematic that individuals are denied the opportunity to mix candidates of both parties in the desired proportion, forced instead for each office to choose D or R.

The logic of metering disappears for individual voters. Limited to a binary choice, the best one can do is alternate D and R over time, a thermostatic control system (Wlezien 1995). But different voter preferences will require different behaviors. Some, whose views approximate one of the parties, will want a steady diet of D or R, others mostly D or mostly R. To work effectively, the system needs a large pool of centrists, indifferent to the D-R choice, who will behave dynamically, voting D when their moderate preferences are violated to the right, or R when they are violated to the left. This requirement is easily met in current American politics. (Probably the parties could not have polarized to the extent they have done had not a very major proportion of moderates first detached themselves from permanent or standing commitments to one side or the other.) Again, we can aggregate the process up to the electorate and recover something like the unitary elector logic.

Elections Evidence

We can resolve the electoral end of this proposition with evidence. If, in fact, the electorate behaves as if it were a unitary decision maker in control of a metering device, measures of its moving ideal points should be closely associated with the mixture parameter, α_t, the proportion of Democrats winning elections for House and Senate. The unitary ideal point is given by our measure of public opinion, public policy mood. The mixture parameter is just election outcomes in seats.

The evidence for mixing is given in Table 6.3. There, regressions of outcomes in Senate (as well as presidential, not shown) elections on public opinion show very strong effects of the expected sort: liberal opinion is associated with Democratic wins. The coefficient on public opinion of 1.01 indicates a one-to-one translation of opinion (with a range of 19 points over the period), strongly leveraging seats (with a 23-point range). The House of Representatives analysis (using percentage seats for comparability) shows a weaker electoral response to changes in public opinion. But even this weaker effect (= .37) is capable of accounting for a seat shift of 7 percent (or 30 seats) between most liberal and most conservative opinion in the historical range, and that is far from a small effect.[7]

I conclude, contrary to a huge literature on individual voting

---

[7] The addition of two elections to the analysis not included in the Dynamic Representation analysis matters for this relationship. The coefficient moved between 1.5 times standard error – an awkward "almost reliable" result – to 2.26 here. Reality hasn't changed much, but the author's burden is eased.

Table 6.3. Democratic Congressional Seats Predicted from Public Policy Mood, Macropartisanship, and Midterm Effects: 1956–94

Variables	House of Representatives	Senate
Seats at t – 1	0.46	0.27
	(0.23)	(0.15)
Public Opinion (Public Policy Mood)	0.37	1.01
	(0.17)	(0.20)
Midterm	–4.93	
	(1.24)	
Democratic Macropartisanship	0.96	1.23
	(0.23)	(0.32)
Intercept	–45.89	–88.64
	(22.81)	(22.47)
Number of Cases	20	20
Adjusted R^2	0.61	0.74

behavior, that the public meets its end of the responsiveness bargain. The American public has moving ideal points that are effectively reflected in the mixtures of parties emerging from congressional elections. Stronger in Senate than House, the preference metering is clearly present in both cases. If government fails to respond to evolving public preferences, it is not for want of a signal.

A Macroanalysis

To assess the party government scenarios, I develop new measures of policy behavior specific to party. Analogous to the ADA and other ratings, these (better) measures tap the percent of times each member or senator votes the liberal position on all roll calls, 1956–94. These are then aggregated by party to produce independent measures of the party tracks over time. These become the operational indicators for the D_t and R_t of equation (3). Their mean, weighted by party proportions, α, becomes a summary of chamber policy-making behavior.

211

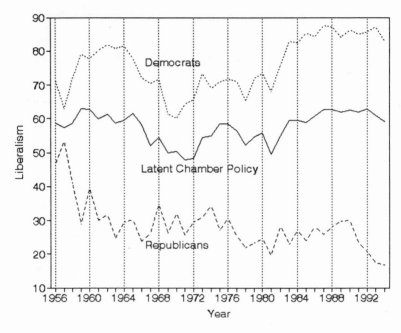

Figure 6.6. House liberalism by party, with estimated latent chamber policy liberalism

Party Government versus Rational Anticipation

Do the Parties Follow the Public Opinion Signal? The micromodel of Dynamic Representation predicts that all individual members of Congress will move in response to the common public opinion signal. It follows that any aggregation of members ought to replicate that signal as well. This works nicely, we have seen, for grand aggregations across the chamber. And it also holds up pretty well in some (unreported) scattered subaggregations we have observed. Thus aggregation by party is expected to reproduce parallel movements to the left (above) and right of the chamber pattern, to be represented by the "state variables" from Table 6.1, estimates of the latent policy making embodied in the various indicators and also linear combinations of the right-hand-side variables, most importantly, public opinion.[8]

The pattern for the House (in Figure 6.6) thus comes as

[8] The state variable metric – mean and variance – is that of the median size of liberal coalition measure, a close analogy to the mixture equation setup.

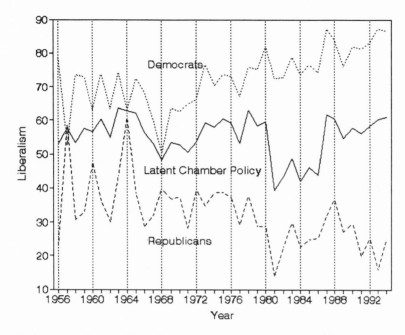

Figure 6.7. Senate liberalism by party, with estimated latent chamber liberalism

something of a surprise. One of the party groups, the Democrats, does regularly move left and right over time with the chamber and with public opinion. Because both parties are trending away from the stationary House norm, trend needs to be controlled in order to examine association of party series with the chamber norm. To do so, little regression models are estimated in which each party's series is a function of linear trend and the chamber norm. Focusing only on the latter, the House pattern is seen to be very much a function of the Democratic pattern ($\beta = 1.39$). The House Republicans, on the other hand, show little such movement ($\beta = .31$). What we see from them instead is a steady drift toward conservatism that seems largely insensitive to the changing electorate.

The story of House policy behavior then is largely that its outcomes are determined by its (then) permanent majority party. Its permanent minority is much less sensitive to changing public views, perhaps because of its permanent minority status. The Senate has a different party history and shows different patterns (in Figure 6.7). There, both parties seem to follow the chamber

213

(and public opinion) signal, with the normal minority Republicans slightly closer ($\beta = .65$) than the normal majority Democrats ($\beta = .48$).

The effect of disaggregation by party is to complicate the responsiveness story, as compared with looking at the fully aggregated macromodels of chamber behavior. Much of that complication arises from the emerging polarization of the parties, a nuisance for modeling, but a fact of some importance for party government scenarios. The evidence to this point is mixed. The parties follow the public opinion signal, but (excepting House Democrats) generally do so less crisply as individual parties than when they are mixed together. That leaves it unclear whether the parties themselves can be carriers of the public's message. That determination is the business at hand.

Testing the Two Alternative Conceptions. We are now ready to compare the alternative models of responsiveness. We have in hand measures of party positions, measures of the latent chamber position, which are linear transformations of public opinion, and knowledge of party mixtures. Each of the models is a restricted model; each fixes one part of the process to observe the other. We can hold party positions constant over time and let mixtures vary, the party government scenario. We can hold mixture constant and let party positions flow with changing preferences, the rational anticipation scenario.[9] We know that both processes contribute something to preference responsiveness.

The question to be addressed is which contributes more – which is the more vital part of the joint process? That question is readily answered by deriving the predictions of each from real data values and comparing them with the estimated latent chamber position, which serves as a baseline responsiveness norm. The presentation of this comparative test is mainly visual, but mean squared error from the prediction of the chamber latent policy variable is an appropriate statistical tool that will tell the same story the eyes can see.

We begin with the party government scenario in the House of

[9] The third alternative, an unrestricted model that lets everything vary, is an accounting identity, except for trivial measurement discrepancies (the mix of party means does not quite produce a median for the chamber), and therefore a test of nothing.

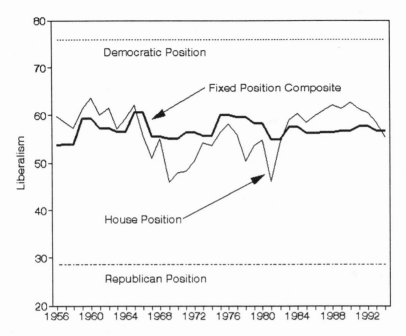

Figure 6.8. The party government model of responsiveness in the House

Representatives. Here we assume constant party positions over time that produce variable outcomes in response to opinion change from the metering behavior of the electorate, changing the party mix. That is captured in Figure 6.8, where each party is fixed at its long-term policy position mean and the mix is allowed to vary to match actual election results.

The series labeled "house position" is the Kalman state variable from Table 6.1 for the House, jointly a dynamic factor score from the four endogenous indicators of policy behavior and a linear composite of public opinion (and also in the House case, the Vietnam casualties variable for control). The "fixed position composite" is an artificial data series constructed on the assumption that parties never change positions, but voters alter the mix of partisans. It is E_t from

$$E_t = \alpha_t \overline{D} + (1 - \alpha_t)\overline{R}_t,$$

calibrated from empirical election results (α_t = percent Democratic seats) and the mean party positions ($\overline{D}$, $\overline{R}$) to predict the latent policy indicator.

215

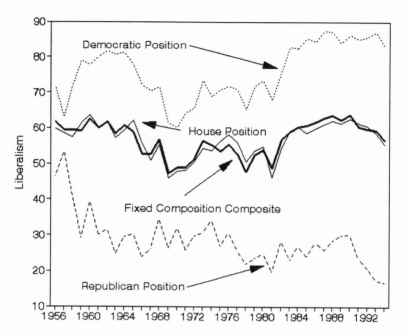

Figure 6.9. The rational anticipation model of responsiveness in the House

What is readily seen in the figure is that the election mix is limited and sluggish relative to the larger and sharper moves of policy behavior in House voting. Not by any means a bad fit, most of the dynamics of one series are seen in more limited form in the other. If we had no basis for comparison, this would be called a success.

But we do have a basis for comparison in the rational anticipation scenario. Here parties are allowed to vary from knowledge of what the public prefers and in anticipation of how it will act at the next election. But the electorate is presumed insensitive, returning a constant mix of parties at every election. The question then is whether the parties change enough to reflect public preferences even without any change of government. The setup is another artificial data series from the earlier equation (3):

$$E_t = \overline{\alpha}D_t + (1 - \overline{\alpha})R_t,$$

where party positions (D_t, R_t) are the actual party positions each year and the mix, $\overline{\alpha}$, is fixed at the mean for the whole period.

It does not require a keen eye to see (from Figure 6.9) that a

216

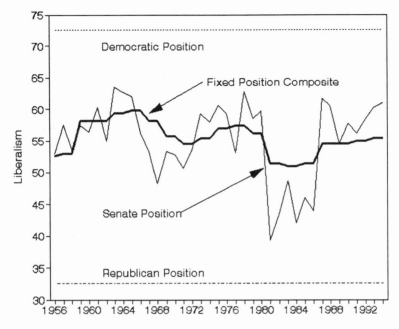

Figure 6.10. The party government model of responsiveness in the Senate

constant mix of moving party positions captures most of what is going on in this policy responsiveness. This near perfect prediction suggests that responsiveness could operate quite nicely in a constant government, albeit one that reasonably feared that the next election might undo its constant standing.

Figures 6.10 and 6.11 perform a parallel analysis for the Senate. They tell the same story. The party government setup performs well in an absolute sense, generally predicting the direction, but consistently failing to predict the amplitude, of policy changes. And the rational anticipation setup again consistently predicts what actually occurred, even under a false assumption that party mixes never change in a body that has even experienced changes of party control in the period.

This evidence is somewhat contrary to the modeling outcomes of Dynamic Representation, where the opinion-elections-policy traditional story of policy responsiveness was dominant for the Senate alone. This newer evidence says that even though Senate composition is highly responsive to preference shifts through elections, such responsiveness isn't necessary. The Senate would

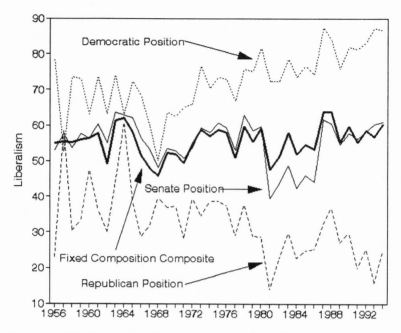

Figure 6.11. The rational anticipation model of responsiveness in the Senate

Table 6.4. Mean Squared Errors for Alternative Predictions of the Responsiveness Signal

Chamber	Party Government Setup	Rational Anticipation Setup
House	26.7	3.1
Senate	21.4	10.0
Average	24.1	6.6

be highly responsive to public preferences even with a fully constant membership.

Table 6.4 summarizes the statistical evidence of model fit. Using mean squared error in predicting chamber position as a criterion, it documents what has already been seen: the rational anticipation setup dominates prediction. The chamber difference reported in Dynamic Representation does reappear here to a limited degree. With an error ratio of almost nine to one, the dominance of rational anticipation is overwhelming in the House. The pattern is more balanced, with a ratio of about two to one, in the Senate.

A Concluding Irony

We started with the political-science view that party government is the best hope for the unlikely prospect of government responsiveness to the dynamics of public preference. We asked whether a party government formulation could be salvaged in view of the emerging polarization of the parties and our new knowledge that policy making does indeed reflect the dynamics of public preference. The answer is yes; we can salvage party government as a credible account of how responsiveness might work.

The irony is that the same evidence that salvages party government as a workable mechanism shows clearly that it is *not* the best hope for responsiveness. Indeed, one does not have to push the evidence very far to conclude also that it is unnecessary. A polity in which the parties were in constant mix – not a bad description of the U.S. House of Representatives before the "Republican Revolution" of 1994 – can produce remarkably adept translation of public preferences into public policies.

We add a prescription. Although never intended for the purpose (indeed, this research project predates the public debate on the matter), these findings speak clearly to a current public debate about democratic procedures, whether or not term limitations for various offices further public control of government. Abstracted from the adversarial rhetoric of public debate, the issue pits contrasting democratic principles against one another. Simple democracy suggests, on the one hand, that voters should get whom they want, not excluding long-serving incumbent candidates. But required turnover, on the other hand, is likely to heighten opportunities for meaningful choices, to make it more likely that changing public preferences will produce changing behaviors of elected officials.

This evidence speaks clearly to the debate. It says without any ambiguity that changing personnel, either within or between parties, is unnecessary for responsiveness. And what is unnecessary cannot weight heavily in a contest with the democratic principle of allowing voters to choose the candidate they prefer.

References

Alesina, Alberto, and Howard Rosenthal. 1995. *Partisan Politics, Divided Government, and the Economy.* Cambridge: Cambridge University Press.

Arnold, R. Douglas. 1990. *The Logic of Congressional Action.* New Haven: Yale University Press.

Bartels, Larry M. 1991. "Constituency Opinion and Congressional Policy Making: The Reagan Defense Buildup." *American Political Science Review* 85: 457–74.

Beck, Nathaniel. 1990. "Estimating Dynamic Models Using Kalman Filtering." *Political Analysis* 1: 121–56.

Durr, Robert H. 1993. "What Moves Policy Sentiment?" *American Political Science Review* 87: 158–70.

Engle, Robert F., and Mark W. Watson. 1981. "A One Factor Multivariate Time Series Model of Metropolitan Wage Rates." *Journal of the American Statistical Association* 76: 774–80.

Kellstedt, Paul, Gregory E. McAvoy, and James A. Stimson. 1996. "Dynamic Analysis with Latent Constructs: The Kalman DYMIMIC Specification." *Political Analysis* 5: 113–50.

MacKuen, Michael B., Robert S. Erikson, and James A. Stimson. 1989. "Macropartisanship." *American Political Science Review* 83: 1125–42.

Mishler, William, and Reginald S. Sheehan. 1993. "The Supreme Court as a Countermajoritarian Institution? The Impact of Public Opinion on Supreme Court Decisions." *American Political Science Review* 87: 87–101.

1994. "Response: Popular Influence on Supreme Court Decisions." *American Political Science Review* 88: 716–24.

Norpoth, Helmut, and Jeffrey A. Segal. 1994. "Comment: Popular Influence on Supreme Court Decisions." *American Political Science Review* 88: 711–16.

Page, Benjamin, and Robert Shapiro. 1983. "Effects of Public Opinion on Policy." *American Political Science Review* 77: 175–90.

1992. *The Rational Public: Fifty Years of Trends in Americans' Policy Preferences.* Chicago: University of Chicago Press.

Segal, Jeffrey A. 1988. "Amicus Curiae Briefs by the Solicitor General during the Warren and Burger Courts: A Research Note." *Western Political Quarterly* 41: 135–44.

Stimson, James A. 1991. *Public Opinion in America: Moods, Cycles, and Swings.* Boulder, Colo.: Westview Press.

Stimson, James A., Michael B. MacKuen, and Robert S. Erikson. 1995.

"Dynamic Representation." *American Political Science Review* 89: 543–65.

Watson, Mark W., and Robert F. Engle. 1983. "Alternative Algorithms for the Estimation of Dynamic Factor, MIMIC and Varying Coefficient Regression Models." *Journal of Econometrics* 23: 385–400.

Wlezien, Christopher. 1995. "The Public as Thermostat: Dynamics of Preferences for Spending." *American Journal of Political Science* 39: 981–1000.

Chapter Seven

Democracy, Elections, and Accountability for Economic Outcomes

Our purpose is to examine the empirical validity of two propositions: that democracy is a political regime distinguished by the accountability of rulers to the ruled, and that elections are the mechanism through which this accountability is enforced. These propositions are obviously related: the first follows from the second one by the definition of democracy as a regime in which rulers are selected by elections. Hence, the structure of the argument we intend to examine is that (1) democracy is a system that enforces accountability (empirical hypothesis), because (2) democracy is a regime in which rulers are chosen by elections (definition), and (3) accountability is enforced by elections (empirical hypothesis). If all of this appears pedantic, hold on.

We begin by spelling out our criteria for classifying political regimes, distinguishing different types of democracy and dictatorship, and providing some background information about their incidence. After we analyze statistically the impact of economic conditions on the survival of heads of governments, we study how rulers are selected under different forms of democracy and focus on the role of elections as a mechanism of accountability. A brief conclusion, mainly a list of doubts, closes the chapter.

Political Regimes

We classify as democracies regimes that during a particular year simultaneously satisfy four criteria:[1] (1) the chief executive

---

[1] For the conceptual justification and historical details, see Alvarez, Cheibub, Limongi, and Przeworski 1996.

is elected (directly or indirectly), (2) the legislature is elected, (3) more than one party competes in elections,[2] (4) incumbent parties have in the past or will have in the future lost an election and yielded office.[3] All the regimes that fail to satisfy at least one of these four criteria are classified as dictatorships.

Democracies are not all the same, and the difference most relevant for our purposes is between parliamentary and presidential regimes. Parliamentary democracies are those in which the legislature can change the executive; presidential democracies are those in which the executive cannot be deposed by the legislature during the term.[4] Other systems are mixed: the president is elected, but the government serves at the confidence of the legislature.[5] All but the Portuguese regime of 1976–81, however, are much closer to parliamentarism than presidentialism, and we lump them together with parliamentary democracies in most analyses that follow.

Dictatorships also differ in several ways, among which we again pick only one. We distinguish institutionalized dictatorships, which we call "bureaucracies," from personalistic regimes, which we term "autocracies." In making this distinction, we rely on Machiavelli's intuition (as highlighted by Bobbio 1989) that collective decision making necessitates some rules of operation for the decision-making body and Montesquieu's distinction between the rule by law and the rule by will, or whim as the case may be.

---

[2] By "party" we mean a list of candidates presented to voters. Various kinds of "fronts," which nominally consist of several parties but present themselves as a single list, are one party by our definition.

[3] This last criterion may appear strange, and it is. The problem one faces in classifying regimes is that there are some cases (in fact 8.3% of the sample) in which all the three previous criteria are satisfied and yet the same party always wins elections, almost invariably by a wide margin. The prototypical case is Botswana. The question that remains open in such instances is whether the party in power would have held elections if it were not sure to win and if it would have yielded office had it lost. Since history has not produced any information that would answer these questions, we must err, either by classifying these regimes as democratic even if they may have not been (type I error) or classifying them as not democratic even if they may have been (type II error). We decided to be prudent and classify these cases as dictatorships.

[4] There are several criteria that distinguish these two systems, but they coincide almost perfectly with those we use. See Lijphart 1992.

[5] Shugart and Carey (1992) introduce several further distinctions among such systems.

We take the existence of an elected legislature to be an indication that both the regime has some rules for internal operation and the rulers announce their intentions to the population in the form of laws, even if they may themselves not be subject to these laws. Hence, we classify as bureaucracies those dictatorships which during a particular year had a legislature and as autocracies those which did not.[6]

Our sample consists of 135 countries (including all democracies) between 1950 or the year of independence or the first year for which economic data are available ("entry" year) and 1990 ("exit" year).[7] The total number of years is 4,126, and we additionally exclude Switzerland, Uruguay until 1966, and post-1980 Yugoslavia, which had a collective executive, to be left with the total of 4,060 years. Altogether, we find 99 democracies (which lasted the total of 1,606 years) and 123 dictatorships (with the total of 2,454 years). Among democracies, we counted 51 parliamentary systems (1,039 years), 9 mixed (147 years), and 42 presidential ones (420 years).[8] There are thus 102 democratic regimes distinguished in terms of their institutions.[9] Among dictatorships, we found 132 bureaucracies (1,785 years) and 98 autocracies (669 years), for the total of 230 dictatorial regimes.[10]

---

[6] Some countries that did not have legislatures during a particular year were obviously experiencing regime transitions. These were appropriately reclassified.

[7] Comparable economic data exist for 141 countries, but we exclude six oil producers. Countries with population in the 1980s larger than one million for which comparable economic data are not available include Albania, Bhutan, Cuba, North Korea, Lebanon, Libya, Namibia, and Vietnam, all dictatorships.

[8] In addition to the United States and to Latin America, where all democracies are presidential, presidential democracies existed in the Congo (1960–62), Ghana (1979–80), Nigeria (1979–82), Uganda (1980–84), Bangladesh (1986–), South Korea (1988–), and the Philippines (1950–64 and 1986–). Portugal between 1976 and 1981 was also classified as a presidential democracy.

[9] Three more than the number of democracies, since there were three changes of institutional systems without a breakdown of democracy: France in 1958 and Brazil in 1961 and 1963.

[10] Transitions between bureaucracies and autocracies are common, which explains why the number of dictatorial regimes is considerably larger when we distinguish types of dictatorships.

Democracy and Accountability

Governments are "accountable" if citizens can discern whether governments are acting in their best interest and sanction them appropriately, so that those incumbents who satisfy citizens remain in office and those who do not lose it. Accountability is a retrospective mechanism, in the sense that the actions of rulers are judged ex post by the effects they have.

Rulers are accountable if the probability that they survive in office is sensitive to government performance; otherwise they are not accountable. Specifically, accountability can be characterized by the derivative of "hazard rate" with regard to the outcomes that were generated during some number of past years, where the hazard rate is the conditional probability that, having been in office for some duration t = 0, 1, 2, . . . , incumbents lose office at (t + dt), dt → 0. Rulers are accountable if their hazard rate increases, and the probability of surviving in office falls when economic performance declines.

As "rulers" we take the chief executives, to whom we refer as "heads" of government, or simply "heads." These are presidents in presidential democracies, prime ministers in the parliamentary and mixed systems, and whoever are the effective rulers in dictatorships. Rulers in the last category can be designated explicitly as dictators, or can bear titles of heads of military juntas, presidents, leaders of the ruling party, executors of the state of emergency, or kings.[11]

No change of heads occurred during 3,386 years, one change in 568, two in 91, three in 13, four and five changes each occurred once. Thus altogether there were 798 changes of heads, on the average once every five years. We observed a total of 792 spells of heads, that is, years of continuous rule by the same person.[12]

---

[11] We coded the number of changes of heads in each year using as sources da Graça 1985, Bienen and Van de Walle 1991, and Banks 1993a. Contrary to Bienen and Van de Walle, we did not make any effort to exclude acting or provisional governments, on the assumption that we cannot distinguish between cases in which heads attempted to consolidate power and failed from cases in which heads did not try to do so.

[12] When we coded spells, we lost the information about the governments that lasted less than one year (for which the changes in HEADS > 1 for a given year). This left us with 674 spells. To these we must add 118 spells that had already begun when we started to observe them.

Of those, 198 were either interrupted because the person died or continued past 1990.[13] In this sense they are "censored." Once we eliminate censored spells, we are left with 594 that ended during the period for nonaccidental reasons.

Some incumbents changed the nature of the political regime while in office. This happened during 55 spells: in 45 the regime changed once without a change of head, in 7 it changed twice, in 2 it changed three times, and in one instance it changed six times. Most of these changes were between different types of dictatorships, due to the opening or closing of legislatures.[14] A few, however, were from democracy to dictatorship or vice versa: for example, from presidentialism to autocracy in Uruguay under Juan Bordaberry in 1973, or from autocracy to presidentialism in Nicaragua under Daniel Ortega Saavedra in 1984. For this reason these regimes must be separated in order to calculate the average duration of incumbents in each regime type. These durations are presented in Table 7.1.

The outcomes we consider include the standard panoply of variables generally utilized in studies of "economic voting," which typically comprise some indicators of income, employment, and inflation. Specifically, we consider the following variables:[15]

G is the rate of growth of per capita income,
CONSDG is the rate of growth of per capita consumption,
GOV is government consumption as a proportion of GNP,

---

[13] We do not distinguish between deaths due to natural causes (as in the cases of Josef Broz Tito in Yugoslavia, Juan Domingo Perón in Argentina, and Bjarni Benediktsoon in Iceland), assassination (Anwar el-Sadat in Egypt, John F. Kennedy in the United States, and Olof Palme in Sweden), suicide (Getúlio Vargas in Brazil and Antonio Guzmán Fernández in the Dominican Republic), or presumed accidents (Samora Machel in Mozambique, René Barrientos in Bolivia, Mohammad Zia ul-Haq in Pakistan, and Ramon Magsaysay in the Philippines).

[14] The most extreme case is Jordan, where the legislature was closed for one year in 1966, in 1974 (until 1984), and in 1985 (until 1989). Other cases of frequent changes of regime without change in the chief executive are Morocco, where the legislature was closed in 1963 (until 1965), 1970 (until 1972), and 1978, and Burkina Faso, where Sangoulé Lamizana allowed an elective legislature to convene in 1970 only to close it in 1974 and reopen it in 1978.

[15] Data for growth of income, consumption, and labor share, as well as for government consumption, are derived from PWT5.6 (see Summers and Heston 1988, 1991, for a description of these data); data for inflation are from the International Monetary Fund (1995). Note that we have only 3,426 observations for inflation; hence, the size of the sample is not the same in all analyses.

Table 7.1. Number of Spells of HEADS and Average Duration of Tenure by Regime (Excluding Censored Spells)

Regime	Number of Spells	Average Duration
Parliamentary	216	3.86
Mixed	51	2.35
Presidential	86	4.34
Bureaucracy	122	7.64
Autocracy	88	3.03
Regime change[a]	31	10.81
All	594	4.81

[a] Since some spells that are censored also had a regime change, this number does not reflect all the spells with regime change.

LFG is the rate of growth of labor force, a proxy for employment, CPI is the rate of change of the Consumer Price Index.

We estimate the probability that a head survives a particular year given the length of tenure and these economic outcomes.

As Table 7.2 (the two upper panels) shows, we learn that survival of heads of governments is independent of all these economic conditions.[16] The only economic variable that appears to matter somewhat for the survival of heads under parliamentary (including mixed) democracies is the growth of the labor force: when employment grows faster, prime ministers are more likely to survive. The growth of per capita income or of per capita consumption, the rate of inflation, or the share of government consumption expenditures does not affect the chances of survival of prime ministers. In turn, none of the indicators of economic performance matters for the survival of presidents

---

[16] In addition to these results, we considered the impact of the change in the rate of inflation, to discover that it never matters. We also experimented with first and second lags of performance indicators. We also considered specifications in which various combinations of these variables were used as well as controls for regions (OECD countries) and periods. The results remained qualitatively the same, with coefficients on labor force growth under parliamentarism hovering around 0.10 confidence level.

Table 7.2. Survival of HEADS by Regime Type (Weibull)

Variable	Coefficient	Standard Error	t-ratio	Prob|t|≥x	Mean of X	Standard Deviation of X
Parliamentarism (censoring interrupted spells)						
G	0.75610E-02	0.1226E-01	0.617	0.53737	2.6880	4.4367
LFG	0.74972E-01	0.4759E-01	1.575	0.11521	1.2764	1.0861
CONSDG	0.62292E-02	0.1096E-01	0.569	0.56969	2.5126	6.9336
GOV	0.34887E-02	0.9281E-02	0.376	0.70700	16.181	6.1317
CPI	-0.16532E-02	0.1852E-02	-0.893	0.37197	12.173	37.155
Presidentialism (censoring interrupted spells)						
G	0.53945E-02	0.9563E-02	0.564	0.57269	0.49800	6.0428
LFG	-0.35251E-02	0.5209E-01	-0.068	0.94604	2.3555	0.98149
CONSDG	0.21748E-03	0.9085E-02	0.024	0.98090	0.99991	4.7490
GOV	0.89785E-02	0.7109E-02	1.263	0.20660	16.055	5.7869
CPI	0.47829E-04	0.8290E-04	0.577	0.56397	237.41	965.93
Presidentialism (censoring interrupted and spells with term limits)						
G	0.21122E-01	0.2197E-01	0.961	0.33644	0.49800	6.0428
LFG	0.13803	0.7924E-01	1.742	0.08152	2.3555	0.98149
CONSDG	0.23803E-01	0.1924E-01	1.237	0.21608	0.99991	4.7490
GOV	-0.10548E-02	0.1425E-01	-0.074	0.94099	16.055	5.7869
CPI[a]						

Note: Performance variables were entered one at a time.
[a] Does not converge.

under democracy, even if we control for periods or for Latin America.

Needless to say, these results are both surprising and dismaying. If democracy is a system in which rulers are chosen by elections and if elections are a mechanism by which voters reward governments that perform well and sanction those which perform badly, we should observe the survival of heads of governments to be sensitive to economic performance under democracy. We find that the survival of prime ministers is slightly sensitive to the growth of employment, but this is all, and even this result is weak. The survival of presidents appears to be completely independent of economic performance.

These results may appear additionally puzzling since many studies based on survey data as well as on aggregate time series of single countries show that people tend to vote for incumbents when economic conditions are good and against them when these conditions are bad (Lewis-Beck 1988: 155; 1991: 1–2).[17] But these effects tend to be small and unstable: Paldam (1981: 181) estimates that "economic indicators explain around 1/3 of the variations in party popularities," while Kiewiet and Rivers (1984: 374–75) sound a cautionary note with regard to the U.S. experience. Moreover, we are far from unique in finding that economic variables do not affect the vote for the incumbent in cross-national analyses of aggregate data. Strom and Lipset (1984; 163 elections between 1950 and 1982) found that inflation mattered after 1973 but not unemployment or industrial output. Lewis-Beck and Mitchell (1990; 27 elections in 5 countries) discovered a moderate effect of inflation and unemployment but not of income growth. Host and Paldam (1990) and Paldam (1991; 197 elections in 17 countries) found mainly that coefficients on inflation often have a wrong sign. Powell and Whitten (1993; 102 elections between 1969 and 1988, 19 countries) discovered that inflation, unemployment, and growth have no systematic effects. Remmer (1993; 21 presidential elections in 12 Latin American countries) found that some economic variables matter for some

---

[17] Exceptions to these findings seem to occur when economic policy is explicitly framed as entailing intertemporal trade-offs. See Stokes 1996a for a general discussion, Przeworski 1996 for Poland, and Stokes 1996b for Peru. Note, however, that Paldam (1991) also observed some unexpected signs for inflation.

political outcomes, but the coefficients are small. Pacek and Radcliffe (1995; 52 elections in 8 developing countries) concluded that incumbents are punished when the economy is declining but not rewarded when it is growing. Hence, it seems that in different samples different economic variables sometimes matter for political outcomes, but the findings are far from robust.

One reason for these unstable findings may be that some additional institutional conditions need to be present to enforce accountability. To examine this possibility, we replicated at least in spirit the findings of Powell and Whitten (1993). Their argument is that some institutional factors affect the ability of voters to discern and punish; therefore, once these factors are controlled for, the relation between economic performance and survival of heads should become stronger. They are particularly concerned about the "clarity of responsibility": whether voters can discern whom to punish. We controlled for the share of the majority party in the legislature, for a dummy variable indicating whether one party has a majority, for the number of effective parties in the legislature, for whether the government is a coalition, and for whether the military meddle in politics.[18] All these variables affect the survival of heads, but what matters for our purposes is that none modifies the relation between survival and economic performance. Hence, "clarity of responsibility" makes no difference for accountability with regard to economic outcomes.

These results are also disturbing. Clearly, the assertion that democracy induces accountability is at least far too broad. Perhaps under some institutional conditions, which we failed to identify, it does. But these conditions are not obvious and may be quite rare.

Democracy and Elections

Surprised and chagrined, all we can do is to question the obvious: that the theoretical link between democracy and accountability passes via elections.[19] If rulers are elected and if facing elections they anticipate the reactions of voters to the outcomes their policies will have generated, then they will be accountable. But are rulers elected under democracy? In some

---

[18] All these variables were taken and updated from Banks 1993a.

[19] For the different views of the role of elections, see Manin, Przeworski, and Stokes (Chapter 1 in this volume).

Table 7.3. Leader Selection by Regime Type

Reason for Change	PARL	PRES	BUR
Elections			
Regular elections	162	66	22
With term limits	—	53	12
Foundational elections	—	—	17
Total due to elections	162	66	39
Other Reasons			
Removal by party/interim	148	4	83
In election years	25	—	5
Change of regime	14	24	32
In election years	6	8	5
Deaths	18	8	28
Total for other reasons	180	36	143
Total	342	102	182
Total Number of Years	1,186	420	1,785

sense they clearly are, but this definitional sense needs to be, yes, deconstructed.

Table 7.3 presents a summary of ruler selection in the three regimes that hold elections.[20] It is true that democracies are regimes in which rulers are more likely to leave office due to elections: 47 percent of prime ministers and 64 percent of presidents left their posts when voters elected someone else, while only 21 percent of bureaucrats did.[21] But many prime ministers

[20] This table and all the data we report have been corrected for the cases in which elections occur in one year and the change of government occurs in the following year. In these cases we considered the year of change in government as the election year.

[21] Since our focus is on democracy, we do not comment on the results concerning the dictatorships. But since it may appear strange that rulers lose office by elections in dictatorships, here is the explanation. Of the 39 changes of bureaucratic heads during election years, 12 were due to term limits: El Salvador (1956, 1967, 1972, and 1977), Honduras (1954), and Mexico (1952,

left office without voters being consulted, while most presidents left it even if voters may have wanted them to stay.

Consider first some background information. We observed altogether 892 legislative elections (870 years in which 1 election occurred and 11 years with 2): 318 under parliamentarism (including mixed systems), 108 under presidentialism, 375 under bureaucracy, and 91 under autocracy,[22] which means that on the average a legislature was elected once in 3.7 years under parliamentarism, 3.9 years under presidentialism, and 4.8 years under bureaucracy. Under presidentialism, there were 86 presidential elections (84 years with 1 election and 2 in Argentina in 1973), or once in every 4.9 years. Under bureaucracy, there were 103 presidential elections, or once every 18 years. Under autocracy, 33 presidents were elected, once every 20 years. Hence, heads of government are on the average subject to popular vote once every 3.7 years under parliamentarism and once every 4.9 years under presidentialism.

But the difference between parliamentarism and presidentialism is much more profound. We need to study these systems separately.

Consider first parliamentarism. As can be seen in Table 7.3, altogether there were 310 peaceful changes of prime ministers, that is, changes not due to death or being overthrown. Of those 162 were due to elections and 148 either to intraparty struggles or to the collapse of a ruling coalition. Hence, 48% of changes of prime ministers are not due to elections: in about one-half of cases it is not voters who sanction the incumbent prime ministers but politicians. Obviously, one could expect that party politicians anticipate the judgment of voters when they replace their leader or decide to leave the ruling coalition. All we can say is that, if this is what motivates them, their efforts are to no avail: the prime ministers who assume office during the electoral term are less likely to be reelected than those who led their parties during the

1958, 1964, 1970, 1976, 1982, 1988). Of these 39 changes, 17 were foundational elections, that is, elections that led to the establishment of a presidential or a parliamentary democracy. The remaining 10 cases consist of single-party regimes or what we call "Type II" dictatorships, as explained in note 3.

[22] The fact that there were legislative elections under autocracy is not incompatible with our definition of this regime: these legislatures were not allowed to convene or were promptly dissolved. In one case, Dominican Republic in 1961, elections took place under democracy, but the congress was closed following a coup d'etat.

Table 7.4. Election in Parliamentary Regimes by Origin of Incumbent and Outcome

Origin of Incumbent	Outcome		
	PM Wins	PM Loses	Total
Middle of the term	24 (29.6%)	57 (70.4%)	81 (100%)
Elections	94 (50.5%)	92 (49.5%)	186 (100%)
Unknown	20	13	33
Total	138 (46.0%)	162 (54.0%)	300 (100%)

previous election. Table 7.4 shows that while only 30% of the former survive elections when they are called, 51% of the latter remain in office after elections. Hence, it is not obvious that the anticipation of voters' reactions drives these changes. In any case, it appears that what we mean by "elections" is selection by politicians subject to ratification by voters. To "elect" is not the same as to select.

We do not pretend that this is a startling discovery: that voters choose from among alternatives presented by competing teams of politicians was exactly what Schumpeter (1942) had in mind. Moreover, once designated by their party peers, the incumbent prime ministers are subject to ratification by voters: of the 148 prime ministers who came into office without elections, 82 were subject to a popular verdict within the next three years (the rest were changed without an election, died or were overthrown in office, or were still around by 1990). On the average, they stayed in office 1.5 years before being subjected to elections.[23] But this fact becomes more significant if we look at it differently: there are periods under democracy when rulers are not those whom voters have elected. People may have voted for their party but (1) they were voting for this party knowing the leader and the eventual

---

[23] Since our data are annual, we attribute 6 months to each of the 18 prime ministers who faced elections in the year they came to office, 1 year to each of the 29 who faced elections next year, 2 years to each of the 22 who waited 2 years before facing elections, and 3 years to each of the 13 who waited 3 years.

head of government, and (2) the appointed prime minister need not be a member of the same party as the deposed one, indeed of any party. The extreme case is Italy, where, as Pasquino (1994: 25) observed, "governing parties seemed to expropriate the voters of the political influence by making and unmaking governments at all levels with very little respect for electoral results." The fact is that 17% of the time, one year in six, parliamentary democracies were led by rulers who were not elected to head their governments.

Let us now turn to presidentialism. Presidents are elected (directly or indirectly) by voters and, short of impeachment, they cannot be removed by representatives. Indeed, as Table 7.3 shows, of the total 70 peaceful changes of presidents, all but 4 were due to elections.[24] Clearly, in presidential systems the candidates are also most frequently selected by fellow politicians. But at least the heads of government are almost never other than those who were elected by voters.

Yet the concept of "electing" is problematic also under presidentialism. While the 86 elections we observed led to departures of 66 presidents, 53 of these departures were necessitated by term limits; voters could not have reelected the incumbent politicians even if they had wanted to.

Simón Bolívar once remarked that "We elect monarchs whom we call presidents," and this fear of presidents turning into monarchs was the reason for imposing term limits. This fear seems to be justified, since it appears that presidentialism gives an excessive advantage to the incumbents: among 22 presidents who faced reelection without impending term limits, only 14 were not reelected, and of those only 6 can be counted as real defeats by incumbents: in the Dominican Republic in 1978, when Joaquín Balaguer lost to Antonio Guzmán Fernández; in Nicaragua in 1990, when Daniel Ortega Saavedra lost to Violeta Chamorro; in the United States in 1977, when Gerald Ford lost to Jimmy Carter, and 1981, when Carter lost to Ronald Reagan; and in the Philippines in 1953, when Elpidio Quirino lost to Ramon Magsaysay, as well as in 1961, when Carlos Garcia lost to Diosdado

[24] The four were Richard Nixon's resignation in 1974; the changes from João Café Filho to Carlos Luz and to Nereu Ramos in Brazil in 1955, following Getulio Vargas's suicide in 1954; and the transfer of power from Velasco Ibarra to Carlos Arosemena Monroy in Ecuador in 1961.

Macapagal. In all the other cases, the incumbent, for various reasons, did not run. These include, for example, Lyndon Johnson in 1969 in the United States, Salvador Jorge Blanco in 1986 in the Dominican Republic, Nereu Ramos in Brazil in 1956, Hector Campora in Argentina in 1973. Hence, there were 14 elections in which the incumbent presidents ran for reelection; given that the incumbent won in 8 and lost in 6, their odds of being reelected were 1.3 to 1, as contrasted with 0.66 to 1 for prime ministers.

Thus, regardless of whether term limits are justified and whether their inclusion in the constitution can be interpreted as putative consent to them by citizens, the fact is that in most democratic presidential systems voters cannot reelect candidates whether they want to or not; as Table 7.5 shows, this was true of 64 out of 86 presidential elections we observed.

In sum, while under parliamentarism about one-sixth of the time the head of government is not someone who had been elected as such, under presidentialism three-fourths of the time it is someone voters cannot elect even if they want to. Whether this is the reason we observe so little accountability under democracy, we do not know. But the link between democracy and elections appears less than definitional.

Elections and Accountability

Since we wanted to compare regimes with different institutional rules – indeed, some without any rules – we allowed for the possibility that heads of government would change in non-election years, which we discovered to be the case even in democracies. But democratic accountability is supposed to work through elections, and our negative results may be due to the fact that we do not distinguish election from nonelection years. We need, therefore, to examine the specific connection between elections and accountability.

In presidential democracies, changes of presidents occur almost exclusively during election years. Yet these changes occur most of the time not because voters evaluate negatively the performance of the incumbent but because they have no chance to reward the incumbents for their performance. It is, therefore, not surprising that economic performance has no effect on the probability that the incumbent survives in office. Once we distinguish (censor) those terms in which incumbent presidents are

Table 7.5. Term Limits in Presidential Elections

Total number of elections	86
Elections that led to change of head	66
Changes due to term limits	53
Changes not due to term limits	13
Incumbents ran and lost	6
Incumbents did not run	7
Elections that led to no change or changes due to other reasons	20
Incumbent won reelection	8
Change not due to election	12
Incumbent faced term limit	11
Incumbent did not face term limit	1
Incumbents who did not face immediate term limit **(13 + 8 + 1)**	22
But who faced later limits	12
Incumbents who did face immediate term limit **(53 + 11)**	64
Incumbents who did face some kind of term limit **(12 + 64)**	76
Incumbents who could be reelected forever	10

not eligible for reelection, the survival of presidents becomes somewhat sensitive to the growth of the labor force, similarly to that of prime ministers (see the lowest panel of Table 7.2). But presidents who can be reelected are few.

In parliamentary democracies, we can distinguish the hazards due specifically to elections from the risks to which prime ministers are exposed during nonelection years, whether of being peacefully replaced or violently overthrown. Making this distinction, however, does not alter the results: an (exponential) multiple hazard model, in which these risks are treated separately, shows again that only the growth of the labor force somewhat affects the survival of prime ministers, in the election and off-election years. Thus, all we can conclude is that parliamentary democracies generate accountability at most with regard to the growth of employment (which probably means unemployment), but only employment.

Since, with the exception of employment for prime ministers and for the few presidents who can be reelected, economic performance does not affect the survival of heads of democratic governments even during the years when elections are held, all we can conclude is that elections do not enforce economic accountability in democratic regimes.

Conclusion

Either our statistical procedures are faulty or governments are not accountable to voters, at least not for economic outcomes. All we can do is to speculate.

1. Voters may care about other things than their material well-being. Since they have only one instrument – the vote – with which to sanction governments for decisions in many realms, voters may decide to keep governments accountable for matters other than economic.

2. Voters may be using their votes to induce the incumbent to act in a representative manner, but they may set the incentive schedule wrong by not giving enough of a chance for incumbents to be reelected when they perform well. Voters may be more likely to vote for incumbents who make them better off but not likely enough to induce politicians to seek reelection rather than give up and extract rents while they can. What is necessary to enforce accountability is not only that the probability of voting for the incumbent increases as economic performance gets better but also that governments that do well have a fair chance to be reelected. And there is evidence that voters tend to vote against incumbents even if they perform well. Remmer (1993) found that in all the twenty-one repeated elections in Latin America between 1982 and 1990, the incumbents' vote share declined. The average decline was 13.1%, and the constant in the regression of the incumbent party's share of the vote on economic performance was about –21%. Paldam (1991: 24) found in turn that, in 190 pairs of elections in the OECD countries, the average change was smaller but still negative: –1.6%. He concluded that "we have to accept that people just don't like to be ruled, or, at least, that they like

237

changes." If people vote against incumbents regardless of what they do, the incumbents do not have an incentive to do anything for them. Hence, if the probability of reelection is low even when economic performance is good, the finding that individuals are more likely to vote for incumbents when the economic conditions are better is not inconsistent with the aggregate finding that economic performance does not affect the survival of the incumbents.

3. Voters may not know enough to be able to evaluate the performance of the incumbent. Specifically, if they do not observe some conditions that governments observe or if they do not know the effects of policies on outcomes, voters cannot be certain how much to expect. Voters will then vote out of office badly performing governments and retain well-performing ones when the objective conditions are in fact bad, but they will indiscriminately reelect governments when conditions are good. We tried to control for such conditions, distinguishing the post-1975 and the post-1982 periods as well as periods during which countries were under agreements with the International Monetary Fund, but to no avail.

4. Making the chances of remaining in office conditional on past performance assumes that voters are myopic, in the sense that at the end of the term they do not take into account the present value of the future, which the incumbent is leaving as the legacy. If voters are fully rational, then their assessment of future prospects enters into the evaluation of the past performance of the incumbent. All we could do to test this hypothesis is to see whether the slope of the economy during the given year (first differences of the performance variables) matters for the survival of heads of government. It does not, but perhaps a better measure of the future prospects would. Yet it is telling that the share of investment (private and public) in gross national product negatively affects the chance of survival of prime ministers;[25] by this test, voters do appear to be myopic.

5. Finally, if voters use the vote prospectively, to choose better governments, governments may be representative just because good policies or politicians are selected, but not because representation is induced by the fear of electoral sanction. Yet note that we should have observed a relation between performance and survival even if voters are using their votes prospectively. Using

---

[25] The coefficient on the share of investment in GDP is -0.0195 with $pr = 0.004$.

the vote prospectively lowers the power of incentives for the incumbent (Fearon, Chapter 2, in this volume), but the past performance of the incumbent still informs the voters how likely it is that a challenger will perform better. Hence, information about the past performance of the incumbent should still matter for the chances of reelection.

Thus, there are good grounds to expect that if governments are representative – whether because they fear retrospective electoral sanctions or because good politicians and policies are selected prospectively – we should observe that incumbents who generate a bad performance are more likely to be thrown out of office. We do not observe it, and, unless our statistical methods are faulty, this implies that elections are not an effective instrument for inducing representation.

Appendix

The purpose of this appendix is to justify the claims made in the conclusion. We develop a simple model of accountability and then show that an incumbent's survival in office will not be systematically affected by his or her performance if (1) the electorate sets the incentive schedule incorrectly, or (2) the electorate cannot observe some conditions that affect the incumbent's performance. We also demonstrate that the relation between survival and performance depends on these conditions. Finally, we point out that even if the electorate uses its votes prospectively, to choose policies or politicians, we should have observed a relation between performance and survival.

The motivation for the model and examples are provided by Manin, Przeworski, and Stokes (Chapter 1, in this volume).

The Basic Model

Time consists of the current electoral term and the future. The sequence of events is as follows. An election takes place. The newly elected government observes some state of nature, β, which characterizes objective conditions. Voters set some criterion, K, which the incumbent will have to satisfy to get reelected with a positive probability. The government decides the amount of rents it extracts during the term. When the term ends, another election

239

occurs. Voters observe their welfare, compare it with the criteria they had set, and vote whether to reelect the incumbent.

Take a single voter (or homogeneous voters or the median voter), to which we will also refer as "the electorate." The change of his or her welfare during an electoral term is

$$\Delta W = \beta - r, \tag{1}$$

where β represents exogenous conditions that determine the maximal level of welfare available and r stands for politicians' rents.

The incumbent's utility is

$$U = r + p(\Delta W(r))V, \tag{2}$$

where $p(\Delta W)$ is the probability that the incumbent is reelected having generated welfare level ΔW for the voter (this is the "accountability function") and V is the value of being reelected.

The incumbent can get $r = U_0$ in one period, which implies that the "individual rationality" ("participation") constraint is

$$U = r + pV \geq U_0, \tag{3}$$

which is satisfied if

$$r^* = U_0 - pV + \varepsilon = U_0^+ - pV, \tag{4}$$

where $U_0^+ = U_0 + \varepsilon$.

Voters' problem is to maximize their welfare, given by (1), by choosing some criterion of welfare, K, such that

if $\Delta W \geq K$, then $p = 1 - \alpha$, $0 \leq \alpha < 1$,

K: $\tag{5}$

if $\Delta W < K$, then $p = 0$,

subject to (3).

If voters believe that politicians are all the same, they set $\alpha = 0$, so that

$$r^* = U_0^+ - V. \tag{4a}$$

This is the basic model.

Retrospective Voting with Full Information

The equilibrium is as follows: voters set $K^* = \beta - r^*$, the incumbent chooses r^*, and voters reelect the incumbent with $p^* = 1$.

If voters were to set $K > \beta - r^*$, the incumbent would not be able to satisfy their participation constraint and would choose $r = U_0$, giving voters $\beta - U_0 < \beta - r^*$. If voters were to set $K < \beta - r^*$, the incumbent would be able to extract rents such that $r = \beta - K > r^*$ and still be reelected, so that voters would be voting for politicians who gave them $\Delta W < \beta - r^*$. Thus, voters would set $K^* = \beta - r^*$. In turn, faced with K^*, the incumbent is epsilon indifferent between extracting r^* and being reelected, which gives them U_0^+ and extracting rents U_0 and giving up on reelection, and chooses r^*. In turn, the electorate, having observed $\Delta W \geq K^*$, votes to reelect the incumbent, since voting for a challenger would not generate a higher level of welfare under the same conditions.

Note that if the electorate sets K too high, perhaps misjudging the participation constraint (4a), then the incumbents are induced to seek excess rents.

Suppose now that the conditions represented by β can be good or bad. Under good conditions $\beta = \beta^G$ and under bad conditions $\beta = \beta^B$. Let the difference between good and bad conditions be $\Delta\beta \equiv \beta^G - \beta^B > 0$. If voters know which conditions hold, they can still set K at K^* (β) and induce politicians to limit their rents to $r = r^*$, regardless of the conditions.

Incomplete Information

Suppose that voters know the magnitude of β^G and β^B but do not know which of them holds. They only know the probability that conditions are good, $\mathrm{pr}\{\beta = \beta^G\} = q$. Then they have the choice of either inducing the government to minimize rents when conditions are bad or giving up when they are bad and inducing rent minimization when conditions are good. Examine first the consequences of each of these rules.

If voters set $K = K^G \equiv \beta^G - r^*$, then the incumbent chooses $r = r^*$ when $\beta = \beta^G$ and $r = U_0$ when $\beta = \beta^B$. When conditions are good, the incumbent can meet its participation constraint, and we already know that it will do it. When conditions are bad, the participation constraint can not be met, the incumbent chooses r = U_0, the electorate gets $\beta^B - U_0$, and voters vote the incumbent out of office. Hence, if voters expect conditions to be good, the incumbent extracts surplus rents whenever they are in fact bad.

If voters set $K = K^B \equiv \beta^B - r^*$, then the incumbent chooses r = r^* when $\beta = \beta^B$. But when conditions are in fact good, $\beta = \beta^G$, the incumbent may be able to extract excess rents and still be reelected. Here we must distinguish two cases. Note that the most the incumbent can extract in rents is U_0. If $\Delta\beta > V$, then $U_0 < r^* + \Delta\beta$, which implies that the electorate (which, to remind, knows the values of β^G and β^B) can distinguish excess rent extraction under good conditions from minimum rents under bad conditions: in the first case, it gets $W = \beta^G - U_0$; in the second, $W = \beta^B - r^*$, and the former is larger. Given that the electorate knows this, it can induce the incumbent to always choose r = r^* by setting K as

if $\Delta W = \beta^G - r^*$, then p = 1,

if $\beta^G - r^* > \Delta W \geq \beta^G - U_0$, then p = 0,

if $\Delta W = \beta^B - r^*$, then p = 1,

if $\Delta W \leq \beta^B - r^*$, then p = 0. (5a)

If, however, $\Delta\beta \leq V$, then the incumbent can extract r = $r^* + \Delta\beta < U_0$. Since the electorate gets $W = \beta^B - r^*$ whether conditions are good and rents excessive or conditions are bad and rents minimal, the incumbent is reelected. Hence, the incumbent sets r = $r^* + \Delta\beta$.

What should voters do? Comparing the expected values of ΔW (K^G) with ΔW (K^B) shows that when $\Delta\beta \leq V$ the electorate is better off by choosing $K = K^G$ when

$$q > \frac{V}{V + \Delta\beta,} = q^* \geq 1/2,$$ (6)

that is, when voters think that conditions are more likely to be good.

The equilibria are thus the following:

1. When $\Delta\beta > V$ and the electorate uses (5a), the full information equilibrium holds even if voters do not in fact observe the conditions.

2. When $\Delta\beta \le V$ and $q < q^*$, the electorate sets $K = K^B$, the incumbent sets rents at $r = r^* + \Delta\beta$ when $\beta = \beta^G$ and at $r = r^*$ when $\beta = \beta^B$, and the incumbent is always reelected.
3. When $q > q^* \ge 1/2$, the electorate sets $K = K^G$, the incumbent sets rents at $r = r^*$ when $\beta = \beta^G$ and at $r = U_0$ when $\beta = \beta^B$. The incumbent is reelected when $\beta = \beta^G$ and it is thrown out of office when $\beta = \beta^B$.

Thus, if voters do not observe something governments do know, they must tolerate excessive rents either when conditions are good or when they are bad. They can make guesses about which to do but are unable to control politicians under some conditions.

Governments Informed about Individual Voters

Suppose that voters are otherwise homogeneous but differ in their estimates of q: the probability that conditions are good. Let the distribution of q_i, $i = 1, \ldots, N$, have the density $f(q)$, so that the proportion of the electorate that will vote to reelect when $\Delta W \ge K^B$ is $F(q^*)$, q^* given by (6). Under majority rule, the incumbent is certain to be reelected, $p = 1$, when the share of the incumbent's votes is $S \ge 1/2$. Suppose now that the government knows the individually specific probabilities q_i and that voters use (5a) when $V > \Delta\beta$ and (5) otherwise.

Assume that the government is limited in what it can extract from each of the N individuals, namely U_0. Then there are several equilibria:

1. When $F > 1/2$, that is, more than half of the voters think conditions are bad, the government is reelected when it gives at least $K^B = \beta^B - r^*$ to each of one-half of the voters and $\beta - U_0$ to each of the rest. Since the government can satisfy the majority even when the conditions are bad, it will always do so and be reelected. The N voters will get in the aggregate

$$\Delta W = (N/2)(\beta^B - (U_0 - V)) + (N/2)(\beta - U_0),$$

subject to the constraint that no individual gets less than $\beta - U_0$, $\beta = \beta^B$ or $\beta = \beta^G$. Hence, the welfare of voters and the share of the vote of the incumbent depend on β and V:

(A) When $\beta = \beta^B$, the level of aggregate level of welfare is

$$\Delta W(F > 1/2, \beta = \beta^B) = N(\beta^B - U_0) + (N/2)V,$$

and the vote share is S = 1/2.

(B) When $\beta = \beta^G$ and $V \le \Delta\beta$, full information equilibrium prevails. The aggregate level of welfare is

$$\Delta W(F > 1/2, \beta = \beta^G, V \le \Delta\beta) = N(\beta^G - U_0) + (N/2)V$$
$$= N(\beta^B - U_0 + \Delta\beta) + (N/2)V,$$

and S = 1/2.

(C) When $\beta = \beta^G$ and $V > \Delta\beta$, the government gives half the voters K^B and the rest $\beta^G - U_0 < K^B$. The aggregate level of welfare is

$$\Delta W(F > 1/2, \beta = \beta^G, V > \Delta\beta) = N(\beta^B - U_0) + (N/2)(V + \Delta\beta),$$

and S = 1/2.

2. When F < 1/2, that is, fewer than half of the voters think conditions are bad, the incumbent is not always reelected. To get reelected, the government must give the larger of K^B or $\beta - U_0$ to the proportion F of voters, and K^G to the proportion (1/2 − F), while it can extract U_0 from the remaining half.

(D) When $\beta = \beta^G$ and $V \le \Delta\beta$, to get reelected, the incumbent will give

$$\Delta W(F < 1/2, \beta = \beta^G, V \le \Delta\beta) = (N/2)(\beta^G - U_0) + (N/2)V$$
$$= N(\beta^B - U_0 + \Delta\beta) + (N/2)V,$$

which is the same as under (B), with S = 1/2.

(E) When $\beta = \beta^G$ and $V > \Delta\beta$, the incumbent gets reelected by generating

$$\Delta W(F < 1/2, \beta = \beta^G) = NF(\beta^B - U_0 + V) + N(1/2 - F)$$
$$(\beta^G - U_0 + V) + (N/2)(\beta^G - U_0),$$

or

$$\Delta W(F < 1/2, \beta = \beta^G) = N(\beta^B - U_0) + (N/2)V + N(1 - F)\Delta\beta.$$

The vote share is S = 1/2.

(F) Finally, when $\beta = \beta^B$, the incumbent cannot satisfy its participation constraint and be reelected. To get reelected, the incumbent must give voters at least

$$NF(\beta^B - U_0 + V) + N(1/2 - F)(\beta^G - U_0 + V) + (N/2)(\beta^B - U_0) =$$
$$(N/2)(\beta^G + \beta^B + V) - NU_0 - NF\Delta\beta.$$

Since the highest level of welfare that can be generated when $\beta = \beta^B$ is $N\beta^B$, if incumbents were to be reelected, their rents would be

$$N\beta^B - (N/2)(\beta^G + \beta^B + V) + NU_0 + NF\Delta\beta =$$
$$NF(F - 1/2)\Delta\beta - (N/2)V + NU_0,$$

which, given that $F < 1/2$, is always less than the reservation utility, NU_0. Hence, when $F < 1/2$ and $\beta = \beta^B$, incumbents give up on reelection. The aggregate level of welfare is then

$$\Delta W(F < 1/2, \beta = \beta^B) = N(\beta^B - U_0),$$

and the vote share is $S = 0$.

The point of all of this is that when governments know what individual voters will be satisfied with, they can fine-tune their policies in such a way as to win reelection whenever possible and extract excess rents at the same time, by exploiting the minority of the more demanding voters. We are not claiming that this is what in fact happens: as Theil (1976: 3) put it, "Models should be used, not believed." Indeed, all we think this model does is to raise the puzzle as to why governments do not always satisfy the lowest bidders. But the model does show that if the very assumption of moral hazard is correct, informational asymmetries allow governments to extract excess rents.

This analysis also has statistical implications, namely, that any function relating the performance of the incumbent to the vote share (or the probability of retaining office) will be unstable. We should expect this function to have a positive slope when conditions are in fact bad and to slope slightly downward when they are good. This is best seen in Figure 7.1, which identifies the equilibria assuming that V and U_0 are constant but F, β, and $\Delta\beta$ can have different values.

Finally, it is easy to show that the electorate is better off when the government does not know individual expectations but only the expectation of the median voter, except when a majority of voters expects the conditions to be good while they are in fact bad, in which case it makes no difference. Thus the asymmetry of information typically assumed in models of accountability – voters do not know what the government can do for them, but government knows what voters will be satisfied with – works against voters.

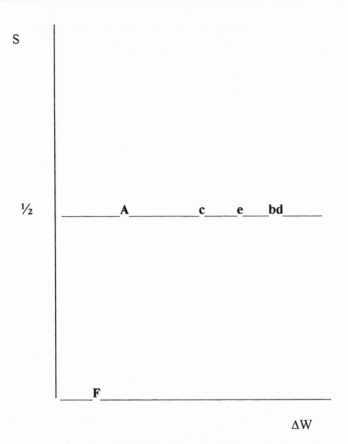

Figure 7.1. Equilibria when politicians know the distribution of voters' criteria, Capital letters show equilibria when $\beta = \beta^B$; lower case, when $\beta = \beta^G$.

Prospective Voting Entails Retrospective Information

Suppose that voters believe that politicians are not all the same and that they are swayed by the prospect of electing better governments. New voters want to use their vote to choose the better type between the incumbent and a challenger.

Formally, the easiest way to model the types of politicians is to characterize them by the value they attach to being reelected.[26] A

---

[26] Alternatively, politicians can differ in their competence, which could be modeled as $Y(\beta)$, with types characterized as $Y^C(\beta)$ and $Y^I(\beta)$.

politician is more public-spirited if he or she wants to occupy public office while extracting lower rents. Let V^I stand for the value of reelection to the incumbent and V^C to the challenger, and let $\text{pr}(V^C > V^I) = \alpha$. Then, everything else being equal, in particular the maximum legally safe level of rents, the incumbent meets his or her participation constraint when

$$r^I = U_0 - pV^I + \varepsilon,$$

and the challenger when

$$r^C = U_0 - pV^C + \varepsilon.$$

If $V^C > V^I$, then the challenger will be induced to extract lower rents by any rule that meets the participation constraint.

The performance of the incumbent is still informative. To keep things simple, assume again that voters know the conditions and the distribution of types of politicians, but are not certain whether the challenger is better than the incumbent. They can then use the performance of the incumbent to arrive at an estimate of α, namely,

$$\alpha(V^I) = 1 - \int^{V^I} f(V)dV = 1 - F(V^I).$$

If voters observe an incumbent who generated welfare W^I, knowing β and U_0, they can infer V^I. They will then vote for the incumbent with the probability $p = 1 - \alpha(V^I)$.

The equilibrium is then as follows: voters set K at $K^* = \beta - [U_0 - (1 - \alpha) V^I]$, the incumbent sets rents at $r^* = U_0 - (1 - \alpha)V^I$, and the incumbent gets reelected with the probability $p^* = 1 - \alpha$.

To see that this is an equilibrium, suppose that the incumbent sets rents at $U_0 - V^I$. Since voters expect the incumbent to set rents at $U_0 - V^I + \alpha V^I$, voters now think that the incumbent is of a better type than they anticipated. But as long as there is some positive probability that the challenger is still better, setting rents at $U_0 - V^I$ does not satisfy the incumbents participation constraint. In turn, if voters set their criterion at $\beta - [U_0 - (1 - \alpha) V^I] < K \leq \beta - (U_0 - V^I)$, knowing that $p = 1 - \alpha$, incumbents will extract U_0. Since voters want the incumbent to limit rents to $U_0 - V^I + \alpha V^I$ and since the incumbent prefers to take these rents and face the chance $p = 1 - \alpha$ of being reelected rather than taking U_0 and losing certainly, neither would want to deviate.

247

Thus, when voters use the vote prospectively, they reduce the power of incentives for the incumbent. But incumbent's performance is still informative for voters' decisions and we should expect a relation between performance and survival.

References

Alvarez, Mike, José Antonio Cheibub, Fernando Limongi, and Adam Przeworski. 1996. "Classifying Political Regimes for the ACLP Data Set." *Studies in International Comparative Development* 31: 3–36.

Banks, Arthur S. 1993a. *Cross-National Time-Series Data Archive.* Binghamton, N.Y.: Center for Social Analysis, State University of New York at Binghamton. Magnetic tape.

——— ed. 1993b. *Political Handbook of the World, 1993.* Binghamton, N.Y.: CSA Publications.

Bienen, Henry, and Nicolas Van de Walle. 1991. *Of Time and Power: Leadership Duration in the Modern World.* Stanford, Calif.: Stanford University Press.

Bobbio, Norberto. 1989. *Democracy and Dictatorship.* Minneapolis: University of Minnesota Press.

da Graça, John V. 1985. *Heads of State and Government.* New York: New York University Press.

Dahl, Robert. 1989. *Democracy and Its Critics.* New Haven: Yale University Press.

Host, Viggo, and Martin Paldam. 1990. "An International Element of the Vote? A Comparative Study of Seventeen OECD Countries. 1948–85." *European Journal of Political Research* 18: 221–39.

International Monetary Fund. 1995. *International Financial Statistics.* Washington, D.C.: International Monetary Fund. CD-ROM version.

Kiewiet, D. Roderick, and Douglas Rivers. 1984. "A Retrospective on Retrospective Voting." *Political Behavior* 6: 369–93.

Lewis-Beck, Michael. 1988. *Economics and Elections: The Major Western Democracies.* Ann Arbor: University of Michigan Press.

——— 1991. "Introduction." In Helmut Norpoth, Michael S. Lewis-Beck, and Jean-Dominique Lafay, *Economics and Politics: The Calculus of Support*, 1–8. Ann Arbor: University of Michigan Press.

Lewis-Beck, Michael, and Glenn Mitchell. 1990. "Transnational Models of Economic Voting: Tests from a Western European Pool." *Revista del Instituto de Estudios Economicos* 4: 65–81.

Lijphart, Arend, ed. 1992. *Parliamentary versus Presidential Government.* Oxford: Oxford University Press.

Pacek, Alexander, and Benjamin Radcliff. 1995. "The Political Economy of Competitive Elections in the Developing World." *American Journal of Political Science* 39: 745–59.

Paldam, Martin. 1981. "A Preliminary Survey of the Theories and Findings on Vote and Popularity Functions." *European Journal of Political Research* 9: 181–99.

———. 1991. "How Robust Is the Vote Function? A Study of Seventeen Nations over Four Decades." In Helmuth Northop, Michael S. Lewis-Beck, and Jean-Dominique Lafay, eds., *Economics and Politics: The Calculus of Support*, 9–31. Ann Arbor: University of Michigan Press.

Pasquino, Gianfranco. 1994. "Shaping a Better Republic? The Italian Case in a Comparative Perspective." Working paper No. 62. Madrid: Instituto Juan March de Estudios e Investigaciones.

Powell, G. Bingham, Jr., and Guy D. Whitten. 1993. "A Cross-National Analysis of Economic Voting: Taking Account of the Political Context." *American Journal of Political Science* 37: 391–414.

Przeworski, Adam. 1996. "Public Support for Economic Reforms in Poland." *Comparative Political Studies* 29: 520–43.

Remmer, Karen L. 1993. "The Political Economy of Elections in Latin America, 1980–1991." *American Political Science Review* 87: 393–407.

Schumpeter, Joseph A. 1942. *Capitalism, Socialism, and Democracy*. New York: Harper & Brothers.

Shugart, Matthew Soberg, and John M. Carey. 1992. *Presidents and Assemblies: Constitutional Design and Electoral Dynamics*. Cambridge: Cambridge University Press.

Stokes, Susan C. 1996a. "Public Opinion and Market Reforms: The Limits of Economic Voting." *Comparative Political Studies* 29: 499–519.

———. 1996b. "Economic Reform and Public Opinion in Peru, 1990–1995." *Comparative Political Studies* 29: 544–65.

Strom, Kaare, and Seymour M. Lipset. 1984. "Macroeconomics and Macropolitics: The Electoral Performance of Democratic Governments." Paper presented at the annual meeting of the American Political Science Association, Washington, D.C.

Summers, Robert, and Alan Heston. 1988. "A New Set of International Comparisons of Real Product and Price Levels Estimates for 130 Countries, 1950–1985." *Review of Income and Wealth* 34: 1–26.

———. 1991. "The Penn World Table (Mark 5): An Expanded Set of International Comparisons, 1950–1988." *Quarterly Journal of Economics* (May): 327–68.

Thiel, Henri. 1976. *Econometrics*. New York: John Wiley.

Part Two

The Structure of Government and Accountability

Chapter Eight

Accountability in Athenian Politics

Other chapters in this volume discuss accountability in modern democracies. As a background to these analyses, this chapter offers an account on accountability mechanisms in the first democracy – Athens in the fifth and fourth centuries B.C.[1] Athenian democracy, all things considered, must be considered a great success largely because of its elaborate system of checks and balances, which prevented rash decisions by the citizens and abuse of power by military and political leaders. In this system, mechanisms of accountability had a central place.

As a direct democracy, the Athenian political system was much simpler than modern representative democracies. In the latter, accountability can be discussed in terms of a threefold principal-agent relationship (see also the Introduction to the present volume). First, the people as a principal choose political repre-

I am grateful to Bernard Manin and Susan Stokes for comments on an earlier draft of this chapter, and especially to Mogens Herman Hansen for detailed written observations.

[1] I am not a historian, and I do not read Greek. In addition to Aristotle's *Politics* and *The Constitution of Athens*, as well as the Greek orators (cited here in the standard reference format), I rely mainly on secondary sources, notably MacDowell 1978, Ostwald 1986, Sinclair 1988, Hansen 1991, Todd 1993, and Cohen 1995. Roberts 1982 is an explicit account of accountability in Athens, with emphasis on historical episodes rather than on legal or institutional aspects. As Mogens Herman Hansen impressed on me in his comments on an earlier draft, historians of Athenian democracy disagree on many of the issues discussed in this article. This puts me in the awkward position of having either to ignore these controversial issues altogether or to take a side in debates that I have no real competence to address. As the former option would impose sharp limits on what I can say, I occasionally opt for the latter. Although I try to minimize my reliance on controversial arguments, I sometimes choose, somewhat arbitrarily, to rely on some secondary sources rather than on others.

sentatives as their agents. Second, in parliamentary systems the legislature chooses the executive as its agent. Third, the executive appoints a bureaucracy of officials as its agents. In Athens, these three relationships collapsed into one. Political leaders (orators in the Assembly) and officials (notably generals) were directly accountable to the citizens at large.

Accountability is an ex post mechanism of control. In modern democracies, control is also exercised ex ante. Voters elect politicians, the legislature nominates the government, and the government appoints officials. In Athens, there was less scope for control ex ante. Each year, some twelve hundred officials were chosen, including the members of the Council of the Five Hundred who prepared cases for the Assembly. Of these, about one hundred were chosen in direct elections, notably holders of all military commands and of the most important financial offices. The remaining were chosen by lot. All officials, whether elected or selected by lot, had to undergo public scrutiny (*dokimasia*) before they could take office. The main purpose of the scrutiny was to ensure that the candidate satisfied formal requirements of birth and citizenship. Competence for the office was not an issue. According to Hansen (1991: 200), *dokimasia* "must have been virtually always a mere formality."[2] For nonelected officials, therefore, accountability ex post was the main control mechanism. Even for elected officials, as we shall see, it was a very powerful method.

I begin by discussing political accountability quite generally, first from a conceptual point of view and then from a cost-benefit point of view. To provide a contrast with later sections, I use examples only from modern political systems. In subsequent sections I give an overview of the working of the Athenian political system as it evolved over time and then discuss the place of mechanisms of accountability within this system.

The Idea of Accountability

When preparing this chapter, I turned first to the *Oxford English Dictionary*. The result was disappointing. There are three

---

[2] Occasionally, broader issues might come up. Reading the four speeches by Lysias (nos. 16, 25, 26, 31 in the Lysian corpus) accusing or defending candidates for office, one has the impression that the scrutiny could be somewhat comparable with American Senate hearings, with emphasis on the candidate's political past and political views.

near synonymous terms, "accountability," "responsibility," and "answerability," which are essentially defined through each other. Yet I learned at least that these concepts have a formal triadic structure: an agent A is accountable *to* a principal B *for* an action X. Implicitly, the definitions also suggest that accountability is individual rather than collective – that is, that nobody can be held accountable for actions done by another member of a group to which he belongs. (For examples of collective accountability, see Heckathorn 1988.) By extension of the concept, we may also talk about *self-accountability*, when A and B are the same agent.

We need to define the idea of "holding accountable." As far as I can see, this can mean one of three things. B may dismiss A without punishing him further, punish him while retaining him as his agent, or dismiss him with additional punishment. In politics, the first mechanism is the most important. Voters can dismiss elected officials by denying them reelection; parliament can vote down a government; the president may be able to dismiss his prime minister. Accountability by dismissal has two subcases. In the first, the dismissal of one agent is automatically followed or accompanied by his replacement with another. This is the case, for instance, with the constructive vote of no confidence.[3] In the second, dismissal and replacement are distinct procedures and may even be entrusted to different organs. In systems with *dual accountability*, in which the prime minister is responsible both to

---

[3] This device was not invented by C. J. Friedrich of the 1949 Bonn constitution, as is usually thought. It has a much older history, as shown by the following passages from Montaigne (1991: 1085): "Pacuvius Calavius corrected that defective procedure, so setting a memorable example. His fellow-citizens had revolted against their magistrates. . . . One day he found the means of locking the Senate in their palace; calling the citizens together in the marketplace he told them that the time had come when they were fully at liberty to take their revenge on the tyrants who had so long oppressed them. He had those tyrants in his power, disarmed and isolated. His advice was they should summon them out one at a time by lots, decide what should be done to each of them and immediately carry out the sentence, provided that they should at the same time decide to put some honourable man in the place of the man they had condemned, so that the office should not remain unfilled." Montaigne further reports that, when Pacuvius's proposal was adopted, "there was as much discord over the elections as agreements over the rejections. Having uselessly exhausted themselves in this quarrel [the citizens] gradually began to slip this way and that out of the meeting, each going off convinced in his mind that an older, better-known evil is more bearable than an old and untried one."

255

the president and to parliament, he may be appointed by the former (subject to the latter's approval) and dismissed by the latter.

The second mechanism – punishment without dismissal – is an important mechanism of control in relations between the executive and its agents. A minister can hold his officials accountable by denying them promotion, demoting them, or moving them sideward to less important positions. This mechanism is also illustrated by the practice of imposing a fine (Australia, Belgium) or loss of job (civil servants in Argentina) on those who fail to vote in general elections.

The third mechanism – dismissal with additional punishment – can be used if the agent is guilty not merely of incompetence but also of criminal dishonesty. Usually, this is not an option within the direct control of the principal. Once the agent is dismissed, the principal may not have any further power to punish him. If the agent was dismissed for behaving criminally, he may be pursued by the criminal justice system. The principal may be able to assist in the prosecution, but except for the case in which the agent is a civil servant the principal cannot prosecute him directly.

In general, the behaviors to be encouraged or discouraged as well as the sanctions that encourage or discourage them can be either dichotomous or continuous. The agent's behavior may be one that is either performed or not, as with voting. It may also be one that can be performed more or less well, as with the conduct of policy. For some behaviors, the principal has only the stark choice between punishing and not punishing. Although a politician may take some comfort from knowing that he *almost* got the requisite number of votes, the margin of loss is dominated by the fact of losing. For other behaviors, the principal may have the choice among varying degrees of punishment, such as dismissal with or without additional sanctions. Citizens, for instance, may be punished more or less severely for failing to vote.

One kind of accountability system involves those in which behaviors match sanctions. The agent may have the choice between performance and nonperformance, and the principal a choice between punishing and not punishing, with neither action allowing of degrees. Conversely, the agent may have the choice between performing more or less well and the principal the choice between sanctioning more or less severely. Another kind involves systems in which continuous variations in performance trigger discontinuous sanctions (denying reelection to politicians) or in which a sanction may be continuously increased until the desirable performance is triggered (fining citizens who don't vote). From a normative point of view, the first kind of system is perhaps preferable, especially when the behavior is one that varies continuously. Yet in practice, winner-take-all systems may be the only feasible ones.

The value of an accountability mechanism may derive from its actual use or from the belief that it might be used. We may refer to the former as "incapacitation" and to the latter as "deterrence." Although deterrence is probably the more important in modern political systems, incapacitation should not be neglected, and in other contexts it may well be the most important. It is now widely believed, for instance, that to justify imprisonment of criminals, incapacitation is more important than deterrence (Gottfredson and Gottfredson 1985). Note, however, that when deterrence works, it is essentially costless. If fear of going to jail keeps people from breaking the law, there is no need to build more than a single jail. By contrast, incapacitation is always costly. (The same is true for attempts to shape behavior by *rewards* rather than by actual or expected punishment.)

Holding accountable or being held accountable can have costs or benefits. There are four cases, depending on whether the costs or the benefits accrue to the principal or to the agent. Whereas the benefits to the principal and the costs to the agent are built into the system, costs to the principal and benefits to the agent also arise.

1. A principal can obviously benefit from dismissing an incurably incompetent or dishonest agent (incapacitation). In the case of a competent but potentially dishonest agent, the principal benefits from the incentive effects generated by his *ability* to dismiss him (deterrence). Benefits of accountability can also arise through more perverse and unintended mechanisms. Thus in the Third and Fourth French Republics there were clear personal benefits to the deputies of holding the government accountable *even when they agreed with what it did*. If the government fell, there was always a chance that they might get a place in the new government. In France, to be *ancien ministre* was a word that opened doors.[4] And when the next government fell, the ministers could just go back to the assembly. The Fifth French Republic solved this problem by attaching a risk to the benefit, namely by

---

[4] For vivid descriptions of this system, see Priouret 1959 and Denquin 1988.

prohibiting ministers taken from the assembly to return to the assembly within the same term of parliament.[5]

2. By definition, an agent suffers from being held accountable. He also suffers from the fact that he *can* be held accountable. The knowledge that he may be punished if he pursues his own interest rather than the interest of the principal limits his ability to pursue the former.

3. The principal may incur costs in holding an agent accountable, if the agent was chosen by the principal in the first place rather than selected by lot or appointed in some other way. For the principal, to dismiss or punish someone he chose to execute his policy is to admit to having made a mistake. In politics, admitting mistakes is always costly. Suppose I vote for somebody and he turns out to perform badly. To vote against him next time around would be to admit I made a mistake. Even if I only admit it to myself, it's still unpleasant. Thus, to avoid cognitive dissonance, I might persuade myself that he hasn't done so badly after all and vote to reelect him.[6]

This is obviously a speculative argument. I am on firmer ground, I think, when asserting that we are reluctant to admit mistakes to others. A president who appoints a prime minister may want to dismiss him if he is incompetent or too independent. On the other hand, he also has a disincentive to dismiss him, because if he does so it will reflect badly on himself. This fact gives the prime minister a certain leverage. If he is indeed independent, he will want to use it. To the extent that competence and independence go together, the president (B) cannot solve the problem simply by appointing a prime minister (A) who is totally loyal to

[5] Alternatively, one might write into the constitution that a deputy who votes for a motion of no confidence that brings down the government is ineligible as minister for some specific time period. This would exclude secret voting, as practiced in the Italian Parliament. In theory, there might also be costs to the deputies of holding the government accountable, namely if the voters hold them accountable in turn, by not reelecting deputies who behave irresponsibly in this respect. In practice, I don't think this has happened. Also, in theory one might impose opportunity costs on the deputies of holding the government to account, by not allowing any given deputy to express lack of confidence in the government more than a given number of times in each term.

[6] Thus according to *New York Times Magazine* of February 28, 1999, a Republican pollster explained the favorable polls for Clinton in the Lewinsky scandal by the argument that "People don't want to admit that the man they voted for as President is so deeply flawed because that says something about themselves."

himself. In determining how far he can go, A must take account not only of B's preferences but also of the cost to B of holding him accountable. Thus A may choose X over Y, knowing that B's preference for Y over X is less intense than his preference for not holding A accountable over holding him accountable.[7]

4. An agent may benefit, finally, from the fact that he will be held accountable if he deviates from the preferred policy of the principal. John Ferejohn (Chapter 4 in the present volume) argues that increasing the degree of accountability in an agency contract can increase the power of the agent, all things considered. Specifically, he argues that agents may have an interest in making it easier for the principal to observe their behavior, in order to get him to trust them with more resources. Hence we might expect the party most favorable to large government to prefer more-transparent party rules. Independently of the substance of policy, a candidate might use his greater transparency as an argument with the voters, thus inducing other candidates to follow suit in a pooling equilibrium.

The Athenian Political System

Athenian democracy begins with the (more or less mythical) reforms of Solon (ca. 590 B.C.) and ends with military defeat and the suppression of democracy in 322. Here, I consider the system as it existed in the fifth and fourth centuries. In this period, Athens was continuously organized as a democracy, apart from two oligarchic episodes: the regime of the Four Hundred (411–410) and of the Thirty Tyrants (404–403). According to one periodization, before 463 and after 403 the emphasis was on the rule of law, whereas in the intermediate period it was on the sovereignty of the people (Ostwald 1986; also Hansen 1991: 174, cited later).

From Solon's reforms up to those of Ephialtes (462), the Athenian political system gradually moved from an aristocracy of birth through an aristocracy of wealth to a (virtually) full-fledged democracy for free male citizens.[8] In this period, the People's Assembly, to which all citizens were admitted regardless of economic status, increasingly took on the more important decision-

---

[7] For a related argument, see Elster 1985, chap. 7.1.2.

[8] Slaves, women, and metics (resident aliens) were excluded from all political functions; *thetes*, the lowest income group, were excluded from office but not from voting in the Assembly or serving as jurors in the Popular Courts.

making functions. An important development was the establishment of the institution of ostracism around 500 B.C. Once a year, the people met to decide whether to hold an ostracism – that is, to send a citizen into exile for ten years without losing his property or other citizen rights. If the vote was positive, there was another meeting two months later at which each citizen wrote on a fragment of pottery (*ostrakon*) the name of the person he wished to have expelled. Debates were not allowed at either meeting. On the condition that at least six thousand votes were cast, the person whose name appeared on the largest number of pottery sherds was ostracized. The device has been interpreted variously as an ex ante control mechanism or as an ex post mechanism of punishment.

At the same time, democratically constituted organs also took on the functions of accountability. Accusations of "crimes against the state" (*eisangelia*) were probably decided in the Assembly by the early fifth century (Ostwald 1986: 28–40). The final step occurred around 462, when *dokimasia* and *euthynai* (an obligatory scrutiny that took place when an official left office) were transferred from the Areopagus to the Council of the Five Hundred. (Later, both functions were for the most part carried out by the courts.) The Areopagus consisted of all former occupants of one of the nine archonships, the highest offices in the city. The archons could only be recruited from the highest income classes; they remained members of the Areopagus for life; and the decisions of this body could not be appealed. For all these reasons, it formed an aristocratic and conservative element in the political system. When officials instead of answering to the Areopagus became accountable to the Council of the Five Hundred, whose members were recruited from all but the lowest income class, the transition to democracy was essentially complete. The Areopagus lost most of its functions apart from judging homicide cases, but regained influence in the fourth century.

The developments over the next century are summarized by Hansen (1991: 174) in a passage that also illustrates an extreme form of accountability:

> Since Ephialtes' reforms in 462 the Assembly had more and more frequently used its increased power to legislate, and the traditional sense of the priority of the laws had given way to a sense that the people in their assembly were the highest power in the state. But in 403 the Athenians returned to the idea that the laws, not the people, must be the highest power and that the laws must be

stable, even if not wholly entrenched. Demosthenes in his speech against Timokrates tells admiringly the story of the Lokrians, who changed only one law in 200 years, because they had the marvelous custom that any proposal for a change of law must be made with a noose round the neck, and if the proposal was defeated the noose was drawn tight.

The orator Andocides (1.87) summarizes the new attitude as follows: "In no circumstances shall magistrates enforce an unwritten law. No decree, whether of the Council or the Assembly, shall override a law. No law shall be directed against an individual without applying to all citizens alike, unless an Assembly of six thousand so resolve by secret ballot." Also, from about 400 onward the Assembly could only pass decrees. Legislation was entrusted to a special body of lawgivers (*nomothetai*), drawn at random (for each session) from a panel of six thousand citizens. Jurors were also drawn randomly (for each trial) from the same panel, which was constituted once a year by drawing lots among all citizens above thirty years of age who presented themselves.

Ostracism disappeared in the fourth century. To the extent that it served as an ex post accountability device, it may be said to have been replaced by the *graphe paranomon*, a legal accusation against a citizen for having made an unconstitutional proposal in the Assembly. Even if the Assembly had passed a decree, its proposer could be punished later for having put it to a vote. More infrequently, citizens were also prosecuted for having proposed an unsuitable *law*. These procedures belonged to a larger array of constitutional principles that served to counteract the dangers of a direct, majoritarian democracy.[9] Other techniques included

---

[9] The Athenians had no constitution in the sense of a body of laws that were more difficult to change, because of delay or supermajority requirements, than other laws. "In contradistinction to the original Solonian laws, the revised corpus of laws [after 403] came to include quite a number of constitutional laws (i.e., norms defining the structure and powers of the organs of government). They did not form a separate and especially protected part of the law code; the Athenians had no constitution in the formal sense, and, though they sometimes used entrenchment clauses to make it more difficult to reverse a law or a decree, such clauses were not attached to what we call constitutional laws" (Hansen 1991: 165). As an instance of entrenchment, he cites a statute (given in Demosthenes 23.62) to the effect that "Whosoever, whether magistrate or private citizen, shall cause this ordinance to be frustrated, or shall alter the same, shall be disfranchised with his children and his property." This does not seem entirely compatible with his statement that "All political decisions in Athens were taken by simple majority" (304).

anapsephisis, a procedure whereby the Assembly could reconsider its decision; delegation of decision making to smaller bodies dominated by the older and more experienced citizens; and two-stage procedures (Hansen 1991: 307). In the case of ostracism, however, the latter device might backfire. "The procedural requirement of two meetings meant that the decision was not hasty. But the interval also gave the opportunity for organising the vote" (Sinclair 1988: 170). In the last recorded case, the two main candidates for ostracism, Nicias and Alcibiades, turned the tables on the proposer, Hyperboles, by using the interval to gather a majority for sending *him* into exile, an abuse that may have contributed to the demise of the procedure.

The four accountability mechanisms I have mentioned – *dokimasia*, *euthynai*, *eisangelia*, and *graphe paranomon* – operated mainly or only through the courts. Whereas the first two took place automatically at the beginning and expiration of office, the last two required a special initiative. The Athenian legal system differed quite radically from modern procedures, especially in that there was no public prosecutor. Not only civil cases but also criminal cases and even crimes against the state depended on the initiative of a private citizen. (But see the subsequent discussion of *apophasis* for an exception.) Many prosecutions over matters of state were in fact parts of private feuds rather than public-spirited interventions (Todd 1993: chap. 9; Cohen 1995). Also, the method for reaching a verdict was quite different from what we are used to. Cases were judged by panels of five hundred jurors (sometimes more). They could not deliberate among themselves, but cast their vote (in secret) after listening to the speeches for the prosecution and the defense. They also heard witnesses for both sides, but cross-examination was not allowed. Once a defendant had been found guilty, the jurors were usually reduced to choosing between the penalty proposed by the plaintiff and that proposed by the defendant. As in modern final-offer arbitration, this procedure may have induced each party to moderation in its proposals (Todd 1993: 134).

There were two main kinds of procedures. A *dike* was a suit in a private matter, broadly conceived. Here, the accuser usually gained financially if he won and suffered no financial loss if he didn't. A *graphe* was a suit in (roughly speaking) public matters – for example, for impiety or military desertion. With some exceptions, accusers did not gain financially if they won the case.

They might be motivated by the public interest, a desire for revenge, or envy, but not by material interest, except in the indirect sense that they might bring a suit to blackmail the accused into paying them for dropping it. If an accuser failed to obtain a fifth of the vote, he was fined and lost the right to bring similar accusations in the future, a practice deemed necessary to prevent frivolous accusations.

Athenian Mechanisms of Accountability

All political systems need devices to hold individuals accountable for their *actions*. The Athenian system was unusual in that it could also hold them accountable for their political *proposals*. In many societies, to be sure, people can be held accountable for inflammatory words and proposals even if they never get translated into action. Even speakers in a legislature may not enjoy full immunity for everything they say. Yet Athens was special in that speakers could be held accountable for the proposals they made in the Assembly. Normally, there is a presumption that an assembly can protect itself against a bad proposal simply by turning it down. If framers believe that the legislature needs to be protected against itself, they can set up a second chamber or rely on judicial review. The Athenians created a further safeguard, by punishing those who made proposals that were later found unconstitutional. (Imagine today a representative or a senator being fined for having proposed a law voted by Congress and later found unconstitutional by the Supreme Court!)

The action-proposal distinction reflects an important reality of Athenian democracy. Roughly speaking, the system had two types of leaders: orators and generals. The former had the main role in proposing policies and getting them adopted, the latter in executing them. In the fifth century individuals such as Themistocles, Pericles, and Alcibiades served both functions, but after the restoration of democracy in 403 there was a "growing specialization of oratory on the one side and military technology on the other" (Hansen 1991: 270). As a result, there also emerged specialized systems of accountability. Those who proposed policies could be held accountable through *probole* and the *graphe paranomon*; those who executed them by ostracism, *euthynai*, *eisangelia*, *apophasis*, and trials in the Assembly. In fact, Sinclair (1988: 152) suggests that the *graphe paranomon* may have been

263

created to close a loophole for the orator who carefully avoided taking executive responsibility for his proposals, for example, by proposing an ambassadorial mission without volunteering to go as ambassador.

I turn to the detail of these mechanisms shortly. First, however, let me comment on the peculiarly strict way in which the Athenians held their leaders accountable for their actions. Their mode of accountability did in fact resemble the legal principle of strict liability (Williams 1993: chap. 3). Theirs was a "results-culture" (Adkins 1972: 61), in which people were held accountable for the outcome of their actions regardless of mitigating or extenuating circumstances. The emphasis on results was linked to the tendency of the Athenians to attach more importance to shame than to guilt (Williams 1993: chap. 4; Cairns 1993: 45) as well as to the perilous situation in which they almost always found themselves. Both points are made with admirable clarity by Kenneth Dover (1994: 231–32, 159–60):

> Shame at defeat or failure, even if I know perfectly well that I did my best and was worsted by overwhelming force or by dishonesty so alien to my character as to be unintelligible and unforeseeable, can still be felt very keenly because I am aware that other people cannot know all the circumstances and may therefore believe that I lacked courage, determination, prudence or common sense. There are few shaming situations to which this consideration is inapplicable, and after all, failure *is* commonly the consequence of sloth, negligence or remediable ignorance. We tend to give the benefit of the doubt, and the Greeks . . . tended not to.
>
> A nation at war turns itself into an organization with a specific and definable purpose, and it deals more severely with negligence and inefficiency than a nation at peace; the more perilous its situation, the less importance is attached to distinctions between incapacity, thoughtlessness and treachery. . . . A Greek democracy, made aware by its experience that external enemies threatened the existence of the nation and that the democratic constitution lay under threat of subversion from within as well as from without, often talked and behaved in ways which remind us much more of totalitarian states than of parliamentary democracies as we know them.

To some extent, of course, all politics is result-oriented. As other contributions to this volume show, politicians often get rewarded or punished for what happens on their watch rather than for what could reasonably have been expected to happen, given their policies, or for how the outcome compares with the counterfactual outcome that would have been produced had another policy been adopted. The example of the Carthaginians who "punished bad counsels in their captains even when they were put right by a happy outcome" (Montaigne 1991: 1057) is certainly atypical. Yet it seems that the Athenians went further in this direction than most other polities. In the notorious trial of the Arginusae generals charged with failure to rescue shipwrecked sailors, the defense that they had been prevented by a sudden storm did not carry the day. Similarly, "the role of envoy could be hazardous," especially "when Athens was not in a strong negotiating position and envoys were likely to return to Athens with proposals or reports that were disappointing or unacceptable to the citizen body" (Sinclair 1988: 152–53). The practice of punishing unsuccessful ambassadors is close to that of punishing the bearers of bad news, a notoriously irrational form of political accountability.

I now proceed to a catalog of the main mechanisms of accountability that we can identify in the Athenian political system. I proceed in a piecewise fashion, as my main purpose in this paper is to illuminate the idea of accountability in general rather than to analyze its role in Athenian politics, a task for which I would not be qualified in any case. Ancient politics like other political systems can be studied not only for itself, but also as a reservoir of examples that can stimulate the imagination and of counterexamples that can keep it in check.

Holding Voters Accountable

I begin with an example from Aristotle's *Politics* (1297a. 15–34), which, although it does not deal with Athenian institutions, provides a useful contrast to them:

> The devices adopted in constitutions for fobbing the masses off with sham rights are five in number. . . . As regard the assembly, all alike are free to attend; but fines for non-attendance are either imposed on the rich alone, or imposed on the rich at a far higher rate. As regards the magistracies, those who possess a property qualification are not allowed to decline office on oath, but the poor are allowed to do so. As regards the law courts, the rich are fined

for non-attendance, but the poor may absent themselves with impunity. . . . In some states a different device is adopted in regard to attendance at the assembly and the law courts. All who have registered themselves may attend; those who fail to attend after registration are heavily fined. Here the intention is to stop men from registering, through fear of the fines they may thus incur, and ultimately to stop them from attending the courts and the assembly as a result of their failure to register. Similar measures are also employed in regard to the possession of arms and the practice of athletics. The poor are allowed not to have any arms, and the rich are fined for not having them. The poor are not fined if they absent themselves from physical training: the rich are.

If we assume, plausibly, that these constitutions are written by the rich and not merely for the rich, the passage illustrates two important ideas. First, as mentioned in the previous section on accountability, there can be benefits to being held accountable (self-accountability in this case). Second, through a form of pre-commitment a group may hold itself accountable, by penalizing undesirable behavior by its members. One set of individuals can enhance their power by limiting their own freedom, while at the same time reducing the power of others by expanding their freedom. These Greek constitutions forced the rich to participate in public affairs by making it costly for them not to do so, while making it less likely that the poor would participate by eliminating any costs to them of abstaining.

In democracies, Aristotle goes on to say, it is the other way around. "The poor receive payments for attendance at the assembly and the law courts; the rich are not fined if they fail to attend." In *The Constitution of Athens* (41.3) he explains how the level of payment was fixed: "At first the Athenians declined to institute pay for attendance in the Assembly. When attendance was poor, and the Prytanes [an Executive Committee of the Council of the Five Hundred that rotated among the ten Athenian tribes] had tried many devices to encourage citizens to come so that the people might ratify proposals by their vote, payment of one obol was instituted as a first move on the proposal of Agyrrhius; Heraklides of Clazomenae, who was called 'the king,' raised it two obols, and Agyrrhius made it three." The sum, which was later raised further, made attendance at the Assembly financially worthwhile to the poorer citizens (Hansen 1991: 150).

As this contrast shows, there may be a choice between

encouraging behavior by rewards and discouraging it by punishments. In most accountability structures, however, the distinction between reward and punishment is a vacuous one. It makes no difference whether we say that voters punish a politician by not reelecting him or that they withhold the reward of reelection. The implicit promise of reelection if he performs well is equivalent to an implicit threat of not being reelected if he performs badly. By contrast, one cannot threaten the voters by saying that if they do not vote they will lose the reward for voting.

Ostracism

If we leave aside the question of the origins of ostracism (Thomson 1972), three main functions have been cited. First, it could be used somewhat like our general elections, to decide between two alternative *policies* by expelling the proponent of one of them (Ostwald 1986: 27).[10] Second, it could be used somewhat like a "vote of no confidence" (Thomson 1972: 140–41, citing Wilamowitz) against specific *individuals*. Third, ostracism could be seen as a vehicle of envy, an interpretation made popular by Plutarch and defended in Walcot (1978). Although the first idea shades over into the second and the second into the third, they are nevertheless reasonably distinct.

On the first reading, ostracism was a form of control ex ante. On the second, it can be seen a mechanism of accountability ex post. Independently of the specific policies he defended, an individual might have accumulated so much power that his presence in the city was viewed as dangerous. There is to my knowledge no indication in the sources that the device, in this use of it, served as a deterrent. In other words, the value of ostracism lay in its actual use (incapacitation), not in the belief that it might be used (deterrence).

Euthynai

This automatic scrutiny of magistrates at the end of their term was especially important in the fifth century. By the fourth century

---

[10] As Mogens Herman Hansen points out to me, the solution to one problem – the risk of a civil war between the adherents of the two policies – could easily give rise to another, namely if the nonostracized leader casts himself as a tyrant.

it had become secondary in importance to *eisangelia* (Todd 1993: 113). Athenian magistrates (including generals) worked in boards, usually with ten members. According to Hansen (1991: 237), "there was some dissonance between collective administration and the Athenian legal system, which was based on individual responsibility, so that only an individual could be brought into a court, not a board of magistrates as such. If a board of ten was required to answer for its administration, that involved ten prosecutions." As we shall see, this principle was sometimes violated in the operation of other mechanisms of accountability.

In the process of *euthynai*, a board of auditors first examined the accounts of any public funds the magistrate had received and spent in office. Next, the magistrate was brought into a court, where the auditors brought accusation against any abuses they might have found. Even if nothing had been found, any citizen could at this stage bring up an accusation of financial mismanagement or bribery. If the magistrate was found guilty, he had to pay back ten times the amount of money involved in cases of embezzlement, or the simple amount in less serious cases. In a further stage, anyone could bring a charge of other kinds of misconduct in office before a special official, who could render a formal condemnation if he thought it well founded. In the fourth century, at least, this condemnation was not final but was passed on to a court for trial. Although *euthynai* was probably more important in the fifth century, the best-known case occurred in 343, when Demosthenes unsuccessfully brought a charge against Aeschines for having mismanaged an ambassadorial mission to Macedonia, an accusation that triggered a prolonged legal feud.

Eisangelia

This procedure was a suit brought by an individual citizen against a fellow Athenian on grounds of religious or political misconduct. Building on Hansen (1975), Ostwald (1986: 525–27) provides a full list of all known fifth-century cases of *eisangelia*. Several of them were for impiety, which does not concern us here. From the point of view of political accountability, the two important cases occurred in the interval between the two oligarchies. After the overthrow of the Four Hundred, three Athenians were tried and two of them executed for the part they had played in the prior overthrow of the democracy. Immediately before the tyranny of the Thirty, a dubious character called Agoratus was manipulated by some of the future tyrants to denounce their enemies. The proper procedures were set in motion, but before they could be concluded, the Thirty came to power. "Riding roughshod over proper legal procedure, they condemned all the accused to death and declared Agoratus a public benefactor" (Ostwald 1986: 527).

From the fourth century, we have a text saying that *eisangelia* can be brought against a citizen on the grounds that he "seeks to overthrow the democracy of the Athenians . . . , attends a meeting in any place with intent to undermine the democracy or forms a conspiracy; or if anyone betrays a city or fleet or a force on land or sea; or if any speaker in the Assembly takes payment to make speeches contrary to the interests of the Athenian people" (Hypereides 4.7–8). There is an interesting omission in this list. Although one can imagine bribery of voters no less than of speakers, citizens could not be held accountable, by *eisangelia* or other procedures, for how they cast their votes (Hansen 1991: 144). With respect to voting in the courts, the Athenians made bribing virtually impossible by selecting jurors by lot on the morning of each trial and by having them vote in secret. Voting in the Assembly, by contrast, was public, and everyone could attend if they came early enough (Hansen 1991: 131). Given the quorum requirement of six thousand, one might think that bribery of a sufficiently large number would be impracticable. This conclusion seems plausible for ordinary decisions by the Assembly, which required the vote of a majority of those present. For ostracisms, however, only a plurality was needed. In excavations at Athens, one has found 191 pottery sherds with the name of Themistocles (who was ostracized ca. 470 B.C.) inscribed on them, written in fourteen different hands only. This indicates at the very least organized political activity, and quite possibly bribery. As the text by Hypereides dates from ca. 330, it is not surprising that he does not mention prosecution of activities that at that time were unlikely to occur. Yet there is no evidence that voters could be held accountable in the fifth century either.

For present purposes the most important fourth-century examples of *eisangelia* were the astonishingly frequent charges made against generals. In the eighty-one years from 403 to 322, we know of some thirty generals who were prosecuted on serious charges (Hansen 1975: 58–65). "Athens had 30,000 full citizens: even in a modern nation state with millions of inhabitants such a large number of political prosecutions would be remarkable" (Hansen 1991: 217). Although "the charge was always framed in terms of corruption or treason, as required by the . . . law," Hansen (1991: 217) argues that "there can be no doubt that a general was often denounced to the people for having lost a battle or being unlucky in a campaign." Sinclair (1988: 151) also notes that conviction rates and severity of penalties were especially high in the unsuccessful periods of Athenian military affairs, confirming the idea that the Athenians were interested in results, not in excuses. Hansen (1991: 217) argues that "the very large number of prosecutions by *eisangelia* faces the historian with an uncomfortable dilemma: either the Athenian Assembly had a notable tendency to elect corrupt and traitorous generals, or else the People's Assembly and the People's Court had a habit of condemning honourable generals on false grounds." This seems true enough, but we should also consider Dover's view, cited earlier, that a nation more or less continuously at war might benefit on rule-utilitarian grounds from punishing generals merely for being unlucky.

Apophasis

Much of what we know about this procedure derives from three speeches by Dinarchus, written for the prosecution of three political leaders (Demosthenes being one) who had been accused of taking bribes from Harpalus, the treasurer of Alexander the Great. *Apophasis*, which was introduced in the 340s and appears to have been used quite frequently, was similar to the *eisangelia* in that it prosecuted attempts to commit political crimes, such as treason, attempts to overthrow the democracy, and bribery. It differed in that the charge was brought not by an individual but by the Areopagus or by the Assembly. In either case, the charge was prepared by the Areopagus, which presented a preliminary verdict to the Assembly. If the verdict was "not guilty," the case was shelved; if "guilty," it was passed on to the Assembly, which could either reject the verdict or confirm it and pass it on to the courts for the final decision (Hansen 1991: 292; MacDowell 1978: 190–91). When the first charge originated in the Assembly, it would have to be made by an individual. When it began with the Areopagus, it represented the only Athenian form of state-initiated prosecution.

Trial by the Assembly

In two important cases, it is possible (although controversial) that officials were tried by the Assembly as a whole rather than by the courts. In both cases, charges were brought against a whole board of officials. In both, the Assembly was swept by emotion, and most of the accused were convicted and executed. In one of the cases, the prosecution respected the principle of individual accountability; in the other, it did not.

The first case (probably ca. 440) concerned the *Hellenotamiai*, a board of ten officials who administered the revenues from the Delian League. All we know about this episode is a passage from a speech by Antiphon (5.69–70): "[The] *Hellenotamiai* were once accused of embezzlement, as wrongfully as I am today. Anger swept reason aside, and they were all put to death save one. Later, the true facts became known. This one, whose name is said to have been Sosias, though under sentence of death, had not yet been executed. Meanwhile it was shown how the money had disappeared. The Athenian people rescued him from the very hands of the Eleven [the officials responsible who carried out the sentences]; while the rest had died entirely innocent." There is no need to stress the implicit condemnation of this impulsive action.

The second case (from 406) arose after an Athenian victory in a naval battle at the Arginusae islands. According to Xenophon (*Hellenica* 1.6–7), the victorious generals were prevented by a storm from rescuing sailors from disabled vessels in the fleet. Later, eight of the ten generals were charged collectively with treason and sentenced to death, and the six of them who were in Athens executed. I shall outline the main steps in the procedure that led to this outcome. (For a full account, see Ostwald 1986: 431–45).

After a preliminary meeting at the Assembly that debated the responsibility of the generals without making any decision, the matter was sent (back) to the Council of the Five Hundred. A member of the council, Callixeinus, persuaded the council to adopt and put before the Assembly a proposal to judge the generals immediately, stating that as the Assembly had already debated the

271

case no further hearings were required. Euryptolemos and others then stated their intention to bring a *graphe paranomon* against Callixeinus for having made this proposal, presumably on the grounds that the proposal treated "as a judicial procedure what had been merely a deliberative meeting of the Assembly" (Ostwald 1986: 439). In the words of MacDowell (1978: 188), the "consequence of this would be that the proposal could not take effect unless Callixeinus was first tried and acquitted on that charge. Uproar followed. There were shouts that it would be intolerable if the people were not allowed to do what they wished. One speaker suggested that Euryptolemos and his supporters should be tried by the same vote as the [generals], and they felt compelled to withdraw their threat of a *graphe paranomon*."

As Xenophon (*Hellenica* 1.7.14–16) continues the story, "when some of the Prytanes refused to put the question to vote in violation of the law, Callixeinus again mounted the platform and urged the same charge against them; and the crowd cried out to summon to court those who refused. Then the Prytanes, stricken with fear, agreed to put the question – all of them, except Socrates." Euryptolemos then made another speech, in which he urged that the generals be given time to prepare their defense and be judged individually rather than collectively. Xenophon concludes his account as follows:

> When Euryptolemos had thus spoken, he offered a resolution that the men be tried . . . separately; whereas the proposal of the Council was to judge them all by a single vote. The vote being now taken as between these two vote proposals, they decided at first in favour of the resolution of Euryptolemos; but when Menecles interposed an objection under oath [*hypomosia*] and a second vote was taken, they decided in favour of the Council. After this they condemned the generals who took part in the battle, eight in all; and the six who were in Athens were put to death. And not long afterwards the Athenians repented, and they voted that complaints [*probolai*] be brought against any who had deceived the people . . . and that Callixeinus be included among them. (*Hellenica* 1.7.34–35)

Deterrence of Frivolous Suits

The Athenians had a number of devices intended to deter "sycophants," individuals who brought frivolous suits for the sake of financial gain. Anyone who brought a *graphe* and failed to get a fifth of the votes at the trial had to pay a fine and lost the right to make similar accusations in the future. The same penalty was imposed if he abandoned a case after starting it, as a blackmailer might do if he succeeded in getting a bribe from his victim (MacDowell 1978: 64). A citizen who abandoned an *eisangelia* once initiated was also liable to a fine. "He was, however, dispensed from the usual further provision than an accuser in a public prosecution was liable to a fine of 1,000 drachmas plus partial *atimia* [loss of civil rights] if he obtained less than a fifth of the votes: treason and political corruption were reckoned as such dangerous crimes that the Athenians wanted no obstacle to stand in the way of an accuser. It may have been just this favoured position of the accuser in the *eisangelia* that led to the abuse of the procedure; and shortly before 330 the Athenians were obliged to apply the customary provision to the case of *eisangelia* as well" (Hansen 1991: 214–15).

The principle of punishing the accuser in an *eisangelia* that failed to get the requisite number of votes amounts to a *two-step accountability device*: holding to account those who held officials to account for no good reason. The principle also applied to those who brought a *graphe paranomon* and failed to get enough votes. Speakers in the Assembly could get around it, however, by hiring sycophants to make risky proposals in their stead (Hansen 1991: 208). Another device that could serve the two-step function was *probole*, an action that could be brought against sycophants and, as in the case of the Arginusae generals, against anyone who deceived the people more generally.

Graphe Paranomon

In the fourth century, this device was a centerpiece of Athenian democracy. As with *eisangelia*, it was used with amazing frequency. Hansen (1991: 209) notes that "the significance of the *graphe paranomon* can best be set in relief by comparing it with the situation in the modern state in which the right of the courts to oversee legislation has been the strongest. The Supreme Court of the United States has had the power to test and overthrow Congressional Acts since 1803. In the period 1803–96 that power was used 135 times: our sources show us that at Athens that figure was nearly reached in two decades."

273

Although often described as "indictment for making an illegal proposal," the institution of *graphe paranomon* had in fact a broader scope. A decree proposed in the Assembly could be nullified, and its proposer punished, if it violated an existing law, was procedurally flawed, or was deemed damaging to the interest of the people (Hansen 1991: 206). In some of the most famous cases of *graphe paranomon*, the accused was charged with having proposed to bestow honors and privileges on an unworthy person. Although the charges were usually phrased in legal terms, this need not mean more than the legal phrasing in cases of *eisangelia* against unsuccessful generals.

Hansen offers another reason for believing that the charges more often than not were substantial rather than formal. A *graphe paranomon* was introduced by a *hypomosia*, an allegation under oath that a particular decree was illegal. This could either be done before the decree had been submitted to a vote or after it had been voted and adopted. If the *hypomosia* occurred before the vote was taken, it was postponed until the court had rendered its verdict. One might expect that after a decision by the court that the proposal was legal, it would be passed on to the Assembly for voting. This may not have been the case, however. Hansen (1991: 210) argues that if the court decided that the decree was legal, it automatically counted as having passed, a practice that makes sense only if it was assessed on substantial rather than formal grounds.

It is not clear to what extent the *graphe paranomon* actually served its ostensible function, which was to keep policy making within the bounds of the law rather than to prosecute or persecute particular individuals. To serve the former function, the charge would have to be brought by a citizen who was genuinely motivated by reason rather than by interest or passion (see Elster 1998 for this trichotomy of motives). The threat by Euryptolemos to bring a *graphe paranomon* against Callixeinus seems to have been motivated by a genuine concern for the public interest. An example of a (more or less) disinterested *graphe paranomon* that was successfully carried out was the accusation made against Thrasybulus after the fall of the oligarchs in 403. Thrasybulus had proposed that all those who had left Athens for Piraeus during their reign be made Athenian citizens when they came back, including foreigners and slaves. "However well intentioned, the proposal will have alarmed the city people: the influx of an unknown number of slaves and of a thousand foreigners would have tipped the electoral balance in their disfavor, and the successful passage of the motion by the Assembly gave their fear substance. In the interest of allaying these apprehensions and of not jeopardizing the reconciliation, Archinus had the decree annulled through a *graphe paranomon*" (Ostwald 1986: 504), not on grounds of its content but on a legal technicality.

These are both fifth-century cases. Over the course of the fourth century, the *graphe paranomon* increasingly became "a major weapon in political warfare" (Sinclair 1988: 153). "Kephalos, a politician at the beginning of the fourth century, boasted that, though he had proposed many decrees, he had never had a *graphe paranomon* brought against him; but the boast of Aristophon, who died in the 330s, was that he had been acquitted in *graphai paranomon* seventy-five times" (MacDowell 1978: 51). The best known of these political cases is a suit brought by Aeschines against Ktesipon for having proposed a decree that the people of Athens should confer a gold crown on Aeschines' old rival Demosthenes. Among the three reasons adduced by Aeschines to show the illegality of this proposal, two are based on technicalities. The third objection, however, is merely pseudolegal. Ktesipon had proposed that the herald should declare that Demosthenes was rewarded by the crown "because he continually speaks and does what is best for the people" (Aeschines 3.49). Yet, Aeschines says, given that "all the laws forbid inserting falsehoods in the decrees of the people" (Aeschines 3.50), he only has to show that the praise given to Demosthenes is false in order to prove that the proposal was illegal. The greater part of his speech, therefore, is devoted to showing that Demosthenes consistently acted against the interest of the people.

Summary and Conclusion

I conclude by highlighting some of the points that emerge from this survey, partly to bring out some unique or unusual features of the Athenian system of accountability and partly to underline commonalities with modern democratic procedures.

1. Any political system rests on a combination of control ex ante and accountability ex post. A system that, like the Athenian democracy, relies heavily on random selection in appointing officials must inevitably give a large place to accountability. The

Athenian device of ostracism is ambiguous in this respect. Depending on the occasion, it may either have served to select policies or to punish individuals.

2. In modern democracies, people are held accountable if they are demonstrably incompetent or demonstrably dishonest. In Athens, they could also be punished for sheer bad luck. This is perhaps the most striking difference between modern and ancient systems of accountability. In addition to the factors I adduced earlier to explain this difference – the dominance of shame over guilt and the imperatives of war – the religious beliefs of the Athenians are also relevant. If an action produces a bad outcome in what appears to be an accidental way, observers may suspect that the situation was engineered by the gods to punish the agent for some blamable prior deed. In a deeply religious society, there are no innocent accidents (Dover 1994: 150).

3. I have distinguished between two purposes of accountability: incapacitation and deterrence. In modern analytical thinking about accountability, as represented by most of the contributions to the present volume, the second approach is by far the predominant one. It would be rash to say that the Athenians were entirely foreign to reasoning in terms of incentive effects. As I mentioned, the principle of strict liability could make sense in a rule-utilitarian perspective. Yet I believe the Athenians were at least equally concerned with ridding themselves of leaders whom they believed to be a threat to the city.

4. The Greek procedures of accountability were part of a system of checks and balances. As in any democracy, there were checks on the people as well as on its agents. To check their leaders – generals and orators – the Greeks used *eisangelia* and *graphe paranomon*, as well as the other procedures that I have discussed. Checks on impulsive or emotional decisions by the people were embodied in *anapsephisis*, two-stage procedures, and the delegation of decision making to smaller bodies.

5. A further check on the people was created by the costs of holding their leaders accountable, notably if competent military leaders were dismissed and executed for sheer bad luck. There were checks on the people in their capacity as checkers of the leaders. Irresponsible prosecutions of orators and generals could themselves be subject to prosecution (two-step accountability). Although Roberts (1982) makes a sustained argument against the view that the Athenian people acted as an emotional mob when

indicting their leaders, the fact is that there were institutional safeguards against such behavior.

6. The converse of this phenomenon – the benefits of being held accountable – is not found in Athenian democracy. In oligarchies, by contrast, the ruling elites may have an interest in holding themselves accountable for fulfilling political and military duties – and in *not* holding the majority of the citizens accountable in the same way. The Athenians made the citizens perform their duties by paying them to do so, not by punishing them for not doing so.

7. The system of checks and balances through mutual accountability had an "unmoved mover" or unchecked checker, in the Athenian people meeting in the Assembly or serving as jurors. The ordinary citizen could not be held accountable for the way he cast his votes. The lack of provisions for punishing citizens who sold their votes represents a lacuna – either in the institutions themselves or in the texts that have come down to us. At the top of the pyramid, the Areopagus was also immune from accountability.

8. The sanctions involved in the Athenian accountability systems were severe. *Eisangelia* and trials in the Assembly often resulted in execution of the accused. *Graphe paranomon* and *apophasis* could lead to crippling fines and loss of civil rights. Moreover, because all prosecutions (before the late introduction of *apophasis*) were left to private initiative, the pattern of accountability was random rather than systematic. Although the combination of result orientation, severity, and arbitrariness strikes a modern observer as undesirable, it took more than two thousand years for a better system of democratic accountability to emerge.

References

Adkins, A. W. H. 1972. *Moral Values and Political Behaviour in Ancient Greece*. New York: Norton.

Cairns, D. 1993. *Aidos: The Psychology and Ethics of Honour and Shame in Ancient Greek Literature*. Oxford: Oxford University Press.

Cohen, D. 1995. *Law, Violence and Community in Classical Athens*. Cambridge: Cambridge University Press.

Denquin, J.-M. 1988. *1958: La genèse de la Vᵉ République*. Paris: Presses Universitaires de France.

Dover, K. 1994. *Greek Popular Morality*. Indianapolis: Hackett.

Elster, J. 1985. *Making Sense of Marx*. Cambridge: Cambridge University Press.

1998. *Alchemies of the Mind: Studies in Rationality and the Emotions*. Cambridge: Cambridge University Press.

Gottfredson, S., and D. Gottfredson. 1985. "Selective Incapacitation?" *Annals of the American Academy of Political and Social Science* 478: 135–49.

Hansen, M. H. 1975. *Eisangelia*. Odense: Odense University Press.

1991. *The Athenian Democracy in the Age of Demosthenes*. Oxford: Blackwell.

Heckathorn, D. A. 1988. "Collective Sanctions and the Emergence of Prisoner's Dilemma Norms." *American Journal of Sociology* 55: 366–84.

MacDowell, D. M. 1978. *The Law in Classical Athens*. Ithaca, N.Y.: Cornell University Press.

Montaigne. 1991 [1580–92]. *Essays*. M. E. Screech, trans. London: Penguin.

Ostwald, M. 1986. *From Popular Sovereignty to the Rule of Law*. Berkeley: University of California Press.

Priouret, R. 1959. *La république des députés*. Paris: Grasset.

Roberts, J. T. 1982. *Accountability in Athenian Government*. Madison: University of Wisconsin Press.

Sinclair, R. K. 1988. *Democracy and Participation in Athens*. Cambridge: Cambridge University Press.

Thomson, R. 1972. *The Origin of Ostracism*. Copenhagen: Gyldendal.

Todd, S. C. 1993. *The Shape of Athenian Law*. Oxford: Oxford University Press.

Walcot, P. 1978. *Envy and the Greeks*. Warminster: Aris and Phillips.

Williams, B. A. O. 1993. *Shame and Necessity*. Berkeley: University of California Press.

Chapter Nine

Government Accountability in Parliamentary Democracy

The chapters in this volume are devoted to the subject of democratic accountability. Most of these contributions focus on the relationship between the performance of institutional agents and the preferences of political principals from the broader polity – citizens, the electorate, or actual voters. This relationship is said to reflect *accountability* if there are instruments available to political principals enabling them to discern and sanction the behavior of institutional agents. In most of the world's democracies, however, institutional agents are (at best) only *indirectly* accountable to these political principals. Most of the world's democracies, that is, are parliamentary, and the essence of parliamentary democracy is the accountability of the government (also called cabinet, executive, or administration) to the *legislature*. Of course, the legislature is exposed to the discipline of the electoral system, and so there may well be a multilinked chain of accountability between government and electorate. Although citizens in parliamentary democracies have no recourse to sanctioning a government directly, they can change the composition of parliament, which, in turn, may force changes in the composition of the cabinet. Whether this broader form of accountability obtains or not, it is still of interest to examine the narrower issue of government accountability to parliament, and, in fact, the latter is necessary for any broader accountability. The purpose of the chapter, as its title indicates, is to concentrate on this arrangement of institutional accountability.[1]

The accountability of the government to parliament is not

---

[1] This argument is elaborated more fully, and tested empirically, in Laver and Shepsle 1996.

merely a normative desideratum of parliamentary democracy. It is also described by the manner in which holding the government or one of its ministers to account is institutionalized. This comes in the form of a privileged legislative motion of confidence or no confidence. When a question of accountability or propriety is raised, about an individual minister or an entire cabinet, such a motion may clear the air. If a confidence motion (moved by the government) is defeated or a no-confidence motion (moved by the opposition) is passed – ordinarily by a simple majority vote – a government (or one of its ministers) is obliged to resign. We rarely see a successful vote of no confidence consummated, however. This is because the mechanism of accountability normally works as a credible threat, a weapon in parliament's arsenal, in short a veritable club behind the door that induces appropriate behavior. Even when it fails to do so, such a motion is rarely brought to a conclusion, because the government anticipates a successful vote against it and resigns in advance of this.

Since as a practical matter cabinets have a firm grip on the day-to-day business of parliament, it might be thought that the executive is in a strong position to block accountability considerations from the agenda. Indeed, were that true, then the executive could either extend its life, even after a legislative majority had lost confidence in it, or engage in activities that would cause a majority to lose confidence in it without fear of subsequent accountability repercussions. Empirically, it happens that in the parliamentary democracies of western Europe (and probably elsewhere as well), motions of no confidence brought by opposition parties are privileged and have relatively easy agenda access. In most parliaments a simple no-confidence motion is in order at any time; sometimes, as in Norway, a second is not even required. Effectively, then, an opposition leader may decide to put such a motion forward while shaving that morning! In our survey of practices in Europe, the most stringent agenda requirement we found was in Greece where a no-confidence motion may not be introduced within six months of a previously failed no-confidence motion (unless it has signatories to it in excess of a parliamentary majority). In general, accountability arrangements are not victimized by agenda machinations.[2]

---

[2] Detail is provided in Laver and Shepsle 1994: 290–91. There we note the interesting fact that, since matters of accountability are the essence of par-

While it is reassuring that governments cannot evade the no-confidence accountability mechanism by agenda manipulation, there are other limits on or restrictions to its use, some of which may be debilitating. The fact of the matter is that parliamentary accountability mechanisms have not been much scrutinized by the political science or political economy literatures.[3] One of the purposes of this chapter is to suggest what might be at stake in such an examination. To preview our analysis, consider a potential mover of a no-confidence motion. What in the world could he or she have in mind? Surely a mover of a motion of no confidence will have forecasts about what will transpire if the motion passes or fails. If it fails, then the status quo is preserved and the sitting cabinet in which (or individual minister in whom) no confidence was alleged would remain in place. (Of course, it is entirely conceivable that the vote itself – both the fact that it had taken place and how near the motion was to passing – has a sobering effect on the incumbent government or minister; thus, it is not quite correct to say that the status quo ante is "preserved.") But what if it passes? What happens then? Passing a no-confidence motion obliges a cabinet (or minister) to resign and parliament, subsequently, to replace it with a feasible alternative. If the prospective alternatives available are unpleasant to a parliamentary majority that is about to oblige its cabinet or a minister to resign, however, then its threat of a vote of no confidence is hardly credible and, in turn, the institution of accountability between executive and legislature in parliamentary democracy is attenuated. That is, *the effectiveness of accountability institutions in parliamentary democracy depends upon the credibility of the no-confidence mechanism, which, in turn, depends upon the alternatives available to replace a sitting cabinet or minister.* A parliamentary majority would be loathe to vote no confidence in a cabinet if it could not then agree on a successor it preferred.

The remainder of this chapter analyzes these microfoundations of accountability. To simplify the discussion we will assume that parliamentary parties are unitary actors. By this we mean that

liamentary democracy, since no-confidence motions cannot be entertained when parliament is not in session, and since parliaments are typically not in session during the long summer recess, strictly speaking most European governments are not accountable in the summertime!

[3] Exceptions include Huber 1996 and Diermeier and Feddersen 1996.

either they consist of collections of like-minded politicians, any one of whom is a copy of any other, or they have members with heterogeneous preferences who nevertheless submit to a party consensus, presumably because of the carrots and sticks available to party leaders.[4] Consequently, the players in our formulation of the game of government accountability are the leaders of the parliamentary parties.

The Institutions of Cabinet Government

The accountability relationship we want to explore is one in which a subset of the players holds the keys to government ministries. They comprise the cabinet or government, and each possesses extraordinary authority within the jurisdiction of his or her ministry. These politicians (or their appointees) turn up at ministerial offices each morning, meet with their senior civil servants, and generally do policy-relevant sorts of things as they carry out their ministry's business. They typically perform these activities as individual ministers within the confines of their individual ministries. They sometimes perform as members of a governmental team, coordinated by the cabinet. This underscores the fact that there really is a sequence of accountability relationships – between senior civil servants and their minister, between individual ministers and the cabinet they comprise, between the cabinet and the parent legislature, and between the legislature and the broader public. We focus on the one between the cabinet and parliament, and so we shall fix by assumption expectations of what happens in all these other relationships.

Before doing so, let's set the terms of discourse. Issues of accountability are inevitably about policy – about whether policy choices in institutional settings are compatible with the preferences of political principals. So we must have a conceptual language in which to talk about policy choice. We employ the generalized spatial model, the simple version of which was popularized by Downs and Black forty years ago. Suppose, therefore, that policy alternatives are represented as points in an n-dimensional Euclidean space. The dimensions of this space

---

[4] This is not to say that our approach does not extend to more-general circumstances of intraparty diversity, only that there is no need to take up this case in the present discussion.

describe the parameters of policy making – pounds spent on military uniforms, francs on school construction, kroners on transportation infrastructure, limits on levels of particulates in the atmosphere, the growth rate target for the money supply, or permissiveness toward divorce, drug use, or sexual preference, and so on. A government policy may be thought of as a parameter setting on each and every one of these policy dimensions. Clearly there are hundreds, perhaps thousands, of dimensions on which governments must make policy.

Unitary political parties are the actors of interest, so we must characterize their preferences and opportunities. As long-lived institutions, parties have a history or reputation, as well as a recent record of campaigning for office. The former consists of the legacy of past campaigns and stints in government; the latter is derived from the most recent party manifesto, campaign speeches by leaders, and identities of shadow ministers. Together these things nail down a party location in the policy space.[5] That is, we assume that a party's preferences are anchored by a point in the policy space – the party's *ideal policy vector* – and that policy satisfaction declines with distance from this ideal point. The party ideal point may be taken to be the set of policies it would implement were it currently in control of all the levers of policy making. The party is assumed to implement these policies either because its members and leaders care intrinsically about policy or because the party is a perfect agent for external constituencies in the larger electoral game. We do not distinguish between these, nor do we assume that parties seek office, per se.[6]

---

[5] We do not specify the mechanism or formula according to which the past and the present are combined into a contemporary party position. One, offered by Fiorina 1981, suggests that voters and other political actors are Bayesian updaters, adjusting a weighted average of past observations in order to incorporate current observations. We do insist that, however arrived at, current party positions are common knowledge.

[6] The classic Downsian premise of office-oriented parties (which formulate policies in order to secure office rather than the reverse, as Downs put it) stands awkwardly alongside the fact that, since the end of World War II, minority governments have prevailed about 25% of the time in Europe. A minority government is one in which the parties in the cabinet have, between them, less than a majority of the seats in the full parliament. If the holding of office were the prevalent motivation, then we should *never* observe minority governments – the majority opposition parties could boot them out and secure the pleasures of office for themselves. If, in fact, we observed minority governments only occasionally, we

283

Policy preferences are not the only thing a political party brings to parliament. It also brings a *weight*, the proportion of seats in parliament it controls. The distribution of parliamentary weights determines the "decisive structure" of the strategic interactions that take place among these parties in parliament. For most purposes, then, we may take party ideals, policy preferences, and weights as the ingredients of a weighted majority rule game that determines who the government is and what policies are implemented.[7]

Now partition the dimensions of the policy space into subsets; each subset of dimensions is a *jurisdiction* over which a government ministry is assigned responsibility. While it might be thought that decisions about which policies will be dealt with by which ministries are discretionary ones, made and unmade at any time, this would be a silly way to proceed. The jurisdictional structure of parliamentary government constitutes a set of standing decisions, at most tinkered with at the margins. It may be thought of as an equilibrium of a larger game, which, for present purposes, may be taken as exogenous.[8] So, at the outset there is a relatively fixed structure to politics and policy given by the jurisdictional responsibilities of ministries.[9]

In this setting we define a *government* as an allocation of ministerial portfolios among parties. The parties that receive portfolios, and hence a place at the cabinet table, are said to be

could attribute the latter to "mistakes" and continue to maintain the office-seeking motivation. However, with minority governments constituting fully one-quarter of all postwar European governments, the empirical facts do not permit this. This means that we cannot treat the cabinet as a sack of trophies to be divvied up among the "winners." Instead, the cabinet must be taken as a policy-making engine.

[7] Our approach would additionally accommodate a set of salience weights for each party, reflecting the fact that its interests vary across policy dimensions. We believe, in fact, that this is typically the case, though it really does not add much to our discussion here so we will ignore it.

[8] Random events, like the oil shocks of the 1970s, for example, may disturb these standing decisions, leading to the creation of new ministries. Likewise, an accumulation of dimensions that have not found a ministerial home may eventually be hived off into a new jurisdiction, as apparently happened in many industrial democracies with the creation of urban affairs ministries to deal with policy regarding urban decline and regeneration.

[9] This is similar to the structure provided by the jurisdictional arrangements of the legislative committee system in American politics.

the parties of government; those that do not are the parties in opposition. If, for example, there were five parliamentary parties and three ministerial portfolios, then the number of feasible governments is 125. (Notice that a government is not merely a *coalition* of parties but also a *distribution* of portfolios among parties.) The accountability of government to parliament depends, as we shall see, on how governments are selected (and deselected) and what governments do once in office. That is to say, the capacity of parliamentary principals to discern agent performance, to sanction it if necessary, and thus to condition, incentivize, and constrain agent behavior so that performance is accountable, depends on the institutional mechanisms available to the principals for making and breaking governments, on the one hand, and the institutional discretion agents have to formulate policies once in office, on the other. In what follows we describe a particular rendering of each of these – called the "portfolio allocation approach" – based on our previous work. But let us be clear that, however one models government formation and ministerial policy making, it is these institutional features that demarcate the accountability relationship between government and parliament.

Government Formation and Ministerial Discretion

The government formation process is the method by which parliamentary principals control their agent, the government. They select the agent in the first instance, monitor its performance, and, on the basis of the latter, either maintain it in office (by approving votes of confidence and defeating votes of no confidence should they arise) or replace it with an available alternative. Thus, "making and breaking governments" is a method for dealing with problems of both adverse selection and moral hazard. Empirically, of course, parliamentary principals do even more than this, involved as they are in the policy-making process (to varying degrees in different parliamentary democracies). We abstract this away, assuming a rather strict division of labor. In our model parliaments make and break governments; governments, in turn, govern.

This means that governments have rather broad discretion in the making of policy. In a sense, they can "do whatever they like." In fact, they do so subject to maintaining the confidence of

285

parliament; they are constrained maximizers. In the portfolio allocation approach, we suppose that ministers have discretion on those policy dimensions that fall within their ministry's jurisdiction. Suppose, for example, that there are five key dimensions of policy and these have been partitioned into the domains of three ministries – two two-dimensional jurisdictions and one one-dimensional jurisdiction. The government, then, consists of three ministries assigned to three (not necessarily different) parties – one controlling the first two dimensions of the policy space, the second the next two dimensions, and the third the last dimension. The first minister will exercise discretion in the sense that she will optimize from her party's perspective by selecting the first two components of her party's ideal point as her ministry's policy. Likewise the second minister will choose the third and fourth components of his party's ideal point as the policy to be pursued by his ministry. Finally, the third minister will select the fifth and final component of its party's ideal as the policy of the last ministry. (Thus, if a single party controls the entire government – that is, all three ministers are drawn from the same party – then that party's ideal point is implemented as policy.) This is how all players in the game (and observers in the larger electoral process) forecast what policy any particular coalition government will pursue.[10]

To summarize, a government is an allocation of portfolios among parties. Each government party, through its ministerial representatives, chooses appropriate components of its ideal point as policy for those ministerial jurisdictions it controls. In effect, each feasible government is a point in the policy space – a forecast of the policies it will implement predicated on ministerial discretion and optimizing behavior. Moreover, all actors, both in and out of government (indeed, in and out of parliament), share common forecasts for what it means in policy terms to select any feasible government.[11] Professional observers of parliamentary

---

[10] The forecast that a minister will choose party-ideal point projections on the dimensions in the ministry's jurisdiction is predicated on the assumption of separable preferences. An interpretation for the case of nonseparable preferences, involving more-intricate reaction functions, is provided in our book, but need not detain us here.

[11] Read the relevant issue of any elite magazine, like the *Economist*, just after a parliamentary government has formed to find the common-knowledge forecast on display for its readers.

politics – politicians, journalists, activists, lobbyists – look at what the government *is*, not at what it *says*; they are thus not fooled by "cheap talk."[12] In this sense, a government is not a pig in a poke. It is a known commodity because the partisan preferences of its ministers are known commodities.

Now that we know what governments do when they are in office, we can model how they are selected in the first place. Before describing that, however, let us make a last point about partisan policy preferences. A party leader with policy preferences, on the one hand, and policy forecasts for each feasible government, on the other, is in a position to express preferences over governments. One allocation of portfolios is preferred to another if and only if the policy forecast for that first government is preferred by the party leader to the policy forecast associated with the second. This derived preference ordering of feasible governments, moreover, is arrived at quite apart from whether the party holding the preferences *participates* in a government. Policy-oriented parties, as distinct from their office-oriented counterparts, care only about the policies expected from alternative feasible governments, not about whether they themselves are sitting around the cabinet table.

Our model of government selection is a sequence that begins with a status quo government. We assume (in a manner compatible with the constitutions of all parliamentary democracies known to us) there is a government in place at all times, consisting of ministers who make policy in their respective jurisdictions until they are replaced. This government is in equilibrium if there is no alternative portfolio allocation that is preferred by a parliamentary majority. If this is the case, then, so long as parliamentary actors exercise foresight, no motion of no confidence can hope to succeed, since there is no feasible replacement for the status quo government that a majority seeks.[13]

---

[12] By this we mean that parliamentary talk is often a sort of mood music that may provide a public relations boost for the government with the general public but does not deceive the professionals. Parties cannot credibly commit to promises about policy that depart from their ideal policies. It is the latter that parties *really* want to implement and, if given half a chance, will do so. The professionals know this.

[13] This sufficient condition for equilibrium, however, is not necessary. There are other circumstances in which a government is in equilibrium that we need not describe here.

287

What is central to our approach is that only a finite number of feasible governments exists; thus, it is entirely possible (and, in fact, is typical for parliamentary settings with small numbers of political parties and/or low dimensionality of the policy space) for one government to be preferred by some parliamentary majority to each and every alternative and, hence, to be in equilibrium. The government formation game, that is, is one involving a finite set of points in the policy space over which the majority preference relation *may* be transitive, or at least have a Condorcet winner, even though the policy space is multidimensional.

Various shocks to a status quo situation may disequilibrate a sitting government that had formerly been in equilibrium. The most common of these is an election that changes the parliamentary weights of parties, and therefore the decisive structure of weighted majority rule. So it is not uncommon to observe a new play of the government formation game just after an election. Against a sitting government (one that will remain in place until replaced), a motion of no confidence is effectively offered by a *formateur* in the form of a proposal for a new government. This proposal is put to the parliament for a vote. Of course, in reality the sitting government may have resigned in anticipation of this; moreover, there need not necessarily be a formal vote (although the newly installed government is, of course, exposed to the prospect of an immediate confidence challenge). These are details that vary from country to country. For our purposes, the important point is that after an electoral shock either the status quo government remains in equilibrium, in which case nothing happens, or it does not, in which case it is replaced by some alternative. Although in reality there may be some slips 'twixt cup and lip, if there is some new equilibrium government fashioned by the results of the recent election, it will eventually be installed.[14]

An election is an obvious shock that may disequilibrate a sitting government and set into motion the process of replacing it. But it is not the only such shock. In advance of an election, public opinion data may indicate an anticipated shift in the decisiveness structure

[14] In the data on government formation in western Europe over the past century, there are, for nearly every country, a few governments that are very short-lived, their lives ranging from several days to several weeks. These may be thought of as mistakes – slips 'twixt cup and lip. They are the out-of-equilibrium selections that do not survive very long.

(were an election to be held at that moment), a shift sufficient to have an immediate disequilibrating effect on the sitting government. The expectation alone, that is, may be sufficient to cause a government to fall and be replaced with another, or for a cabinet reshuffle of portfolios to take place. Elsewhere we have referred to this as a "public opinion shock" (Laver and Shepsle 1998). Alternatively, events in the broader world, like wars, economic downturns, environmental catastrophes, or whatnot, may have the effect of making some dimensions of public policy more salient than they were. These we call "agenda shocks," which are represented by changes in policy preferences of political parties that may render a sitting government out of equilibrium.[15] Even more dramatically, parties may actually change their ideal points for reasons of party strategy in the larger electoral game, because one party leader has been replaced by another or one leadership faction by another, or because of events in the larger world. These "policy shocks," too, may disequilibrate a situation.

What we have suggested so far, then, is that a sitting government – a status quo allocation of portfolios among parties – takes policy decisions a jurisdiction at a time in a manner consistent with forecasts commonly held by all parliamentary actors. A parliamentary majority, should it prefer some alternative allocation of portfolios, can replace the sitting government whenever it wishes. If no parliamentary majority wishes to replace the status quo, then it is an equilibrium. In effect, then, we are claiming that *a government is accountable to its parliamentary principals when it is an equilibrium government.* Only then is it both doing what is expected of it and not majority-dominated by some alternative government.

Accountability in Parliamentary Democracy

To liken accountability of governmental agents to parliamentary principals to the idea of an equilibrium in the government formation process gives considerable precision to the

---

[15] Technically, changes in salience weights alter indifference curves (e.g., making spherical ones elliptical), which may have the effect of making a once invulnerable government newly vulnerable to some feasible alternative government.

accountability concept. A government is said to be accountable to parliament when parliament has no reason to replace it with an alternative. The accountability mechanism comes into play, on the other hand, when a government is out of equilibrium either because it has changed policies that were formerly in equilibrium or because some exogenous shock disequilibrates its equilibrium policies. The possibility then arises for a successful no-confidence maneuver, or a government resignation in anticipation of this. Activation of the accountability mechanism, in short, is a response to an out-of-equilibrium situation.

There is a second sense in which we may identify the activation of an accountability mechanism with out-of-equilibrium phenomena. To this point we have proceeded under the broad "protection" of assumptions of common knowledge and complete information. All parliamentary actors know everything there is to know – they know everyone else's weight and preferences; they know the rules of the game regarding government formation; they know exactly what a collection of governing parties will do if allocated ministerial portfolios; and they know that they all know these things. In short, the strategic interaction is characterized by complete information and common knowledge. This is a stricture of no mean proportions. If we suppose that information is incomplete – that forecasts about what particular governments will do if installed in office are shrouded in some uncertainty because it is not known for sure what a party's policy preferences are – then a government may be "in equilibrium" ex ante in an expectational sense, but "out of equilibrium" ex post once the veil of ignorance is lifted and the uncertainty is resolved.

In this remaining section we want to explore these two variations on the theme of accountability and equilibrium. We have been building toward a point of view about accountability in parliamentary systems. We observed that an accountability relationship between institutional agents and the public is at best a mediated one. Institutional agents in parliamentary democracy – members of the government or cabinet – are accountable to the legislature, which, in turn, is accountable to the broader public through elections. The mechanism of institutional accountability is the no-confidence procedure (or threat thereof). Our characterization of accountability has three important facets. First, the connection between cabinet and parliament – between agent and principal – is an *equilibrium* phenomenon. Second, though policy is infinitely malleable, and policy parameters are continuously variable, the fact of the matter is that there are only a *finite* number of ways to form a government. This affects the efficacy of any accountability mechanism because it constrains the credible threats a principal may make against its agent. Third, adverse selection and moral hazard problems with which an accountability mechanism must contend are complicated by *uncertainty in forecasting*. If a principal does not know for sure either what its agent stands for or what the effects are of difficult-to-observe environmental factors on agent decisions, then it will be handicapped in implementing accountability processes. We take each of these three issues up seriatim.

Equilibrium

Consider a sitting government going about the business of governing. Each minister is implementing, for each parameter (dimension) in the minister's jurisdiction, the level given by his or her party's ideal point. Suppose now that a motion of no confidence is moved. This suggests that something about this policy-making setting is amiss. Either someone has moved no confidence in an equilibrium government, the motion fails, and the government remains in place; or something occurred to disequilibrate a previously in-equilibrium government (the disequilibration was sufficient to bring on a successful no-confidence procedure and the replacement of the now out-of-equilibrium government with an alternative); or the original status quo government was not in equilibrium in the first place (it was a short-lived mistake and the no-confidence procedure serves as a corrective); or, finally, no government is in equilibrium.

The first possibility is best dealt with as an instance of incomplete information, something we examine shortly. The second possibility suggests, quite plausibly we believe, that governments live in a stream of exogenous shocks. These are the lightning bolts out of the blue that cannot and are not anticipated when a government takes office. Some perturb ideal points of parliamentary parties; others alter the salience of dimensions and ministerial jurisdictions; still others affect party weights – a by-election result, the fusing or splitting of parliamentary parties, and so on. These shocks buffet the sitting government around, and some are sufficient to induce the initiation of a successful no-confidence procedure. A government that was seen to be operating in an accountable manner before a shock is no longer doing so and is, consequently, held to account.[16] Having equated accountability with equilibrium, what we are now suggesting is that shocks sufficient to destroy this equilibrium are also sufficient to trigger accountability proceedings.

The third and fourth possibilities just mentioned allow for the possibility that accountable performance may simply not be in the cards. As we observed earlier, it is possible in nearly every country to find very short-lived governments – undoubtedly "mistakes" (some of which, like the Indian government of mid-1996, are known in advance to be mistakes!) – that trigger the accountability mechanism. The subsequent vote of no confidence or resignation in anticipation of it then sets the matter right – unless, of course, it simply isn't possible to set the matter right. In neither our model nor any other (multidimensional) approach with which we are familiar is equilibrium assured. Absent an existence theorem, our equating of equilibrium with accountability means that in some circumstances it simply will not be possible to install ministerial agents who perform in a manner accountable to the preferences of parliamentary principals.

Finite Number of Feasible Governments

Generally speaking, if there are m ministerial portfolios and p parliamentary parties, then there are $(p)^m$ feasible governments. Associated with each such government is a policy forecast. These are the possibilities on the table, and, in comparison to an incumbent government's policy, a parliamentary majority must determine whether any of the $(p)^m - 1$ alternatives to it is preferable. If not, then the government in place is in equilibrium and, as we have conceived it, is performing in an accountable fashion.

We know from general treatments of multidimensional spatial models that *almost never* does a policy exist against which no

[16] This means that, before the shock, no decisive parliamentary majority could settle on an alternative government whose forecast policies are preferred to those of the existing government. It's not enough that a parliamentary majority is "unhappy" with government performance; it must also have a superior alternative in mind.

other policy is preferred by a majority. This nearly universal absence of a Condorcet-winning policy means that *almost always* there will be an "unhappy" parliamentary majority, unhappy in the sense of being willing to exchange the existing policy for some feasible alternative. But *policies* are not the same as *governments*. If we switch attention from policies to governments, the finite number of the latter comes into play. It is possible for there to be a government whose forecast policy has the property that no other government's forecast policy is preferred by a parliamentary majority to it. This government would be an equilibrium and, according to our argument, will perform in an accountable manner. *This does not mean there are no policies a majority would prefer to those of this (allegedly accountable) government. It does mean there are no governments available to implement any of these policies.*

What we are saying then is that parties, and coalitions of parties (viz., governments), are long-lived entities with histories and reputations. They cannot change their spots overnight. This means that parties cannot continuously adjust expectations of what policies they will implement if installed in power. Consequently, parliaments must make do with the finite number of governments available and, thus, with the finite menu of policy alternatives available. An equilibrium in this world is one in which: (1) the government in power is performing as expected; (2) that performance is accountable in the sense that it does not trigger the accountability mechanism; but (3) parliamentary majorities need not be particularly pleased with the policies implemented; and yet nevertheless (4) parliament cannot credibly threaten to vote no confidence in the government. Accountable agent performance does not mean that the principals necessarily are happy campers.

Uncertainty in Forecasting

If parliamentary actors are uncertain of one another's preferences, then they will not know for sure what policies will be implemented by any government they might install. Although information is incomplete, actors often will possess *some* information that will permit them to entertain probabilistic beliefs. Assuming common knowledge for ease of exposition, it is certainly conceivable, in these circumstances, that there will be an equilibrium *in expectational terms*. What does this mean? It says that parliamentary actors prefer the policies expected of the government installed to those expected of any alternative government.

Expectations, however, are ex ante. In equilibrium, they motivate parliamentary majorities to act on their beliefs and install the government in question. But then, ex post, the uncertainty dissipates, the veil of ignorance is lifted, and the government in question actually begins implementing policies. If the implemented policies are as expected, then no parliamentary majority will feel differently ex post than it had ex ante. If, on the other hand, expectations are not fulfilled, then it is possible for a parliamentary majority to regret its decision. In short, surprises – whether the exogenous shocks to which any government is subjected during its tenure in office or the unexpected actions of a government on which other parliamentary actors had only partial information ex ante – can undermine accountable performance.

Conclusion

There are two major points developed in this chapter. The first is that, in most of the world's democratic orders, political accountability is mediated. The political officials who implement the policies that have impact on citizen welfare are *not* directly accountable to those citizens. Rather, they are accountable to *representatives* of those citizens. The representatives, in turn, are accountable to citizens to a greater or lesser extent depending on properties of the electoral system and the state of electoral competition. Most of the chapters in this volume are concerned with matters of accountability between citizens and their political agents. The present chapter, in contrast, takes those political agents as principals and inquires about the degree to which *their* agents – the cabinet in parliamentary systems – are accountable or not.

The second point of this chapter is to align the idea of accountability with the notion of equilibrium. A political agent is *accountable* to his or her principal, according to this view, when the principal, having the means to do so, has no inclination to replace him or her with a feasible alternative. There is no question but that this property characterizes an equilibrium in a principal-agent relationship. Agents are not perfect substitutes for principals. So, the question in a principal-agent relationship is whether the principal is content with the services of an imperfect agent. Here, "content" means the principal has no alternative that he or she would wish to substitute for the incumbent agent. Thus, a content principal reflects a principal-agent relationship in equilibrium.

But why does it also, as we allege, reflect a relationship characterized by accountability? The latter relationship is one in which the agent's behavior reflects the prospect of being monitored and sanctioned by his or her principal. We have maintained that the vote-of-no-confidence procedure in parliamentary democracies permits parliamentary principals to observe and sanction their agents, the members of the cabinet. In the portfolio allocation approach, agent behavior is rigidly fixed exogenously – parties "do their own thing" in the ministries for which they are given responsibility in response to electoral imperatives in the larger, extraparliamentary world. So they are not conditioning their government behavior on any system of incentives inside parliament. They are accountable, therefore, only in the sense that, as known commodities, they have been selected by their parliamentary principals in a process in which those principals were quite free to choose any of several different alternatives. So long as the selected agents perform as advertised, they will not be replaced (i.e., sanctioned).

Consequently, *accountability is both a state (equilibrium) and a mechanism (e.g., confidence procedure).* The latter can only be observed as a retrospective acknowledgment of an out-of-equilibrium situation. The very presence of the accountability "club" standing behind the door is, to be sure, an ex ante influence that may well keep an agent who is disposed to drift from doing so. But it is only observed in action – it is only hauled out from behind the door, so to speak – when accountability has failed, when a parliamentary agent has violated expectations in such a manner as to make it vulnerable to replacement. In these circumstances the government falls and is replaced by a new set of ministers. So, in a somewhat ironic locution, mechanisms of accountability may be seen to work only when accountability has failed.

References

Diermeier, Daniel. and Timothy Feddersen. 1996. "Cohesion in Legislatures: Procedural and Policy Coalitions." Paper presented at the annual meeting of the American Political Science Association, San Fransisco.

Fiorina, Morris P. 1981. *Retrospective Voting in American National Elections*. New Haven: Yale University Press.

Huber, John D. 1996. "The Vote of Confidence in Parliamentary Democracies." *American Political Science Review* 90: 269–82.

Laver, Michael, and Kenneth A. Shepsle, eds. 1994. *Cabinet Ministers and Parliamentary Government*. Cambridge: Cambridge University Press.

  1996. *Making and Breaking Governments: Cabinets and Legislatures in Parliamentary Democracies*. Cambridge: Cambridge University Press.

  1998. "Events, Equilibria, and Government Survival." *American Journal of Political Science* 42: 28–55.

Chapter Ten

Mixing Elected and Nonelected Officials in Democratic Policy Making: Fundamentals of Accountability and Responsibility

This study focuses on one part of the principal-agent relationship in democratic governments, that of department heads, who are usually career officials, and their elected principals, in this case ministers in the Australian commonwealth government. It does not consider the dual role in which most elected and career officials find themselves, that of principal in some aspects of their position, and that of agent in others. Nor does it examine any of the multitude of principal-agent relationships that ultimately seek to tie the street-level public servant to the policy preferences of the electorate. It seeks expanded understanding of the way that public bureaucracies respond to elected officials' policy preferences.

Many scholars note the increasing size, function, and power of public bureaucracies during the past century (Crenson and Rourke 1987; Weber 1958; Wilson 1978). The bureaucracy's growth in power poses important problems in a democracy because it creates the possibility that unelected officials can decisively impact policy, potentially in ways that disregard public preferences. This, in turn, makes the task of elected officials of especial importance since they must oversee the bureaucracy, infuse it with democratic preferences, and make it accountable to democratic processes. Many scholars have thus studied the relationship between the two (Gaus 1936; Hyneman 1950; Laver and Shepsle 1994; Michaels 1995; Redford 1969; Wood and Waterman 1994; Worsham and Ringquist 1994). Despite this attention, neither organization

297

theory nor democratic theory provides consensus on what Aberbach and Rockman call the proper "mesh" of elected and unelected officials in "an optimal mix" (Aberbach and Rockman 1988: 606). The mix between the two constitutes an important component of democratic theory, because that mix determines the extent to which government reflects more nearly the preferences of elected officials or the preferences of unelected public servants.

Responsiveness, Accountability, and Responsibility

This study utilizes the concepts of accountability and responsibility in the context of the principal-agent relationship between elected and administrative officials to explore how this relationship translates public preferences, as defined by elected officials, into policy. Mechanisms that impose accountability and provide definition of responsibility ultimately seek to achieve responsiveness. How do accountability and responsibility help achieve a bureaucracy responsive to elected officials' preferences?

Accountability at its most basic means answerability for one's actions or behavior (Dwivedi 1985; Dwivedi and Jabbra 1988: 5; Kernaghan and Langford 1990: 157; Pennock 1979; and Uhr 1993b: 2). Accountability focuses on the obligation owed by all public officials to the public, the ultimate sovereign in a democracy, for explanation and justification of their use of public office and the delegated powers conferred on the government through constitutional processes (Uhr 1992, 1993a; Banfield 1975: 587–88). An accountability plan constitutes an arrangement of obligations owed by one set of officials to another and ultimately to the public (Uhr 1992, 1993a). The accountability plan should define to whom one must answer (Caiden 1988: 34–35). Such arrangements vary widely across modern democracies, but they commonly require that the representatives of the public owe the public an explanation of their tenure in office. Because unelected officials exercise much influence in democratic governments, effective accountability involves two accountability transactions: one set of officials, such as the bureaucracy, who give an account of their activity, to another set, such as legislators, who take due account and feed their own considered account back into the political system and, through that mechanism, to the people.

For accountability to sustain responsiveness, it must be supported by sanctions and awards. In the relationship between the electorate and elected officials, the electorate can sanction by withholding or withdrawing support, and ultimately possibly defeating elected officials at the next election. Removal from office constitutes the obvious ultimate sanction. This sanction may also exist in the relationship between elected and unelected officials, although rules protect many public servants from dismissal except for criminal conduct. In the principal-agent relationship between elected and unelected officials, however, elected officials have sanctions other than, or in addition to, removal from office. These include demotions, embarrassment in the media, investigations, and budgetary penalties, among others (Peters 1978: 207–29). Principals can also provide positive rewards for those who account well for their work (Friedrich 1950: 398).

"Responsibility" constitutes another concept useful for examining the appropriate mix between appointed and elected officials in democratic government. Responsibility refers to the charter of delegated powers entrusted to the government, to the grants of power conditionally made available by principals to public official agents to do the things that they have the capacity to take charge of, act on, or provide. The definition of responsibility often emphasizes empowerment and discretion (Burke 1986: 11–15; Freund 1960: 37; Pennock 1960: 4, 27). A principal can rely on and leave in charge an agent who is responsible (Lucas 1993: 11). Principals thus expect agents to act responsibly by showing policy and administrative initiative and leadership, but also to accept accountability when initiatives do not work well or become publicly suspect (Friedrich 1960; Pennock 1979: 267; Uhr 1993b).

Responsible agents also possess internal characteristics that interact with the external charge of responsibility that principals give them. Responsible agents have a sound concept of their duties, and act in accordance with due deliberation, sound reasoning, and consideration of relevant facts and circumstances (Pennock 1979: 267). Responsibility may be based on "a course of action derived from some set of ideals" (Burke 1986: 9). Mosher called this kind of responsibility subjective or psychological responsibility because it indicates "to whom or for what one *feels* responsible and *behaves* responsibly" (Mosher 1968: 8; see also Burke 1986: 8–13; Kernaghan and Langford 1990: 158; Marx

299

1957: 44–45). This sense of responsibility also builds energy into the important place of anticipation on the part of the agent, a process that extends a principal's influence over the agent. But even in this sense of responsibility, where the agent provides self-definition of responsibility, agents must consider the consequences of their actions, for which they are accountable (Freund 1960: 29–30).

Implicit but *very* important in the definition of responsibility is the requirement that principals provide sufficient definition of agents' duties so that definition may guide agents' actions as well as provide a basis for principals to appraise agents' actions through accountability mechanisms. Overall, responsibility suggests an empowerment of agents by principals through assignment of authority, an acceptance of the responsibility of that authority by agents, and discretion to act on that authority.

The requirement that agents be accountable to their principal for the way they act on their responsibilities by exercising authority and carrying out their duties indicates the interrelationship of accountability and responsibility (Caiden 1988: 25; Uhr 1993b: 4). John Uhr notes that accountability "defines the boundaries within which official responsibilities are acted out" (Uhr 1993b: 4). Agents consider or anticipate the consequences of their actions as they exercise discretion. Without accountability their discretion would be unfettered and might lead to unresponsive actions. Accountability seeks to assure that agents will take their responsibilities seriously and act on those responsibilities in a way that principals will approve. Further, well-defined responsibilities provide to agents guidance to inform their discretion and provide principals a basis on which to judge agents' actions.

Accountability and responsibility provide a starting point for considering the appropriate mix between elected officials and the public service in democratic governments. But they provide just a starting point, because scholars of democratic governments do not agree what that mix should be. This study aims to examine empirically these concepts as they play out in the relationships between high-level elected and nonelected officials in a democratic country. The findings identify key components in the mix between these groups of important officials that would take us closer to understanding how this relationship works.

Australian Commonwealth Government

To examine these concepts for insights into the way that elected and unelected public officials relate in a democracy, this study will rely on interviews with top Australian commonwealth government officials. Australia represents a hybrid in the family of democratic nations. It offers a unique definition of government that lies somewhere between the U.S. government and that of Great Britain. The Australian commonwealth (i.e., federal) government has been described as "the Washminster system" in reference to its combination of Westminster-derived principles of the British model of responsible parliamentary government and U.S.-inspired principles of federalism, a written constitution, and a bicameral legislature, with each house having substantial powers (Thompson 1980). In contrast to the American system, however, it does have responsible political parties and operates as a parliamentary democracy, although not in so pure a Westminster fashion as Great Britain (Emy and Hughes 1991: 343–50).

Australia comprises a good setting for this study. The Labor government, headed by Prime Minister Robert Hawke, assumed power in 1983 and developed reforms designed to increase the responsiveness of the bureaucracy. These reforms, described later, redefined the relationship between ministers and the heads of departments. By exploring that relationship, the study seeks to increase understanding of accountability, responsibility, and responsiveness in democratic governance.

The data for this study come from two sets of interviews with Australian commonwealth government officials. The author conducted the first set of interviews between October and December 1992. At the time of these interview the cabinet included seventeen senior ministers, plus the prime minister. In addition, a number of "junior" ministers held responsibility for some part of a given department's functions. The 1992 interviews include seven current or former cabinet ministers, nine persons who headed departments in Australian national government (who typically had many years of experience in the Australian Public Service prior to being appointed department secretary), and nine staff members to the ministers, six of whom held the designation of "senior adviser."

The author conducted the second set of interviews in October

1996. This set of interviews offered the opportunity to interview new ministers, as the Coalition parties (the Liberals and Nationals) defeated the Australian Labor Party in March 1996 after thirteen years of power. It also provided an opportunity for senior Labor ministers to offer observations from the perspective of many years in office, but now serving in opposition. Although the Coalition government reduced the number of departments from twenty to eighteen, it maintained the basic department organization of the previous Labor government, with the concomitant continuation of senior and junior ministers. The new government incorporated fourteen ministers, in addition to the prime minister, as cabinet ministers.

The 1996 interviews included five cabinet ministers, four senior staff members of the remaining nine cabinet members, four former Labor government cabinet ministers (all of whom had been interviewed in the previous set of interviews), five current department heads (one of whom had been included in the previous set of interviews), and two former department heads (both of whom had been interviewed in the previous round of interviews).

The interviews with the ministers averaged about thirty minutes in length; with the staff members, about forty-five minutes in the first set of interviews, and about thirty-five minutes in the second set; and with the secretaries, about one hour in the first set of interviews and about forty-five minutes in the second set. All interviews were recorded and transcribed, with the respondents being promised that they would not be identified with any quotations utilized in the study in return for their agreeing to the interview.

Mixing Ministers, Ministerial Staff, and Department Heads

Seeking Responsiveness

Ministers expect responsiveness from departments. One minister voiced this expectation by stating that "[i]t's as simple as the department is there to serve the government-of-the-day in a professional way, exercising at all times loyalty, not entering at any time into politics" (interview, October 1996). Politicians desire reelection. They must construct a record that will muster voter approval at the next election (Manin 1997: 178–79). They believe that controlling the resources of the bureaucracy contributes to this goal (Silberman 1993: 54). Colin Campbell and John Halligan write that by the 1970s in Australia, "The bureaucracy was seen as too elitist, too independent, too unrepresentative and insufficiently responsive. . . . The reaction was to challenge the public servants' monopoly over advice to ministers and to question their indispensability to the processes of government" (Campbell and Halligan 1992: 201–2). Many Labor Party leaders formed their views of the bureaucracy from the party's experience in government from 1972 to 1975, when they assumed power after the Coalition parties had held power for over twenty years. One department secretary explained:

> It was a public service in which security of tenure of department heads was absolute, in which the only people in the service were the ones who had joined at the bottom and gradually worked their way up to the top. There'd been one government for twenty-three years, and therefore there was a certain satisfaction with the status quo. And the public service was seen or perceived to be an obstacle to rapid change. (Interview, department secretary, October 1992)

With this background, the Hawke government changed the selection process of department heads to elicit more responsiveness from the commonwealth bureaucracy. The change provided the prime minister and the minister of the department more control over the appointment. Prior to 1987, when a vacancy in one of these positions developed, the Public Service Board created a short list of public servants available to fill it, with the minister and prime minister usually choosing from the list. Since 1987 the secretary of the Department of Prime Minister and Cabinet, appointed by the prime minister, performs the function previously performed by the Public Service Board. This shifted control over these appointments to the government of the day (Campbell and Halligan 1992: 50, 206–8; Halligan and Power 1992: 89–91; Hawke 1989; Hyslop 1993: 73–75). Further, the Labor governments appointed department heads to five-year terms, although some were replaced prior to the end of their appointments, usually by shifts to other departments. In fact, department heads served in given departments during the Labor governments (1983–96) an average of thirty-nine months, just over three years (Dunn 1997: 45). Finally, the Hawke government

303

appropriately changed the title of the department head from permanent head to department secretary. The advent of the new Coalition government indicated just how much this control has shifted. The new government replaced six of twenty department heads. Two others departed by late 1996. The new department heads, though, usually had extensive public sector experience.

A second Hawke government reform focused on increasing the ability of ministers to achieve responsiveness from the bureaucracy by providing more staff resources to ministers. This process began in the early 1970s, with the advent of an earlier Labor government, but diminished somewhat when the Liberal-National government resumed control in 1975. The Hawke government reemphasized and strengthened ministerial staff resources when it assumed power in 1983 (Campbell and Halligan 1992: 202–3; Forward 1977; Halligan and Power 1992: 75, 76, 81–84; Mediansky and Nockles 1975, 1981; Smith 1977; Warhurst 1988: 336–39; Weller, 1980, 1983; and Yeend 1979). The Hawke government started with 224 staff members in 1983 (Walter 1986: 115) and the last Labor government under Prime Minister Paul Keating ended with 481 (*Ministerial Directory* October 1995). When Labor lost power, the typical cabinet minister had from 10 to 12 staff members with policy-related responsibilities. Noncabinet ministers generally utilized 5 to 7 individuals in these categories, while parliamentary secretaries had 2 to 4. Additional staff included 2 or 3 secretarial-administrative staff members for both kinds of ministers and 1 for parliamentary secretaries and, usually, 3 electoral office staff members for both ministers and parliamentary secretaries. The new Coalition government continued heavy staffing, although the total number decreased to 423 (*Ministerial Directory* July 1996). In general each ministerial and parliamentary secretary office in the new government contained 1 or 2 fewer staff members in the policy-related categories compared with its Labor counterpart at the end of their thirteen years in power.

Although both the Hawke government in 1993 and the Howard government in 1996 adopted central review procedures for ministerial staff appointments, the individual ministers chose their staff members. Historically, ministerial staff included persons assigned from the departments, and this continued. But the augmenting of staff assistance by the Labor governments included hiring staff members with much greater diversity of background than had previously been the case. Further, the ministers assigned staff members more-important responsibilities so that they became key players in the definition of responsibility and the exercise of accountability, as noted later.

Defining Responsibility

For bureaucracies to be responsive, political leaders must define the responsibilities of the bureaucracies. Until that happens, those in the bureaucracy may be less likely to act in ways that conform with the preferences of their elected superiors because they will not know these preferences or how they translate from the present into different policies or implementation practices. Thus the translation of politically defined preferences into administrative policy can fail because elected leaders do not provide clear decisions to bureaucracies. Three months after Australians elected the new Coalition government in early March 1996, Department of Defense officials complained that they did not know what their new minister wanted:

> However, 100 days of Coalition government have come and gone with McLachlan [the defence minister] on the bridge at Defence and the engine-room watch is becoming irritable at the inactivity. "We are in the engine-room down below but nothing much is coming down on the telegraph," says one senior officer. "We are all watching the pointer, but it just doesn't move." (Lague 1996)

This minister subsequently appointed a study committee to examine the Australian Defence Department that reported in 1997, possibly providing the "engine-room" with signals after that point. But this example illustrates how the failure of elected officials to provide direction to the bureaucracy makes it difficult for career officials to be responsive. A department secretary, speaking of a Labor minister reported, "There's one minister who I had where . . . there was an underlying lack of trust, but it was more a failure to articulate clearly the vision that he had. The department struggled to know what the hell he wanted" (interview, October 1996). Another department secretary explained the difficulty of ministers sending clear signals to the bureaucracy: "frequently it's because ministers don't know what they want until

305

they see it. And they need something to rub up against, respond to" (interview, October 1996).

How do ministers define the responsibilities of their departments? Effective ministers recognize the importance of their role in providing this definition. Ministers can provide clear direction. One minister noted the formula for getting the department to respond:

> Well, I suppose I get the best out of people by being very demanding. . . . I know pretty much what I want and how I want to get it and I demand extremely high quality work. But . . . I do try and give constant feedback, both in terms of hopefully identifying with some precision what it is I want – not leaving people floundering around without guidance or with mixed messages, that's important. And secondly, if I don't like something . . . telling people why I don't like it rather than just, "[I] don't like it, do it again." (Interview, December 1992)

Another minister voiced a similar view: "Well, it is the capacity to just tell the departments they're wrong. To say, 'That is not what we're going to do'" (interview, November 1992). A third minister offered this observation:

> I do think it's very important that a minister establish the political lines. What I mean by that, I don't mean the partisan ones, but a minister lets the department know the minister is boss and that's it. I have the sort of personality that I can do that very quickly. But I also think that you get a better response out of departments if they respect [you]. (Interview, October 1996)

Australian ministers and department heads report that providing direction to departments occurs best in two-way, back-and-forth communication about policy matters between the minister and the department during the development of new policy. They further report that in almost all cases a complementary relationship develops between ministers and departments in policy development. For example, secretaries believe that their departments must play a strong role in policy development. One secretary reported:

> [W]e've had very close relationships with the . . . ministers and their offices. The process of deciding on what issues will be brought to the cabinet in the budget is one which goes through a budget policy committee, and that consists of the minister, some

of the members of the minister's staff, and the senior people in the department. . . . [I]t is a genuine attempt to identify what the priorities are, to set down very clearly what the facts are and what the issues are, and to come up with the right sort of proposals, solutions which can be turned into proposals. (Interview, October 1992)

Not all ministers create such a formal meeting to plan policy initiatives for a given year. But departments nevertheless find ample opportunity to provide input into policy development. One department secretary noted, "But my general view is that the department ought to put forward proposals or recommendations in all cases. And you shouldn't just give options. You can give options, but they say, 'Well, I think you ought to go for this one' " (interview, October 1992). Departmental input into policy development also includes evaluating the positions of various players in the process. According to a department head, "the influence I think that I have, indeed that the department has, is to bring a balance to the various interest groups to ensure that parliamentarians and indeed the minister, particularly the minister, is made aware of the likely impacts on the broader economy of any particular . . . interest group's [position]" (interview, October 1992).

Ministers fully expect the involvement of departments in policy development. One minister stated that "the adviser [on the minister's personal staff] may have the idea or the minister may have given the adviser the idea or talked about the ideas – but the development of that would be very much dependent on the policy resources of the department" (interview, November 1992). As one minister stated:

Theoretically, I would say that essentially the minister is responsible for policy direction to the department and also for the political direction, that is, when not so much policy issues but problems arise which have very clear political implications, then, direction comes from the minister. On the other hand, it does not really always work like that in practice in the sense that the department plays an enormous policy-making role because it has resources that neither the minister nor the party has. So while I think it would be true to say at least in two of the three departments that I have been in charge of the general policy directions are determined by the minister, . . . a lot of the development of significant parts of the policy very much come from the department. (Interview, November 1992)

Part of the policy input of departments consists of their warning ministers of potentially negative policy consequences. As one minister stated, "I've said I want to be told the pros and cons of anything, so I don't go out and live in a fool's paradise. After all, I've got to defend whatever decision I make. And if I don't know the negatives, then I'm not prepared to answer them. I may decide to go ahead regardless of the negatives, but I need to know what they are" (interview, October 1996).

Ministers report that departments influence the policy direction that ministers give back to the department. As one minister described it, "the minister's intentions in policy are often much moderated as a result of interchange between the minister and his office and the department" (interview, November 1992). Part of the reason that departments can change the direction that ministers might have otherwise given to them stems from ministers' desire to avoid blunders that generate political costs. One minister explained this rationale: "[I]t's a case of not just sensible public policy making. I think it's good political sense. It's a good way of protecting your own ass because, I mean, the last thing I think any minister wants is a bunch of bureaucrats that are ... trying to tell you what you want to hear" (interview, November 1992). This minister noted the usefulness of the experience of the bureaucracy in achieving his goals, and explained why most want reactions and advice strongly put by public servants (Attlee 1954: 310).

Overall, the information that "moderates" ministers' intentions no doubt varies from case to case and from minister to minister. This information may include practical administrative implications for new policy thrusts (Young and Sloman 1982: 30–31), explanations based on the institutional memory of the bureaucracy, or analysis that relates the minister's proposal to present policy. This process suggests a policy development process that emphasizes a blending of the perspectives of the ministers and the departments. The minister obviously must bring the preferences and reality as defined by politics (Blondel 1991: 6–7; Attlee 1954). But the bureaucracy also participates in policy development because ministers believe that the direction they ultimately provide to departments benefits from information provided to the minister by the departments. Thus departments participate in the definition of responsibility given to them by ministers. Their participation in that definition provides an enriched perception by the department of ministerial preferences that define departmental responsibility as the department further develops policy ideas or implements policy that cabinet and parliament eventually approve.

The ministerial staff also plays a key role in defining the responsibilities of departments in Australian commonwealth government. One minister explained, "I think [name of staff member] would agree that monitoring in some senses is almost the most important responsibility that we have. In terms of the simple ongoing work of the department, yes. But it becomes more than simply monitoring. It's direct interaction whenever policy changes or reactions to situations that arise become the order of the day" (interview, October 1996). The staff becomes, in this sense, extensions of the minister in providing directions to the department, feedback from the minister, and interpretation of what the minister wants. One staff member explained:

> Well, a lot of [the staff's task] involves conveying to the department the minister's views on particular issues. And often he'll annotate submissions and the views go back that way, and when his views are clearly expressed in that way, our role is merely just transliterating his handwriting. But at other times he will ask for certain views of his to be conveyed to the department or he'll give some extra background supplementing what he's written, and either because we're asked or because we think it makes sense, we convey those additional thoughts to the department to help guide their implementation and formulation of policy. (Interview, November 1992)

Ministerial staff also works to facilitate the department's contact with the minister. How does this occur? One staff member indicated that department personnel often asked for guidance, saying "we're not quite sure how to play this. . . . What do you think" (interview, November 1992)? One staff member stated the extensiveness of this contact, usually initiated by the department, "Oh, I could have anywhere between ten and forty phone calls [from the department], depending on the day. . . . I would easily get twenty e-mails a day from the department" (interview, October 1996). A department head explained the reason for this extensive interaction:

> They [the staff] know the minister's mind much better than most of the department does, so when he writes on something, "I don't agree with this, please do such and such," the officer in the

department can ring the ministerial staff member and say, "Well why did he say this?" And they can explain the background, or ... if the meaning isn't clear, they can ring up and say, "Well, do you know what this means?" (Interview, October 1992)

Ministerial staffs' frequent interaction with ministers provides them great opportunity to learn the minister's views, likely reactions, and plan. They can utilize this information then to give definition to departmental responsibility. One staff member stated:

Well, we have a meeting with him every morning that he's here. Our staff.... [H]e tells us how he feels about everything.... But I think also that you, after working for a minister for a fairly long time, that you have a pretty good sense of how they're going to react. And because of the nature of the beast, you wouldn't really be working for them in these jobs unless there was a certain simpatico. (Interview, November 1992)

Much informal interaction occurs between ministers and their staffs, and this also provides the opportunity for learning the ministers' preferences. One staff member indicated that "In sitting periods when the parliament is in session, he works in that office over there and our doors are open so we're constantly sort of talking to each other. We would probably talk twenty or thirty times a day, and maybe every day you'd have perhaps half an hour or more to have sort of a more lengthy sort of brainstorming session about what ... we are doing" (interview, October 1996). Frequent formal and informal interaction usually results in a deep understanding of the minister and his or her preferences, even how the minister likely thinks about or views a variety of situations. One staff member stated, "I find that you develop a sort of almost an ESP-type relationship where you try to anticipate what they think and most times you get it right" (interview, October 1996). The staff thus extends the minister's ability to define the department's responsibility.

Exercising Accountability

The minister, the department, and the ministerial staff work together in various ways to define the department's responsibility in policy formulation. That definition then becomes the basis on which the minister can hold the department accountable as it implements policy. The accountability relationship between principal and agent flows more in one direction in democratic governance, from the elected official to the bureaucracy, than the flow in both directions noted in establishing the department's responsibility. But, importantly, the processes of responsibility and accountability often interrelate, as reflected in policy formulation in Australia. For even as the department engages in actions that help the minister to define its responsibility, the minister and ministerial staff engage in accountability exercises with the department.

The ministerial staff plays a large role in the accountability relationship with departments, and does so in a variety of ways. In policy development the staff evaluates the written work of the department before it goes to the minister. Ministerial staff also evaluates briefs, drafts of submissions to cabinet, policy proposals, drafts of speeches, or any other matter prepared by the department. One minister stressed the basic role of staff evaluation: "[T]he advisers are here as filters to . . . deal with the stuff coming to me from the department. And . . . telling me whether it's good, bad, or indifferent, or responsive to questions I've asked, if I've asked for something. Or whether it's . . . sensible and sound in terms of . . . what objective we're trying to pursue" (interview, December 1992). One staff member explained the detailed way that staff works in most ministerial offices to analyze departmental proposals:

> But when a submission comes up, it will go to the relevant policy adviser for their consideration and comment. Now at that stage it may well be that they need some further advice [from the department] – the submission is not clear in a particular area. Or they know that the minister will want a particular angle looked at. . . . [W]e may well choose to go back to the department at that stage to seek further information or clarification. Once they have looked, it comes to me. I look at everything before it goes to the next stage. . . . And at that stage, I may also choose to go back to one of my advisers or go back to the department to seek information and clarification. And then we will write our own recommendations and put all those submissions to the minister, who then looks at them with the knowledge of the department's recommendations, our own recommendations and as complete a picture as possible that we can give him, and he will then make his decision.

311

Sometimes he will discuss the issues with us, sometimes he won't. Sometimes he will discuss them with the department before he makes a decision on a particular issue. (Interview, October 1996)

Once the minister makes a decision on policy direction, the office expects the department to follow that decision in developing the details of the policy, and later to implement the policy in ways that conform with the goals of the policy. When departments fail, either because of resistance or because they do not understand the minister's position, the ministerial staff responds. One staff member explained:

It's the department that, when the decision is made, it goes away and implements the decision. They also, when they're faced with a new situation or implementing policy, they will quite often come back to the minister with recommendations with how that might be done and so forth. . . . Do these recommendations accord with the intention of the policy? And we'll quite often say, "Well look, this is not what was in mind when the government set down this policy direction, this policy path." Sometimes that means it will go straight back to the department. You say "I'm sorry, start again." I've just done that with one last week. I said, "Look, this is not at all what the minister was seeking. He's given you a very firm and clear direction as to the path he wants to go down. You're setting him off on a different path. You're ignoring a policy decision that's already been made. So please take that into account at the outset and come back with recommendations that relate to that decision." (Interview, October 1996)

Overall, department secretaries report that most ministers and their offices do not involve themselves in the day-to-day work of the department once a new policy has been developed. One minister explained the rationale for this feature of ministerial involvement in management:

My secretary, and this might sound self-evident but I don't think it is, I actually expect him to administer the department. And the reverse of that is that that means I don't administer the department, I keep out of it. . . . I can't hold him accountable for administering his department if I stick my fingers in it. I, actively, stay out of it. Then, he is fully responsible, for the good and the bad. (Interview, October 1996)

But ministers intervene, either directly or through their staff, when a department makes an error that leads to negative political consequences or bad publicity. One minister, discussing the way that public servants could properly exercise discretion, explained:

> [T]he general rule that I run is that they have to make a judgment as to whether there will be political consequences, that is, unfavorable publicity, questioning of what's been done. If they think it is likely to have those consequences, then, I think, anything like that they would talk to their immediate superiors, go ahead and make the decision, whether it is something that needs to be brought to my attention or whether it is something they can handle themselves, recognizing that if they handle it themselves and the thing blows up, then they bear the consequences of that. (Interview November 1992)

The periodic meetings that most ministers have with department personnel also provide the setting for exercising accountability. One department secretary explained: "With most ministers you'd meet, say, once a week, at a set time and just go over all the issues that were around from the minister's point of view. Then they have the opportunity to say that things are going very badly – 'I've heard terrible reports about this particular area, how the staff are being rude or whatever it is,' that sort of stuff" (interview, October 1996).

The fact that most ministers and department secretaries report that ministers do not involve themselves in day-to-day administration does not mean that political direction of everyday department activities does not occur. The fact that departments know that ministers and their staffs may subject them to periodic monitoring has an impact. The fact that departments may not predict when such monitoring will occur increases its potential impact. Beyond this, however, the oversight function provided by ministers provides information that departments then use to *anticipate* reactions from the ministry. This anticipation becomes a way that department personnel then define their responsibility, thus looping accountability mechanisms and their impact back into processes that help nonelected officials define their responsibilities.

Achieving Responsiveness

Evaluation by elected officials of the relationship between themselves and the bureaucracy constitutes an important test of how well political control of the democracy works. Ministers seek responsiveness so that they can accomplish their political goals. They want to impact policy and achieve influence over it. They want others to be able to evaluate their impact similarly to what one staff member volunteered:

> [My minister] is quite a good example of . . . a minister who's broken new ground in a portfolio. . . . [H]e demonstrated not just an ability to administer effectively a big department of state, but I think he very ably demonstrated an ability to fashion policy, strategy, in ways which had very far-reaching consequences and in ways which were often not in harmony with the thinking of the departmental advice. (Interview, December 1992)

Ministers do report resistance from the bureaucracy that required persistence on their part to win the day with the bureaucracy:

> I can remember in the early days [of his career as a minister] one particular issue where a powerful public servant had particular views which disagreed with mine. And it was a very painful process because you would find that what you wanted changed was changed only marginally. And it was a series of operations through a number of trenches. . . . [I]f a minister wants to do something which really is running against what a department wants to do, . . . then it is a much more costly process in time and effort than when what the minister wants is roughly in accord with what the department wants. But most of . . . the leading departmental figures see themselves as basically working to the minister, but bringing their own expertise. And that's where the sort of debate that I would put it, in nearly all cases, that's a productive and creative situation. (Interview, November 1992)

Overall, though, Labor government ministers reported a productive relationship with departments and departmental personnel, and that they believe they found a responsiveness by the bureaucracy to political direction. One minister related this view:

> We have a system essentially where for the most part public servants obey the ministers. . . . No one comes in here and tells me that they're not going to do something. They may make good reasons for why they shouldn't do it, and I listen. There's no obstruction of orders by the public servant. It's fairly much a

democratic-centralist command system in this process. (Interview, November 1992)

Another minister expressed the most typical attitude toward the department's role in policy formulation:

[T]hey know the direction in which the government would be coming from. And for that reason, the majority of the advice you get is advice that you have no difficulty with. But, as I said, they don't hesitate to try it on. And I think that's a good thing, personally, because my view is that . . . at least you get people that are strongly motivated about the portfolio and have got a view on it and, . . . providing you then learn to recognize what that bias is, you know that people are constantly going to be coming from a particular direction, and if you disagree with it you can discount the advice to that end and then get to a stage where you just agree to disagree with bureaucrats that have that view and tell them precisely what it is you want. That's not a problem. (Interview, December 1992)

Most ministers emphasized the collaborative character of their relationship with their departments, which permits melding together the various perspectives of ministers and departments. The newly minted Coalition ministers provide another, and corroborating, view of responsiveness by the bureaucracy in Australia. They came to power after 13 years in opposition expecting resistance from the departments. But four of the five interviewed for the study reported satisfaction with their departments and expressed surprise at how responsive they had been. One indicated that "The relationship with the department has gone amazingly well. We had a major reform agenda. They were not a department that were viewed as being sympathetic to this agenda, but I treated them like professionals and they have acted like professionals and have really not resisted this in the way that I thought that they might" (interview, October 1996).

Based on these interviews, how can we best summarize the relationship between elected and appointed officials in the Australian national government, especially as obtained in the Hawke-Keating Labor governments? To help in this task, let us examine a model proposed by Laver and Shepsle that seeks to capture the varying ways that the mix between public servants and elected officials takes place, particularly in parliamentary settings. The model builds on varying relationships between

315

ministers and the cabinet, the larger legislative body, and the civil service. A "bureaucratic government" focuses the power to make and implement public policy in the permanent civil service. A "legislative government" decides all policy in the legislature, with the cabinet mechanically implementing it. In "prime-ministerial government" a powerful prime minister dominates a collective executive. In "party government" the powerful executive consists of members subject to the discipline of a well-organized party. Caucuses exercise great power. In "cabinet government" a powerful executive takes collective decisions binding all members. Finally, a "ministerial government" which Laver and Shepsle favor, features a powerful executive in which individual ministers, as heads of major departments, have significant impact on policy that falls under their jurisdiction (Laver and Shepsle 1994: 5–8).

The overall relationship between the political and the administrative in Australia makes it a ministerial government category as defined by Laver and Shepsle. In Australia, both elected and appointed officials recognize the need for cooperation and good communication. Both groups of officials respected the relative contributions that each can bring to the policy process. Resistance to ministerial direction does occur, but those instances do not dominate the discussion. In fact, resistance that crosses the line of the department presenting its views in a satisfactorily aggressive way does not occur often, according to those interviewed in this study. When resistance does cross the line, ministers believe they have the necessary power and influence to counter such moves effectively. The level of satisfaction of ministers with respect to the relationship between politics and bureaucracy constituted an important measure of the effectiveness of that relationship. By that measure, Australian ministers pronounce the relationship as an effective one.

Discussion

Democratic theory provides no final, definitive answers when it comes to stating clearly the responsibility of the bureaucracy or the most appropriate ways through which the elected officials of particular representative institutions can take account of the bureaucracy's actions. Nor is it clear which forms of taking account relate most appropriately to which oversight institutions. Given these ambiguities, one must take care in drawing lessons from one democracy and applying them to others. But the Australian example does provide important signals about what is important in developing accountability and responsibility processes that achieve responsiveness in democratic governance. What can we conclude from the interviews with top-level bureaucrats and politicians in Australia with respect to the most fundamental dynamics of accountability and responsibility and of the mix between them for assuring responsiveness by the bureaucracy?

The Australian Labor governments strengthened the responsibility-accountability components of the ministerial-department relationships during their period of governing between 1983 and 1996. The more-direct control by elected leaders of department head appointments sought to put in place those persons competent to lead and manage departments and who either shared the goals of the government or were willing to help the government achieve its goals. The Hawke government intensified this process in 1987 by developing a reorganization plan that set up new departments, offering the opportunity to replace or move department heads. The net result, according to one minister, was that "what tended to happen in all of those departments is highly energetic and innovative bureaucrats got placed in charge of them, and not just in charge of them, but down the line at the deputy secretary and first assistant secretary level. And they were frequently quite devoted to the idea of change. Now, so you wouldn't have said you had a problem there of bureaucratic inertia" (interview, November 1992). In these cases the department secretary made the appointments lower in the hierarchy, but generally took into account the ability of persons in those positions to work well with the minister. Also, these individuals, as did the department heads, almost always came from the ranks of career public servants.

Developing more political control over the appointment and continuation of department heads also provides possibilities of rewards and punishments that can enhance responsiveness. One minister observed that

> the minister ultimately controls the fate of the head of the department, and it is clear that the head of the department recognizes that so (a) if you have a good relationship with the top bureaucrat and he is sensitive to the concerns [of the minister] that we are talking about, then (b) I think that the minister can rely on the chief departmental executive to be sure that the minister's

views tend to prevail and his concerns are met. (Interview, November 1992)

The Australian system of department-minister relationships also establishes an important potential award for department heads and departments whom ministers view as trustworthy and able. They can be influential participants in formulating policy with ministers and their staffs. The better that relationship, the greater the department's influence with the minister. This potential award can, of course, also provide a potential sanction. Departments that do not perform well carry less influence with ministers. Thus, as ministers evaluate department heads, or take account of their work, there can be consequences for the department heads, and for that reason they can anticipate those consequences as they perform their work.

Providing direction requires more from elected officials than appointing department heads. The way in which the mechanisms of responsibility and accountability work in the Australian system hinges strongly on the relationship between the minister and the department head. The parliamentary system permits direct contact, much of it informal, between department secretaries (as well as other senior executives in the department) and ministers. Contacts between the minister and department personnel occurred frequently. This permits department heads and other top management to develop an understanding of ministerial priorities and interests that guides them in their work. Over time the secretary and the minister develop a working relationship (Hyslop 1993: 14). Secretaries indicated how they come to know their ministers' needs and positions in several ways:

> You don't go and say, "Okay, Minister, what are you interested in here?" You observe over the first month or so of them being there what it is that emerges as their interest. I mean, you do all the right things up front by drawing their attention to the whole spectrum of activities. But you soon just work out what he's interested in, soon recognize what the political hot issues are or, whatever.... [S]ometimes there's things you just have to interest him in whether he wants to be or not. And in terms of sort of spotting his interests, I think the only way you can do it is to let it emerge. (Interview, October 1992)

In the end this kind of relationship fosters a situation in which the department secretary can anticipate what the minister wants and how a given decision situation affects him or her (Attlee 1954: 310). And this has a powerful impact on what a department secretary does as it provides a framework in which the minister defines the department head's responsibility and provides cues that the department head uses to define his or her sense of that responsibility. The department secretary who understands what her minister wants then possesses sufficient information to do as one indicated she did in determining action on discretionary matters: "I would do what I think the minister would do in this situation. And by and large, on discretion matters, I would follow that. That doesn't mean that I would follow that in giving advice to the minister, because that's a separate issue" (interview, October 1992).

The Labor governments' emphasis on a vitalized ministerial staff also provided a important strengthening of the responsiveness of departments to ministerial direction. The staff greatly augments ministerial ability to evaluate information provided by the department, to oversee departmental policy development, and to monitor department action and implementation. The staff also provides an important enhancement of information available from the minister to the department. This can occur at the department's initiative in gathering information about the minister's preferences and reactions, or at the initiative of the staff or the minister to provide information to the department. Ministers can, if they wish, and see the need to, provide ongoing monitoring that in effect requires those in the public service to answer to him or her, which helps achieve responsiveness from these officials. As with the department management positions, the number of staff members appointed has remained small enough to retain direct contact between the staff and the minister, thus enhancing the minister's ability to communicate effectively with the staff and, through the staff, with the department.

The Australian reforms thus did not extend the number of political appointments beyond the minimum necessary to achieve effective delivery of the political preferences and directions of elected officials that define the responsibility of the bureaucracy. The number of officials appointed has remained small enough that elected officials can take care in making appointments of persons who have sufficient qualifications and experience for the office. Keeping the number of appointed officials small also avoids diffusing the message of the principal by cluttering the commu-

319

nication paths with excessive numbers of political or patronage appointments, which ultimately dilutes the power of elected principals. Australian elected officials can maintain direct communication with appointed officials.

The relationship between responsiveness, responsibility, and accountability also works well in Australia because fairly clear norms exist that help define the responsibility of public servants and provide a context in which accountability occurs. What norms define the general responsibilities of departments, within which appointed officials can appropriately exercise discretion? In the first place, reforms took place in a context that recognized the importance of a collaborative effort between ministers and departments to achieve effective policy making. The ministers interviewed seemed genuinely interested in and grateful for departmental input as policy matters were being debated in the earliest stages of development. In this interaction, ministers may find their views "moderated" or influenced by the information that departments can bring to bear on a policy question. They found valuable the sharing by departments of practical administrative implications of policy options, and the provision of knowledge from department expertise and experience. They also noted that advice from departments has saved them embarrassment and provided information useful to them as they formulate policy. This means that the responsiveness of departments during the Labor governments occurred in a context that permitted departments to give advice without fear or favor. The working norms thus assure that the possibility of strong negative sanctions occasioned by the more direct engagement of elected leaders in the appointment of department heads does not infringe upon the traditional Westminster notion of departments providing strong warnings to these elected leaders when necessary. Importantly, the Australian bureaucracy under the Labor governments exercised strong impact on policy making so that the expertise, experience, and institutional memory of the bureaucracy could impact policy changes emanating from elected leaders in the government.

Norms also protect department officials from being asked by ministers or their staffs to involve themselves in partisan political, rather than policy, matters. Department personnel know that the ministerial staff will most often take information provided by the department and give it the appropriate political spin. They can almost always count on ministerial advisers to establish a liaison with party organizations within parliament. The Labor governments continued an emphasis on the neutral, partisan-insulated public service, which provided important cues to the way in which Australian politicians expect the public service to define its responsibility.

The study also indicates the importance of elected leaders developing clear objectives for the public service to provide an appropriate relationship between politics and administration. Developing these objectives provides unelected officials a definition of their responsibility. It also provides to elected officials a basis by which they may take account of the actions of department heads. John Burke notes that public servants can play a part in this definition: "One of the major ways in which bureaucrats can contribute to policy formulation is by ensuring that policy is clearly and properly defined by relevant political authorities" (Burke 1986: 58). No democratic government finds it easy to define clear objectives because policy must often serve a variety of goals. Yet even in the United States, where a governmental structure based on separation of powers makes defining clear policy goals deliberately difficult, studies of successful direction of the bureaucracy stress the important impact of clear objectives (Randall 1979). Campbell and Halligan found in their extensive interviews of Australian public service personnel that ministers in the Hawke government more than their predecessors took initiatives in policy formulation and indicated what they wanted from departments (Campbell and Halligan 1992: 61–62). To do this, ministers had to develop clear policy objectives and communicate them effectively to the department. In this study both ministers and department secretaries stressed the importance of elected leaders developing clear objectives and communicating them effectively to the department. Ministers also stressed the will to back up their positions, as noted earlier.

The Australian experience under the 1983–96 Labor governments thus suggests that democracies can develop mechanisms of accountability and responsibility that define the relationship between elected officials and top appointed officials in the bureaucracy in a way that elicits responsiveness from the bureaucracy. This requires both elected and nonelected officials to act in ways that give active meaning to responsibility and accountability mechanisms, as noted in this study. The forging of strong accountability and responsibility relationships between elected and nonelected officials stands at the heart of democratic governance, and thus deserves more attention than is sometimes received from elected and nonelected officials, as well as from scholars.

References

Aberbach, Joel, and Bart A. Rockman. 1988. "Mandates or Mandarins? Control and Discretion in the Modern Administrative State." *Public Administration Review* 48 (2): 606–12.

Attlee, Clement R. 1954. "Civil Servants, Ministers, Parliament and the Public." *Political Quarterly* 25 (4): 308–15.

Banfield, Edward C. 1975. "Corruption as a Feature of Governmental Organizations." *Journal of Law and Economics* 18 (December): 587–605.

Blondel, Jean. 1991. "Cabinet Government and Cabinet Ministers." In Jean Blondel and Jean-Louis Thiébault, eds., *The Profession of Government Minister in Western Europe*, 5–18. New York: St. Martin's Press.

Burke, John P. 1986. *Bureaucratic Responsibility.* Baltimore: John Hopkins University Press.

Caiden, Gerald E. 1988. "The Problem of Ensuring the Public Accountability of Public Officials." In Joseph G. Jabbra and O. P. Dwivedi, eds., *Public Service Accountability*, 17–38. West Hartford, Conn.: Kumarian Press.

Campbell, C., and J. Halligan. 1992. *Political Leadership in an Age of Constraint.* Sydney: Allen and Unwin.

Crenson, Matthew A., and Francis E. Rourke. 1987. "By Way of Conclusion: American Bureaucracy since World War II." In Louis Galambos, ed., *The New American State*, 137–77, 213–17. Baltimore: Johns Hopkins University Press.

Dunn, Delmer D. 1997. *Politics and Administration at the Top: Lessons from Down Under.* Pittsburgh: University of Pittsburgh Press.

Dwivedi, O. P. 1985. "Ethics and Values of Public Responsibility and Accountability." *International Journal of Administrative Sciences* 51 (1): 61–66.

Dwivedi, O. P., and Joseph G. Jabbra. 1988. "Public Service Responsibility and Accountability." In Joseph G. Jabbra and O. P. Dwivedi, eds., *Public Service Accountability: A Comparative Perspective*, 1–16. West Hartford, Conn.: Kumarian Press.

Emy, Hugh V., and Owen E. Hughes. 1991. *Australian Politics: Realities in Conflict.* 2d ed. South Melbourne: Macmillan.

Forward, Roy. 1977. "Ministerial Staff under Whitlam and Fraser." *Australian Journal of Public Administration* 36 (2): 159–67.

Freund, Ludwig. 1960. "Responsibility – Definitions, Distinctions, and Applications in Various Contexts." In Carl J. Friedrich, ed., *Responsibility*, 28–42. New York: Liberal Arts Press.

Friedrich, Carl J. 1950. *Constitutional Government and Democracy.* Boston: Ginn and Company.

——— 1960. "The Dilemma of Administrative Responsibility." In Carl J. Friedrich, ed., *Responsibility*, 189–202, New York: Liberal Arts Press.

Gaus, John. 1936. *The Frontiers of Public Administration.* Chicago: University of Chicago Press.

Halligan, John, and John Power. 1992. *Political Management in the 1990s.* Melbourne: Oxford University Press.

Hawke, R. J. L. 1989. "Challenges in Public Administration." *Australian Journal of Public Administration* 48 (1): 9–16.

Hyneman, Charles S. 1950. *Bureaucracy in a Democracy.* New York: Harper and Brothers.

Hyslop, Robert. 1993. *Australian Mandarins: Perceptions of the Role of Departmental Secretaries.* Canberra: Australian Government Publishing Service.

Kernaghan, K., and J. W. Langford. 1990. *The Responsible Public Servant.* Halifax, Nova Scotia: Institute for Research on Public Policy.

Lague, David. 1996. "Sabre Ruttling in Russell." *Sydney Morning Herald*, June 25. Internet version.

Laver, Michael, and Kenneth A. Shepsle. 1994. "Cabinet Ministers and Government Formation in Parliamentary Democracies." In Michael Laver and Kenneth A. Shepsle, eds., *Cabinet Ministers and Parliamentary Government*, 3–12. Cambridge: Cambridge University Press.

Lucas, J. R. 1993. *Responsibility.* Oxford: Clarendon Press.

Manin, Bernard. 1997. *The Principles of Representative Government.* Cambridge: Cambridge University Press.

Marx, Fritz Morstein. 1957. *The Administrative State.* Chicago: University of Chicago Press.

Mediansky, Fedor, and James Nockles. 1975. "The Prime Minister's Bureaucracy." *Public Administration* (Sydney) 34 (3): 202–18.

——— 1981. "Malcolm Fraser's Bureaucracy." *Australian Quarterly* 53 (4): 394–418.

Michaels, Judith E. 1995. "A View from the Top: Reflections of the Bush Presidential Appointees." *Public Administration Review* 55 (3): 273–83.

Ministerial Directory. 1995. Australian Government Publishing Service. October.

——— 1996. Australian Government Publishing Service. July.

Mosher, Frederick C. 1968. *Democracy and the Public Service*. New York: Oxford University Press.

Pennock, J. Roland. 1960. "The Problem of Responsibility." In Carl J. Friedrich, ed., *Responsibility*, 3–27. New York: Liberal Arts Press.

——— 1979. *Democratic Political Theory*. Princeton: Princeton University Press.

Peters, B. Guy. 1978. *The Politics of Bureaucracy*. New York: Longman.

Randall, Ronald. 1979. "Presidential Power versus Bureaucratic Intransigence: The Influence of the Nixon Administration on Welfare Policy." *American Political Science Review* 73 (3): 795–810.

Redford, Emmette. 1969. *Democracy in the Administrative State*. New York: Oxford University Press.

Silberman, Bernard S. 1993. *Cages of Reason*. Chicago: University of Chicago Press.

Smith, R. F. I. 1977. "Ministerial Advisers: The Experience of the Whitlam Government." *Australian Journal of Public Administration* 36 (2): 133–58.

Thompson, Elaine. 1980. "The 'Washminister' Mutation." In Patrick Weller and Dean Jaensch, eds., *Responsible Government in Australia*, 32–40. Victoria, Australia: Drummond Publishing.

Uhr, John. 1992. "Public Accountabilities and Private Responsibilities: The Westminster World at the Crossroads." Paper presented at the annual meeting of the American Political Science Association, Chicago.

——— 1993a. "Parliamentary Measure: Evaluating Parliament's Policy Role." In I. Marsh, ed., *Governing in the 1990s*, 346–75. Melbourne: Longman Cheshire.

——— 1993b. "Redesigning Accountability: From Muddles to Maps." *Australian Quarterly* 65 (2): 1–16.

Walter, James. 1986. *The Ministers' Minders: Personal Advisers in National Government*. Melbourne: Oxford University Press.

Warhurst, John. 1988. "Reforming Central Government Administration in Australia." In Colin Campbell and B. Guy Peters, eds., *Organizing Governance Governing Organizations*, 327–43. Pittsburgh: University of Pittsburgh Press.

Weber, Max. 1958. *From Max Weber*. H. H. Gerth and C. Wright Mills, eds. New York: Oxford University Press.

Weller, Patrick. 1980. "Controlling the Structure of the Public Service." In Patrick Weller and Dean Jaensch, eds., *Responsible Government in Australia*, 197–203. Richmond, Victoria, Australia: Drummond Publishing.

——— 1983. "Transition: Taking over Power in 1983." *Australian Journal of Public Administration* 42 (3): 303–19.

Wilson, James Q. 1978. "The Rise of the Bureaucratic State." In Francis E. Rourke, ed., *Bureaucratic Power in National Politics*, 54–78. 3d ed. Boston: Little, Brown.

Wood, B. Dan, and Richard W. Waterman. 1994. *Bureaucratic Dynamics: The Role of Bureaucracy in a Democracy.* Boulder, Colo.: Westview Press.

Worsham, Jeff, and Evan Ringquist. 1994. "A Theory of Political Influence of Bureaucracy." Paper presented at the annual meeting of the American Political Science Association, New York, September 1–4.

Yeend, G. J. 1979. "The Department of Prime Minister and Cabinet in Perspective." *Australian Journal of Public Administration* 38 (2): 133–50.

Young, Hugo, and Anne Sloman. 1982. *No, Minister.* London: British Broadcasting Corporation.

Part Three

Overview

Chapter Eleven
Situating Democratic Political Accountability

Democracy differs from anarchism most sharply in accepting both the need for and the propriety of public and collective action and thus, arguably, in accepting the reality and legitimacy of politics. For there to be public action at all, there must be potentially binding public choice, and hence a system for making such choices and for ensuring that they do, in the appropriate circumstances, bind. There has to be a system of authority, within which, however fluid the movement of persons between the two statuses, it will at best very often be true that those who command are different from those who obey (Maistre 1965: "Study on Sovereignty," 93). Democracy fully shares with anarchism, whether philosophical (Wolff 1970; Simmons 1993) or comparatively practical, the recognition that this vertical relation of authority is inherently hazardous. It seeks to provide, if with necessarily imperfect success, at least some degree of remedy for such hazards, short of simply abandoning the practice of public action. Unlike anarchism, it cleaves to the practice of public action because it views the state of nature, the continuous individual practical interpretation of how it is permissible to act, unmediated by any structure of institutionalized authority, as generically far more dangerous than vertical subjection to such authority (Dunn 1990: chap. 3; 1996). This is merely a vague probability calculation, and in the worst possible cases – the Holocaust – it comes out badly wrong. But in the modal case it is an eminently reasonable assessment (Hobbes 1991; Dunn 1990: chap. 3; 1995: chap. 4).

There are essentially two approaches to the task of limiting these hazards. One is seeking to structure (and hence constrain) the moment or process of public choice itself, whether from the inside (by selecting what ingredients go into determining this) or the outside (by setting external limits to its legitimate scope). Votes and constitutionally protected civil rights are familiar examples of internal and external structuring of public choice. (Public choice here, plainly, is to be read as a phrase in ordinary English, not in academic American.) While the two are much confounded in application (Dunn 1990: chap. 5), the first corresponds broadly to the project of ancient liberty, and the second broadly to that of modern liberty (Constant 1988: 313–28).

The second approach is holding the key agents and implementers of public choice effectively responsible for the manner in which they make and implement these choices.[1] It will have a very different flavor if it is aimed principally at the intentions of such public agents or at the unwelcome consequences that prove to follow from their actions. The locus of democratic accountability is this second approach to limiting the inherent hazards of political subjection. Its key terms are action, subjection, and the tension between intention and consequence in political, as in most other (arguably all other), forms of action. The rationale of democratic accountability must give priority to democratic subjection over accountability; otherwise it would plainly be better advised to cleave to anarchism and strive to prevent, as effectively as it can, the genesis of concentrated coercive authority in the first place. In the states of today, practices of democratic accountability form the key site of putative recon-

[1] Can the conception of accountability offer an effective approach to securing the opportunities of political life, as well as to limiting its hazards? Hardly so. Such sanctioning as it can hope to provide can only work by taking as its target highly determinate conceptions of action. It needs to pin down both intention and readily predictable consequences, and to do so distinctly more precisely than visual (evidential) opportunities normally (or perhaps ever) permit. Discerning and seizing opportunities is an ineliminably entrepreneurial matter. It can seldom or never rest on compelling evidence of what is already fully the case. The proof that the opportunities genuinely are there (that they are not simply fantasized) can in most instances only be provided by seizing them. The asymmetry between seizing opportunity and limiting hazard is important because it means that any modeling of an entire political system through the mutual capacities of its participants to sanction one another's conduct needs either to be wholly external to the agents concerned (a God's-eye view that prescinds from their patterns of attention and temperamental attitudes), or to register the inherently speculative, heuristic, and hence analytically hazy (and from a human point of view onto-logically indeterminate) character of political action.

ciliation between the norm of democracy and the apparently antithetical implications of state authority (Dunn 1992: conclusion). Any reasonably dependable program for vertical political accountability will be parasitic on a well-entrenched and effective practice of subjection, of effectively enforced and binding rules, a government of rules and not of persons. Accountability, thus understood, is an arrière-pensée to such a practice of subjection, designed to accommodate the fact that any government of rules will always in fact be implemented (or not implemented) by persons.

All this, of course, is a conceptual proposal, not a matter of semantic fact. Besides the vertical hazards that we face from our rulers, all humans also face many hazards from one another – horizontal hazards. Anarchists, for whatever reason, prioritize vertical over horizontal hazards. Democrats, however nervously, prioritize horizontal over vertical hazards. But the systems of rule that they establish in the effort to do so are far from eliminating horizontal hazards. They seek, naturally, to limit such hazards in the interaction between citizens by establishing and enforcing a system of civil and criminal law. Even this system, however, must in the end be interpreted, authoritatively and vertically, through the structure of the democratic state, the system of subjection itself.

It is therefore (if in some instances, like the United States, exceedingly intricately) at the mercy of the security (or otherwise) that this system offers its subjects within the process of public choice itself. Modern political thought has struggled with this conundrum for several centuries without making notable headway. It seems by now likely that there is limited headway to be made – that there is probably no way in principle of structuring the process of public choice so that it can be relied upon to furnish a high degree of security for all subjects in relation to everything that is of decisive significance for them. In the process of public choice, familiarly, horizontal hazards between groups of citizens (spite, competitive greed) are transposed into vertical hazards. Democratic political accountability is no specific for this threat. Ancient Greek expedients – *graphe paranomon* or ostracism (prophylactic democratic accountability: warding off in good time occasions for future regret) – erratic though they inevitably were, offered more-direct remedies (Finley 1983: 50, 53–55, 102; Hansen 1974, 1975, 1976, and 1991: 205–12, 35–38; Ober 1989:

95–97, 301–3, 73–75). The distinguishing characteristic of modern democratic political accountability is the attempt to control such hazards not at the moment of (or in advance of) public choice, but on the basis of subsequent assessment and initiative. (No retrospectively applied remedy stands much chance of proving prospectively reliable: of consistently averting the outcomes it seeks to avoid.) Utilitarians may see this as an instance of bolting the stable door after the horse has fled. But, like the practice of punishment more generally, it can also be viewed less literally, and seen instead very much as an orientation toward the future: an attempt to specify and install an effective system of sanctions that will generate a large surplus of desired over undesired behavior and minimize the forms of behavior that are especially unwelcome (a paradigm utilitarian objective).

As with punishment itself, however, this way of viewing the matter – for all its agreeable astringency and its putatively clear-headed grasp of the requirements for practical rationality – is not in the end imaginatively sustainable. Democratic accountability is therefore better captured by seeing it as a bold, if perhaps somewhat muddled, approach to mediating the strains of political membership than by seeing it as a narrow and robustly instrumentally rational set of devices for minimizing (let alone eliminating) the vertical dimension of the risks of collective political life. This is just what we should expect, if the main weight of political hazard for given groups of subjects comes not from the predicament of subjection itself but from the injection of the wills and purposes of other groups of subjects into the content of public choice: in other words, from transposed horizontal risk. It would be a poor example of democracy in which this was not certain to prove so. Even in the most ideal of democracies we cannot all win all the time; and when we lose, we can be sure that, sooner or later, each of us will mind very badly. By using the future as a space in which to vindicate and enforce our judgments that we did not deserve to lose, democratic political accountability assuages the bitterness of political defeat, and gives those who would otherwise have little motive to do so a reason for staying in the game.[2] But it can do so, of course, only insofar as it is not a mere ideological fiction, but a relatively determinate and palpable political fact. This means that to a very large degree,

[2] For the importance of such reasons, see Przeworski 1991.

and over a great many burning issues, it simply in practice cannot do so.

One important, if minimal, sense of political accountability bears directly on the relation between those who hold authority and those who are subject to it. This sense specifies as a necessary condition for the authority's legitimacy that the term over which it lasts should be decided, not by the discretion of its holders, but, within some set of established and observed rules, by those who are subject to it. In the case of democratic accountability, in modern political speech, this minimal sense becomes redundant, since no plausible understanding of what the term democracy means could exclude such minimal accountability. (Compare the contortions of the *Beijing People's Daily*'s description of Taiwan's first democratic presidential election as "the activity by which a change of Taiwan region's leader was engineered.")[3] The thinnest sustainable modern usage of democracy requires that the *demos* can expect to play at least some causal role, sooner or later, in the activity by which changes in their leaders are engineered (Dunn 1992: conclusion). Where even this minimal condition is not satisfied, the harm that it is reasonable for the *demos* to fear is the harm of oppression. Modern democracy purports to exclude the possibility of oppression (at least, of the people as a whole by their rulers as such) through its structuring of the process of public choice. The plausibility of its claim to have succeeded in doing so depends very largely on the plausibility of viewing the people as a whole. It is weakened by salient and durable divisions of class or ethnic (or perhaps even gender) interest, and virtually eliminated in some instances by national divisions. (Consider the challenge to formulate a cogent structure for full democratic political accountability for the government of Northern Ireland.) This minimal sense of political accountability is of overwhelming importance. But in any plausible candidate for a modern democracy, seeing the issue of accountability principally as one of rulers to ruled is almost certain to mislead, since the main oppressive hazard to any particular group in such circumstances is likely to be a transposed horizontal hazard, emanating from other groups of citizens, not a hazard inherent in vertical subjection itself.

The distinctive problem of democratic accountability lies in the

---

[3] Tony Walker et al., "China Raises Hopes of Bilateral Summit," *Financial Times*, March 25, 1996, p. 4.

relation between the people distributively and the public agents of popular sovereignty (whether the latter exercise executive, legislative, or judicial powers themselves, or act as the more or less docile instruments toward their fellow citizens of those who do exercise these powers). It is best conceived as a relation between persons ("Person is a Forensick Term appropriating Actions and their Merit," Locke 1975 [1689], bk. II, xxvii, 26; p. 346). Persons need not be single individuals. Groups or institutions can often plausibly be seen as collective agents and hence as persons. The state itself is a persona ficta (Hobbes 1991, chap. 17, 120–21). Within this relation, one set of persons either can or can not hold another set of persons effectively liable for their actions. In any well-ordered and effectively implemented system of democratic political membership, those who exercise public powers *ex hypothesi* can, over time, hold all their fellow citizens effectively accountable for any types of action for which they have earlier, and through due process, chosen to hold them accountable. By the same token, it is only under very unusual circumstances and through normatively precarious rationales, that they are entitled to hold their fellow citizens accountable for types of action that have not been duly preidentified in this way (Hart 1968: chap. 7).

If elections are contested and their outcomes implemented in practice, if participation is widespread, and if citizens enjoy political rights and liberties, it is reasonable to hope that governments will be responsive to citizens. (For extensive evidence that this is indeed so, see, e.g., Stimson, MacKuen and Erikson 1995.) At the very least, it is reasonable to expect greater responsiveness under these conditions than under those in which elections (if held at all) are not contested or their results resolutely ignored, participation is narrow or absent, and citizens enjoy few, if any, political rights or liberties. (It is instructive, if perhaps unsurprising, that the links between these conditions and the outcomes of governmental activities should prove under analysis to be so weak; see Cheibub and Przeworski, Chapter 7 in this volume.) In this restricted sense, contested elections (the punitive resources of retrospective voting) might still be a necessary condition for accountability, but they were always certain to fall some way short of being a sufficient condition. Most of the weight, in seeking to secure accountability, has to be carried by the vigor of citizen participation and by the scope of rights and liberties open to citizens.

One could think of accountability in this sense as a relation of power or force between citizens and their rulers – an interactive game, the payoff structure of which, more or less effectively, rationally sanctions the behavior of the latter through the threats and offers that it is open to the former to make and execute. This is unlikely to prove very instructive.

Why? Fundamentally, because of the inherent opacity of all human action, and the added informational obstacles that most citizens face in sanctioning most public officials in most ways in which, in retrospect, they might wish to have been able to sanction them. (For the practical importance of this see, e.g., Stokes, Chapter 3 in this volume.) Since in any modern state most citizens most of the time cannot really have even the foggiest conception of most of what is politically going on, citizens need to be very highly selective in their foci of political attention and pretty fortunate even in their access to information about these fields, to work out how it is in their interest to promise or threaten their actual or potential rulers. The idea of well-calibrated instrumental sanctions has had a very good run for its money in modern political thinking and has an evident role in prudent institutional design. But in epistemic terms it is an astonishingly optimistic way of envisaging political relations. Acknowledging the full bleakness of political experience leaves little alternative to recognizing that much of politics must be handled by other modalities (if it is to be handled at all).

Democratic accountability is best seen as a relation between the past acts of those who exercise public power and their future personal liabilities. Its core site is the degree to which our rulers, in a democracy, are effectively compelled to describe what they are doing while ruling us, and to explain why they take this to be appropriate: to give us, as Felipe Gonzalez said, reasons for their actions (Maravall, Chapter 5 in this volume). So conceived, the relation of accountability holds fully where persons exercising public powers are (1) liable for their actions in exercising these powers, (2) predictably identifiable as agents in the exercise of these powers to those to whom they are liable (in the democratic case, ultimately to the *demos* distributively), (3) effectively sanctionable for these acts once performed, and (4) knowably so sanctionable for them in advance. Even Jacobin levels of surveillance proved insufficient to implement accountability in this strong sense; and the institutional structures through which the Jacobins eventually sought to enforce their conception of accountability

335

were fairly drastically alienated from the agency of the *demos* itself.

It remains important, however, to recognize that the formal apparatus of the modern constitutional representative constitutional democracy is far from ensuring accountability in any of these four senses. Not even a multiplicity of parties, with real electoral followings and a history of vigorous ideological contestation over more than four decades of continuous history within such a republic, as the experience of Italy has recently underlined, is sufficient to ensure anything of the kind. An effective conspiracy of career politicians as an occupational group, directed against the people at large, as in the Italian case, can be proof against all accountability-favoring features of competitive electoral politics and the rising fury of the rest of the population, unless and until other public agents prove able and willing to come to the latter's rescue. What is necessary, as Montesquieu long ago explained, is that one power should be in a position to stop another: to bring it to a halt (Montesquieu 1989 [1748]: XI, 4, p. 155; I have emended the translation).

At the very least, an analysis of how accountability can reasonably be hoped to work must take in a sophisticated division of political labor (a cast with many types of political actor, among both professionals and amateurs), and a far wider range of transactions than giving or witholding one's vote, and winning or losing elective office. (For an exemplary instance, commending models in which career politicians often attempt, and are even judged to be attempting, to act responsively within the constraints that they face, rather than shamelessly extracting rents because they are confident of being wholly unaccountable, see Stokes, Chapter 3 in this volume). Political accountability today cannot be direct, peremptory, and reliable. To work benignly (and, over time, probably to work at all), it must be very elaborately mediated, somewhat tentative, and mutually pretty patient.

A highly illuminating microcosm of the impact of these requirements in practice is given in Delmer Dunn's analysis of the potentially conflicting conceptions of representation incorporated into the roles of public bureaucrats and elected politicians, and the delicate choreography of mutual adjustment that results from these. Both bureaucrats and elected politicians purport to be (in the technical sense) agents of the same principal. But in the modern representative republic (Fontana 1994; Manin 1997), elected politicians constitute both legislatures and executives; and the latter pair compete with one another for the title of intermediary principal over the unmistakably agent bureaucracy. Bureaucrats unsurprisingly view the matter more ambivalently. All that is missing in this account is a sense (or lack of sense) of the continuing presence of a third type of agent, also a contender for the role of intermediary principal, whose assigned task it is to interpret and enforce the framework of public law that alone confers the title to exercise any public power at all on behalf of a common ultimate principal, the People themselves.

The intrinsic deliberative complexity of politics has always made accountability precarious (Finley 1983). The overwhelming deliberative complexity of contemporary politics renders it increasingly metaphorical, and permanently threatens to reduce it to a purely symbolic status.

Modern democracies possess essentially two avowable approaches to establishing adequate democratic surveillance of their rulers and public officials. One is through the criminal law, where the latter are held to, and potentially prosecuted under, the explicit rules governing the powers that they exercise, and punished, then or later, for their more flagrant breaches of these rules. Establishing that the rules have been flagrantly broken can call on the entrepreneurial energies of a wide variety of more or less publicly motivated agents. The United States is the historically privileged terrain for exploring these possibilities (though there were, of course, earlier pioneers with their own battle honors: above all, the Dreyfus case). It has had some notable successes at the very highest level. Recently, even such initially unpromising sites as Mexico and South Korea have also begun to make some headway. The fraudulent or illegal exercise of public power can be shown to be accountable, if, and only if, the fraud or illegality is put on trial in an effective and well-secured judicial system. But the most formidable challenge is to get it to court in the first place. Public prosecutors stand in a long political tradition. But, in the nature of the case, they are inherently unreliable when it comes to prosecuting their fellow rulers. The main burden of meeting this challenge cannot reasonably be consigned to a simple institutional fix. Instead, it must be distributed across the full range of political initiative among the citizenry at large, exercising all its rights and liberties.

Prosecuting rulers or public officials for fraud or other illegality in the exercise of their responsibilities may often be a practically arduous assignment. But it is a relatively simple objective; and its point is pretty transparent. It requires a presumption of mens rea in the agents who are to be indicted (that one cannot prosecute in this setting for lethargy or stupidity, or even for gross cowardice as such, let alone for hardness of heart, but only for well-formed acts, consciously recognized by their perpetrators as breaching public law).[4]

The key point, one of the greatest political importance, and far from effectively attended to by modern political thinkers, is that accountability in this sense (accountability *stricto sensu*) will only handle a fairly modest proportion of the hazards we face from our rulers and which it is reasonable for us to wish to minimize. In particular, it will certainly not handle the hazards that flow from conduct which is abject or disgraceful but which may be validly legally exculpated in face of the criminal law by a skilled advocate. There are some very important examples of such relations in the recent political experience of (for example) Britain, France, Italy, and Japan (no doubt plenty in the United States, too): public provision of AIDS-contaminated blood supplies, the deliberate governmental suppression of documents crucial for the defense in public prosecutions for illegal trading (the Matrix Churchill case), British governmental response (or lack of it) over time to the trajectory of bovine spongiform encephalopathy. Intermittent punitive voting between teams of politicians is not a promising approach to sanctioning such behavior in advance. While it may offer a certain psychic relief, and some expressive potential, in retrospect, it is too aggregated, and too confounded with other considerations, to address the issue with any energy and precision.

What other approach to addressing it is open to modern democratic politics? The sole plausible candidate (none too

[4] This is probably too strong, as it stands. To make it more realistic, it would need to be reexpressed in terms of the awareness of the constraints of public law, which it is incumbent on the holders of public roles to exhibit. At one end of the continuum in question, this may well be a matter of strict liability. What needs to be epistemically determinate is that the public agent has indisputably performed a particular act, and that the act, under whatever the appropriate interpretative criteria are deemed to be, is plainly in conflict with public law. (Not that the agent in question necessarily in fact paid the slightest attention to this relation: just that in retrospect he plainly legally should have done – it was clearly his official duty to have done so.) But to set the issue up, it is better to express matters as simply as possible.

plausible at that) is a regime of freedom of information. It is characteristic of the demand for accountability in such instances that the conduct in question look in retrospect both furtive and ignoble, however brazen its perpetrators may show themselves when it comes out into the open. The main weight of democratic accountability (even if sanctioned in the last instance by highly intermittent opportunity for punitive voting between teams of career politicians) has to fall here: on the attempt to maximize the degree to which politically consequential conduct by rulers and their subordinates is always in the open. The scale of the obstacles to this endeavor is all too obvious, both in the subjective motivational sets (Williams 1981: chap. 8) and behavioral repertoires of actually existing politicians, and any likely successors to them, or in the fundamental form of the polity itself. Reason of state is profoundly and self-righteously committed to the arcane as such – to judging the state and its custodians in rapt privacy for itself and themselves, and to confounding it and them with the utmost determination. But democracy is necessarily at odds with this tradition. The reason of a democratic state cannot be wholly at ease with furtiveness as such.

As Stokes admirably stresses, citizens can only choose on the basis of what they are enabled to know (Stokes, Chapter 3; and see Manin, Przeworski, and Stokes, Chapter 1 in this volume). A political system in which accountability is enacted on the basis of ignorance and incomprehension is unlikely to benefit anyone with much consistency. State discretion is a clear inroad into democratic accountability, and state furtiveness is a frontal assault upon it. The demand for privacy in ruling is an attack on the core charter of a democratic state: virtually a confession of sinister interest on the part of its rulers. Or at any rate, this must be so if the demand for privacy is permanent: a demand never to be fully found out. The democratic demand to be ruled in broad daylight – to be able to see what is politically happening (which certainly requires being able to look for oneself, the right to try unimpededly to find out) – and the classic claims of prerogative (the power of doing public good without a rule: Locke 1988 [1689], II, para. 166, ll. 20–21; Dunn 1969, chaps. 11, 12), can not be conceptually reconciled simultaneously. If we really succeeded in eliminating prerogative from political life, we would not merely discomfit professional politicians (and even reasonably ambitious bureaucrats) so radically that the supply of them might dry up, we would also

find that we had achieved very many plainly undesirable consequences at the same time. To be able to rule beneficially, political
leaders need to be able to act, and sometimes to act boldly. They
need a considerable degree of freedom. The more we bind them,
no doubt, the less they will be able to do against us, but the less,
too, and at least equally consequentially, they will be able to do
for us. Paralyzing rule is not a recipe for ensuring that it has a
surplus of desired over undesired consequences.

Any possibility of reconciling the demand for rule in public
with the continued exercise of prerogative power must involve
the passage of time. In this sense, democratic accountability is
inherently retrospective, not just tautologically, in that what is held
accountable is always actions, and there is no conceptual possibility of calling future acts to account in the present, but also
because present-tense freedom is only compatible with full
political visibility if the latter is a deliberate artifact and fashioned
later. It is still far from clear how these conceptual structures
interrelate at this point. One reason why full political visibility
cannot be temporally simultaneous – a standing present – may well
be epistemic: a matter of conceptual barriers to making windows
into persons' souls. But another reason is clearly a consequence
of the structure of political practices. The best of regimes of
freedom of information would always be open to infinite
manipulation and largely at the mercy of fluent hypocrisy. Most
actually existing regimes of this kind lie some distance away from
the best. But the development and deepening of practices of public
exposure – of putting politically consequential conduct tendentially
under the floodlights – must be essential to any coherent project
of rendering the most democratically generated of rule effectively
accountable.

It is a precondition for being able to identify the agents (the
"real movers," as Burke [1989: 59] calls them),[5] for ascertaining
what they did in fact do, and how far in fact even they appreciated
what its consequences were likely to prove, and thus for judging

---

[5] "The effect of liberty to individuals is, that they may do what they please.
. . . liberty when men act in bodies, is power. Considerate people, before they
declare themselves, will observe the use which is made of power; and particularly
of so trying a thing as new power in new persons, of whose principles, tempers,
and dispositions, they have little or no experience, and in situations where those
who appear the most stirring in the scene may possibly not be the real movers"
(Burke 1989: "Reflections on the Revolution in France," 59).

how far we have reason to view their intentions as excusable or as radically discreditable. If the central strand of political relations, across the potential division of labor in a modern democratic state, lies in the treacheries and seductions of trust, it is only insofar as we can ever hope to learn what our rulers have in fact done that we can ever ascertain just how far we have been betrayed. As democrats, we must favor illumination, clarification, seeing as sharply as possible just what has been done by those who rule us in our own name. We must do so, not in the inane expectation that we can expect to enjoy recognizing what has been done, or to enjoy each others' several contributions to its having been done, but because it is only by identifying and understanding it that we can ever coherently judge just how far the claim of those whom we have collectively chosen to rule in our name that they are truly doing so on our behalf is any more than a brutal travesty. The practices needed here are almost wholly still to be made – invented, refined, and established in operation. But the need for them is plain enough (Manin, Przeworski, and Stokes, Chapter 1). Perhaps, too, there is already quite a widespread awareness of this need. The degree of popular disaffection from career politicians and incumbent governments across the world at present might just be a simple function of the recent performance of the economies over which they preside. But it may also connect quite peremptorily with an awareness of this need, and with the secular shift in the balance of subjection that accompanies (and perhaps permits a growing awareness of) just this need.

The quest for democratic accountability is not best seen as a search for magically efficacious causal mechanisms for rearing the fabric of felicity by the hands of reason and of law (Bentham 1970 [1789]: 11). Rather, it is an attempt to draw an ever brighter line between the freedom of action that professional political agents require in order to act boldly and effectively, and the degree of personal privilege that they can excusably claim for their actions from the citizens on whose behalf they purport to act. It reconciles the formers' freedom at one time with their responsibility then and later by insisting on the citizens' right of informational access to (their right to know about) these actions, once they have been performed: not necessarily immediately, but at least at some definite point in the future.

Criminal liability is one element in such responsibility, with a long and intricate history of its own behind it (see especially

341

Hansen 1974, 1975, 1976, and 1991: chap. 8, esp. 205–24). But it is just as inadequate to restrict the idea of responsibility to criminal liability as it would be unjust to extend criminal liability to all political actions to which a majority of citizens subsequently take exception.

If democracy (the experience of ruling and being ruled by turns [Aristotle 1932: 1261b, pp. 72–74; 1317b, p. 490], or the attempt to banalize rule [Dunn 1992]) were just an instrumental facility for securing a minimally disagreeable stream of experience for the citizenry, it might be terminally discouraging to learn that there is no way of ensuring prospectively that professional political agents act as more of the citizens would wish them to do. But if the experience of being ruled, democratically as much as otherwise, is seen as a somewhat richer existential drama of trust and betrayal (Dunn 1990),[6] pride and humiliation, it may be easier to capture why political accountability should still seem so important. Most citizens emphatically prefer less disagreeable to more disagreeable experiences in most instances. But they have more on their minds and in their emotions than is captured in this simple preference. Just as they value the right and opportunity to reject their rulers (to say no; Dunn 1997), without necessarily overestimating the consequential benefits they can hope to secure by exercising it, so too they value the sense that, under democracy, those who rule in their name are in the end personally answerable to them.

The core of the matter is how democracy is in the end conceived. What is fundamental is to acknowledge that democracy is one (very broadly defined) form of being ruled: in the modern world, one broadly defined form of state. It is not, and cannot be, an alternative to being ruled (Dunn 1993, chap. 1). To be ruled is both necessary and inherently discomfiting (as well as dangerous). For our rulers to be accountable to us softens its intrinsic humiliations, probably sets some hazy limits to the harms that they will voluntarily choose to do to us collectively,[7] and thus diminishes some of the dangers to which

---

[6] There is plenty of evidence that it is so seen: see Maravall, Chapter 5, and Stokes, Chapter 3. When it is, elections can make robust sense as the choice of preferred persons (Fearon, Chapter 2), without the slightest presumption that such a choice will compel the chosen to act in any particular way.

[7] No modern political system (and probably no political system that has ever existed) sets reliable limits on the harms that may be inadvertently inflicted by rulers.

their rule may expose us. To suggest that we can ever hope to have the power to make them act just as we would wish them to suggests that it is really we, not they, who are ruling (cf. Ferejohn, Chapter 4 in this volume). This is an illusion, and probably a somewhat malign illusion: either a self-deception, or an instance of being deceived by others, or very probably both. A political science that did justice to democracy (in all its ambiguity) would have to be one in which the presence of these perceptions and sentiments was recognized and explained, and their consequences accurately assessed, not one in which their existence was denied or dismissed as irrational in the first instance.

References

Aristotle. 1932. *Politics*. H. Rackham, trans. Cambridge, Mass.: Harvard University Press.

Bentham, Jeremy. 1970 [1789]. *An Introduction to the Principles of Morals and Legislation*. J. H. Burns and H. L. A. Hart, eds. London: Athlone Press.

Burke, Edmund. 1989. *The Writings and Speeches of Edmund Burke*. Vol. 8. L. G. Mitchell, ed. Oxford: Clarendon Press.

Constant, Benjamin. 1988. *Political Writings*. Biancamaria Fontana, trans. Cambridge: Cambridge University Press.

Dunn, John. 1969. *The Political Thought of John Locke*. Cambridge: Cambridge University Press.

1990. *Interpreting Political Responsibility*. Princeton: Princeton University Press.

ed. 1992. *Democracy: The Unfinished Journey*. Oxford: Oxford University Press.

1993. *Western Political Theory in the Face of the Future*. 2d ed. Cambridge: Cambridge University Press.

1994. *The Identity of the Bourgeois Liberal Republic*. In Biancamaria Fontana, ed. *The Invention of the Modern Republic*, 206–25. Cambridge: Cambridge University Press.

1995. *The History of Political Theory*. Cambridge: Cambridge University Press.

1996. "The Contemporary Political Significance of John Locke's Conception of Civil Society." *Iyyun* (Jerusalem) 45 (July): 103–24.

1997. "The Transcultural Significance of Athenian Democracy." In Michel Sakellariou, ed., *Democracy and Culture in Ancient Athens*. Athens: The Academy of *Athens*.

John Dunn

Finley M. I. 1983. *Politics in the Ancient World*. Cambridge: Cambridge University Press.

Fontana, Biancamaria. 1994. *The Invention of the Modern Republic*. Cambridge: Cambridge University Press.

Hansen, Mogens H. 1974. *The Sovereignty of the People's Court in Athens and the Public Actions against Unconstitutional Proposals*. J. Raphaelsen and S. Holboll, trans. Odense University Classical Studies 4. Odense.

1975. *Eisangelia: The Sovereignty of the People's Court in Athens in the Fourth Century BC and the Impeachment of Generals and Politicans*. Odense University Classical Studies 6. Odense.

1976. *Apagoge, Endeixis and Ephegesis against Kakourgoi, Atimoi and Pheugontes: A Study in the Athenian Administration of Justice in the Fourth Century BC*. Odense University Classical Studies 8. Odense.

1991. *The Athenian Democracy in the Age of Demosthenes*. Oxford: Blackwell.

Hart, H. L. A. 1968. *Punishment and Responsibility*. Oxford: Clarendon Press.

Hobbes, Thomas. 1991. *Leviathan*. Richard Tuck, ed. Cambridge: Cambridge University Press.

Locke, John. 1975 [1689]. *An Essay concerning Human Understanding*. Peter H. Nidditch, ed. Oxford: Clarendon Press.

1988 [1689]. *Two Treatises of Government*. Peter Laslett, ed. Cambridge: Cambridge University Press.

Maistre, Joseph de. 1965. *The Works of Joseph de Maistre*. Jack Lively, ed. New York: Macmillan.

Manin, Bernard, 1997. *Modern Representative Government*. Cambridge: Cambridge University Press.

Montesquieu, Charles-Louis de Secondat, Baron de. 1989 [1748]. *The Spirit of the Laws*. A. Cohler, B. Miller, and H. Stone, trans. Cambridge: Cambridge University Press.

Ober, Josiah. 1989. *Mass and Elite in Democratic Athens*. Princeton: Princeton University Press.

Przeworski, Adam. 1991. *Democracy and the Market*. Cambridge: Cambridge University Press.

Simmons, A. John 1993. *On the Edge of Anarchy*. Princeton: Princeton University Press.

Stimson, James A., Michael B. MacKuen, and Robert S. Erikson. 1995. "Dynamic Representation." *American Political Science Review* 89: 543–65.

Williams, Bernard. 1981. *Moral Luck*. Cambridge: Cambridge University Press.

Wolff, Robert Paul. 1970. *In Defense of Anarchism*. New York: Harper.

Author Index

Subject Index

40–44, 100, 126
and elections, 10–14, 29, 16–19, 50–51
descriptive, 32
mandate conception of, 16–17, 22, 30–31, 100, 120, 126
and responsiveness, 10, 12

and structure of government, 19–22

separation of powers, 20

term limits, 61–62, 113
time preferences, 14